Netscape™ FastTrack Server

How to Order:

For information on quantity discounts contact the publisher: Prima Publishing, P.O. Box 1260BK, Rocklin, CA 95677-1260; (916) 632-4400. On your letterhead include information concerning the intended use of the books and the number of books you wish to purchase. For individual orders, turn to the back of this book for more information.

Netscape™ FastTrack Server

Allen L. Wyatt

Prima Publishing

ISBN: 0-7615-0691-8

Library of Congress Catalog Card Number: 96-69344

Printed in the United States of America

96 97 98 99 BB 10 9 8 7 6 5 4 3 2 1

Publisher:
Don Roche, Jr.

Associate Publisher:
Ray Robinson

Senior Editor:
Tad Ringo

Senior Acquisitions Editor:
Alan Harris

Acquistions Editor:
Deborah F. Abshier

Development Editor:
Tim Huddleston

Project Editor:
Anne Owen

Technical Reviewer:
Greg Newman

Assistant Acquisitions Editor:
Jill Byus

Administrative Assistant:
Ruth Slates

Indexer:
Sharon Hilgenberg

About Allen L. Wyatt

Allen Wyatt, an internationally recognized expert in small computer systems, has been working in the computer and publishing industries for over 15 years. He has written more than 35 books explaining many different facets of working with computers, as well as numerous magazine articles. His books have covered topics ranging from programming languages to using application software to using operating systems. Through the written word, Allen has helped millions of readers learn how to better use computers.

Besides writing books, Allen has helped educate thousands of individuals through seminar and lectures about computers. He has presented seminars and lectures throughout the United States, as well as throughout Mexico and Costa Rica. His books, which often form the basis of his presentations, have been translated into many languages besides English, including Spanish, French, Italian, German, Greek, Chinese, and Polish.

Allen is the president of Discovery Computing Inc., a computer and publishing services company located in Sundance, Wyoming. Besides writing books and technical materials, he helps further the computer book industry by providing consulting and distribution services. With his wife and three children, he lives on a 390-acre ranch just outside of town, on the edge of the Black Hills. In his spare time, he tends his animals, has fun with his family, and participates in church and community events.

If you would like to send e-mail to Allen, his address is *awyatt@dcomp.com*.

Discovery Computing Inc.
20101 US Highway 14
PO Box 738
Sundance, WY 82729
800-628-8280
307-283-2714 (fax)
Send comments to: *Webmaster@dcomp.com*

Contents at a Glance

Part I   **Creating Your Site**

1   Your Hardware 3

2   Your Software 21

3   Your Internet Connection 46

Part II   **Installing and Developing Your Web Site**

4   Installing Your Web Server 61

5   Converting from Another Server 93

6   Troubleshooting Your Web Installation 107

Part III   **Basic Content Development**

7   Planning Site Content 125

8   Basic Web Publishing 133

9   Creating Pages with Netscape Navigator Gold 183

10   Interfacing with Other Services 211

Part IV   **Advanced Content Development**

11   Working with Scripts 229

12   Working with WinCGI 265

13   Working with JavaScript .289

14   Working with Java 323

Part V   **Server Security**

15   Basics of Security 357

16   Internet Services and Security 389

Part VI   **Managing Your Site**

17   The Netscape Serve Manager 409

18   Day-to-Day Management 429

19   Utilizing Log Files 451

20   Monitoring and Improving Performance 467

     Index 483

Contents

Part I   **Creating Your Site**

Chapter 1   **Your Hardware**

The Network View 4
    Servers 4
    Workstations 7
    Network Hardware 8
CPU and Speed 9
    The 80486 Family 9
    The Pentium Family 11
    The Pentium Pro 11
Memory Requirements .13
    Quantity 13
    Speed 14
Disk Drive Requirements 15
    Speed 15
    Space 16

Other Elements 17

    CD-ROM Drives .17

    Video 18

Summary 19

Chapter 2   Your Software

Client/Server Essentials .22

Services in the FastTrack Server 23

    Web Server 24

    Netscape Navigator Gold 25

    Netscape Server Manager 25

    Internet Service Manager 31

Requirements for Running the FastTrack Server . . .26

    Windows NT Server 3.51 26

    Windows NT Server 3.51 Service Pack 27

Other Services for Your Site 28

    DNS Server 28

    E-Mail Server 33

    FTP Server 34

    Gopher Server 35

    Remote Access Service 36

Windows NT Tools 36

    The Control Panel 37

    The User Manager .40

    The Event Viewer 41

The Performance Monitor 42

The Registry Editor 48

Summary 43

Part II   **Installing and Setting Up Your Site**

Chapter 3   **Your Internet Connection**

Understanding the Internet 46

Internet Versus Intranet 47

Internet Providers 48

Connection Types 49

Equipment Required 50

Selecting a Provider 54

Getting Set Up 55

Your Domain Name 55

Your IP Address 57

Lead Times 57

Summary 58

Chapter 4   **Installing Your Web Server**

Setting Up a Directory Structure 62

Understanding URLs 62

Directory Considerations 64

A Word on Directory Indexing 65

Setting Up the Web Server 65

    Installing the Service Pack 66

    Checking Your System 68

    Installing Netscape FastTrack Server 69

Configuring the Web Server 76

    Setting the Default File 76

    Controlling Directory Indexing 80

    Changing the Default Port Setting 81

    Using Additional Document Directories 83

    Hosting Multiple Sites 85

Summary 91

Chapter 5   Converting from Another Server

Server Differences 94

    Operating System Differences 94

    Directory Structure .95

    File and Directory Names 95

    Using Log Files 96

    Scripts 97

    Security Differences 99

    Map Files 99

    HTML Differences .100

    Virtual Servers 101

A Sample Conversion 101

    Planning Your Move 102

    Bringing Down Your Old Server 103

    Installing the Netscape FastTrack Server 104

    Converting Your Information 104

    Checking Your Installation 105

Summary 105

Chapter 6 Troubleshooting Your Web Installation

Testing Your Installation 108

Starting and Stopping the Server 109

    From the Services Applet 109

    From the Netscape Server Manager 110

Common Problems and Solutions 111

    People Can't Locate My Server 112

    When Connecting to My Server,
the User Gets a URL Error 113

    People Can't Access Some Files and
Directories on My System 113

    Additional Document Directories
Aren't Visible 114

    I Need to Reinstall My Web Server in a
Different Directory .114

    I Just Converted to FastTrack,
and My Web Documents Don't Show Up . . .115

When People Connect to My Server,
All They See Is a Directory 116

I Can't Get in the Netscape Server Manager .116

Removing Your FastTrack Server 117

Removing through Windows NT 118

Removing through Netscape 120

Residual Files and Cleanup 121

Summary 122

Part III   **Basic Content Development**

Chapter 7   **Planning Site Content**

Your Directory Structure 126

Information at Your Site 127

Focus, Focus, Focus 127

Copyrighted Information 128

Compressed Files .128

A Word on File Formats 130

Graphics Files 131

Audio Files 131

Summary 132

Chapter 8   **Basic Web Publishing**

Understanding HTML Documents 134

     Document Structure 135

     Formatting Paragraphs 139

     Formatting Characters 151

     Including Graphics in a Document 154

     Adding Links 157

     Miscellaneous Tags 160

Understanding Image Maps 163

     The HTML Tags .164

     The Map File 165

Creating Tables 166

     Borders and Other Table Attributes 168

     Skipping Cells 170

     Spanning Columns 171

     Spanning Rows 174

     Aligning Cell Contents 175

     Graphics in Tables 178

Summary 182

Chapter 9   **Creating Pages with Netscape Navigator Gold**

What Is Netscape Navigator Gold? 184

The Navigator Gold Interface 184

     Browser Window Interfaces 185

The Editor Window .186

Setting Up the Editor Preferences 189

Creating a Page 193

    Blank Pages 194

    From a Template 194

    Using a Wizard 196

    An Existing Page 198

Editing a Page 199

    Working with Text .200

    Adding Graphics 204

    Adding Links 206

Saving Your Work 207

Hand Crafting 208

Summary 209

Chapter 10   Interfacing with Other Services

Access Basics 212

Accessing FTP Files from Your Web Site 213

    Establishing a Directory Link 213

    Establishing a File Link 217

Accessing Gopher Files from Your Web Site 222

Sending Electronic Mail 224

Summary 226

Part IV   **Advanced Content Development**

Chapter 11   **Working with Scripts**

Scripting Basics 230

    Understanding Scripts 230

    Understanding Forms 231

Creating a Form 231

    Submitting a Form .233

    Limiting Input 237

    Using Check Boxes and Radio Buttons 239

    Using Pull-Down Lists 244

    Using Text Boxes 246

Creating a Script 249

    Submission Methods 249

    The *ACTION* Attribute 250

    Choosing a Scripting Language 251

    What the Script Sees 252

    Returning Information to the Server 256

    Writing the Script .257

Allowing Your Script to Run 261

Summary 264

Chapter 12   **Working with WinCGI**

What Is WinCGI? 266

HTML Links to WinCGI 267

   Using a Form 267

   Using a URL 268

How Information Is Passed 270

Creating the Program 271

   The Framework File 271

   Adding Your Code 275

   Compiling Your Program 279

A Simple Sample Program 279

A More Complex Sample Program 281

Allowing Your Script to Run 284

   Configuring FastTrack Server 285

Setting Your Directory Permissions 287

Summary 288

Chapter 13   <u>Working</u> with JavaScript

What Is JavaScript? 290

Adding JavaScript to Your Pages 291

   Hiding the JavaScript Code 292

   Using Functions 294

Understanding Objects .296

   The Window Object 299

   The Document Object 302

   The Location Object 305

   The History Object .306

Working with Events 307

    User Events 307

    Simulated Events 308

Data Types and Variables 309

    Conversion Functions 311

    More About String Summary 312

    Arrays 315

Other Scripting Considerations 316

Example Scripts 317

    A Changed Link Page 317

    Formatting Input .319

Summary 321

Chapter 14   Working with Java

What Is Java? 324

    The Virtual Machine Concept 325

    Applications vs. Applets 326

    Server-Side vs. Client-Side 327

The Building Blocks 327

    Data Types 327

    Operators 328

    Arrays and Strings 329

    Objects, Objects, Objects 329

    Memory Management 332

Developing Java Programs 332

Creating Your First Java Applet 335

Compiling the Applet 337

Adding the Applet to a Web Page 338

A More Elaborate Java Applet 339

Applet Methods 341

The HTML Document 342

Passing Parameters to Applets 345

A Template for Applets .348

Developing Your Skills .350

Resources in the JDK 350

Newsgroups 352

Web Sites 352

Summary 353

Part V   Server Security

Chapter 15   Basics of Security

Windows NT Security 358

The NTFS File System 358

Setting Effective Account Policies 359

Understanding User Accounts 361

Working with Permissions 371

Understanding Auditing 375

The Secure Sockets Layer 376

    Implementing SSL 377

    Usage Differences 387

Summary 387

Chapter 16   Internet Services and Security

Developing Your Security Plan 390

    Developing a Written Plan 391

    Making Backups 392

    Using Log Files 393

    Watching Your Directory Structure 393

    Watching Programs Used 394

    Enforcing Passwords 395

    Adding Gateway Machines 395

    Using Secure Machines 396

Security Issues for Your Site 396

    The User Account .396

    Document Files 399

    Executable Files 400

    Limiting Access to Your Server 400

Reviewing Events 403

    Viewing Event Logs 403

    Configuring Log File Settings 405

    Managing Your Log Files 406

Summary 406

Part VI   **Managing Your Site**

Chapter 17 **The Netscape Server Manager**

Starting the Netscape Server Manager 410

The User Interface 411

    The Toolbar 412

    The Category Choices 413

    The Configuration Window 413

The Configuration Categories 414

    System Settings 415

    Access Control 416

    Encryption 418

    Programs 419

    Server Status 420

    Config Styles 421

    Content Mgmt 422

Using Netscape Server Manager
Over the Network 424

Summary 426

Chapter 18 **Day-to-Day Management**

Meaningful Error Messages 430

    Creating the Error Pages 432

    Configuring FastTrack 434

Testing Your Error Messages 436

Managing Content Pages 436

Moving or Removing Pages 436

URL Forwarding 438

Managing Server Users 440

Controlling Users 441

Controlling Groups .442

Putting Users and Groups to Work 443

Using Configuration Styles 444

Defining a Configuration Style 444

Editing Styles 447

Using Your Styles 447

Establishing Management Checklists 448

Summary 449

Chapter 19 Utilizing Log Files

Accessing the Error Log 452

Access Log Formats 454

EMWAC Log Format 454

Common Logfile Format 455

Logging Options 456

What to Record 458

Log File Format 458

What to Exclude 459

Archiving Your Access Log 459

Using Log Files 461

   The Log File Analyzer 461

   Custom Programs .463

   Managing the Log Files 464

Summary 465

Chapter 20   **Monitoring and Improving Performance**

The Task Manager 468

The Performance Monitor 470

   The User Interface .470

   Monitoring Objects 474

   Refresh Rate 475

   Printing Reports 477

FastTrack Performance 478

Improving Performance 479

Summary 481

Index   **483**

PART I

Creating Your Site

Chapter | 1

Your Hardware

The foundation of any computer system is the hardware you use to build that system. Therefore, any Internet site you start must, at the lowest level, rely upon hardware. Very few people take a look at hardware, or are so confused by it that, in effect, the hardware becomes an impediment to a successful site.

This chapter focuses on the hardware you need to run an effective Internet site. Here you learn what hardware is required, as well as what hardware can improve your Internet site's performance.

The Network View

When you develop a Web site, by default you are establishing a network environment. Even if your site uses a single computer, it becomes part of the World Wide Web, which in turn is part of the Internet. By definition, the Internet is a network of computers that can share information by using a common set of protocols. The same is true of all other Internet services, such as Gopher or FTP. They all operate within and take advantage of a networked environment.

Because you are establishing your own network environment, looking at the two main components of that environment—servers and workstations—makes sense.

Servers

The computer system on which you run your Internet server software is called a *server*. Notice that this statement makes a distinction between *server software* and *server hardware*. Although this distinction may sound confusing, server hardware is just the computer system on which you run your server software, as Figure 1-1 illustrates.

For your Internet site, your server software is the Netscape FastTrack server. Thus, your server hardware must conform to the requirements of the FastTrack server and the operating system on which you choose to run FastTrack.

> **NOTE:** Chapter 2, "Your Software," fully discusses the software components of a Web site, including FastTrack server.

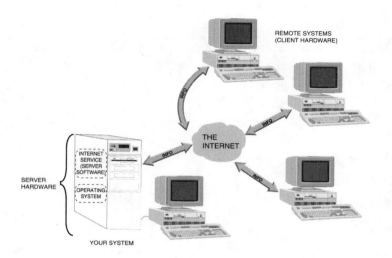

FIGURE 1-1

The relationship between server hardware and software.

After you have established the foundation of your server hardware, you can run your server software. Server software allows client software, in this case Web browsers from around the Internet, to connect to your server to retrieve information.

In reality, very little difference exists any more between server hardware and any other high-powered computer system; if you purchase a high-powered computer system, you generally can use it as a server. The hardware requirements for establishing a Web server using the FastTrack server software are very specific, however. Your system requirements can be divided into the following categories:

- Computer
- Hard drive
- Memory
- CD-ROM drive
- Video system

Each of these items is covered in detail in the following sections. As you read through the sections, remember that these system requirements presented are *minimums*. (Anyone who has used computers for any length of time realizes that for adequate system performance, you need more robust hardware.) Later in this chapter you will learn more about how to select hardware that will fulfill more demanding needs.

Your Computer

Netscape FastTrack is available for either UNIX or Windows NT. If you plan to run FastTrack on a UNIX system, your computer can come from any number of vendors. The following UNIX versions are supported:

- ◆ OSF/1 2.0
- ◆ HP-UX 9.x or greater
- ◆ AIX 3.2.4 or greater
- ◆ IRIX 5.2 or greater
- ◆ SunOS 4.1.3
- ◆ Solaris 2.3 or greater

As long as your computer meets the minimum requirements for one of these operating systems, you can run the UNIX versions of FastTrack. If, on the other hand, you are planning to use a Windows NT environment, your computer must use either the Intel 80486, Pentium, Pentium Pro, or DEC Alpha chips. Even though Windows NT will run on other hardware platforms, FastTrack does not support those other platforms.

In most small- to medium-sized businesses, chances are good you'll be running FastTrack on the Windows NT platform using an Intel chip. This is not to say the other platforms are not acceptable; on the contrary, you can get very good performance from any of the platforms on which FastTrack runs. For the purposes of this book, most examples and screen shots are from the Windows NT version of FastTrack.

Your Hard Drive

The amount of disk space you need for FastTrack depends, again, on the platform on which you are installing the software. If you are installing it on a UNIX platform, you should have at least 10 MB of hard drive space available. For the Windows NT versions, you need at least 50 MB of available hard drive space.

For most systems, these requirements present no big problems. The recommendations allow room for both the installation of the server software and the log files you might generate. If you anticipate having a very busy Web site, you may want to increase the recommended minimums by about 50 percent.

> **NOTE:** The disk drive space requirements noted here are for *additional* hard drive space. This is in addition to any other hard drive requirements for your operating system or other software.

The internal structure of Windows NT also requires disk space for use as virtual memory. This virtual memory, called a *swap file,* is used as a temporary storage place for information normally stored in RAM. For efficient use of FastTrack, particularly at heavy loads, you need at least 150 MB of disk space set aside for use as a swap file.

Your Memory

Regardless of the platform you are using with FastTrack, you need to have at least 32 MB of RAM in your system in order for the server to work properly. Under some circumstances, you can make FastTrack work with only 16 MB, but under such constraints you will notice very slow response times. In order for FastTrack to work as it should, Netscape raised the minimum memory requirement to the stated 32 MB.

Your CD-ROM Drive

If you ordered your copy of FastTrack on CD-ROM, directly from Netscape, you will need a CD-ROM drive in your system. If you downloaded your copy of FastTrack from the Internet, you can get by without the CD-ROM drive but may want it for your operating system files or for use with other programs.

Your Video System

The video system within a computer is comprised of a video card and a monitor. The size and type of monitor you get is not important (as long as it works with your video card), but different operating systems do have different requirements for your video card. For example, Windows NT requires—at a minimum—a VGA card. You should check your operating system documentation to see which type of card you require.

Workstations

You don't *need* a workstation to establish your Internet site. You will quickly find, however, that having a workstation separate from your server is advantageous. The workstation enables you to do development work without taxing the server. In effect, you can develop resources for your server without slowing the response time of your server, which should be handling requests across the Internet.

The workstations you use can run any variety of operating systems; thus, they can have any number of hardware requirements. Most often, however, you will use a workstation operating system that is compatible with the operating system used on your server. For instance, you would use Windows NT Workstation, Windows 95, or Windows for Workgroups 3.x with Windows NT Server.

The UNIX operating systems with which FastTrack will work do not make a distinction between the server and the workstation operating systems, as does Windows. If you are running a variant of UNIX on the machine designated as your server, chances are good you are also running the same version of UNIX on your workstations. The difference is how you have each machine configured to work in the network as a whole.

Network Hardware

The type and complexity of network hardware you need depends on two main items: your network topology and the number of nodes in your network. The topic of network configuration can be quite complex and is definitely beyond the scope of this book. If you have a network already in place, information in relation to network hardware is probably pointless, anyway—you must work with what you have.

If you haven't set up a local area network, you need the following items:

♦ A *network interface card* for each computer connected to the network. These cards must all use the same protocols. For example, if you are establishing an Ethernet network, all the interface cards must use Ethernet.

♦ A *hub* or *concentrator*. This device provides a central, localized connection for each computer on the network. Hubs and concentrators do essentially the same thing, but different network protocols refer to them by the different names. You need a hub or concentrator only if you are connecting more than two computers in your network.

To use your network hardware effectively and efficiently, you should refer to a good book on network basics. You also may want to employ the services of a knowledgeable network technician. The time savings alone can more than justify the cost of paying such an individual.

> **NOTE:** The type of hardware required to establish a local area network differs from what you need to connect your network to the Internet. For information on this latter topic, see Chapter 3, "Your Internet Connection."

CPU and Speed

As you learned earlier in this chapter, the most common CPU platform for both servers and workstations is based on chips from Intel. Although you can run your operating system on systems based on other types of chips, such as the DEC Alpha or MIPS Rx400, for cost-conscious small- and medium-sized businesses, the expense of such platforms can be prohibitive. This fact implies that most readers of this book will use Intel-based computer systems.

Because the system requirements for FastTrack allows for an 80486 or greater CPU, you can select from any of the following CPUs:

- ◆ 80486
- ◆ Pentium
- ◆ Pentium Pro

The following sections can help you determine exactly which type of Intel CPU is appropriate for the system on which you will run your FastTrack server.

The 80486 Family

The 80486 made its debut in 1989, although systems using this chip didn't appear on the market until 1990. All else being equal (including clock speeds), a system using a 486 will run approximately 75 percent faster than one using a 386. This degree of improvement was made possible by changing the internal design of the CPU itself. Features such as an internal memory cache and an integrated numeric coprocessor mean that the 486 can fly through most computing tasks, when compared with the 386.

Almost a dozen different variations on the 486 chip exist, if you count versions from other companies than Intel. You can find versions of the 486 from companies such as AMD, Cyrix, IBM, and Texas Instruments. Following are the different configurations available:

- **486DX.** The original 80486, introduced by Intel. Versions are also available from AMD and Cyrix.
- **486DX2.** An 80486 that runs at double speed internally.
- **486DX4.** An 80486 that runs at triple speed internally. Clock speeds of between 99 and 100 MHz make this chip the fastest 486 on the market.
- **486SX.** An 80486 with the math coprocessor disabled.
- **486SL.** An 80486 with a limited address bus, thereby limiting memory access to no more than 64 MB. (An unlimited 486 can access 4 GB of RAM.) Separate versions have been created by Intel, and by Intel for IBM use. This chip is used primarily in laptop computers and thus won't be found in systems considered as a Web server.
- **486SLC.** This chip is really a cross between a 386 and a 486, created by Cyrix as a competitor to the higher-priced Intel line.
- **486SLC2.** This chip is the low-power IBM version of the 486SX. This chip includes design improvements that boost its performance over both the 486SX and the 486SL.
- **Blue Lightning.** An IBM version of a 486 that runs internally at triple speed. In many ways, this chip is similar to the 486DX4, but it has internal design differences that result in lower power consumption and a greater internal cache. It also lacks the internal numeric coprocessor present in many other 486 chips.
- **486DLC.** This 486 chip is produced by Cyrix. Functionally, the only difference between this chip and a normal 486 is that the internal cache is only 1 KB in size.
- **486Rx2.** This Cyrix 486DLC chip has been modified internally to run at double speed.

Many 486 systems are still on the market today. The higher-speed members of this CPU family are quite adequate for running servers, particularly servers carrying a low load. (We use a 66 MHz 486 for our server, and have had very satisfactory performance.) If you are running a site that typically has a dozen or more people accessing information at the same time, however, you will find the performance of all but the absolute fastest 486s inadequate. In this case, you should look at either a 100 MHz DX4 or pass on the 486 family entirely and choose a member of the Pentium line.

The Pentium Family

The Pentium chip was introduced in early 1993, and by the end of the year systems were appearing that used the chip. Although this delay may not seem significant when compared with availability delays in earlier systems, part of the reason for the problem was the revolutionary design of the Pentium chip.

Many observers felt that the 486 chip was about as fast as anyone could make a microprocessor. Intel introduced superscalar technology in the Pentium, however, which modified the method by which the individual CPU instructions were executed. Instead of a single path through the CPU, superscalar technology uses dual data pipelines, allowing two instructions to be executed at the same time. The design changes of the Pentium resulted in a large leap in computing speed. When comparing the 66 MHz Pentium to a 66 MHz 486DX2, for example, the newer chip can process nearly twice the information in the same amount of time.

The primary variations of the Pentium CPU have revolved around clock speeds, which started at 60 MHz and have now increased to 166 MHz. Intel may release even faster versions of the Pentium, as there is talk of a 200 MHz version among industry pundits.

Recently, the price of the Pentium has dropped dramatically. This price drop has been precipitated by the release of clone competitors and by Intel's next-generation chip, the Pentium Pro (see the following section). This price drop means that the Pentium is not only powerful, but suddenly very affordable. As a network server or fast workstation, the Pentium can't be beaten on a price/performance comparison. The availability of lower-speed Pentiums is giving way to higher-speed models, and considering anything below a 120 MHz or 133 MHz model is inadvisable. At these speeds, your server can keep up with virtually any demands placed on it.

The Pentium Pro

In the fourth quarter of 1995, Intel introduced the next generation of CPU. In another surprise naming move, the CPU's name implied that it is a member of the Pentium family—the Pentium Pro. In reality, the Pentium Pro is an entirely new CPU that implements a radical new design for increased performance.

The Pentium Pro uses state-of-the-art technology to improve performance. Three base technologies are together referred to as *Dynamic Execution* by Intel:

- First, a technology known as *multiple branch prediction* helps the Pentium Pro to anticipate modifications in instruction flow, and then dynamically adapt how the CPU works in order to match the needs of the program.

- Second, *data flow analysis* allows the CPU to examine data it receives and then determine the optimal processing sequence.

- Finally, *speculative execution* allows the CPU to actually process instructions ahead of time. Based on the multiple branch prediction technology, the CPU can execute instructions before they are needed, and hold them until they are needed.

In addition to improved architecture, the Pentium Pro includes a secondary memory cache built into the chip. The secondary cache, often called an *L2 cache*, can be either 256 KB or 512 KB in size. This cache allows for faster memory processing and helps relieve potential bottlenecks for the CPU.

Perhaps the biggest issue to keep in mind with the Pentium Pro is that it was designed specifically for 32-bit operating systems. This fact means it works great for Windows NT (both Server and Workstation) or for some variations of UNIX, but not for Windows 95 (which includes some 16-bit code) or Windows for Workgroups. In fact, if you run 16-bit operating systems on a Pentium Pro, your software will run more slowly than on a regular Pentium.

While the 32-bit orientation of the Pentium Pro may not appear to be a drawback when running a 32-bit program such as FastTrack on a 32-bit operating system such as Windows NT, it can be a problem if you add additional software to the server that is based on 16-bit technology. If you decide to select a Pentium Pro, make sure all your software components are designed exclusively for 32-bit systems.

Systems based on the Pentium Pro are still quite expensive. This fact isn't surprising, as systems based on the vanguard chip from Intel always carry a price premium. The question, then, is whether the additional cost and performance is worthwhile for your server. (Unless you have a specific need such as video or high-end graphics processing, the cost of a Pentium Pro system is prohibitive for general workstation use.) For low- and medium-traffic Internet sites, a regular Pentium system probably will do just fine. If you anticipate heavy traffic, and you also use the server for many in-house workstations, you may want to consider using a Pentium Pro.

Memory Requirements

I could reminisce for hours on the "old days" when 16 KB of memory was more than adequate for a computer system. When the IBM PC was first introduced, the 640 KB memory maximum was considered more than enough. (In fact, most systems only had 16 KB or 256 KB of memory installed.) Then came memory hogs such as Lotus 1-2-3, and finally Windows. Most systems being sold these days have at least 8 MB of memory, with provisions to install upwards of 64 MB of memory.

Exactly what should you look for in your system, as far as memory is concerned? The answer is two-fold, really. You need to be concerned not just with the *amount* of memory installed, but the *speed* of that memory, as well. The following sections discuss these issues.

Quantity

Earlier, this chapter mentioned that the minimum memory requirement for FastTrack is 32 MB. To some people, this requirement may seem like a lot of memory, but remember that this amount is only the *minimum*. If you want decent system performance, you should install at least 48 MB of memory in your server, and possibly 64 MB.

Because an Internet server can have quite a few services running on it, a large amount of memory is required. If the memory isn't available in the form of RAM, Windows NT uses disk space as virtual memory. This situation means a slower response time, as information is shuffled back and forth between RAM and storage on disk. Thus, the first rule of improving system performance is to add RAM; this change provides the largest increase in performance—even more than upgrading the CPU.

Perhaps an illustration is in order. We used a 66 MHz 486 system for our server, and it had only 16 MB of memory. (Yes, we ran early versions of FastTrack with only 16 MB of memory.) If we had to bring down the server, it sometimes seemed like forever before we were back online. The reason is the number of services that are intrinsic to running our Internet server. (You learn more about these services in Chapter 2, "Your Software.") The problem is that the services must all be running at the same time, which means they all occupy a portion of memory. As the services all vie for memory, Windows NT spends a great deal of time moving information between disk and memory. You would think that by increasing the RAM to 32 MB in the system, we would see a 100 percent performance improvement. (Twice the memory, half the time required, means 100 percent improvement, right?) In reality, the performance improved much more than 100 percent, because more can be done in RAM rather than the disk swap file. While adding the extra 16 MB of memory (to grow from 16 MB to 32 MB) is expensive, it is well worth the cost in the long run.

Speed

The type of memory used in your computer system also can affect overall performance. Many technical considerations exist in regard to memory, but the factor with perhaps the largest impact is memory speed.

Memory speed is measured in *nanoseconds*. Each second contains 100,000 nanoseconds—the amount of time necessary for light (and electricity, which travels at near the speed of light) to travel 11.72 inches. The speed of memory chips used in a small computer system can vary greatly—anywhere from 10 to 200 nanoseconds. The lower the number, the faster the RAM chips. Thus, you should seek out systems that have RAM speeds at 70 nanoseconds or below.

Typically, you can't improve the performance of an existing system by replacing your existing memory chips with faster chips. The reason is that the timing specifications of the motherboard are set when the board is designed. Thus, even though you may add RAM chips that are capable of faster speeds, the motherboard is still designed to deliver and access information at the slower speed. Memory speed is something you need to check when you first purchase a computer system.

NOTE: There are several specialized types of memory available on the market these days. These include EDO RAM, Fast Page Mode RAM, and SDRAM. These types of RAM are fundamentally different from traditional RAM because the way in which information stored in the RAM is accessed has changed. This doesn't mean anything to the user, however, except that the RAM is faster. While you will pay a premium for systems using such RAM, you should consider doing so if you want the fastest performance possible.

Disk Drive Requirements

For many people, hard drives are often an afterthought when putting together a system. When you are providing services to others on the Internet, system performance becomes a big issue. In this regard, your disk drive can either enhance or impair your overall system.

When planning your hard drive, consider these two areas: the speed of the drive, and the amount of space on the drive. The following sections discuss these issues.

Speed

In any computer system—and especially in servers—the speed of your hard drive matters quite a bit. Hard drive speed is typically measured in many ways. You may run across several terms, each measuring a different aspect of speed:

- ◆ *Seek time.* The average amount of time necessary to move the read/write heads from the current cylinder to another random cylinder.

- ◆ *Latency.* This has to do with the average amount of time necessary to locate a sector after the read/write heads have positioned themselves over the proper cylinder. Latency is purely a function of the rotational speed of the hard drive.

- ◆ *Access time.* The average amount of time necessary to find a given sector on the disk, starting from any other sector. In reality, access time is the sum of the seek time and the latency for the drive.

- ◆ *Transfer rate.* A measure of how much data can be transferred per second by the disk drive to the computer. Typically, the transfer rate is provided in millions of bits per second (*Mbps*). The higher the transfer rate, the better your system performance.

When you look through advertisements for disk drives, the speed mentioned in the advertisement is generally the access time. If you compare the access time from one drive to the access time from another, you are comparing apples to apples, and you can make a rough guesstimate of the relative performance of the drives.

If you run across an advertisement that specifies seek time rather than access time, you should temper this claim by looking at the rotational speed of the drive (measured in

RPM, or *revolutions per minute*). The faster the drive spins, the lower the latency, and thus the lower the access time. You want a drive that has a high rotational speed, low seek time, and (in all cases) a high transfer rate.

> **TIP:** If you are shopping for a new hard drive, it may become clear from looking at advertisements that seek times and access times have been confused. A good policy is to ask the vendor whether the drive speed advertised refers to seek time or access time before you make a decision.

Space

Earlier in this chapter, you learned the minimum hard drive space requirements for various operating systems. The figures provided refer to the amount of hard drive space required for just FastTrack-related files, not for anything else you may want to store on your system. In many ways, determining your overall space requirements simply boils down to a little detective work. You need to figure out how much space your operating system files consume, how many applications or services you will be running, along with the data file requirements for those programs. You also need to determine how much information you want to place on your server for access by other users. Don't make the assumption that Internet programs don't take much space—downloading the FastTrack Server alone takes over 10 MB of disk space!

> **Tip:** Before settling on a final disk drive size, see Chapter 2, "Your Software," for a full discussion of the software needs for an Internet site.

In general, hard drive space is cheap. The prices of hard drives seem to be lower every week. As of this writing, you can find fast 1 GB hard drives for under $200. Although you may think that 1 GB is quite a large drive, if you are running an active FTP site (in addition to your Web site), or if you have files available for download through your Web site, you can easily eat up such "limitless" space. Because hard drive space is so inexpensive, I suggest getting at least 1.5 to 2 GB of drive space. With EIDE drives and SCSI drives, you can easily add drive space by simply adding another drive at a later time.

> **CAUTION:** Make sure that when you purchase your hard drive, you also have a way to back it up. When you start providing information over the Internet, backups become critical; downtime for lost data can seriously impair the popularity of your site.

Other Elements

Other items are critical to the usefulness and performance of your system, and you can always add more gadgets to customize your system exactly as you want it. When looking at what hardware you should get for your server or workstation, you should examine at least a couple of additional areas. Primary among these are a CD-ROM drive and your video card.

CD-ROM Drives

CD-ROM drives are becoming standard equipment on computer systems. More and more software programs (including operating systems) are being distributed on CD-ROM—a direct outgrowth of the complexity and size of the products on the market today.

CD-ROM drives have their roots based in the CD audio technology that has swept the recording industry. It was a relatively easy (and logical) step to begin storing computer data, rather than musical data, on the 4.7-inch CD. After all, the CD is well suited to the task because it stores the musical data in digital format.

When you are looking for a CD-ROM drive for your system, the primary factor you need to consider is drive speed. You can make do with a single-speed drive, but you greatly improve performance by using a faster unit. Drive speed designations refer to the rotational speed of the CD and are indicated by a number followed by an X. Thus, a 3X drive runs at a rotational speed that is three times that of a single-speed drive. You can find 2X, 3X, 4X, 6X, and even 8X drives on the market these days. The purpose of increasing the rotational speed is that the data on the CD is moved under the read heads faster, thereby allowing it to be accessed more quickly.

Prices of CD-ROM drives are largely related to rotational speed. Although finding single-speed and 2X drives on the market is becoming more difficult, it is still possible, and at a very attractive price. If you are in the market for a CD-ROM drive, however, budget for at least a 3X or 4X drive. You will pay only a little more money than for a single-speed drive, and you will be much happier with the performance of the drive in your system.

Video

The minimum video requirement for running Windows is a VGA card, and other operating systems used with FastTrack have their own requirements. If you are running FastTrack under Windows NT, the VGA requirement should be viewed as the "least common denominator." The type of video card you get for your server or workstation depends on the type of work you are going to do. In an Internet services context, this translates to the type of information you are going to make available.

For example, if you are providing a few simple graphics, you probably will be happy with a VGA card or a graphics accelerator (see the sidebar). On the other hand, if you are providing high-resolution JPEG images or full-motion video, you will find a more powerful or specialized video card helpful.

Types of Video Cards

Any number of video cards are available. From a Windows perspective, the least powerful card is the plain-vanilla VGA. This standard has been around for years and has been somewhat improved by the release of various SVGA (superVGA) cards. SVGA cards provide the same capabilities as VGA cards but include higher video resolutions.

The biggest improvement in video technology revolves around the introduction of *graphics accelerators*. The difference between a video adapter and a graphics accelerator is that the latter can process video information more quickly than a standard video adapter, typically by implementing a special video processor chip in the circuitry. This fact easily distinguishes the more modern graphics accelerator—sometimes labeled simply as a *graphics adapter*.

Many SVGA cards on the market incorporate the specialized circuitry that qualifies them as graphics accelerators. The effect of using these cards is quite simple: if you speed up the video, you speed up the entire computer system because you don't need to wait as long for one of the slowest parts of your computer system.

Most out-of-the-box computer systems sold today include a fairly decent video card. These cards are adequate for use in workstation environments using typical development tools. If you are doing specialized graphics, pay special attention to the video card and make sure that it meets your needs.

> **TIP:** If you are buying a computer touted as a "network server," be sure to review the type of video adapter included. Because many system developers assume that you will be doing predominantly text-based work at the server, they don't include a very powerful video card. If you are using Windows NT, make sure your new system includes at least an SVGA graphics accelerator.

Summary

The basis of any computer system—including the one you use for your Internet services—is the hardware. In this chapter, you have learned what you need to make a good system and how you can make a good system better. Although Netscape publishes minimum hardware requirements for the FastTrack server, going beyond the minimum can improve your performance and productivity.

In the next chapter, you learn what is required for your Internet server from a software standpoint.

Chapter | 2

Your Software

After you have laid the foundation of your system through intelligent selection of hardware, you are ready to build the next layer—the software. The software you select determines what services you offer over the Internet. In this chapter, you learn what software you need for your site, how services function on the Internet, and what services are included with the FastTrack Server. You also learn what other services you can offer and how you can get those tools.

Client/Server Essentials

In traditional computer processing, information presented to a computer user is transferred across a network in a straightforward manner. The user begins by requesting information from a program running on his or her computer. This program accesses a remote database and requests the information it needs to fulfill the user's request. The information in the database is transferred to the user's computer, where it is processed, and the answer is finally provided to the user. Under this processing model, the raw data is actually transferred across the network to the user's computer.

In most respects, this approach to data processing is unnecessarily wasteful of computer resources. The problem is that a precious commodity—time—is used to transmit large amounts of raw data over the network. While the data requested by the user is being transmitted, no other data can be transmitted over the network. This problem may not be significant when only a couple of users are on the network, but it quickly becomes significant on a network like the Internet, where millions of users are online at the same time. To overcome this drawback, a different model of network processing was developed, called the *client/server model*.

Under the client/server processing model, the local host (the *client*) doesn't request raw information; instead, it requests final answers. Processing of the information is done at the remote database (the *server*). In this way, only the answer is transmitted across the network, thereby requiring less time and network resources.

The vast majority of information on the Internet is provided through this client/server relationship between two programs. The site that publishes information establishes a server; the site that wants to access the information uses a client. The *client software* communicates with the server software, and the requested information is transferred over the Internet between the two systems. Figure 2–1 illustrates this process.

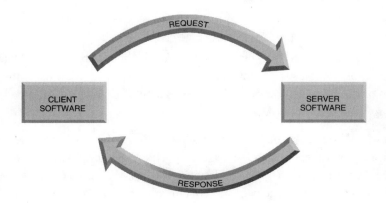

FIGURE 2–1

Client and server programs work with each other to provide information on the Internet.

As an example, consider the World Wide Web. If you want to establish a Web site, you need to run a piece of software called a *Web server*. This software responds to requests from a *Web browser*, which is the client software. The communication between the two (server and client) is done using a protocol called *HTTP*, which stands for *Hypertext Transport Protocol*. Using HTTP, the client issues a command that is received by the server. The server then responds to the command, providing information to the client. The client then can use the information received as desired. In most instances, it displays the information on the browser screen or processes it in some other way (such as playing a sound or downloading a file).

Other Internet services such as FTP and Gopher work the same way. They use the same client/server approach, even though a different protocol is used for each service.

Services in the FastTrack Server

The Netscape FastTrack Server is the entry-level Web server product from Netscape Communications, a premier Internet services company. The FastTrack server allows you to make information available over the Internet. In essence, the FastTrack server provides the server part of the client/server pair discussed in the preceding section. The FastTrack server is composed of several different components, including the following:

- ◆ A World Wide Web server
- ◆ Netscape Navigator Gold
- ◆ Netscape Server Manager

The following sections introduce each of these components.

Web Server

Most readers probably are already familiar with the World Wide Web. The Web enables you to publish and/or view all sorts of information. In many respects, the Web is the multimedia portion of the Internet. You can publish text, graphics, sounds, full-motion video, and programs, to name a few options.

Information on the Web is published as a series of *pages*. Be careful not to confuse a page on the Web with a physical page, such as a page of this book. Some similarities exist, but many differences exist as well. The biggest difference is that a Web page can be as big as the designer chooses to make it. The page can contain any of the data types already discussed, along with links to other pages on the Web. Figure 2–2 shows an example of a Web page, as seen within a browser.

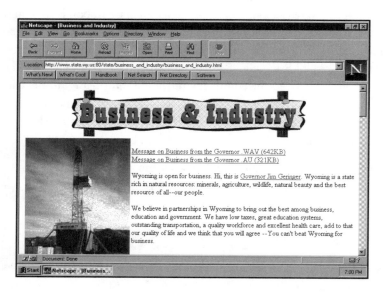

FIGURE 2–2

A Web page can contain many different elements.

Notice that the Web page in Figure 2–2 contains underlined text. Underlined items denote links to related information elsewhere on the Web. As the person using the browser moves the mouse pointer over the link, the status bar indicates where the link goes. When the user clicks the link, the browser software contacts the server at a remote location, which transfers a page over the Internet, and the browser displays the new page.

Over the past couple of years, the Web has experienced the largest growth of any single service available on the Internet. Accurate figures on actual growth of the Web are hard to come by, but estimates indicate that millions and millions of people are actively using the Web on a daily basis.

The Netscape FastTrack Server is, by nature, a Web server. Using the FastTrack server, you can publish information on the Internet. Alternatively, you can use the server to publish information for your own local area network, setting up an *intranet*. Either way, you follow the same basic steps and publish information in the same basic way. The second section of this book (beginning with Chapter 4, "Installing Your Web Server") provides the information you need to set up your Web site with the FastTrack server.

Netscape Navigator Gold

There are many Web browsers on the market these days, each of which allow you to connect to a Web server and retrieve information. The Web browsers from Netscape own the lion's share of the browser market. Navigator Gold is only one of the browsers available from Netscape, and it is included with your FastTrack server.

Navigator Gold is much more than a simple Web browser, however. The most exciting aspect of the product is that you can also use it to create your own Web pages. Thus, Navigator Gold is also an *authoring tool* you can use to create your own content. In Chapter 9, "Creating Pages with Netscape Navigator Gold," you learn how to use this unique tool for that very purpose.

Netscape Server Manager

The Netscape Server Manager provides a consistent interface for managing every aspect of your Web site. From the Netscape Server Manager, you can access configuration information for different areas of the Web server, such as performance, access, and execution. Figure 2–3 shows the Netscape Server Manager.

Notice that the Netscape Server Manager is browser-based, meaning you use a familiar Web browser interface to change the configuration of FastTrack server. You learn more about how to use the Netscape Server Manager throughout this book, but particularly in Chapter 17, "The Netscape Server Manager."

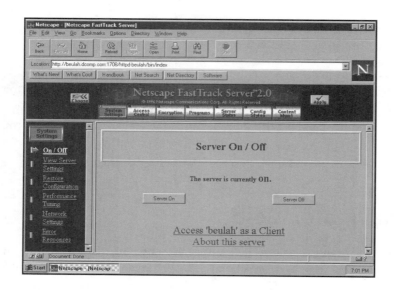

FIGURE 2–3

The Netscape Server Manager enables you to control your Web site.

Requirements for Running the FastTrack Server

In Chapter 1, "Your Hardware," you learned about the computer hardware you need to set up your own Internet services using Netscape FastTrack Server. Hardware is only part of the story, however. Software requirements for using the product include the following items:

- ◆ Windows NT 3.51
- ◆ Windows NT 3.51 Service Pack

The following sections discuss each of these items.

Windows NT 3.51

According to Netscape specifications, you must be running at least Windows NT 3.51 to use FastTrack. This means that you can run the server on any of the following operating system versions:

- ◆ Windows NT Workstation 3.51
- ◆ Windows NT Server 3.51

- ◆ Windows NT Workstation 4.0
- ◆ Windows NT Server 4.0

In addition, these operating systems can be running on any of the hardware discussed in Chapter 1, "Your Hardware." If you try to run FastTrack on any other operating system (such as Windows 95), the services will not work properly.

If you are running an earlier version of Windows NT (such as 3.5), you can get upgrades at a very reasonable cost.

Windows NT 3.51 Service Pack

Periodically, Microsoft issues service packs for its operating systems. These service packs contain minor upgrades to correct problems, bugs, and errors. The service packs aren't widely publicized, but they come out fairly regularly. Service packs are issued cumulatively, which means that service pack #4 includes everything in service pack #3, which includes everything in service pack #2, and so on. If you are using Windows NT 3.51, you need to get at least service pack #4 in order for FastTrack to work properly. If you are using Windows NT 4.0, you won't need this service pack.

> **NOTE:** Since Microsoft regularly issues service packs, it is a good idea to check their Web site to see what the latest service pack is. Always install the latest service pack for use with your system.

Service packs are available from any of the normal download sites for Microsoft. If you already have an Internet connection, you can get the requisite service pack by using your Web server with the following URL:

```
http://www.microsoft.com/isapi/support/bldqpage.idc?ProductPage=q_
➥servpk&ProductTitle=Windows+NT+Service+Packs
```

If this URL doesn't work (URLs are known to change from time to time), try http://www.microsoft.com and browse around the site looking for the service packs.

Other Services for Your Site

In addition to a Web server, you can install additional Internet services on your system. Some of these services are basically mandatory; others serve only to provide a more rounded collection of services for your site.

DNS Server

A *DNS server* is a program that translates between the two types of addresses used on the Internet: domain addresses and IP addresses. The translation is necessary because computers cannot understand domain addresses directly; they can understand only the numeric IP addresses.

Understanding Domain Addressing

Everything you do on the Internet in some way involves the use of an address. The addresses that most people use are called *domain addresses*. These are the addresses that people put on their business cards. Consider the following domain address:

```
awyatt@dcomp.com
```

This is an actual address—mine. This address functions in much the same way as my physical address (which you would use to send me a physical letter or package). The part of the address before the @ sign is my user id, in this case awyatt. The portion of the address after the @ sign is the *domain*, with periods between each *level* of the domain. Domains are nothing but different organizational levels. These levels are increasingly general, from left to right. It is this part, on the right side of the @ sign, that is translated by the DNS server so that computers can understand it.

The domain naming system provides a method of uniquely identifying different organizations and computer systems on the Internet. Because the system allows for different domain levels to be included in an address, at times the domains can appear rather complex. For instance, take a look at the following fictional address:

```
vic@carlton.state.wy.us
```

This domain name has four levels. If you start at the end of the domain and work backwards, you can get a more specific idea of where this domain is located. The us level indicates that this is a geographic domain, located within the United States, and the wy indicates that it is in the state of Wyoming; state is the name of a subdomain within Wyoming, and carlton is the name of a particular server within the state subdomain. Each level of the domain may contain other subdivisions. For example, the state subdomain may contain more than one server, and within wy more than a single subdomain is likely.

Notice that this explanation uses terms like "probably" and "may." No hard-and-fast rule exists. The domain naming system has developed over years, and at times may be used inconsistently. The important thing for you to remember is that domains help to identify the location of a computer or network. This system is essential for accessing resources and directing information across the Net.

Top-level domains (those appearing at the right side of a domain address) can be either of two types: organizational or geographical. Table 2–1 describes the seven possible organizational domains.

Table 2–1   Organizational domains.

Domain	Purpose
com	Commercial entities, such as businesses
edu	Educational institutions
gov	Non-military U.S. government institutions
int	International institutions, such as NATO
mil	U.S. military institutions
net	Network resources, including Internet service providers
org	Nonprofit organizations

For the most part, any domain name ending with an organizational domain can be assumed to be physically located within the United States. For domains outside the United States, and for state and local governments within the United States, the top-level domain is geographical in nature. This top-level domain consists of two letters that indicate the country in which the domain is located. At last count, more than 90 geographical domains existed; Table 2–2 gives an example of some of the geographical domains.

Table 2-2 Sample geographical domains.

Domain	Country
aq	Antarctica
au	Australia
br	Brazil
ca	Canada
ch	Switzerland
cn	China
de	Germany
dk	Denmark
es	Spain
fr	France
hk	Hong Kong
il	Israel
it	Italy
jp	Japan
mx	Mexico
nz	New Zealand
pl	Poland
ru	Russian Federation
tr	Turkey
uk	United Kingdom
us	United States
va	Vatican

Understanding IP Addressing

As mentioned earlier, a DNS server converts a domain name into an IP (Internet Protocol) address. You may already know that the IP address is numeric in nature. Each IP address is unique, meaning it identifies a single location on the Internet. These IP addresses consist of four 8-bit numbers, represented in decimal notation, but separated by periods. Thus, the following is an example of an IP address:

`205.163.44.2`

Each of the four numbers in an IP address is called an *octet*. Because each octet represents eight bits of the address, no single octet can have a value above 255. The lowest possible

IP address is 0.0.0.0 and the highest is 255.255.255.255 (although this fact is misleading, because the network itself uses some IP addresses for overhead purposes).

IP addresses are assigned to networks based on the size of the network. Only three classifications of networks exist: A, B, and C:

♦ Class A networks are very large, and few IP addresses are available for these types of networks—only 126 possible Class A addresses exist in the world. Each Class A network can have in excess of 16 million computers in its individual network. For Class A networks, the first octet of its IP address is between 1 and 126, and all the remaining octets are used to identify members of that network.

♦ Class B networks are a bit smaller; they can have up to approximately 65,000 workstations. For these types of networks, the first octet of the IP address is a number between 128 and 191, and the second octet further denotes the network address. Thus, approximately 16,000 Class B networks can exist in the world. The last two octets of the IP address denote individual workstations.

♦ Class C networks are the smallest. These networks can include up to about 250 workstations per network. The first octet of the IP address has a value between 192 and 223, and the second and third octets further define the network. The final octet identifies the workstation on the network. A couple of million Class C networks are possible.

When You Need a DNS Server

When you provide an address for an Internet operation, you can use either the domain name method or the IP address method. Most people use the former because it's easier for humans to read and understand. The DNS server converts the domain name to the IP address completely behind the scenes. If you are setting up an Internet service, and you have reserved your own domain name, you are entirely responsible for that domain, and you should have your own DNS server.

For example, my company has a reserved domain name of dcomp.com, and that domain has a Class C address assigned to it. This means we are responsible for everything that happens within that domain. If we add servers, we assign the fourth octet number of the IP address to the machine. However, for the rest of the Internet to be aware of this new addition, we need a DNS server to handle the resolution from the domain name (such as www.beulah.dcomp.com) to the IP address (such as 205.163.44.8).

Where to Get a DNS Server

You can get a DNS server in many places. Some are free, and others cost money. You can download free DNS servers from the Internet; they fall into the category of shareware or that of beta software. The best (and most stable) freeware DNS server for Windows NT is a port of BIND, the standard DNS server for the UNIX environment. You can download this program by connecting to the Web site at

```
http://www.software.com/prod/bindnt/bindnt.html
```

If you are a brave soul, you can also get the Microsoft version of a DNS server for free. This product is considered a beta, and is improved only sporadically. (A beta is a program that is still in testing; it has not been thoroughly debugged, nor is it considered complete.) The consensus of most network administrators around the Internet is that the product isn't really stable, and that you shouldn't rely on it. But, if you want it, you can download a copy by using FTP to connect to the following site:

```
rhino.microsoft.com
```

Log in as dnsbeta and also use dnsbeta as your password. As of this writing, the files are in the files directory. Read the file CONTEXT.TXT at the FTP site for information on which files you should download.

> **NOTE:** If you use the Microsoft DNS beta with Windows 3.51, no technical support is available. However, Microsoft has indicated that its DNS server will be out of beta soon and provided free of charge with Windows NT 4.0.

Several commercial DNS products are available for Windows NT. If you want more information about commercial versions, contact the following vendors:

MetaInfo
(206) 523-0484
http://www.metainfo.com

FBLI
(514) 349-0455
http://www.fbli.com

NOTE: Setting up a DNS server can be frustrating and complicated. Follow the instructions provided with your DNS server software exactly. Getting additional explanatory material also is helpful. A good book on the subject, recommended by many sites on the Internet, is *DNS and BIND* by Paul Albitz and Cricket Liu, published by O'Rielly and Associates.

E-Mail Server

E-mail is unquestionably the single largest use of the Internet. This fact makes sense because the Internet is a medium for communication, and e-mail is the standard way of communicating electronically. If you are responsible for your own domain, you may want to set up a mail server for your site.

You may be familiar with e-mail from the user side of the fence: When you need your mail, you fire up your e-mail program (such as Eudora, MS Mail, or E-Mail Connection) and manage your messages. These programs are called *User Agents*; they enable you (the user) to manage your mail by using an interface with which you are comfortable.

User Agents don't take care of all the behind-the-scenes tasks related to e-mail, however. You may remember that when you first set up your e-mail program you provided the name of an e-mail server with which the program should connect. From the network administrator's viewpoint, this server (called a *Message Transfer Agent*, or *MTA*) is the key program required for e-mail. If you manage your own domain, you may want to install your own MTA program, or e-mail server.

Several e-mail servers are available for Windows NT. Some are shareware and others are available as commercial products. On the shareware side, you may want to look at the following programs:

- ◆ *EMWAC.* This free version of a mail server also includes the capacity to run your own mailing list. You can get additional information on the software at http://www.emwac.ed.ac.uk.

- ◆ *Internet Shopper.* This shareware product by Brian Dorricott has recently come out and looks quite full-featured. You also can get quite a few utilities that work with the product to provide special management features. Prices vary, depending on the capabilities of the program, but useful

systems start at about $200. You can get more information at
http://www.net-shopper.co.uk/software/ntmail/index.htm.

The commercial side offers several programs that provide server capabilities. You can contact any of the following companies—be sure to ask for their server products (although I am most fond of post.office from Software.com):

♦ *IRISoft.* A relative newcomer to the market, Mi'Mail appears to be a very good value for commercial mail servers. At only $99 for a full version, you can download a test version and use it for 30 days before making your final decision. For more information, connect to http://www.irisoft.be/en/ntserv.htm (notice that IRISoft is located in Belgium).

♦ *Lotus.* cc:Mail includes not only a user interface (the User Agent discussed earlier), but a server that runs in the background 24 hours a day. This product comes in several configurations, based on the number of users. Prices start at $825 for your local network, with an additional fee in excess of $3,400 to provide gateway access to the Internet. You can find out more at http://www.lotus.com/ccmail/.

♦ *Microsoft.* The BackOffice portion of Microsoft Mail, which is Microsoft's mail server, is available for a base price of at least $1,300. (Don't be surprised, however, if your price goes up as you add connectivity features to various systems.) You can learn more about this product at http://www.microsoft.com/Mail/.

♦ *Software.com.* Their post.office product retails for $495, but you can download a fully-functional copy from the Web for a 30-day trial. Installation is easy, and configuration is done using a Web page (really cool!). Information is available at http://www.software.com.

FTP Server

FTP is the name of the program used to transfer files from one system to another. In reality, FTP is an acronym for File Transfer Protocol. From a user's standpoint, this program accomplishes several tasks:

♦ Establishes a connection between your machine and a remote site

♦ Enables the user to perform limited directory-related operations at that site

♦ Transfers files between the remote site and the user's machine, or vice versa

Because FTP enables files to be transferred, it is one of the most popular programs used on the Internet—particularly popular with people who have been using the Internet for a while. (Many newer users think that the World Wide Web and the Internet are synonymous; therefore, they don't try additional programs such as FTP.)

Literally thousands of FTP sites are available around the Internet. FTP sites are particularly well-suited for file-related materials. For example, you may sell computer products and want to make drivers available on the Internet. Or you may have an outstanding collection of sound files that you want to make available. These needs lend themselves very well to a solution involving FTP.

There are many places you can get an FTP server. If you are using the UNIX versions of FastTrack, an FTP daemon should have been included with your operating system. If you are using Windows NT, you can find an FTP server in the Windows NT Resource Kit. This is a version of the shareware FTP server distributed by EMWAC.

> **TIP:** The EMWAC FTP server included with the Windows NT Resource Kit may be a bit dated. You should check the EMWAC Web site at http://www.emwac.ed.ac.uk to determine if a more recent version of the server is available.

Gopher Server

Gopher is one of the most widely used tools on the Internet, particularly in the educational and government arenas. Gopher enables a user to retrieve information stored in Gopher servers at various sites across the Internet. Developed in early 1991 by the University of Minnesota's Minnesota Microcomputer, Workstation, and Networks Center, the Gopher software has been widely accepted and implemented over much of the Net.

The main reason that Gopher has been successful is that finding information on the Internet can be difficult. Most people who were looking for files or other information on the Net found that locating an uncommon file or resource was more of a chore than a learning adventure. It often took hours of tracking and investigating to find the right information. Considerable time still may be needed to find obscure information, but locating information now is much easier than before, thanks in large part to Gopher.

In a nutshell, Gopher is a program that enables you to access databases from all around the Internet. More specifically, as its name implies, it will "go for" the data or topic you specify. But instead of forcing you to blindly search a database for your desired topic, Gopher always presents your choices in a series of menus from which you can make choices. Each choice represents a resource that you can use. These resources can be on a local computer system or from virtually anywhere on the Internet.

The most popular and low-cost way to set up your own Gopher server is to download the shareware version from the University of Minnesota. You can find several versions for various platforms (including UNIX and NT) at the Gopher site at gopher.tc.umn.edu.

Remote Access Service

Remote Access Service (RAS) is provided with Windows NT Server. It enables dial-in access to your network from any computer, using a modem. Access is account- and password-protected, and you can control what information dial-in users can access. Dial-up is easiest from other systems using Windows, particularly Windows 95, where Dial-Up Networking (the Windows 95 equivalent of RAS) can be used.

After a remote user has connected to your system by using RAS, he has access to all network resources for which you have provided permission. This includes access to the Internet, as RAS connections are established using PPP or SLIP protocols. RAS is a great way for employees on the road to stay in touch, and you also can start your own Internet access service for other people.

> **NOTE:** Effectively using RAS is beyond the scope of this book. However, I would suggest that before you try to enable RAS you have a firm understanding of how it works and what it implies for your system. RAS, if implemented improperly, can compromise the security of your entire network. Get yourself a good book on the subject of remote networking, specifically for Windows NT networks.

Windows NT Tools

If you have been working with a Windows NT network for some time, you may already be familiar with many of the administrative tools built into the operating system. If your background lies in other areas, however (for example, managing Internet services on a UNIX-based system), you may not be familiar with the Windows NT tools yet.

Windows NT provides many tools that may at first seem esoteric or hard to find, but they are nonetheless beneficial to administering an Internet site. The following tools, in particular, are helpful:

- Control Panel
- User Manager
- Event Viewer
- Performance Monitor

It is not the purpose of this chapter to provide detailed information on how to use each of these tools. That being said, the following sections do provide some introductory material that you may find helpful in getting started with the tools. The best way to learn how to use the tools, quite honestly, is to start using them and studying the online help provided with each tool.

The Control Panel

The Control Panel is the heart of how you configure Windows NT. You access the Control Panel by choosing the Settings option from the Start menu, and then clicking on the Control Panel option. When the Control Panel opens, it looks just like any other program group window, as shown in Figure 2–4.

Not all the icons within the Control Panel (called *applets*) are useful for an Internet site, but two of them can be critical. These applets—Network and Services—are described in the following sections.

The Network Applet

If you double-click the Network applet within the Control Panel, you have an opportunity to change the configuration of your network (see Figure 2–5). Chances are good that you had this set up when you first installed your local area network, but you will undoubtedly be visiting it again as you configure for your Internet services.

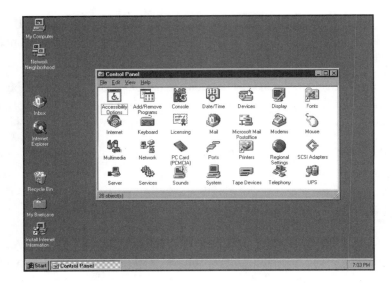

FIGURE 2–4

The Control Panel contains various configuration elements for a Windows NT system.

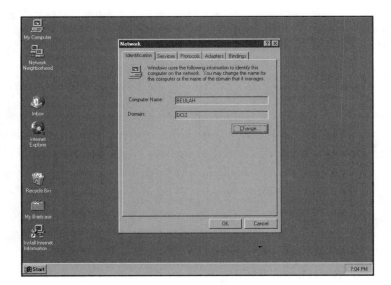

FIGURE 2–5

The Network applet enables you to modify your network configuration.

NOTE: If you haven't already configured your network for the TCP/IP protocol, you need to do so. The Internet uses TCP/IP for all communications, and you use the Network applet to make your changes for TCP/IP. If you need help in this area, refer to your Windows NT documentation or to a good text on TCP/IP.

As you decide to add various servers to your Internet site, you are, in effect, adding network services. Many of these services end up in the Network applet, and you need to return here from time to time to configure the services.

The Services Applet

In the Windows NT environment, *services* are programs that run in the background and provide functionality that can be called on by other programs. In the UNIX environment, services are known as *daemons*, because they run all the time in the background. When you double-click on the Services applet, Windows NT displays the Services dialog box shown in Figure 2–6.

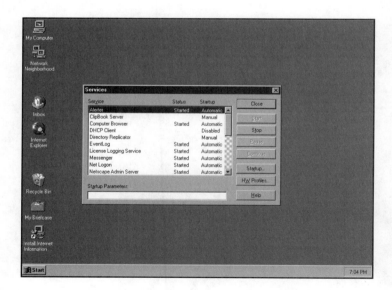

FIGURE 2–6

The Services applet provides a way to control all the services installed as part of Windows NT.

Notice that the Services dialog box lists each service alphabetically, along with an indication of the service's status (started or paused) and how the service initially starts. You can modify a service by double-clicking the service name.

Internet services are designed to run around the clock. To do this, they must run as Windows NT services. After you have successfully installed a service (such as your Web server), it appears in the Services dialog box. By using this dialog box, you can control whether the service runs or modify how the service is started.

The User Manager

The User Manager is where you control who has access to your domain. Many Internet services utilize the User Manager to control who has access to the information on your system. (The FastTrack server does not rely on the User Manager; it uses its own security information.) It's a good idea to know how to use the User Manager to modify account access rights if you need to do so.

To start the User Manager, choose the <u>P</u>rograms option from the Start menu, then choose Administrative Tools (Common), and finally User Manager for Domains. (Under Windows NT Workstation the menu choice is simply User Manager.) Windows NT opens the User Manager window, as shown in Figure 2–7.

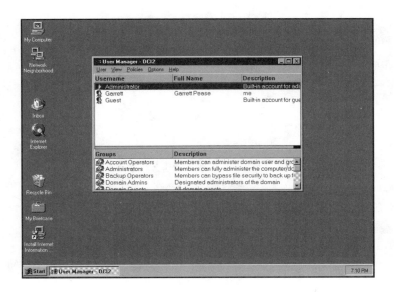

FIGURE 2–7

The User Manager displays a list of your defined user accounts and groups.

At the top of the User Manager window are the user accounts that have been defined for your domain. At the bottom of the window are the user groups that you have set up. If you want to change user account information, double-click the user's name. Likewise, if you want to change a group, double-click the group name.

> **NOTE:** The menus at the top of the User Manager window manage the various users and groups on your system. Perhaps the most important menu options are under the Policies menu. Here you set the default rules for using your network. To fully understand the implications and importance of these settings, get a good book on Windows NT network management—you'll find it well worth the investment.

The Event Viewer

As Windows NT runs, events crop up from time to time. These events may be triggered by a software program or by the operating system itself. If desired, you can have these events recorded in a log file so that you can review them as you deem necessary. When you want to review the events, you use the Event Viewer.

To start the Event Viewer, choose the Programs option from the Start menu, then choose Administrative Tools (Common), and finally Event Viewer. Windows NT posts the Event Viewer window, as shown in Figure 2–8.

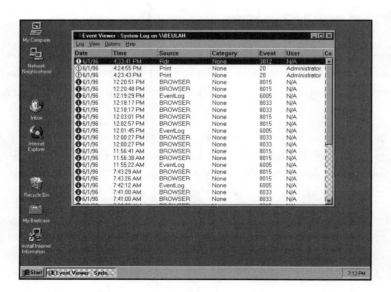

FIGURE 2–8

The Event Viewer enables you to review and manage the event log files.

Using the Event Viewer, you can review any of the three log files maintained by Windows NT. The three log files and their purposes are as follows:

- ◆ *System.* This log file records events that occur in managing the operating system. For example, a device not responding as expected by Windows NT might be a recordable event.

- ◆ *Security.* This log file records events generated by the security system of Windows NT. For instance, if someone tries to log into the system by using a bad password, this event ends up in the security log.

- ◆ *Application.* The application log file records events generated by your programs. Different programs can generate different types of events, such as a word processor indicating when it got an unexpected result from a system query.

You select which log file is displayed in the Event Viewer by using the File menu. You can see more information about a specific event by double-clicking the event in question.

After you install your Internet servers, they behave like a part of your system. (Remember that the servers run as services on your system.) The servers log events as they occur, and you may need to review those events from time to time.

The Performance Monitor

The performance of a computer system always seems of interest to certain users. In reality, it should be of great interest to network administrators. If the performance of your network is slowed in any way, it doesn't just affect a single user—it can affect *all* users on the network.

Windows NT includes a tool to help experienced users evaluate the performance of their systems. You access this tool, Performance Monitor, by choosing the Programs option from the Start menu, then Administrative Tools (Common), and finally Performance Monitor (the Performance Monitor window is shown in Figure 2–9).

Using the Performance Monitor, you can monitor different system objects or subsystems by adding them to the window. To do this, you select the Add to Chart option from the Edit menu. You can also specify how often you want these objects sampled, and then the Performance Monitor displays the results of its monitoring. By thoughtful use of the Performance Monitor, you can discover areas where you can tweak your system to improve throughput.

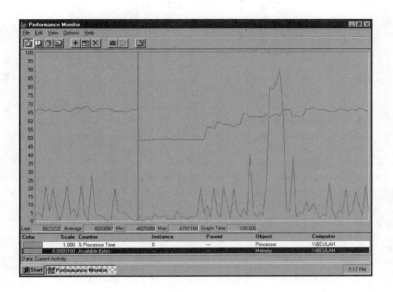

FIGURE 2–9

The Performance Monitor enables you to view how different parts of your system are responding over time.

Summary

Software is the key to accomplishing anything with a computer, and your Internet server is no exception. Without the proper software, you can't effectively offer any Internet services. This chapter has introduced you to the software that—together with your hardware—provides the basis for your Internet services. Here you have learned about each of the software products you need, as well as how they work together.

In the next chapter, you learn about the third component of any Internet server—the actual Internet connection.

Chapter | 3

Your Internet Connection

After you have your hardware and software in place, you are ready to connect to the Internet. Actually creating your Internet connection is perhaps the most expensive part of providing Internet services. In this chapter you learn the ins and outs of the Internet and getting connected. You even learn the difference between the Internet and the latest networking buzzword—an intranet.

Understanding the Internet

The Internet seems to be the hottest craze in computing these days. You can't seem to read a single article about a program or a piece of hardware without the Internet being mentioned somewhere. Everyone wants Internet connectivity to be built into their programs, and every business seems to be advertising on the Internet.

So exactly what is the Internet? It has been described by some experts as a "network of networks." Technically, this definition is correct. Thousands and thousands of networks (local area networks, generally) around the world have been connected to each other by using the Internet. Although this description is technically correct, however, it falls short of conveying the breadth and depth of the Internet.

Because of the vast wealth of information that is available on the Internet, some people have aptly described it as a tool—a new computing tool. This is also a very good description. You can find information about virtually anything on the Internet, and the number of resources are growing daily. People just like you are connecting to the Internet and making information available in staggering numbers.

The roots of the Internet are found in the mid-1960s when researchers, experimenting with computer communications, developed a fast and reliable method of sharing information over ordinary phone lines. This communication method, known as *packet switching*, involved breaking down a message (regardless of its size) into small packets that were sent individually over the communications channel. The packets then were reassembled at the other end of the communications link. The use of packets allowed other people to share the same communications link (with their own packets). It also allowed the packets to take various routes to the same destination, which meant that the communications links that defined the network were *dynamic* in nature. This dynamic approach to networking means that even though one route between two nodes on the network might go down, the packets can travel a different route to get to the same destination. The result is less potential for down time.

Over the years, packet switching has been used in networks of all sizes. As local networks grew at individual research facilities and universities, connecting these networks to share information between the differing facilities became desirable. These interconnections were treated as extensions of the original, individual networks. In 1969, the Department of Defense, through their Advanced Research Projects Agency (ARPA), created an experimental packet-switched network called ARPANET, an early forerunner of the Internet. In 1982, ARPANET joined with MILNET (the military network) and a few other networks, and the Internet was created from this consolidation. Internet is a shortened version of *internetwork system.*

Today, the Internet is a phenomenally-fast-growing communications medium. Millions of networks and individual computers are being connected to the Internet, and the result is very exciting to watch. You have probably felt this excitement, as well, or you would not be considering offering your own services over the Internet.

Internet Versus Intranet

As the Internet has grown, and particularly in the past couple of years, a number of computing tools have emerged that were designed specifically for use on the Net. Remember that the Internet is simply a huge network—this fact means that those tools will work not only on the Internet, but also on local area networks within organizations.

This is the distinction between the Internet and an intranet: The Internet is a network connection with computers *outside* your organization, and an intranet provides similar connections and services for use *within* your organization (see Figure 3–1.) Many large companies are using the tools originally developed for publishing information over the Internet, but limiting those tools to use within the company. For example, Eli Lilly and Company, a pharmaceuticals concern based in Indianapolis, IN, has established a Web site that isn't open to everyone on the Internet. Instead, it is used on their own internal network to disseminate information quickly and easily.

From a technical standpoint, not much difference exists between the Internet and an intranet. Indeed, the same networking concepts are used, and the same tools come into play. As you work through this book, remember that everything discussed about the Internet can also be adapted for use within your own organization.

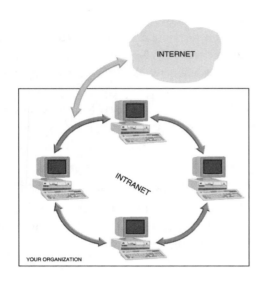

FIGURE 3–1

The relationship between the Internet and an intranet.

Internet Providers

An *Internet provider* (sometimes called an *Internet Service Provider*, or *ISP*) is a company that provides a way for you to access the Internet. Establishing a full-time connection to the backbone of the Internet is expensive, at the very least. In fact, it's so expensive that not many organizations can afford it. To overcome this problem, hundreds of smaller companies have sprung up that establish the expensive link, and then resell limited access to their link for a smaller amount of money.

Providing access to the Internet is not a regulated business. ISPs are therefore free to charge whatever they feel the market will bear. This situation is one reason why Internet access in large metropolitan areas costs less than in smaller areas—more competition exists between different ISPs. This setup drives prices down and ultimately helps the consumer. Because prices charged by different ISPs can vary quite a bit, you should shop around and find the right mix of services and price from an ISP.

You can divide the functions of an Internet provider into four categories:

- ◆ **Equipment.** Establishing a reliable connection to the Internet requires a fair amount of specialized equipment. An ISP takes care of purchasing the computers, routers, multiplexors, and phone equipment necessary for maintaining the link with the Internet.

◆ **Communications.** Not only does providing Internet access deal with computer equipment, but it is also intimately related to phone service. (Phone lines provide the communications medium for the Internet.) The provider takes care of setting up and maintaining the high-speed communications lines between its facilities and the Internet.

◆ **Service.** Providers often supply telecommunications consulting services as well as Internet access. At the least, they should provide a help desk that can aid you when you're having connection problems.

◆ **Billing.** Because you aren't the only customer for the provider, each provider must have some way to bill you and all its other customers. The billing process involves metering time on the system and making sure that billings and collections are handled properly.

If you aren't establishing an Internet service, but instead are using Internet tools on an intranet, you don't need to work with an ISP. Instead, the physical network within your organization becomes your communications medium. (For example, the LAN that you already have in place.)

Connection Types

Before you can select a provider, you need to determine exactly what type of Internet service you need—what type of connection you should get. You can connect to the Internet in many ways, but not all types of connections are appropriate for offering services to others. In general, you can establish two types of Internet connections: dial-up or dedicated. These options are discussed fully in the following sections.

Dial-Up Service

Dial-up service uses a modem to connect with the Internet provider's computers, and in turn with the Internet. This scheme is great for people who want to use the Internet only once in a while; if you want to provide services, however, a dial-up system could severely cramp your plans. Remember that the services are offered on your computer, and people can reach your computer only when the dial-up modem link is active. Unless you plan to leave the connection open 24 hours a day, your services may not be available at all times. If people find your services unavailable when they need them, they simply won't visit your site anymore.

Dedicated Service

A dedicated Internet account is the opposite of a dial-up account. Where a dial-up account requires you to establish a modem connection every time you want access, a dedicated account is available 24 hours a day, 365 days a year. Establishing a dedicated account involves setting up your own Internet gateway and paying to have a direct, full-time link with the network. Your computers, in effect, become a full-time part of the Internet.

Because dedicated accounts offer a full-time connection to the Internet, this is the type of account you need if you are providing Internet services. If you establish a Web site, for example, the Internet makes that site accessible all over the world. If your site is in Denver, and someone wants to access it from France, that time difference is eight hours. If they access your site in the morning (France time), the time may be the middle of the night in Denver, but your Web site is still expected to be available.

To establish a dedicated service account, you still need to work with an Internet provider. This type of service is where the providers really start to differ, however. Some providers can only supply low-volume dedicated accounts; others may charge exorbitant fees for setting up dedicated accounts. You must do some heavy comparison shopping to find the deal that is right for you.

Equipment Required

Whereas a dial-up connection only requires a modem, a dedicated connection requires additional hardware to work properly, as well as a dedicated phone line. These items are covered in the following sections.

> **NOTE:** Remember that the requirements described in these sections are in addition to what you learned about in Chapters 1 and 2—you still need the proper computer hardware and software to make it all work.

Router

A *router* is a computer device that inspects data packets it encounters to determine where they should be sent. In layman's terms, a router acts as a "traffic cop," to determine what information gets sent where. A router is essential to direct information between your network and the Internet at large (and vice versa).

Routers are available from any number of sources. In fact, the fortunes of companies that produce and sell routers have risen with the popularity of the Internet. Routers aren't something that you can walk into a computer store and purchase off the shelf, because they are rather specialized. To purchase a router, you must contact the manufacturer directly, contact a distributor, or work through your Internet provider.

Depending on the provider you use, you may be able to lease a router from the provider, get suggestions on which one to purchase, or buy a router outright. Some ISPs even require you to use their routers, in order to guarantee compatibility with their equipment. Routers typically cost anywhere from $2,000 to $10,000, depending on the complexity of your network and the capabilities of the router itself.

> **TIP:** If you decide to get a router from your Internet provider, make sure that you understand whether you are leasing or buying. The key point is who will own the router if you decide to switch providers at some point in the future.

In general, routers are pretty easy to use. In most installations, you set them up once and then forget about them. Routers have several plugs on the back; the simplest routers have only two plugs. One plug connects the router to your network, with a network cable that runs from the router to your hub or concentrator. The other plug connects the router to the DSU/CSU (described in the next section).

DSU/CSU

Between the router and the phone line is a device known as a *DSU/CSU* (data service unit/channel service unit). These devices used to be separate units—the DSU serviced the data terminal equipment (the router) and the CSU serviced the digital data service (the phone line). Today, however, the DSU/CSU is typically a single device, about the size of an external modem.

In technical terms, the CSU portion of the device is used to terminate the digital phone circuit through line conditioning and equalization. The DSU then converts the signaling protocol (the way in which communications signals are transferred over the wires) from the phone company's format to the format needed by the router.

The capabilities of the DSU/CSU must be matched to the bandwidth (capacity) of the phone line and the needs of the router. For this reason, most people purchase the DSU/CSU at the same time as the router. This strategy not only means a single source for equipment (less finger-pointing if things don't work), but also a better chance that the DSU/CSU has been tested with the router.

Phone Lines

If you were connecting to the Internet by using a dial-up account, you could use normal phone lines to establish a link. When you set up a dedicated account, however, you need to lease a communications channel between your location and that of your Internet provider. In most instances, securing a communications channel involves working with your local phone company. If you and your Internet provider aren't located in the same city, it may involve working with several phone companies. Some providers may be willing to help you to get the phone link set up; others may not.

> **NOTE:** If your ISP is unwilling to at least help with getting the necessary data line, you may want to look for another ISP. If you need to work with multiple phone companies, the process can be frustrating, at best.

Dedicated links come in several varieties, each distinguished by the capacity (*bandwidth*) of the channel. In general, four types of dedicated links are available:

- ◆ **56Kb channel.** This is a common small-capacity dedicated channel. A 56Kb channel can handle up to 56 kilobits of information per second, which means it will handle twice the throughput of the fastest asynchronous modems on the market today.

- ◆ **T1 channel.** This type of connection is equivalent to 24 56Kb channels, operating at a bandwidth of 1.544Mbs. T1 service refers to the type of wiring used in the connection, not the data rate and composition, however. (That is called the *DS1*.) A T1 line is often called a *point-to-point connection*, because you bypass the normal phone company switches entirely. When you use a T1 channel, you need special phone company equipment at your office, as transmission is done over fiber-optic cable. The channel begins at your location and ends at the phone company switch, where your data signal is compressed onto high-capacity phone company lines. This signal then ends up at the phone company switch serving your Internet provider, where it is split off the normal phone company lines and routed directly to the provider's facilities.

- ◆ **T3 channel.** The fastest connection you can get is a T3 channel, which operates at 45Mbps. At this bandwidth (called *DS3*), the link has 28 times the capacity of the T1 line and 672 times the capacity of the 56Kb line.

- ◆ **ISDN channel.** *ISDN* is an acronym for *Integrated Services Digital Network*. This type of link is available in many larger metropolitan areas, but hasn't been pushed heavily by most phone companies. ISDN allows transmission of data at 64Kbps per channel over normal phone lines, and up to 128Kbps for pure data. Using an ISDN line is less expensive than a regular 56Kb channel, and you can get multiple ISDN lines to effectively increase your bandwidth.

The phone line component of a dedicated link has the potential of being the most expensive part of your Internet connection. The costs vary, depending on the capacity of the link and the distance between you and your provider. If you are within the same exchange, 56Kb links can go for up to $400 per month, while T3 channels can easily run well above $10,000 per month. Interestingly, most ISDN lines are available for around $50 to $75 per month.

If you are just starting to provide Internet services, you can easily get by with a 56Kb line or an ISDN line. As your traffic grows, you can look at expanding and adding lines. You need to do some very serious Internet work to require the bandwidth provided by or justify the cost incurred with a T1 or T3 connection.

Internet providers use these same types of dedicated links to connect to the Internet. The weakest providers use 56Kb lines, and the strongest use direct T3 connections to hook into the Internet backbone. You can judge the capacity of your provider by asking what type of lines they use to connect to the Internet.

> **TIP:** If you are considering using a T1 or T3 channel, you should be talking to only the largest national Internet providers. Many of the smaller regional providers rely on 56Kb or T1 links, and your needs would easily strip them of their capacity.

Selecting a Provider

After you know the type of service you need from your provider, you can go about selecting the provider. Internet providers are springing up all over the place, and so are their ads. Take a look in any phone book, under the general heading of *Internet*. If you look in the back of many popular magazines, you can often find advertisements placed there by Internet providers. The interesting thing is that these advertisements aren't limited to computer magazines. Take a look at the classifieds in *Business Week*, for example. There are—literally—ads everywhere you look.

Even though advertisements are starting to appear in lots of places, the best place to start is with people that have a situation similar to yours. For example, you may know of another business in your community that has dedicated access to the Internet. Talk with them and find out who they use as their provider. Other businesses also can be a valuable resource when it comes to identifying the problems in getting connected.

The next step is to start calling around to different Internet providers. Take your time; your selection process should be thorough, especially if many providers are available in your area. Ask each provider some questions that satisfy the following key points:

- **Services.** Does the provider offer the type of service you need? Do they use an Internet link that is of a higher capacity than you are thinking of installing? (If not, their link becomes a bottleneck, as they try to place additional demands on their other links.)

- **Cost.** What does the provider charge for the services you require? What about up-front or setup charges? Are there any hidden charges? What are the terms of payment?

- **Security.** How secure is the provider's system? Can they help you make sure that your system is secure?

- **Support.** Is user support provided at no additional charge? How knowledgeable are the customer support personnel? Can the provider help you with telecommunications consulting, if necessary?

Getting Set Up

When you have the proper equipment, a dedicated phone line, and a provider, you are almost done, but you still have a few hoops to jump through. The biggest concerns are getting a domain name and an IP address, as described in the following sections.

Your Domain Name

The good news about selecting a domain name is that you get to select your own name. The bad news is that if someone else has already registered the name, you can do very little about it except to select a different name.

After you have chosen a domain name, you need to register it with the InterNIC. The *InterNIC* is the shortened name for the *Internet Network Information Center*, which is actually a service provided by three different companies. The information compiled, maintained, and distributed by the InterNIC is divided into three categories:

- ◆ **Registration Services.** These services relate to registering domain names so that they are not used by other people. (Remember—domain names must be unique.) InterNIC Registration Services are provided by Network Solutions, Inc.

- ◆ **Directory and Database Services.** These services include information about different databases and resources on the network, as well as a white pages and yellow pages directory of Internet addresses. InterNIC Directory and Database Services are provided by AT&T.

- ◆ **Information Services.** This category of services includes training and newsletters in how to utilize the Internet more effectively. The information disseminated by this part of InterNIC is particularly directed toward technical people responsible for organizations and networks already connected to the Internet. InterNIC information services are provided by General Atomics/CERFNet.

It is probably obvious from the foregoing that the part of InterNIC responsible for domain names is Registration Services. To have your domain name registered, you need to follow these steps:

1. Contact your Internet provider and indicate that you want to register your domain name.

2. Determine the domain name you want to use. Remember that domain names must be in the appropriate top-level domain, as discussed in Chapter 2, "Your Software." Thus, if you run a commercial business named Joe's Widgets, it would be appropriate for you to register the name widget.com.

3. If you want to save time in the registration process, do a preliminary search to see whether the name you have selected is already in use. You can do this by using Telnet to connect to internic.net and use the whois server at that location to search for the name. (Instructions on how to use the whois server are found at the InterNIC site.)

4. Determine who will provide DNS server functions for your domain name. (DNS servers were covered in Chapter 2, "Your Software.") It is a good idea for you to provide DNS services for your own domain, your Internet provider can do this as well. You need an IP address for both a primary and secondary DNS server. (Getting your IP address is discussed in the next section.)

5. Fill out the registration forms required by InterNIC Registration Services. These are available on-line at http://rs0.internic.net/rs-internic.html.

6. Submit the forms to Registration Services via e-mail. The address to which you submit the forms is included in the forms themselves.

> **TIP:** Make a copy of your forms before you submit them. This can help you if any problems occur in the registration process.

As of September, 1995, InterNIC charges a fee for registering a domain name. The initial fee is $100, which registers your unique name for two years. After that, the renewal fee is $50 per year. For more information on this fee, you may want to review the document at http://rs.internic.net/announcements/fee-policy.html.

After submitting your forms, approximately two weeks are required for the domain name to be registered (assuming no conflicts or problems). The actual amount of time required depends on the workload of Registration Services. If you think the process is taking overly long, contact your Internet provider to enlist help.

Your IP Address

The easiest way to get an IP address is to talk to your Internet provider. Providers generally have a block of IP addresses from which they can assign yours. The IP address assigned should be a range of addresses based on the size of your network. Most Internet users fall into the category of Class C networks, as described in Chapter 2, "Your Software." This means that you are assigned the first three octets of the IP address, and then you can administer the final octet.

For example, when we worked with our Internet provider to make our domain functional, our provider assigned us the address 205.163.44. Notice that this is an incomplete IP address; it is only the first three octets. The final octet can range from 0 to 255, based on our needs.

> **NOTE:** Remember that you will need to assign a static IP address to your router and to your DNS server. As these are two of the first addresses assigned, you may want to assign .1 and .2 to this purpose.

Lead Times

Everything in life takes time—often, longer than we would like. The amount of time you need to get your domain up and running depends, in large part, on how diligent you are in accomplishing the steps. As a general guideline, the following may be helpful in figuring out how much time to allow:

Choose a provider	3 days
Data line	2–3 weeks
IP address	1 day
Domain name	2 weeks
Router, DSU/CSU	1 week

Obviously, some of these time frames may vary. If you live in a rural area with only a single Internet provider, you can save a lot of time, even if you may not save much money. In addition, no time is included in these guidelines to implement the information covered in Chapter 1, "Your Hardware," and Chapter 2, "Your Software."

Some of the items on the list can be accomplished at the same time because you are actually waiting on others. For example, you can order the data line and the IP address and register the domain name at essentially the same time. Then from start to finish the tasks listed above can take from two to three weeks, or more.

Summary

Setting up an Internet services site is exciting and, at first, a bit bewildering. Although many people feel comfortable with computer hardware and software, the idea of establishing the actual Internet connection may seem beyond reach. This chapter has focused on how you can establish that connection with the least number of problems. The key to the whole process boils down to choosing your Internet provider intelligently and then working with the provider to accomplish your goals.

In the next chapter, you start to learn how to put your Web site together.

PART II

Installing and Setting Up Your Site

Chapter | 4

Installing Your Web Server

The Netscape FastTrack Server is a full-featured program that includes many tools to help run a professional Web site. In this chapter, you learn how to install the Web server, as well as how to get it up and run for the first time. By the time you have completed this chapter (and if you have been working along up to this point), you should have a fully functional Web server, ready to publish information on the Internet.

> **TIP:** If you have already been running a server (from a different vendor) at your site, and you are switching to the FastTrack server, you may want to read Chapter 5, "Converting from Another Server," before completing the steps in this chapter.

Setting Up a Directory Structure

Before making your Web server operational, you should give some thought to how you want to organize your server directories. The structure of your directories affects how other users access your site, as well as how you create the content pages you publish on the Web. The next several sections assist you in determining how to structure your site.

Understanding URLs

You locate information through a Web browser by using URLs. *URL* is an acronym for *universal resource locator*; think of it as an expanded form of the domain addressing discussed in Chapter 2, "Your Software." The difference is that a URL also includes an indicator of the type of resource at a particular location, and may contain directory and file name information as well.

As an example, consider the following URL:

```
http://www.beulah.dcomp.com
```

This URL contains an indicator of what is located at the address (the `http:` part), as well as a domain name for the server containing the information (`www.beulah.dcomp.com`). The resource type and the domain name are separated by two slashes.

> **CAUTION:** If you use a URL with only a single slash after the resource type, most browsers generate an error. Two slashes are required for proper syntax. Also, make sure you use forward slashes instead of backslashes.

When you use the URL in a browser, the server at the specified address is contacted, and an HTTP command is issued that is received by the server, which then responds. In this example (`http://www.beulah.dcomp.com`), the server returns the default HTML page, located in the root WWW directory for the server. (HTML is the mark-up language used to create Web documents. You can specify the file name to be used as the default. This capability is covered later in the chapter.) The server returns the default file because no file name is specified at the end of the URL.

> **NOTE:** Instead of using a domain address for a server, you could specify the IP address. Doing so is risky, however, as IP addresses are known to change periodically. (For example, when a company changes from one Internet provider to another.) Using the IP address, you would type `http://205.163.44.8` rather than `http://www.beulah.dcomp.com`.

Now take a look at another URL:

`http://www.beulah.dcomp.com/sundance`

This URL is very similar to the first, except that a directory name has been appended. In any URL, the first element is the resource type (`http`), the second is the server address (`www.beulah.dcomp.com`), and anything after that is considered a directory path. In this case, the URL points to a directory named sundance. When the server is contacted, it looks for the sundance directory, and then returns the default file from that directory. Again, the default file is returned because no file name is specified in the URL. The following URL is a little more different:

`http://www.beulah.dcomp.com/sundance/dtower.htm`

Here a full specification is provided, including a file name. In this case, the server returns the specified file (`dtower.htm`) to the browser. If you understand these basics of how a URL works, you can feel a lot more confident about using them as you work with the Web.

Directory Considerations

How you put your Web directories together is entirely up to you, but you should keep in mind that, unlike your personal computer, your Web site may be accessed by many, many people around the Web, who will need to work through your directories. Therefore you should give some thought to how those directories are structured *before* you start putting together your site.

The reason for planning your directory structure ahead of time is that robots wander around the Web, gathering information to appear in high-powered search engines such as Lycos or Alta Vista. Many people use those search engines to locate the information at your site. If you change your directory structure after the robots have cataloged your site, you run the risk of having bad URLs in the search engines. This situation can frustrate users and signal missed opportunities.

If you are running a very small Web site, with a single purpose, the organization of your site is quite easy. In fact, you may be able to get by with only a single directory—the root directory—for your server. If your content is quite diverse, you should set out an organization up front.

As an example, Discovery Computing Inc. (`http://www.dcomp.com`) provides Internet advertising services for a number of businesses in Northeastern Wyoming. The natural way for these businesses to be organized is by town. Thus, our directory structure appears as follows:

```
Aladdin
Art
Class
DCI
Hulett
Misc
Moorcroft
Newcastle
Sundance
```

Each of these items is a subdirectory within the root directory for the Web server. With the exception of the Art, Class, DCI, and Misc subdirectories, each represents a town in our area. The other directories have the following purposes:

- ◆ **Art.** A directory of common art files: icons, buttons, wallpaper, and the like.
- ◆ **Class.** A directory for an Internet classified service we run.
- ◆ **DCI.** A directory for documents related directly to our company.
- ◆ **Misc.** A directory for documents that don't fit into any of the other directories.

I'm not trying to say that this system is the only way to organize your directories. On the contrary—I am saying only that this method has worked for us. The key is that you need to think through how to organize your site before you start publishing documents.

A Word on Directory Indexing

Earlier, this chapter pointed out that when someone tries to contact your server and access a directory (without specifying a particular file name), the server returns the default file from that directory. This is true as long as a feature called *directory indexing* isn't enabled.

> **CAUTION:** If directory indexing is disabled, and no default file exists in the directory, the server generates an error to the remote browser.

Directory indexing enables remote users to view the contents of your Web site directories. At some sites, this feature may be beneficial, particularly for an intranet. Directory indexing enables users to step through directories and make choices as to which files they see. For example, Figure 4–1 shows an example of what a browser would display with directory indexing enabled at a site.

Later in this chapter, you learn how to enable and disable directory indexing for your site.

Setting Up the Web Server

Setting up your FastTrack Web server isn't particularly difficult, but you need to go through specific steps, in the right order. These steps include the following:

- ◆ Installing the service pack
- ◆ Checking your system services
- ◆ Installing the FastTrack software

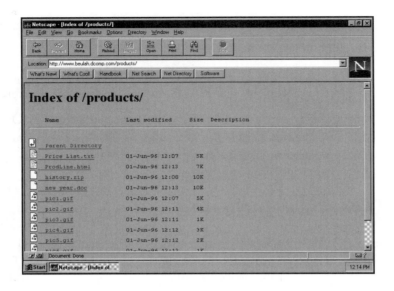

The following sections cover each of these tasks in detail.

Installing the Service Pack

If you are using Windows NT 3.51, you must install the latest Windows NT 3.51 Service Pack. If you are using Windows NT 4.0, you can skip this section entirely; there is no need to install the service pack.

In Chapter 2, "Your Software," you learned where to locate the free service pack, and you also learned that you should use the latest service pack available. Now that you have it on your hard drive, it's time to install it.

Decompressing the Files

When you downloaded the service pack, it was saved on your disk in a compressed format. Before you can use it, you must decompress the files by following these steps:

1. Create a temporary directory on your drive.
2. Copy or move the file `sp4_351i.exe` to the temporary directory. (If you have a later service pack, your file will have a different name.)

3. If you have not already done so, open an MS-DOS window in which to perform the remaining steps.

4. Make the temporary directory the current working directory.

5. Enter the following command at the command prompt (if you have a later service pack, you should substitute the proper file name):

```
sp4_351i
```

Running the downloaded file decompresses the files it contains. When you are through, all the files are located within the temporary directory you used.

> **CAUTION:** When you fully decompress the service pack, it consumes approximately 24 MB of space on your hard drive. Make sure you have enough space available before decompressing.

Updating Your System

With the service pack decompressed, you are ready to perform the update. You do this by opening an MS-DOS window and changing to the temporary directory you used in the preceding section. Enter the following command at the command prompt:

```
update
```

Shortly you should see a couple of screens (the first of which is shown in Figure 4–2) designed to guide you through the update process. In essence, the Update program replaces Windows NT system files with newer versions. This change is made primarily to fix system bugs that have been discovered (and fixed), but also to add features necessary for products such as the FastTrack server.

After you click the OK button to start the update, the new system files are copied to their proper locations. Depending on the speed of your machine, the update takes about a minute. When the update is done, a message appears to inform you that you need to restart your machine. After restarting, you can safely delete the contents of the temporary directory.

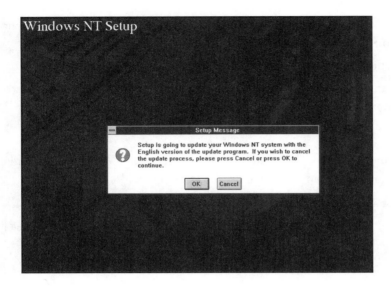

FIGURE 4–2

The Update program guides you through the process of installing the service pack.

TIP: Updating all your Windows NT 3.51 machines with the service pack is a good idea. You can run the Update program on both workstations and servers.

Checking Your System

Before you install your Web server, you should do a few things. For most readers, these items are no big deal—chances are good that you won't have to do anything. However, some programs, if running at the same time as FastTrack, can cause your system to act unreliably. To head off any potential problem, look through the following list and take any actions necessary on your system:

- ◆ **Beta versions.** If you were running a beta version of FastTrack, remove it from your system.

- ◆ **DNS servers.** Make sure your DNS server (described in Chapter 2, "Your Software," is up and running. If you are connected to the Internet, FastTrack requires a properly installed and configured DNS server in order to even install fully.

- **Web servers.** If you are running any other Web servers, disable them before installing the FastTrack server.

- **Administrator privileges.** To install the Web server properly, you must be logged on to the server with administrator privileges.

- **Browser.** You must have a copy of Netscape Navigator or Navigator Gold installed on your system to successfully complete the installation.

Installing Netscape FastTrack Server

The installation of your Web server is really quite quick and painless, and there are only a couple of hoops through which you must jump. This section describes the installation process, in detail. The steps here are based on installing the server under Windows NT Server 4.0. If you are installing under a different operating system, your steps (and definitely the screens shown here) will differ. The information provided in this section should give you a rough idea of what you need to do, however.

> **CAUTION:** You need at least 37 MB of free space on your hard drive to install FastTrack server, depending on your operating system. (This number includes size of the file you may have downloaded from the Netscape Web site.)

To start the installation process, browse through your system until you find the f32d20.exe program. Once located, run the program; shortly you will see the dialog box shown in Figure 4–3.

To continue with the installation, click on the Yes button. The installation program then decompresses, from the distribution file (f32d20.exe), the files it needs to install FastTrack. These files don't take very much room; they are copied to whatever temporary directory you have defined for your system. Typically this is the C:\TEMP directory, or some similar name. (These files are deleted when the installation is complete.) After a short time decompressing, the Setup program is started, as shown in Figure 4–4.

This welcome screen serves two purposes. First, it lets you know that you are nearly ready to install FastTrack. Second, it informs you that you should shut down any open programs running on your system. When you are ready to proceed, click the Next button.

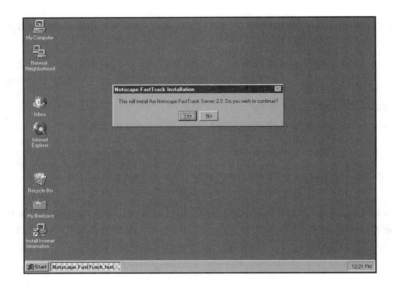

FIGURE 4–3

When you first run the FastTrack installation program, you are asked if you want to continue.

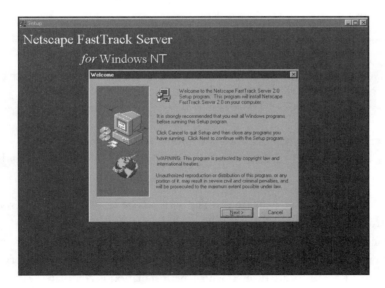

FIGURE 4–4

The first screen of the Setup program suggests that you close all open programs running on your system.

At this point you may see a message indicating that Netscape Navigator Gold was not found on your system. (In other words, you have not installed it yet.) This product is distributed on the CD-ROM with FastTrack, or you can download it from the URL shown in the dialog box on the screen. (As of this writing you can download the file from http://home.netscape.com/comprod/mirror/index.html.)

If you don't have Navigator Gold or Navigator (non-Gold) installed on your system, you won't be able to finish installing FastTrack server. If this is the case on your system, install the products and then run the setup program again.

If you do have Navigator (but are missing Navigator Gold), you can continue with the installation. Click on the OK button to continue. Shortly you will see the license agreement for FastTrack, as shown in Figure 4–5.

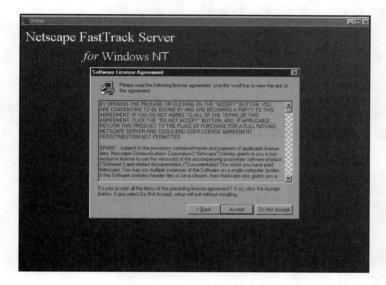

FIGURE 4–5

FastTrack includes a standard software license agreement which is displayed during installation.

License agreements are always a pleasant reminder of our society and a particularly pleasing part of any installation. You can read through the agreement, or feel free to take your entire computer system to your lawyer's office to have the agreement reviewed. When you are satisfied that you understand it, click on the Accept button to continue. This displays the screen shown in Figure 4–6.

At this point you can specify where you want the FastTrack files installed. By default, the files are installed in the C:\Netscape\Server directory. If this setting is unacceptable, you can change to any other existing directory by clicking on the Browse button.

When you are ready to continue, click the Next button. Setup begins to copy files from the temporary directory and from the distribution file (or CD-ROM) to the final directory where your Web server is to be installed. This doesn't take particularly long, depending on the speed of your system. When Setup is through copying files, you will see the screen shown in Figure 4–7.

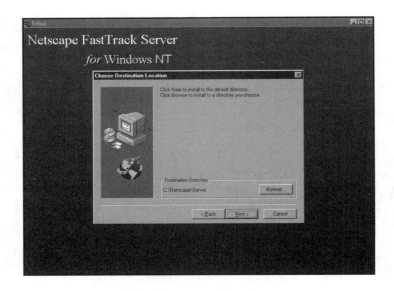

FIGURE 4–6

You need to specify where you want the FastTrack files installed.

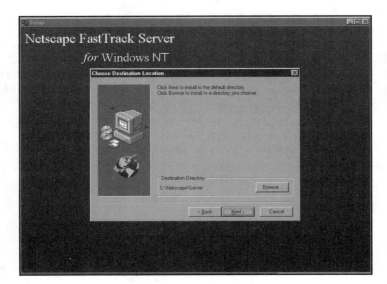

FIGURE 4–7

Setting up FastTrack includes some basic configuration of the server.

The purpose of this screen is to just let you know that the file copying is complete and that you are about to configure your server. The configuration information provided in the next few questions is just the bare essentials necessary to get your server up and running. When you are ready to proceed, click on the Next button. This displays the screen shown in Figure 4–8.

FIGURE 4–8

FastTrack needs to know the Internet address of your server.

Here you are being asked for the Internet address of the Web server you are creating. The default information shown on the screen is pulled from the TCP/IP configuration information for the machine on which you are installing FastTrack. If the information is not correct, then you should exit the installation and make sure your TCP/IP information is set up correctly.

> **CAUTION:** If you are connected to the Internet, the DNS name you supply at this screen must already be defined and configured in your DNS server. If you are setting up an intranet, then the name you supply must be a host on your local network. If neither of these conditions are met, you will not be able to complete the installation process beyond a couple more steps.

When you are ready to continue, click on the Next button. This displays the screen shown in Figure 4–9.

This screen allows you to specify the user name and password to be used for access to the Netscape Server Manager. The information you enter here does not need to match your user ID and password used for access to your NT domain. You can use any name and password desired, but you need to remember it so you can access the configuration portion of your server later. When you are satisfied with the user name and password (which you must enter twice), click on the Next button. This displays the screen shown in Figure 4–10.

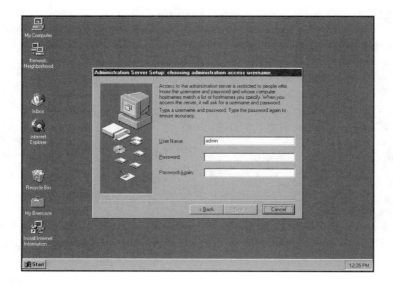

FIGURE 4–9

The information provided in this screen is used to control access to the Netscape Server Manager.

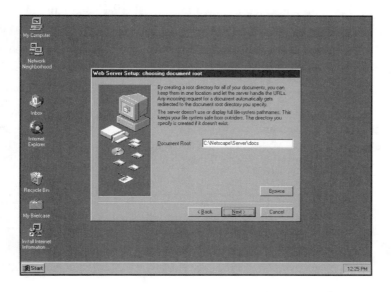

FIGURE 4–10

Setup needs to know the directory you want used as the home directory for your server.

Earlier in this chapter you learned about setting up your directory structure. Here is where you first specify the home directory for your content pages. All other directories in your server are subordinate to the directory you specify in this dialog box.

The default home directory suggested by Netscape is the \docs directory, within the directory where you installed FastTrack. If you want to use a different directory, enter the full path in the Document Root field, or click on the Browse button to select an existing directory. When you are through specifying the directory, click on the Next button.

At this point you are done with the Setup program, and you will see the notice shown in Figure 4–11. Click on the Finish button to end the Setup program.

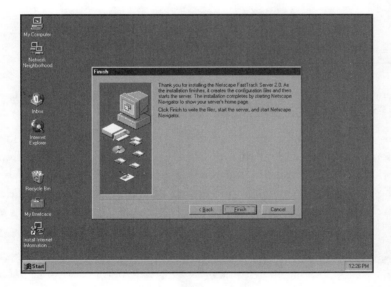

FIGURE 4–11

The Setup program is done installing FastTrack.

As a parting gesture, the Setup program starts Netscape Navigator (Netcape's browser program), if it is installed on your system. The connection is made to your new Web server, and your screen should appear similar to Figure 4–12.

Your Web server is now up and running, and anyone with access to your server can view the same page you are seeing at this point.

FIGURE 4–12

Your new Web server is up and running.

Configuring the Web Server

After your Web server has been installed, you are ready to configure your server. Most of the configuration settings control how your Web server reacts to HTTP requests from the outside world. If you have worked through this chapter to this point, you probably already know how you want to configure your server. The following sections detail different areas to which you should pay attention, right off the bat.

> **NOTE:** The information in this chapter is designed as a step-by-step sequence of how to change FastTrack for the first time you use it. If you want detailed information on how to use the Netscape Server Manager (which is used to configure FastTrack), refer to Chapter 17, "The Netscape Server Manager."

Setting the Default File

As you learned earlier in this chapter, the default file is returned to the browser by FastTrack when the URL specified by the browser doesn't include a file name. FastTrack allows you to specify default file names to be returned. You can specify a single file name, or multiple file names. These file names are valid for all directories on your server. Suppose you have the following directory structure for your site:

```
WWWRoot
Artwork
Hulett
Moorcroft
Newcastle
Sundance
```

If someone pointed her URL at the Hulett directory, the file with matching one of the default file names in that directory would be returned. Likewise, if she pointed her URL at the Newcastle directory, one matching the default file names from that directory would be returned.

When you first install FastTrack, the default file names are set to `index.html` and `home.html`. To change the default file names to something else, follow these steps:

1. Choose the <u>P</u>rograms option from the Start menu. This displays the Programs menu.

2. Choose the Netscape option from the Programs menu. This displays the Netscape menu.

3. Click on the Administer Netscape Servers option. This starts Netscape Navigator, and shortly you will see a security dialog box asking for your user name and password (as in Figure 4–13).

FIGURE 4–13

Before you can change server settings, you must enter a name and password.

4. Enter your user name and password as you specified it when installing FastTrack, then click on OK. This displays the Server Selector page, as shown in Figure 4–14.

5. Scroll through the Server Selector page and click on the server name you want to configure. (In our case, the server name is beulah, as in beulah.dcomp.com.) This displays the Netscape Server Manager, as shown in Figure 4–15.

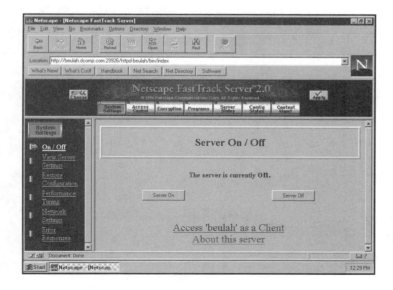

FIGURE 4–15

The Netscape Server Manager is used to configure your Web server.

6. On the toolbar in the top frame, click on Content Mgmt at the far right side. This changes the information displayed in the lower frames.

7. In the lower-left frame, click on the Document Preferences option. This changes the information displayed in the lower-right frame. Your screen should now look as shown in Figure 4–16.

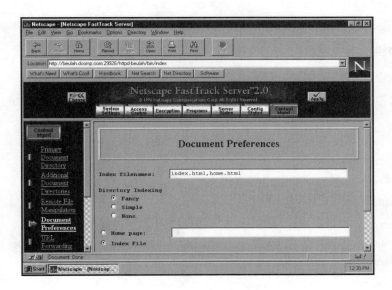

FIGURE 4–16

The Document Preferences frame is used to configure how FastTrack handles your base documents.

8. In the Index filenames field, change the default file names to those you want used as your document defaults.

9. Scroll through the lower-right frame until you find the OK button, then click on it. This sends your configuration information to the server and changes the page displayed in the lower-right frame.

10. Scroll through the lower-right frame and click on the Save and Apply button. Shortly you will see a dialog box indicating your changes were accepted.

11. Click on OK to close the dialog box.

Controlling Directory Indexing

By default, FastTrack has directory indexing turned on. Many sites would rather not have people browsing through their directories; for other sites, allowing indexing makes sense. If you have any of the following needs, keeping directory indexing enabled is appropriate:

◆ You have a lot of non-HTML files for people to download.

◆ The files available in a directory change rapidly and often.

◆ You want others to see how neat your directories look.

To disable directory indexing, follow these steps:

1. If you did not close the Netscape Server Manager pages after the last section, jump to step 7.

2. Choose the <u>P</u>rograms option from the Start menu. This displays the Programs menu.

3. Choose the Netscape option from the Programs menu. This displays the Netscape menu.

4. Click on the Administer Netscape Servers option. This starts Netscape Navigator, and shortly you will see a security dialog box asking for your user name and password (as shown earlier in Figure 4–13).

5. Enter your user name and password as you specified it when installing FastTrack, then click on OK. This displays the Server Selector page, as shown earlier in Figure 4–14.

6. Scroll through the Server Selector page and click on the server name you want to configure. (In our case, the server name is beulah, as in beulah.dcomp.com.) This displays the Netscape Server Manager, as shown earlier in Figure 4–15.

7. On the toolbar in the top frame, click on Content Mgmt at the far right side. This changes the information displayed in the lower frames.

8. In the lower-left frame, scroll down until you find the Document Preferences option, then click on it. This changes the information displayed in the lower-right frame. Your screen should now look as shown earlier in Figure 4–16.

9. Under Directory Indexing, choose the None option.

10. Scroll through the lower-right frame until you find the OK button, then click on it. This sends your configuration information to the server and changes the page displayed in the lower-right frame.

11. Scroll through the lower-right frame and click on the Save and Apply button. Shortly you will see a dialog box indicating your changes were accepted.

12. Click on OK to close the dialog box.

> **NOTE:** You can turn directory browsing on or off only for the *entire site*, not by directory. If you want people to be able to browse one directory but not another, you may be out of luck.

Changing the Default Port Setting

When a TCP-based message is sent to a server, it is directed to a specific port. Different software servers on the physical server listen to different ports. In this way, you can run multiple services on a single server, and each service listens only to the appropriate messages.

By default, HTTP commands (understood by Web servers) are sent to port 80. The FastTrack server listens to this port, but you can change the port setting, if desired. Why would you want to do this? For any of the following reasons:

- You are running a different service on port 80.
- You want to increase security a bit, by using a port of which only authorized users would be aware.
- You are running your Internet Web server on port 80, but want to set up an intranet server on a different port.
- You hate following conventions and just want to be different.

In most cases, you don't need to worry about the port setting. After all, most of the Web servers currently in use on the Internet already use port 80, and if you want to maximize visits to your site, you should use port 80 as well. If you are determined to change the port, you can do so by following these steps:

1. If the Netscape Server Manager is still visible on your screen, proceed to step 7.

2. Choose the <u>P</u>rograms option from the Start menu. This displays the Programs menu.

3. Choose the Netscape option from the Programs menu. This displays the Netscape menu.

4. Click on the Administer Netscape Servers option. This starts Netscape Navigator, and shortly you will see a security dialog box asking for your user name and password (as shown earlier in Figure 4–13).

5. Enter your user name and password as you specified it when installing FastTrack, then click on OK. This displays the Server Selector page, as shown earlier in Figure 4–14.

6. Scroll through the Server Selector page and click on the server name you want to configure. This displays the Netscape Server Manager, as shown earlier in Figure 4–15.

7. On the toolbar in the top frame, click on System Settings (this choice may already be selected). This changes the information displayed in the lower frames.

8. In the lower-left frame, click on the Network Settings option. This changes the information displayed in the lower-right frame. Your screen should now look as shown in Figure 4–17.

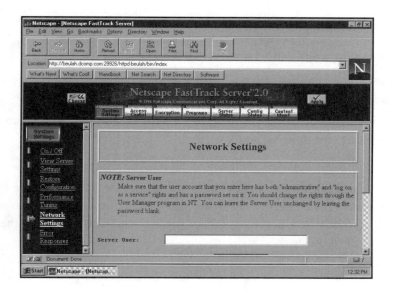

FIGURE 4–17

The Network Settings frame is used to configure how FastTrack relates to your network and the Internet.

9. Scroll through the Network Settings frame until you see the Server Port field. Change the value to the port number you want to use.

10. Scroll through the lower-right frame until you find the OK button, then click on it. This sends your configuration information to the server and changes the page displayed in the lower-right frame.

11. Scroll through the lower-right frame and click on the Save and Apply button. Shortly you will see a dialog box indicating your changes were accepted.

12. Click on OK to close the dialog box.

After changing the port, it is a good idea to stop and restart the server, as discussed in the next chapter.

Using Additional Document Directories

When someone connects to your Web server, everything they access is relative to your home directory, as discussed earlier in this chapter. For instance, one of our Web servers uses the directory e:\basis as a home directory. When someone connects to the server and uses the following URL,

```
http:\\www.beulah.dcomp.com\products\new\
```

they are actually accessing files in the e:\basis\products\new directory. FastTrack takes care of the transition between the URL and the actual directory path.

If you have been around computers since the early days of DOS, you may remember the JOIN command. This command (which was dropped from recent versions of DOS) enabled you to treat a different disk as if it were a directory on the current drive. FastTrack allows you to define additional directories, which are not beneath your home directory, to be accessible through your Web site.

Suppose that your main Web directories are on drive D:, but you have a directory on drive F: that you want to make available from the Web. Instead of duplicating the contents of the directory, you can create an additional directory that points to drive F:. As far as visitors at your site are concerned, the directory is part of your Web site.

To set up an additional directory, follow these steps:

1. If the Netscape Server Manager is still visible on your screen, proceed to step 7.

2. Choose the <u>P</u>rograms option from the Start menu. This displays the Programs menu.

3. Choose the Netscape option from the Programs menu. This displays the Netscape menu.

4. Click on the Administer Netscape Servers option. This starts Netscape Navigator, and shortly you will see a security dialog box asking for your user name and password (as shown earlier in Figure 4–13).

5. Enter your user name and password as you specified it when installing FastTrack, then click on OK. This displays the Server Selector page, as shown earlier in Figure 4–14.

6. Scroll through the Server Selector page and click on the server name you want to configure. This displays the Netscape Server Manager, as shown earlier in Figure 4–15.

7. On the toolbar in the top frame, click on Content Mgmt, all the way at the right side of the toolbar. This changes the information displayed in the lower frames.

8. In the lower-left frame, click on the Additional Document Directories option. This changes the information displayed in the lower-right frame. Your screen should now look as shown in Figure 4–18.

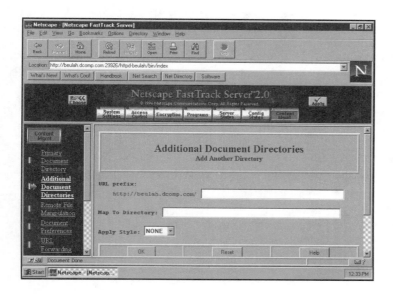

FIGURE 4–18

The Additional Document Directories frame is used to define and manage content directories elsewhere on your system.

9. In the URL Prefix field, enter the URL to be associated with this directory.

10. In the Map to Directory field, enter the directory path on your hard drive.

11. At the bottom of the Additional Document Directories frame, click on the OK button. This sends your configuration information to the server and changes the page displayed in the lower-right frame.

12. Scroll through the lower-right frame and click on the Save and Apply button. Shortly you will see a dialog box indicating your changes were accepted.

13. Click on OK to close the dialog box.

Hosting Multiple Sites

Most organizations are interested in running only a single Web site, but you may have a special need for more than one server. FastTrack provides several ways you can handle this at your site, depending on how the servers will be accessed and what your needs are.

- ◆ Software virtual servers
- ◆ Hardware virtual servers
- ◆ Multiple FastTrack instances

Each of these approaches is discussed in the following sections.

Software Virtual Servers

When you use software virtual servers, it appears to the outside world as if you have multiple Web sites, even though they are all being managed by a single copy of FastTrack server. They are called software virtual servers because the information about which pages to used is determined by the HTTP request received by FastTrack, not by the IP address to which the request was made. Thus, you can have multiple domains which resolve to the same IP address, and then FastTrack determines which content to display based on the domain used.

As an example, let's say you have the following three domains:

- ◆ widget.com
- ◆ layout.com
- ◆ faxsavers.org

You (or your Internet provider) have configured your DNS server so that all three domains resolve to a single IP address. When the HTTP request comes down the line from a remote browser, it is resolved to the single IP address. Thus, FastTrack would see a request to any of these as an attempt to access information at a single Web site. Most modern browsers, however, also send the URL to which they are connecting in the HTTP request.

This is where software virtual servers come into play. Even though FastTrack sees the requests come in on the same IP address, it examines the request and finds that different domains were used in the URLs. Based on this information, it looks in the software virtual servers you have defined to determine what home directory to use for the domain.

> **NOTE:** If someone connects to your site using a very old browser (one that doesn't put URL information in the HTTP request), then they will see the default page for the main domain at your site. This is not necessarily a problem. As long as you know it may happen, you can account for it in the content you develop.

To define software virtual servers, follow these steps:

1. If the Netscape Server Manager is still visible on your screen, proceed to step 7.

2. Choose the Programs option from the Start menu. This displays the Programs menu.

3. Choose the Netscape option from the Programs menu. This displays the Netscape menu.

4. Click on the Administer Netscape Servers option. This starts Netscape Navigator, and shortly you will see a security dialog box asking for your user name and password (as shown earlier in Figure 4–13).

5. Enter your user name and password as you specified it when installing FastTrack, then click on OK. This displays the Server Selector page, as shown earlier in Figure 4–14.

6. Scroll through the Server Selector page and click on the server name you want to configure. This displays the Netscape Server Manager, as shown earlier in Figure 4–15.

7. On the toolbar in the top frame, click on Content Mgmt, all the way at the right side of the toolbar. This changes the information displayed in the lower frames.

8. In the lower-left frame, scroll down until you find the Software Virtual Servers, then click on it. This changes the information displayed in the lower-right frame. Your screen should now look as shown in Figure 4–19.

FIGURE 4–19

The Software Virtual Servers frame is used to define and manage the appearance of additional sites.

9. In the URL Host field, enter the DNS name of the domain to be added as a software virtual server.

10. In the Home Page field, enter the directory of the home page for this domain.

11. Scroll through the lower-right frame until you find the OK button, then click on it. This sends your configuration information to the server and changes the page displayed in the lower-right frame.

12. Scroll through the lower-right frame and click on the Save and Apply button. Shortly you will see a dialog box indicating your changes were accepted.

13. Click on OK to close the dialog box.

Hardware Virtual Servers

Hardware virtual servers are similar to software virtual servers, with one major difference—hardware virtual servers are delineated by the IP address used in the HTTP request received by FastTrack server. Thus, hardware virtual servers assumes you have set up (in your DNS configuration) different IP addresses to which the different domains can be resolved. This method also assumes that you have bound those different IP addresses to your network card (or cards) using the standard methods applicable to your operating system.

The other caveat of using hardware virtual servers is that each server shares the same configuration information. The biggest drawback that this presents is that you cannot mix-and-match security on different hardware virtual servers. Thus, one server could not be secure and the other one unsecure. If this presents a kink for your needs, then you will need to use multiple instances of FastTrack server, as described in the next section.

To set up hardware virtual servers, follow these steps:

1. If the Netscape Server Manager is still visible on your screen, proceed to step 7.

2. Choose the <u>P</u>rograms option from the Start menu. This displays the Programs menu.

3. Choose the Netscape option from the Programs menu. This displays the Netscape menu.

4. Click on the Administer Netscape Servers option. This starts Netscape Navigator, and shortly you will see a security dialog box asking for your user name and password (as shown earlier in Figure 4–13).

5. Enter your user name and password as you specified it when installing FastTrack, then click on OK. This displays the Server Selector page, as shown earlier in Figure 4–14.

6. Scroll through the Server Selector page and click on the server name you want to configure. This displays the Netscape Server Manager, as shown earlier in Figure 4–15.

7. On the toolbar in the top frame, click on Content Mgmt, all the way at the right side of the toolbar. This changes the information displayed in the lower frames.

8. In the lower-left frame, scroll down until you find the Hardware Virtual Servers option, then click on it. This changes the information displayed in the lower-right frame. Your screen should now look as shown in Figure 4–20.

9. In the IP Address field, supply the IP address to which requests for this new domain will be directed.

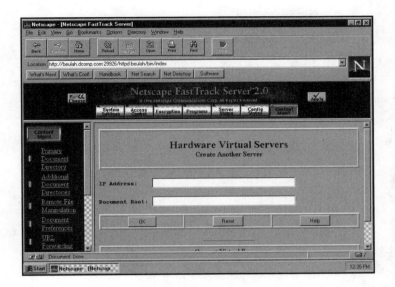

FIGURE 4–20

The Hardware Virtual Servers frame is used to define and manage the appearance of additional sites according to IP address.

10. In the Document Root field, specify the home directory for this new server.

11. In the lower-right frame click on the OK button. This sends your configuration information to the server and changes the page displayed in the lower-right frame.

12. Scroll through the lower-right frame and click on the Save and Apply button. Shortly you will see a dialog box indicating your changes were accepted.

13. Click on OK to close the dialog box.

Multiple FastTrack Instances

In some rare instances you may need to add an instance of FastTrack server. Typically this is done only when you already have another server defined, and your new server (the one you want to add) meets any of the following criteria:

- ◆ You want to use a different port number than was used in the other server
- ◆ This new server will be secure, while the other is insecure, or vice versa

If you need to add another server, you don't do it by running the Setup program again. Instead, you follow these steps:

1. Choose the Programs option from the Start menu. This displays the Programs menu.

2. Choose the Netscape option from the Programs menu. This displays the Netscape menu.

3. Click on the Administer Netscape Servers option. This starts Netscape Navigator, and shortly you will see a security dialog box asking for your user name and password (as shown earlier in Figure 4–13).

4. Enter your user name and password as you specified it when installing FastTrack, then click on OK. This displays the Server Selector page, as shown earlier in Figure 4–14.

5. Scroll through the Server Selector page and click on the Install a New Netscape FastTrack Server button. This displays the page shown in Figure 4–21.

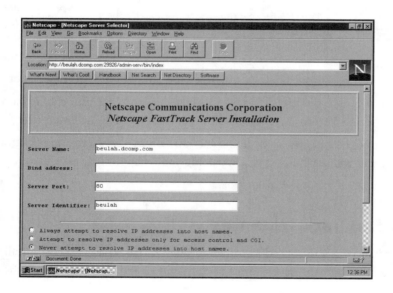

FIGURE 4–21

Adding a new server instance only requires answering a couple of questions.

The form that now appears on your screen must be filled in so that FastTrack can know how to treat the new server. The following information needs to be provided:

♦ **Server name.** Type the fully qualified DNS name for your server. An example might be web.widgets.com.

♦ **Bind address.** If your new server will be using an IP address different from your other servers, enter the IP address here.

- ◆ ***Server port.*** If your new server will be using a different port number, enter it here. (You must use a different port number if the new server is using the same IP address as other servers.)
- ◆ ***Document root.*** Enter the home directory to be used by this server.

In addition, you can specify how FastTrack server should resolve IP addresses on this new server. Typically, HTTP requests received by a server never have the DNS name of the initiating host. Instead, only an IP address is included. For reporting purposes, you may want to have IP address resolved to their DNS names. (This can be much nicer in reporting.) The default selection, which is to never do IP resolution, is much better for a high-performance or heavily used site. Resolving IP addresses can take quite a while (in computer time). When you stop to think that any given visit by an individual can generate anywhere from four to forty HTTP requests, each of which would need to be resolved, you can begin to see how resolving the addresses can slow down your site.

Once you have provided all this information, click on the OK button. Your new server is created, and you are returned to the Server Selector page. Your new server should appear in the list of available servers. You can now configure this new server independently from your original server.

Summary

The Web is the hottest area on the Internet these days, and by using the Netscape FastTrack Server you can quickly be up and running with your own Web site. This chapter has discussed, in depth, how to install the Web server on your Windows NT system. You also learned how to configure the server to best match your needs.

In the next chapter, you learn what considerations you should take into account if you are converting from a different Web server to the FastTrack server.

Chapter 5

Converting from Another Server

Obviously, the FastTrack server isn't the first Web server on the market, nor is it the only server on the market. The Web has been around for the past several years. The first Web servers were available for UNIX systems, but in the past two years or so more and more Web servers appeared specifically for Windows NT. This fact implies that you may already have installed a Web server on your system, but now are thinking of changing over to the FastTrack Web server.

The information in this chapter can help you to make the transition easier. Here you learn the benefits of changing systems, as well as how much work you may have to do when you finally make the leap.

Server Differences

Essentially, every Web server available does the same thing—they just go about it in different ways. The FastTrack server accomplishes the task common to all Web servers—answering HTTP commands by transferring information over a TCP/IP network—but it also does some tasks differently than other servers. In addition, it adds some bells and whistles you can't find elsewhere.

The following sections are in no particular order; they are provided so you can understand the differences you need to watch for when changing to the Netscape FastTrack Server.

Operating System Differences

The cost of any Web server must include the cost of the operating system required to run that Web server. For sites that already have Windows NT installed, the operating system issue isn't a big deal. For sites that migrate from other operating systems, the cost in dollars and time can be significant.

In Chapter 2, "Your Software," you learned exactly what you need in the way of an operating system for the FastTrack server. FastTrack can operate on a wide variety of operating systems. If you are converting from your current operating system to another one, you need to take the differences between the operating systems into account.

For example, if you are converting to Windows NT in order to establish your Web site using FastTrack, then you need to learn how to use Windows NT. In day-to-day use, Windows NT is similar to other versions of Windows, although it's more complex in administration. If you are coming from a UNIX environment, you may find the way in which Windows NT approaches familiar issues (such as security) to be a bit disorienting. The same can also be said if your conversion is going in the other direction—toward UNIX instead of away from it.

Regardless of which way you are going, if you are migrating to a new operating system at the same time you are migrating to FastTrack, you should understand that you will need a significant investment of time and (by extension) money in order to make the complete transition.

Directory Structure

In Chapter 4, "Installing Your Web Server," you learned something about the directory structure used in the FastTrack server. You learned about home directories, additional document directories, and directories for virtual servers. The FastTrack server is quite flexible when it comes to how you set up your directories. Your current Web server probably uses some other scheme for tracking or setting directories. You need to understand not only your current directory structure, but how you can translate that structure to the FastTrack environment.

In many cases, the conversion from old to new can go quite smoothly. For example, you may only need to point the FastTrack server to your old home directory, and you will be all set. However, if your old server requires some esoteric structure, you probably will want to make changes as soon as you are using the FastTrack server.

> **CAUTION:** Remember that if you make changes to your directory structure, the changes affect any links that may exist to your site. You should make directory structure changes only when absolutely necessary.

File and Directory Names

The FastTrack server is quite flexible with file and directory names. You can use any legal Windows NT name, with one exception—spaces. You can't use spaces in file names or directories if those files or directories will be accessible from the Web.

For users of most other servers, this restriction doesn't present a problem. It's conceivable, however, that some servers may allow spaces. If you have a Web site that uses spaces, converting to the FastTrack server could prove a bit painful. When converting, make sure that you perform the following steps:

1. Remove spaces from all published directories and file names.
2. Check all links in your HTML documents to make sure that they use the newly changed file and directory names.
3. Attempt to update external links to your site, wherever possible, so that they are correct.

As an alternative, you can leave all your directory and file names as they are and simply update the references (links) to those directories and files instead. For instance, if you edit your links so that spaces in file and directory names are replaced with plus signs (+), you should have no problem.

Using Log Files

Web servers keep log files, as do most other servers that have their roots in the Internet. Log files track who has visited your site and what they did there. These log files are typically stored as plain text, and are restarted periodically. For example, the server may start a new log file every day.

Programs are available on the Internet that enable you to analyze log files and use them to generate statistics about your site. In fact, you may have developed a custom program that you use to pick apart your log files and develop really meaningful statistics. Many sites have even developed CGI scripts that display counters or other information about the site—all originally derived from log files.

Unfortunately, no standard log file format exists for Web servers. A log file used by one server may be similar to a log file used by another—but seldom is it identical. This situation means that an analysis program developed for one type of log file doesn't work on another. If you change servers, you need to make changes to your log file analysis programs. For some sites, this requirement can mean extensive work.

> **NOTE:** You may have heard of the *Common Log File Format*, an attempt at standardizing log file formats used by Web servers. Some servers use it; others don't. Alas—the standard everyone desires hasn't truly arrived.

In Chapter 19, "Utilizing Log Files," you learn more about how the FastTrack server creates log files, how to understand them, and what you can do with them.

Scripts

Chapter 11, "Working with Scripts," describes how the FastTrack server handles scripting. In essence, scripts are nothing more than a way to run interactive programs on your Web server. Because scripting is intimately tied to the server, different servers have different scripting capabilities.

The biggest areas to consider are in relation to script locations and script languages and conventions, as described in the following sections.

Script Locations

Most servers are fairly flexible about where you can store scripts, although some common conventions about script storage have sprung up. Many Webmasters store their scripts in a directory with a name similar to /cgi/bin, or a variation such as /cgi-bin.

FastTrack is a bit more detailed about where scripts are located. Since FastTrack allows you to use many different types of scripts, it also allows you to specify many different locations for those scripts. Figure 5–1 shows the Netscape Server Manager configuration screen for the CGI script directories.

Notice in the lower-left frame of Figure 5–1 that there are several different choices you can make for program file locations. If the server from which you are converting uses a different directory structure, you will need to give some thought to how you want your scripts organized under FastTrack. In particular, you need to pay attention to the following issues:

   ◆ If your scripts reference information in multiple directories, you may need to change the scripts so that they reference your new directories.

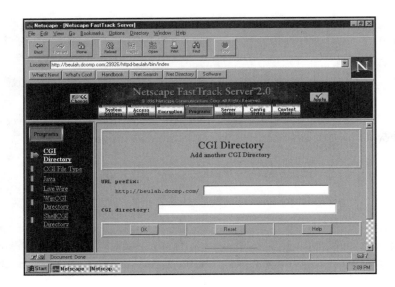

FIGURE 5-1

When you configure the FastTrack server, you can specify the physical location of your script files.

- If your scripts read from or write to a disk file, you will need to make sure the affected directories have the proper permissions set so the scripts will run without error.

- Your scripts run under Windows NT, using the user accounts that FastTrack uses. You need to make sure the user account has sufficient security privileges to access the data it needs.

Script Languages and Conventions

The FastTrack server accepts virtually any language you want to use in conjunction with the server. This flexibility is quite nice, but you (as programmer) need to do some research to discover exactly how you should establish the interface with the server.

The FastTrack server follows several conventions for script interfacing. Most readers may already be familiar with *CGI* (*common gateway interface*). You can find information about how to use CGI in Chapter 11, "Working with Scripts." FastTrack also allows you to use WinCGI, which allows your scripts to work with Visual Basic programs. WinCGI is discussed in Chapter 12, "Working with WinCGI." Other interfaces that FastTrack allows you to establish include JavaScript and Java, which are also covered in their own chapters later in this book.

Security Differences

The different approaches to security in the computer world are astounding. The operating system usually has its own security system, but that doesn't stop Web servers (and, indeed, many other programs) from establishing their own security procedures.

If you are converting from a Web server that relies on the security provisions of the operating system, you need to realize that FastTrack approaches security entirely differently. It does not rely on the operating system; instead, you can control access to individual directories and files made available through the Web server. This doesn't make the conversion to FastTrack impossible, it just means you have one more thing to consider and then follow-up on after the conversion is complete.

Map Files

If you have been using the Web for any time, you are familiar with image maps—graphics that are "clickable." You can point to an area of the graphic, click the mouse button, and thereby instruct the server to do something.

Most often, the coordinates of your click are passed to the server, which then compares the coordinates with the contents of a map file. The map file contains information that directs the server as to where to make the next link. Exactly how you create image maps for the FastTrack server is covered in Chapter 8, "Basic Web Publishing." You should know, if you are converting to FastTrack, that at least two ways exist for constructing the map files associated with an image map: CERN and NCSA.

The CERN Format

The CERN map file format features the default URL on the first line, followed by *shape definitions*. Each shape definition includes an indicator of the shape type (rectangle, circle, or polygon), followed by pairs of coordinates that define the limits of the shape. The last thing included in each shape definition is the URL associated with that region of the map. For example, the following is a map file in the CERN format:

```
default http://www.dcomp.com/crookcounty/crookcounty.htm
rect (266,114) (331,143) http://www.dcomp.com/crookcounty/crookcounty.htm#aladdin
rect (216,267) (300,297) http://www.dcomp.com/crookcounty/crookcounty.htm#sundance
circle (57,176) 25 http://www.dcomp.com/Sundance/Dtower.htm
```

```
rect (113,285) (208,332) http://www.llbean.com/parksearch/parks/195LLN90LL.html
rect (134,131) (190,160) http://www.dcomp.com/crookcounty/crookcounty.htm#hulett
```

The NCSA Format

The NCSA map file format contains much the same information as the CERN format. The difference is that the URL is included in each shape definition right after the shape type, instead of at the end of the line. In addition, the coordinate syntax for the circle shape is just a little different. The following is the same map file, only now in the NCSA format:

```
default http://www.dcomp.com/crookcounty/crookcounty.htm

rect http://www.dcomp.com/crookcounty/crookcounty.htm#aladdin 266,114 331,143

rect http://www.dcomp.com/crookcounty/crookcounty.htm#sundance 216,267 300,297

circle http://www.dcomp.com/Sundance/Dtower.htm 57,176 82,176

rect http://www.llbean.com/parksearch/parks/195LLN90LL.html 113,285 208,332

rect http://www.dcomp.com/crookcounty/crookcounty.htm#hulett 134,131 190,160
```

FastTrack Map Files

The FastTrack server uses the CERN format for image maps. If your old server uses the NCSA format, you must convert all your map files so that they function properly.

> **TIP:** Some map programs, such as MapEdit, enable you to convert from one file type to the other simply by loading and resaving the map file. (You can find more information about MapEdit at `http://www.boutell.com/mapedit/`.)

Image maps are discussed in more detail in Chapter 8, "Basic Web Publishing."

HTML Differences

Some servers extend the flexibility of content pages by adding extensions to the regular HTML tags. If your server adds server-specific HTML statements, and you have taken advantage of those statements, then a safe bet is that they aren't supported by FastTrack. Depending on how heavily you relied upon them, this problem could mean a fair amount of work to make your HTML documents work properly under FastTrack.

TIP: When you transfer all your documents to FastTrack, step through them with your favorite browser to make sure they still appear as you intended.

Virtual Servers

Chapter 4, "Installing Your Web Server," describes how you can set up multiple servers under FastTrack. This ability is not unique to FastTrack; indeed, you can find the same ability in many commercial Web servers. It seems, however, that the name applied to the ability to establish multiple servers goes by many different names, depending on the server in question. In some servers it is called *multihoming,* while in others it simply goes by the name of *virtual servers.*

It makes sense that the process of establishing multiple servers is implemented differently under different Web servers. You need to carefully examine how multiple servers were implemented under your old server, as well as under FastTrack. Pay attention to the following items:

- How do you specify multiple domain names under the old server? How does this translate to the way FastTrack requires them to be specified?
- What are the differences in how IP addresses for each domain name are specified to the server?
- How are paths mapped to different servers?
- How are differing configurations for each server handled under your old server?
- How many servers did you have set up on your old system?

After you answer these questions, you should be able to set up your multiple servers under FastTrack with a minimum of trouble.

A Sample Conversion

To better understand how to make the switch from another Web server to the Netscape FastTrack Server, perhaps an example conversion walkthrough is in order. When Netscape introduced FastTrack, they lowered the prices of their Web servers. Thus, it is conceivable that before FastTrack, many people found the cost of a Netscape server to be too expensive, opting instead for looking elsewhere. There are several free servers on the market, which is always a safe bet for "trying your hand" at Web publishing. For example, Microsoft always suggested that Windows NT networks use the EMWAC server, which was free in a basic configuration. In fact, Microsoft included a copy of the EMWAC server with the Windows NT Server Resource Kit.

Because the EMWAC server was free, and because it has been around longer than any other NT Web server, a lot of people have used it as the basis for their sites, and a lot of these same people will consider moving to the new FastTrack server. For these reasons, this sample conversion assumes you are currently running EMWAC and you want to change to FastTrack.

> **NOTE:** Remember that the exact steps you follow in converting from your old server depend on the server you are using and how your content is organized.

Planning Your Move

Before starting, plan exactly how you are going to do your conversion. Questions to keep in mind include the following:

- When will you convert? Pick a time when you historically have little traffic on your system.

- Do you understand what to do? You should read through all conversion information before you attempt to do it, to make for a smoother transition.

- Can someone else help with the conversion? The old adage that two heads are better than one is certainly applicable to Web site conversion. If you have someone else at your site that you can bounce ideas off, you should do it.

- Have you made a backup of your server site? Being prepared never hurts, and your site documents are probably quite valuable.

Bringing Down Your Old Server

The first task you must accomplish is to stop and remove your old server. You do this by following these steps at the server console:

1. Select the Settings option from the Start menu. This displays the Settings menu.

2. Choose the Control Panel option from the Settings menu. This opens the Control Panel window.

3. Double-click the Services icon to see the Services dialog box, as shown in Figure 5–2.

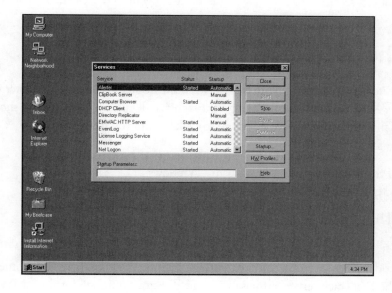

FIGURE 5–2

You can shut down the EMWAC Web server from the Services dialog box.

4. In the list of services, highlight the EMWAC HTTP Server item.

5. Click the Stop button.

6. When asked to confirm your action, click the Yes button. The service is then stopped and the services list is updated.

7. Click the Close button to close the Services dialog box.

8. Close the Control Panel.

9. Choose the <u>P</u>rograms option from the Start menu. This displays the Programs menu.

10. Click on the Command Prompt option from the Programs menu. This opens a command prompt window.

11. Change to the directory in which the https.exe program is located.

12. Type **https -remove** from the command prompt, and then press Enter.

13. In the \WINNT\System32 directory, delete the files HTTPS.HLP, HTTPS.CPL, and HTTPS.EXE (if there).

At this point, you may want to check your deletion by opening the Services dialog box (from the Control Panel) and verifying that the EMWAC HTTP Server item is, indeed, gone from the listed services. You are now ready to install your new FastTrack server.

Installing the Netscape FastTrack Server

Installing your new Web server is quite easy. Just follow the steps covered in Chapter 4, "Installing Your Web Server." Rather than go through the detailed steps here, you should read through Chapter 4 (if you have not done so). Make sure you understand how to accomplish the following tasks:

- Install the service pack (if you are using Windows NT 3.51).
- Check system services.
- Install the FastTrack software.
- Configure the Web server.

Make sure that during installation (or later, during configuration) you point the home directory for the FastTrack server to the same home directory you used for the EMWAC server.

Converting Your Information

Earlier in this chapter you learned about differences you should check for when switching to the FastTrack server. Much of what you have done using the EMWAC server is portable to the FastTrack environment. For instance, all your map files should work just fine.

One area you may want to check really closely is your CGI scripts. Remember that the directory structure used for executable scripts is a bit different under FastTrack. You should copy your CGI scripts to the directories you specified when you configured FastTrack. After this is done, you need to modify your HTML documents to make sure that references to the location of the scripts is correct.

Checking Your Installation

To check your installation, follow the general guidelines discussed in Chapter 6, "Troubleshooting Your Web Installation." The guidelines and steps contained there can help you ensure that your new FastTrack server is responding to requests from remote browsers.

After ensuring that the Web server is up and running, you will want to ensure that all your content pages are functional. The only real way to do this is to spend some time with a browser, looking through your own site. All your pages should look the same as they did under the EMWAC server.

Summary

Converting from one server to another need not be a harrowing experience—but it could be. The difference is in how well you understand what you are doing and how well you have prepared. In this chapter, you have learned the factors that go into a good transition and what you should look out for.

In the next chapter, you learn how to troubleshoot your newly installed Web server.

Chapter | 6

Troubleshooting Your Web Installation

Assuming that you already have installed the FastTrack Web server, you are ready to give it a test drive and make sure that everything is working as it should. This chapter focuses on testing your Web server and troubleshooting any problems you may discover. If you are lucky, you may never need the information in this chapter. On the other hand, understanding the principles and information covered here doesn't hurt.

Testing Your Installation

After you have your Web server installed, you should test the installation to make sure that users can see the information you want to publish. Before you can go through the testing steps, however, you need to make sure that HTML files are available in your home directory.

> **NOTE:** When you install the Web server, FastTrack automatically installs a default HTML page. This page is provided for example use only; it contains links to other Netscape sites. This page is more than adequate for testing purposes.

Right after the installation program was completed, you may remember that it stated Netscape Navigator and connected to your new server. While this ensures that your Web server is available on the same machine on which it is installed, a better test is to make sure it is available from other machines. When you are ready to conduct tests, follow these steps:

1. Locate another computer that has access to the Internet, or to your local area network (if you are using an intranet).

2. Start a Web browser program on the testing computer. (It does not have to be Navigator.)

3. In the URL field of the browser, enter the URL for your new server. (Be sure to include the `http://` specification at the front of the URL.)

   The default page for your server should appear on the browser's screen.

Notice that the testing steps are really quite simple. When you are done, you may want to contact a friend across the country and ask him or her to follow the same steps. If all is working right, he or she should be able to see your information just as easily as you did.

> **NOTE:** If you run into problems testing your installation, follow the applicable trou-
> bleshooting steps covered later in this chapter.

Starting and Stopping the Server

You already know that the FastTrack server runs as a service under Windows NT. This
setup means the server is available all the time, even when you aren't logged into the system. At times, however, you may need to stop and restart the Web server, by stopping
and starting the service. You can do this either from the Services applet or from the
Netscape Server Manager.

> **CAUTION:** When your Web server service has been stopped, your Web server isn't
> operational. People can't connect to your server until you restart the service.

From the Services Applet

To stop the Web server service from the Services applet, follow these steps:

1. Choose the Settings option from the Start menu. This displays the Settings
   menu.
2. Choose the Control Panel option from the Settings menu. This displays the
   Control Panel window.
3. Double-click the Services icon to see the Services dialog box, as shown in
   Figure 6–1.
4. In the list of services, highlight the Netscape FastTrack Server item.
5. Click the Stop button.
6. When asked to confirm your action, click the Yes button. The service is then
   stopped and the services list is updated.
7. Click the Close button to close the Services dialog box.

To restart the Web server, follow steps 1 through 4, but then click the Start button.

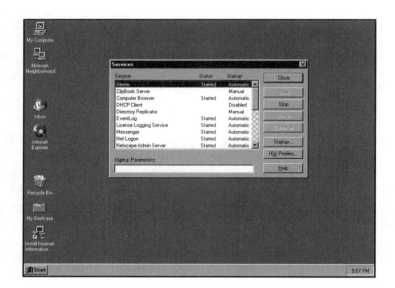

FIGURE 6–1

The Services dialog box controls how system services are executed in Windows NT.

From the Netscape Server Manager

To stop the Web server service from the Netscape Server Manager, follow these steps:

1. Choose the <u>P</u>rograms option from the Start menu. This displays the Programs menu.

2. Choose the Netscape option from the Programs menu. This displays the Netscape menu.

3. Click on the Administer Netscape Servers option. This starts Netscape Navigator, and shortly you will see a security dialog box asking for your user name and password (as in Figure 6–2).

FIGURE 6–2

Before you can change the properties of your server, you must enter a name and password.

4. Enter your user name and password as you specified it when installing FastTrack, then click on OK. This displays the Server Selector page, as shown in Figure 6–3.

FIGURE 6–3

The Server Selector screen allows you to choose different servers to administer.

5. Scroll through the Server Selector page until you can see the name of the server you want to stop.

6. Click on the light-switch control to the left of the server name. When the control says "ON," the server is running; when it says "OFF," the server is stopped.

Common Problems and Solutions

By and large, running a Web server is fairly straightforward and easy. At times, however, you may bump into something that puzzles you. The following sections provide some guidance for common problems you may encounter.

People Can't Locate My Server

This is a common problem for new Web sites. To narrow down the problem, determine the IP address of your Internet server. Then go to another computer (preferably outside of your organization), and try to connect to your Web server, using the IP address in the URL. Thus, if your IP address is 205.163.44.8, you would use the following URL in a browser:

```
http://205.163.44.8
```

If the connection works, but using the domain name doesn't, the problem lies with your DNS server or the DNS entry for your site. If the connection doesn't work, the problem is in your Web server. Both these potential problem areas are covered in the following sections.

> **NOTE:** If neither method works (IP address or domain name), then one of two things happened. First, the IP address or the domain name may have been typed incorrectly. Second, the user may not have an active connection to the Internet. Both problems are beyond the scope of this book to correct.

DNS Problem

If the problem is your DNS server, try the following solutions:

- ◆ Check to see that your DNS server is functioning. You can do this by checking the Services area of the Control Panel on the server which serves as your DNS server. If the DNS service hasn't been started, start it.

- ◆ Check your DNS configuration files to make sure that your spelling and syntax are correct. DNS configuration files can be tricky, so look for small things, like missing periods or misspelled server names.

- ◆ If your DNS server seems to be functioning, contact the Internet provider for the computer from which you did the original checking. Their DNS server may not be providing a correct resolution to your domain name. Talk over your problem with their tech support personnel.

Web Server Problem

If the problem is related to your Web server, try these potential solutions:

- ◆ Check to make sure your FastTrack server is actually running. You do this by using the Netscape Server Manager, as described earlier in this chapter.

- ◆ Make sure your TCP/IP configuration is correct. You do this by using the Network applet in the Control Panel.

- ◆ Make sure you have a valid Internet connection to the server. The best way to determine this is to use the Ping command from the server to verify the existence of an outside server. (I always try the command ping internic.net at the command prompt.) If you get a response, you have an active connection; if you don't, you have a connection problem.

When Connecting to My Server, the User Gets an Error

This is caused most often by the user not specifying a file to load when entering a URL. For example, the user may enter the following as a URL:

```
http://www.beulah.dcomp.com/widgets
```

Because no file name is indicated here, the browser and server assume that it's a directory. If the widgets directory contains no default document, and directory indexing is disabled, an error is generated. Three possible solutions exist for this problem:

- ◆ Create a default document for the widgets directory.

- ◆ Leave the problem as is. (You may want to force the user to specify a document name.)

- ◆ Enable directory indexing, as discussed in Chapter 4, "Installing Your Web Server."

People Can't Access Some Files and Directories on My System

There could be several causes for this problem, but all of them should be relatively easy to fix.

First, check to make sure the documents and directories are within the home directory you created for your Web server. As an alternative, you could make a directory on another drive accessible as another document directory, as discussed in Chapter 4, "Installing Your Web Server."

Next, make sure none of the file names or directory names contain spaces. Even though Windows NT and most other operating systems allow spaces in names, Web servers tend to ignore such conventions.

Additional Document Directories Aren't Visible

Chapter 4, "Installing Your Web Server," explains how you can set up additional document directories using FastTrack. If you have directory indexing turned on, users may comment that they can't see the additional directories. Unfortunately, although an you can add additional directories, and they are accessible, they are not visible. Thus, additional directories are of use only when you are explicitly linking to a resource in the directory.

By way of example, say you have a page containing several links. One or more of the links can point explicitly to documents or other files in the additional document directory. When the user clicks on the link, the information in the additional directory is loaded with no problem. However, if you have directory indexing turned on, the user doesn't see the additional directory in any directory list.

I Need to Reinstall My Web Server in a Different Directory

You may need to reinstall the FastTrack program files in a different directory than the original. If this situation occurs, you need to remove FastTrack and reinstall it in the other directory. To do this, follow the steps outlined later in this chapter, in the section on removing FastTrack. You can then reinstall FastTrack according to the instructions in Chapter 4, "Installing Your Web Server."

I Just Converted to FastTrack, and My Web Documents Don't Show Up

When you run a Web site, you make a huge investment in the documents you publish. When you convert to FastTrack, it is understandable that you want your Web documents to be available. If you convert to FastTrack and you see the default Netscape Web page (as shown in Chapter 4, "Installing Your Web Server"), then your home directory may be set incorrectly. You can check this out with Netscape Server Manager by following these steps:

1. Choose the Programs option from the Start menu. This displays the Programs menu.

2. Choose the Netscape option from the Programs menu. This displays the Netscape menu.

3. Click on the Administer Netscape Servers option. This starts Netscape Navigator, and shortly you will see a security dialog box asking for your user name and password (as earlier in Figure 6–2).

4. Enter your user name and password as you specified it when installing FastTrack, then click on OK. This displays the Server Selector page, as shown earlier in Figure 6–3.

5. Scroll through the Server Selector page until you can see the name of the server you want to configure; click on the server name.

6. On the toolbar in the top frame, click on Content Mgmt at the far right side. This changes the information displayed in the lower frames, as shown in Figure 6–4..

7. Change the Primary Directory field to reflect the path to the home directory of your Web files. This should be the same directory you used as a home directory under your previous Web server.

8. Click on the OK button in the lower-right frame. This sends your configuration information to the server and changes the page displayed in the lower-right frame.

9. Scroll through the lower-right frame and click on the Save and Apply button. Shortly you will see a dialog box indicating your changes were accepted.

10. Click on OK to close the dialog box.

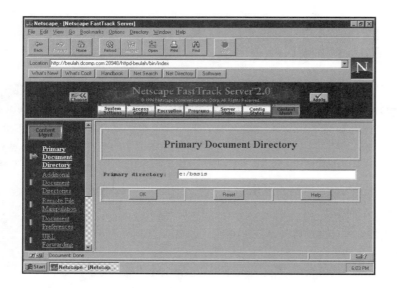

FIGURE 6–4

The Document Preferences frame is used to configure how FastTrack handles your base documents.

When People Connect to My Server, All They See Is a Directory

This problem occurs when two conditions are met. First, you have enabled directory browsing. Second, you don't have a default document file available. Both topics are covered in some detail in Chapter 4, "Installing Your Web Server."

I Can't Get in the Netscape Server Manager

In order use the Netscape Server Manager, you need to know both the user name and password you used when you first installed FastTrack. If you have forgotten the password, you have two options. First, you can delete FastTrack entirely and reinstall. Typically this is only a viable option if you are running a single server and you have done much configuration work.

The other option is to edit the password file to "fudge" your way past the problem. To do this, follow these steps:

1. Browse through your system until you find the admserv directory, within the directory where you installed FastTrack. Thus, if you installed FastTrack in C:\Netscape\Server, then you would look in C:\Netscape\Server\admserv.

2. Using a text editor such as Notepad (not a word processor), load the file admpw, which is located in the directory. The file should contain a single line of text, similar to this:

```
admin:asl234asdf
```

This is your user name (to the left of the colon) and password (to the right of the colon) for the Netscape Server Manager. The password is encrypted, the user name is not.

3. Erase everything after the colon, but not the colon itself.

4. Save the altered file, using the same name (admpw).

5. Choose the Programs option from the Start menu. This displays the Programs menu.

6. Choose the Netscape option from the Programs menu. This displays the Netscape menu.

7. Click on the Administer Netscape Servers option. This starts Netscape Navigator, and shortly you will see the security dialog box, asking for your user name and password.

8. Enter your user name, which you saw in step 2. *Do not enter a password.*

9. Click on OK to enter the Server Selector page.

10. Scroll down to the bottom of the Server Selector page and click on the Configure Administration button. This displays the page shown in Figure 6–5.

11. Click on the Access Control link. This displays the page shown in Figure 6–6.

12. Enter a new password in the Authentication Password field, and then enter it again in the next field below it.

13. Click on the OK button to save your changes.

14. Close Navigator and try to access the Netscape Server Manager again, this time using the new password.

Removing Your FastTrack Server

There may come a time, for one reason or another, when you want to remove the FastTrack server from your system. There are two ways you can accomplish this task: through Windows NT or through Netscape. Regardless of which method you choose, there are also some residual files which you may need to delete when you are done.

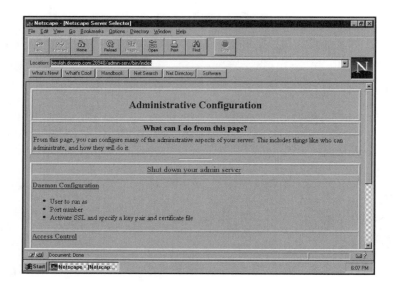

FIGURE 6–5

The Administrative Configuration page allows you to configure access to the Netscape Server Manager.

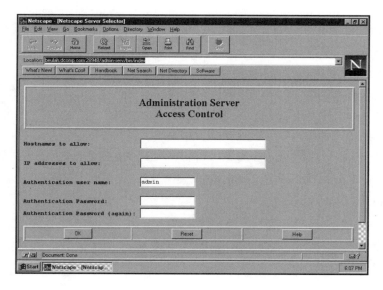

FIGURE 6–6

This page allows you to change your Netscape Server Manager user name and password.

Removing through Windows NT

If you have Windows NT 4.0 installed on your system, you can use the Add/Remove Programs applet in the Control Panel to remove FastTrack. You accomplish this by following these steps.

1. Choose the Settings option from the Start menu. This displays the Settings menu.

2. Choose the Control Panel option from the Settings menu. This displays the Control Panel.

3. Double-click on the Add/Remove Programs icon in the Control Panel. This displays the Add/Remove Programs Properties dialog box, as shown in Figure 6–7.

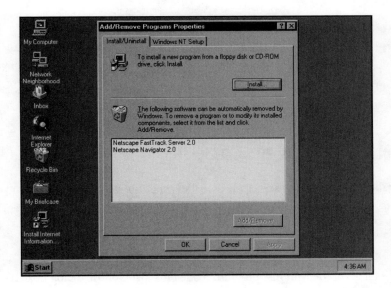

FIGURE 6–7

Removing programs is easy under Windows NT 4.0.

4. In the list of programs at the bottom on the dialog box, highlight the Netscape FastTrack Server 2.0 entry.

5. Click the Add/Remove button. This displays a dialog box asking if you are sure you want to remove the program.

6. Click on the OK button. This displays the dialog box shown in Figure 6–8.

7. Click on the OK button. The FastTrack files are removed from your hard drive.

8. When prompted, click OK to acknowledge your remove.

9. Close the Add/Remove Programs Properties dialog box.

When you are through, there are still some residual files which must be cleaned up, as described shortly.

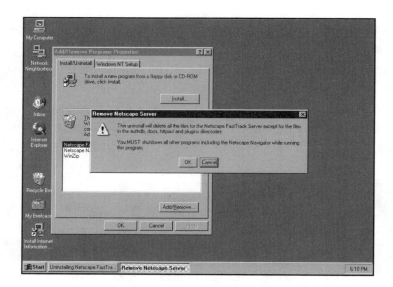

FIGURE 6–8

Before removing program files, you are given one last chance to change your mind.

Removing through Netscape

When you installed the FastTrack server, an uninstall program was also installed on your system. To access this program, follow these steps:

1. Open a window displaying the contents of the directory in which you installed Netscape FastTrack Server.

2. Double-click on the nsuninst program icon. This displays the dialog box shown in Figure 6–9.

3. Select the first check box, which is labeled Netscape FastTrack Server.

4. Click on the OK button. This displays the warning dialog box shown earlier in Figure 6–8.

5. Click on the OK button. The FastTrack files are removed from your hard drive.

6. When prompted, click OK to acknowledge your remove.

The uninstall program removes your FastTrack program files and the Web server. When completed, you should still work through the next section as well.

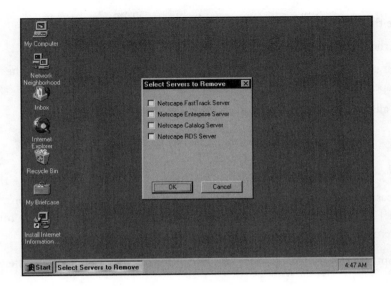

FIGURE 6–9

*FastTrack server also
includes an uninstall
program.*

Residual Files and Cleanup

Regardless of which method you use to remove FastTrack server, there are a few items which are left on your hard drive. The primary reason is that there are directories which may contain documents or scripts you have created. To clean up these directories, you should first move your scripts and documents to another directory, if you want to keep them. Then delete the entire directory in which you first installed FastTrack server.

The other item which needs to be cleaned up applies only to Windows NT 4.0. When FastTrack was first installed, there were a couple of shortcuts installed in your menu structure. These shortcuts now point at non-existent programs—you have removed them from your system. To remove the shortcuts, follow these steps:

1. Right-click on the Start button. This displays a context menu.
2. Choose the <u>O</u>pen option from the context menu. This displays the Start Menu window.
3. Double-click on the Programs folder icon in the Start Menu window. This displays the Programs window.
4. Double-click on the Netscape folder icon in the Programs window. This displays the Netscape window.
5. Delete the Administer Netscape Servers shortcut.

6. Delete the FastTrack README shortcut.

7. Close the Netscape window.

8. If, after step 6, there were no more icons in the Netscape window, delete the Netscape folder icon from the Programs window.

9. Close all the windows you opened in steps 2 and 3.

Summary

Installing the FastTrack server is fairly easy, but that fact doesn't mean that you won't have problems. This chapter has focused on testing your installation and troubleshooting it in case problems arise.

In the next chapter, you learn the basics of how to put together your own Web content pages.

PART III

Basic Content Development

Chapter | 7

Planning Site Content

After your Web site is up and running, you need to give some thought to what it should contain and how it's put together. There's a good chance that you gave this some thought before setting up your site; you at least needed to know what you would provide for a home page.

This chapter discusses some of the issues you must consider when you are planning what to offer at your Web site. The focus here is on content and organization of that content. If you are the person responsible for your Web site, you will undoubtedly find this information handy in your planning.

Your Directory Structure

Once you have established the home directory for your Web site, and you start providing information, you will find that the number of documents, figures, files, and the like that end up at your site can quickly add up. This means that sooner or later you must determine how you want to organize your information.

How you put your Web directories together is entirely up to you, but you should keep in mind that, unlike your personal computer, your Web site may be accessed by many, many people around the Web, who will need to work through your directories. Therefore you should give some thought to how those directories are structured *before* you start putting together your site.

The reason for planning your directory structure ahead of time is that robots wander around the Web, gathering information to appear in high-powered search engines such as Lycos or Alta Vista. Many people use those search engines to locate the information at your site. If you change your directory structure after the robots have cataloged your site, you run the risk of having bad URLs in the search engines. This situation can frustrate users and signal missed opportunities.

If you are running a very small Web site, with a single purpose, the organization of your site is quite easy. In fact, you may be able to get by with only a single directory—the home directory—for your server. If your content is quite diverse, you should set out an organization up front.

As an example, Discovery Computing Inc. (`http://www.dcomp.com`) provides Internet advertising services for a number of businesses in Northeastern Wyoming. The natural way for these businesses to be organized is by town. Thus, our directory structure appears as follows:

```
Aladdin
Art
Class
DCI
Hulett
Misc
Moorcroft
Newcastle
Sundance
```

Each of these items is a subdirectory within the root directory for the Web server. With the exception of the Art, Class, DCI, and Misc subdirectories, each represents a town in our area. The other directories have the following purposes:

- **Art.** A directory of common art files: icons, buttons, wallpaper, and the like.
- **Class.** A directory for an Internet classified service we run.
- **DCI.** A directory for documents related directly to our company.
- **Misc.** A directory for documents that don't fit into any of the other directories.

I'm not trying to say that this system is the only way to organize your directories. On the contrary—I am saying only that this method has worked for us. The key is that you need to think through how to organize your site before you start publishing documents.

Information at Your Site

If you have ever visited a busy Web site, you probably noticed all sorts of documents, graphics, sounds, files, and the like. Amassing huge amounts of information isn't particularly difficult, it just takes time. To manage the information at your site, however, you need an understanding of both your site and the information you are providing. The next several sections are very helpful in this regard.

Focus, Focus, Focus

With the cost of disk space these days, it's very easy to start believing you can create and store huge documents at your site, and then make them available to the world. The problem with this theory is that, although disk space may be cheap, your Internet pipeline is not. The more people you have using your site, the greater the opportunity for creating a bottleneck.

To get around this problem, you should try not to publish every piece of neat information you run across. Instead, focus on the unique topic (or topics) you want to provide. You may want to become the ultimate Web site for information related to the U.S. Civil War. While this topic is still broad, it's much more focused than simply publishing everything about a larger topic, such as warfare in general.

As another example, if the primary reason for the existence of your site is to support your company's marketing and support efforts, then you already have a built-in focus for the information you make available. Realizing your purpose for existence allows you to define which information is acceptable and which isn't.

Copyrighted Information

If you are providing information on your server in which your company has a proprietary interest, you need to make that interest known to all those who visit your site. For example, you may make your product documentation available at your site. In this case, you should make sure that copyright notices exist within the documentation pages or files (if you allow complete files to be downloaded).

Conversely, if you are running a general-interest Web site (for example, the U.S. Civil War site mentioned earlier), you need to be sure you have the right to post and publish the information at your site. In many respects this area is still gray, and you need to be as conservative as your insurance agent and lawyer suggest that you be. For example, if you started posting electronic copies of textbooks about the U.S. Civil War, you are probably violating U.S. copyright law.

> **CAUTION:** If you are in doubt as to what you can safely publish at your Web site, check with qualified legal advisors.

Compressed Files

If your site includes files which can be downloaded by visitors, you will probably want to consider compressing the files so they can be transferred quicker. This approach to offering your files makes quite a bit of sense, since both you and your visitors benefit. Compressed files take less disk space and transfer over the Internet faster. This means your visitor receives their file faster and you free up bandwidth quicker.

Many compression programs and standards are in use around the world. Typically, compression standards crop up around various operating systems. As you are browsing various Internet sites, you can tell which compression programs are being used by looking at the file name extension for a file. Table 7-1 lists some of the more common file compression standards you will run into on the Internet.

Table 7-1 Common file name extensions for compressed files.

Extension	Platform	Program
.arc	DOS	ARC
.lh	DOS	Lharc
.lzh	DOS	Lharc
.sit	Macintosh	Stuffit
.tar	UNIX	Tar
.Z	UNIX	Compress
.z	UNIX	Pack
.zip	DOS/Windows	PKZIP; WinZip
.zoo	DOS/UNIX	zoo210

Even though the information in Table 7-1 indicates a platform for the various file extensions, programs are available on the Internet that allow you to decompress (or compress) files using any given compression standard on virtually any type of computer system.

Which compression standard should you use for your files? That depends on the type of files you are compressing and who your typical user is. If the file you want to make available at your site is an executable program for a UNIX system, for example, you should use the TAR standard. However, if the files are transportable to a wide variety of platforms (this is typically the case with audio, graphics, text, or video files), you may want to keep several different compressed versions of the files.

TIP: Compressing single files doesn't make much sense unless the single file is quite large. If you can, compress entire collections of related files.

A Word on File Formats

One of the issues you need to be concerned with when publishing information on the Web is the format in which your information will be stored. It goes without saying that the majority of your documents will be in HTML format. This is the format used for Web pages, as discussed fully in Chapter 8, "Basic Web Publishing." Beyond this, however, there is quite a bit of latitude and even more confusion. The following sections discuss your options when publishing graphic and audio information.

Graphics Files

Even though the Web originally began as a text-only Internet service, these days there are very few Web pages that don't include graphics. If you have been around computers for any length of time, you know that there are literally dozens of ways you can format and store a graphics file. Table 7-2 indicates just a few of the common graphics file formats.

Table 7-2   Common file name extensions for graphics files.

Extension	Format
.bmp	Windows or OS/2 bitmap
.cdr	CorelDRAW!
.cgm	Computer graphics metafile
.clp	Windows clipboard
.cut	Dr. Halo
.drw	Micrografix Draw
.gif	Graphics interchange format
.jpg	JPEG format
.mac	MacPaint
.msp	Microsoft Paint
.pcx	ZSoft Paintbrush
.psd	Adobe Photoshop
.ras	Sun raster image
.tga	Truevision Targa
.tif	Tagged image file format
.wmf	Windows metafile
.wpg	WordPerfect graphic

Even though you can create graphics in any of the formats shown in Table 7-2, it doesn't necessarily mean you should. Not all of the graphics file formats can be displayed by all browsers. Your visitors could download helpers or browser add-ons that will allow them to view virtually any type of graphics file, but why put them through that trouble?

The most common graphics file formats used on the Web are GIF (pronounced either with a hard G or as *jiff*) and JPG (pronounced jay-peg). These formats are understood by every popular browser available, so it is a fair bet that your graphics will not go unappreciated.

Typically, GIFs are used for small, low-color (256 or less) images. Thus, they are great for icons and small artwork. The strengths of GIF files are as follows:

◆ ***Small file size.*** GIF files are saved using automatic compression, which means they consume fewer bytes than many formats and can be transmitted quickly.

◆ ***Interlacing.*** When working with large graphics, you can direct the image to be saved in an interlaced format. This means that it appears to your visitor that the image is loaded quicker since the image is loaded in multiple passes.

◆ ***Transparency.*** Under some GIF variations, you can direct that a specific color in the image be treated as "transparent." This means that when the color is encountered by a browser, the background appears in the place of that color instead of the color itself.

These benefits do not mean you should always choose GIF files. If you have a need for higher quality, try the high-resolution, high-color capabilities of JPG files. Images saved in this format are highly realistic, although the files can be rather large.

Your job, as a site administrator, is to pick the image format that is best for your intended uses. Think about your images, your desired effect, and your visitors, then pick the format that is right for you.

Audio Files

There are just about as many audio file formats as there are graphic formats. Audio files are making great inroads into the Web, although they are not as widespread as graphics. The reason for this is that your visitor must have a sound card and speakers in order to appreciate your audio selections. If you decide to include audio clips at your site, however, you can save them in many different ways. The most common audio file formats are WAV and AU, both so-named because of the file extensions used for sounds saved in that format (.WAV and .AU).

The WAV format is typically used on Windows-based systems. The format was originally designed by Microsoft, but can now be played on quite a number of hardware platforms. The AU format is widely accepted in the UNIX environment, and is making large strides into the Windows world. The format originated on Sun and NeXT systems. Typically there is not much difference in file sizes between WAV and AU files, nor is there much sound quality difference for the types of sounds typically found on the Internet. In addition, most browsers understand the WAV format automatically, and a good number of new browsers understand the AU format. Thus, your decision about which format to use can be based on who you anticipate your visitors being—UNIX or Windows users.

> **TIP:** If you want additional information on audio file formats, check out some of the search engines on the Internet, such as Alta Visa. Use the search words "audio file formats."

Summary

Running a good Web site takes time and energy. Exactly how much you devote to your site is up to you, but any skills you can develop and knowledge you can attain will assist you in your efforts. This chapter has presented some of the things you can do and remember to make your site more professional and "user-friendly."

In the next chapter, you begin to learn how you can create your own Web documents.

Chapter | 8

Basic Web Publishing

Now that you have your Web server up and running, you may be wondering how you can create documents to publish on the Web. If you previously used a different Web server, you may know all about creating documents; in this case, you may want to skip most of this chapter. On the other hand, if Web publishing is new to you, chances are good that you can benefit by at least reading through the information here.

The purpose of this chapter is to introduce you to the basics of using HTML to publish your documents. In particular, you learn how to use HTML within the Netscape FastTrack Server environment. This chapter isn't intended as an end-all reference to HTML; other books on the market can help in that respect.

> **TIP:** If you want a dynamic look at HTML from a reference standpoint, check out http://www.willcam.com/cmat/html/crossref.html. For content, this site is better than most HTML reference books I have seen.

Understanding HTML Documents

You publish documents on the Web using plain ASCII text files that have special tags inserted throughout the text. The syntax of these tags is collectively known as *HTML*, which is an acronym for *Hypertext Markup Language*. HTML was created specifically for use on the Web, but is related to an older standard known as *SGML*, which stands for *standard generalized markup language*.

HTML tags are inserted within a document by enclosing the tag within angle brackets (the less-than and greater-than signs). For instance, the following is a simple HTML tag:

<STRONG>

Many HTML tags also have counterparts that are "terminating" tags. For example, the <STRONG> tag turns on strong type, typically causing the browser to display a bold font. To turn off the strong type, you use the following tag:

</STRONG>

Notice the use of the slash within the tag. This signifies that the browser should turn off whatever attribute the tag represents. HTML tags are not case-sensitive, meaning that <STRONG> is interpreted the same as <strong> or even <StRoNg>.

> **NOTE:** The exact interpretation of most HTML tags is left up to your browser. For example, one browser may display headings differently than another browser, although the same tag is used on both of them.

Different versions of HTML are available, with the latest version being 3.0. Most browsers these days support HTML 3.0, but most browsers also add their own little enhancements to the standard. Thus, some tags work only with Netscape's browser; others work only with Microsoft's. Fortunately, if a browser receives a tag it doesn't understand, it completely ignores it. Suppose that a Web document includes the following tag:

```
<abcdefg>
```

This is a meaningless tag; no browser would know what to do with it. Rather than generate an error, the browser simply ignores the rogue tag.

Document Structure

Every HTML document has a basic structure that you must follow. If you don't follow this basic structure, the effects on a browser are undefined. This means that the document may be displayed on one browser, but not on another.

The two parts of a document are the *head* and the *body*. The head of the document contains information used to define the purpose and layout of the document, and the body contains the text to be displayed in the browser window. To mark the document head, you use the <HEAD> and </HEAD> tags. Likewise, to mark the body you use the <BODY> and </BODY> tags. The following example shows how this is done within the document file:

```
<HTML>
<HEAD>


</HEAD>
<BODY>


</BODY>
</HTML>
```

Everything between <HEAD> and </HEAD> is considered the document head, and everything between <BODY> and </BODY> is the document body. Notice also the <HTML> and </HTML> tag pair surrounding all the other tags. These tags are required in any document, as they mark the limits of the HTML document.

You already know that an HTML file is straight ASCII text. Outside of that, and the structure just shown, nothing is special about an HTML document. You don't need to put one tag per line, or separate tags with spaces. In fact, your document could be all scrunched together on a single line, if desired. This isn't a good idea, however, because HTML tags are a lot easier to understand if you space them out a bit. Spacing is desirable for humans, but not necessary for the computer.

What's in the Document Head?

As mentioned earlier, the document head specifies identification information for your document. You do this with a series of tags that specify what type of information you are including. The following example could be the start of a document for a home page:

```
<HTML>
<HEAD>
<TITLE>Discovery Computing Inc.</TITLE>
<META NAME="description" CONTENT="Home page for Discovery
Computing Inc., a company specializing in providing
information services.">
<META NAME="keywords" CONTENT="computer books consulting
programming technical editing Sundance Wyoming WY
Web Advertising fulfillment distribution writing authoring">
</HEAD>
<BODY>

</BODY>
</HTML>
```

This example includes two new sets of tags in the head portion of the document. The first is the <TITLE> and </TITLE> pair. This tag specifies the title that you want assigned to the document—the title that appears in the title bar for the document browser whenever a user displays the page. It's also the name that appears in a bookmark, if the user bookmarks your page in his or her browser.

> **NOTE:** The titles of Web documents are often grabbed automatically and placed in Web indexes. That's why, if you contact indexes like Alta Vista, you may see entries that say "NO TITLE." These are documents that didn't have the <TITLE> and </TITLE> tags specified in the document head.

The other tag used in this example is <META>. This is a tag that allows you to provide specialized information to another program that may access your page. In this case, the <META> tag specifies information that is accessed by several types of indexing robots (see the sidebar) that browse through the Web. The other words within the <META> tag (NAME and CONTENT) are referred to as attributes. (You learn more about attributes later in this chapter.) Whether you include the <META> tag, and exactly what you put in it, is up to you. (In other words, this tag is optional.)

Web Robots

Several indexing services on the Web are very helpful when locating information. These services compile their information automatically by sending out *robots*. These are nothing but specialized programs that browse around the Web, looking for information to include in the index.

When a robot encounters a page, it pulls the URL, the document title, any indexing information (from the <META> tags), and perhaps the first couple of lines of text. This information is stored in a database accessed when people visit the index's Web site. The robot also works its way through the other links stored in the page, indexing them as well.

What's in the Document Body?

The body of your document is where you place information that you want displayed on the browser of the person viewing your page. Whatever you type here is displayed in the remote browser, but not in the same format as you type it. Consider the following HTML file:

```
<HTML>
<HEAD>
<TITLE>Discovery Computing Inc.</TITLE>
<META NAME="description" CONTENT="Home page for Discovery
Computing Inc., a company specializing in providing
information services.">
<META NAME="keywords" CONTENT="computer books consulting
programming technical editing Sundance Wyoming WY
Web Advertising fulfillment distribution writing authoring">
</HEAD>

<BODY>

                    Welcome to Discovery Computing Inc.

Discovery Computing Inc. (DCI) is a multi-faceted company providing
a host of services to many different companies and individuals. As
a corporation, we have been in business for just under ten years,
helping many companies solve problems, increase sales, and improve
productivity.

In essence, our services can be boiled down to the following:
        Authoring
        Consulting
        Publishing Services
        Order Fulfillment

</BODY>
</HTML>
```

From examining this file, you might think that this text would display information about Discovery Computing, nicely formatting on the screen. Figure 8–1 shows what actually appears when you view this document.

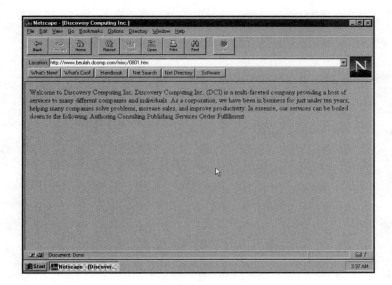

FIGURE 8–1

The best presentation of information in a document isn't done hastily.

Notice that the words are all bunched together, and they don't look anything like they do in the text file. This problem occurs because HTML doesn't recognize "white space," including extra spaces, tabs, or carriage returns. Instead, all text is displayed with only a single space between each word.

Thus, the first thing to remember when developing HTML documents is that including text is easy—the hard part is displaying it in the format you want. You do the formatting with special HTML tags, as the following sections explain.

Formatting Paragraphs

The first task in formatting your document text is to break it into paragraphs with the <P> and <BR> tags. These tags don't require closing tags, although some designers advocate the use of a </P> tag.

The <P> tag causes a paragraph break. Wherever you include the tag, the browser at the other end ends the paragraph, skips a line, and starts the following text at the beginning of a new line. The following text shows the earlier HTML document, with the <P> tag inserted at the beginning of the first paragraph.

```
<HTML>
<HEAD>
<TITLE>Discovery Computing Inc.</TITLE>
<META NAME="description" CONTENT="Home page for Discovery
Computing Inc., a company specializing in providing
information services.">
<META NAME="keywords" CONTENT="computer books consulting
programming technical editing Sundance Wyoming WY
Web Advertising fulfillment distribution writing authoring">
</HEAD>

<BODY>

                 Welcome to Discovery Computing Inc.

<P>Discovery Computing Inc. (DCI) is a multi-faceted company providing
a host of services to many different companies and individuals. As
a corporation, we have been in business for just under ten years,
helping many companies solve problems, increase sales, and improve
productivity.

<P>In essence, our services can be boiled down to the following:
<P>      Authoring
<P>      Consulting
<P>      Publishing Services
<P>      Order Fulfillment

</BODY>
</HTML>
```

Now, when you display the page, it appears as shown in Figure 8–2. Notice that the added paragraph breaks makes the document look a bit closer to what is intended. (They certainly makes it more readable.)

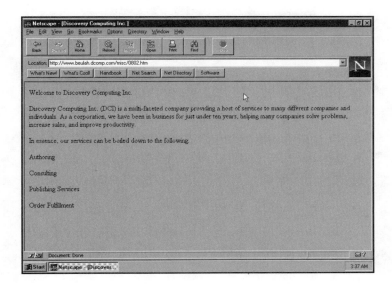

FIGURE 8–2

The <P> tag starts a new paragraph.

NOTE: If you add multiple <P> tags to your document, without any intervening text, the additional tags are ignored by most browsers. Thus <P><P><P> has no different effect than a single <P>.

Look at Figure 8–2 again. Notice that some areas have *too* much space. For example, the list of services probably would look much better without the extra line between each paragraph. This is where the <BR> tag can come in handy. This tag means *break*, and it does just that—it breaks the line where the browser encounters the tag, and then picks up again at the beginning of the next line. You can modify your HTML file to use this tag as shown here (Figure 8–3 shows the resulting browser screen):

```
<HTML>
<HEAD>
<TITLE>Discovery Computing Inc.</TITLE>
<META NAME="description" CONTENT="Home page for Discovery
Computing Inc., a company specializing in providing
information services.">
<META NAME="keywords" CONTENT="computer books consulting
programming technical editing Sundance Wyoming WY
Web Advertising fulfillment distribution writing authoring">
```

```
</HEAD>

<BODY>

                    Welcome to Discovery Computing Inc.

<P>Discovery Computing Inc. (DCI) is a multi-faceted company providing
a host of services to many different companies and individuals. As
a corporation, we have been in business for just under ten years,
helping many companies solve problems, increase sales, and improve
productivity.

<P>In essence, our services can be boiled down to the following:<BR>
        Authoring<BR>
        Consulting<BR>
        Publishing Services<BR>
        Order Fulfillment

</BODY>
</HTML>
```

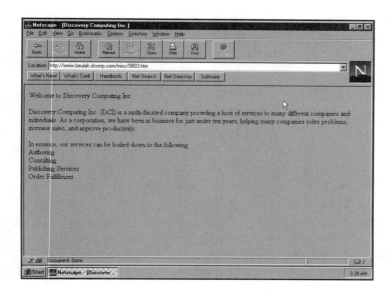

FIGURE 8–3

The <BR> tag breaks the line; the text following the tag starts on the next line.

Designating Headings

The HTML standards enable you to specify special headings (also just called *heads*) for the body of your document. Don't confusing these heads with the document head (mentioned earlier in the chapter), which the browser doesn't display. Headings are a typographical treatment of text that organizes the document. For example, the words *Designating Headings* at the beginning of this section are a type of head.

To add headings to your document, you use the <H1> and </H1> tags. In reality, you use this same format for up to six levels of headings, each of which looks different. Thus, you can have <H1>, <H2>, <H3>, and so on, all the way to <H6>. The way in which each level of heading appears is entirely up to the browser viewing your page. In general, however, the lower the heading number (with <H1> being the lowest, by number), the larger and bolder the text appears.

Adding a heading to our sample document makes it look much better on a browser. The natural heading, in this case, is the first line of text. Following is the HTML document with the new heading tags inserted:

```
<HTML>

<HEAD>

<TITLE>Discovery Computing Inc.</TITLE>

<META NAME="description" CONTENT="Home page for Discovery
Computing Inc., a company specializing in providing
information services.">

<META NAME="keywords" CONTENT="computer books consulting
programming technical editing Sundance Wyoming WY
Web Advertising fulfillment distribution writing authoring">

</HEAD>


<BODY>


<H1>                  Welcome to Discovery Computing Inc.</H1>


Discovery Computing Inc. (DCI) is a multi-faceted company providing
a host of services to many different companies and individuals. As
a corporation, we have been in business for just under ten years,
```

```
helping many companies solve problems, increase sales, and improve
productivity.

<P>In essence, our services can be boiled down to the following:<BR>
      Authoring<BR>
      Consulting<BR>
      Publishing Services<BR>
      Order Fulfillment

</BODY>
</HTML>
```

Notice in the code that the <P> tag that started the paragraph following the heading was removed. The <H1> tag, as displayed by a browser, includes additional space after the heading and before the following text—so you don't need the <P> tag. Figure 8–4 shows how the addition of the heading changes the look of the document.

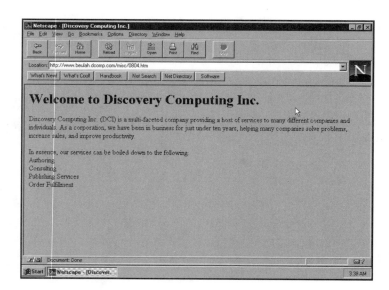

FIGURE 8–4

Adding headings to an HTML document enables you to organize your text.

Centering Information

Centering information horizontally on the screen is often more pleasing than have everything butted up to the left side of the window. To center information, use the <CENTER>

and </CENTER> tag pair. For example, I like to have my first-level headings centered. (Call it a personality flaw, if you like.) To achieve this look, all you need to do is remove the extra spaces at the beginning of the heading (they don't help anything, anyway), and include the proper tags. The result is shown in the following text lines:

```
<HTML>
<HEAD>
<TITLE>Discovery Computing Inc.</TITLE>
<META NAME="description" CONTENT="Home page for Discovery
Computing Inc., a company specializing in providing
information services.">
<META NAME="keywords" CONTENT="computer books consulting
programming technical editing Sundance Wyoming WY
Web Advertising fulfillment distribution writing authoring">
</HEAD>

<BODY>

<CENTER><H1>Welcome to Discovery Computing Inc.</H1></CENTER>

Discovery Computing Inc. (DCI) is a multi-faceted company providing
a host of services to many different companies and individuals. As
a corporation, we have been in business for just under ten years,
helping many companies solve problems, increase sales, and improve
productivity.

<P>In essence, our services can be boiled down to the following:<BR>
      Authoring<BR>
      Consulting<BR>
      Publishing Services<BR>
      Order Fulfillment

</BODY>
</HTML>
```

Originally, the <CENTER> tag started as an extension available only in Netscape, but it has been adopted since then by other browsers. Most browsers understand the tag (and you may recall that if the browser doesn't understand the tag, it's ignored anyway). The result of using the <CENTER> tag, from the browser's point of view, is shown in Figure 8–5.

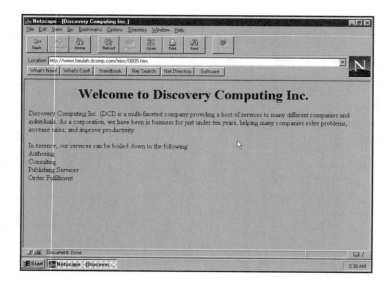

FIGURE 8–5

The <CENTER> tag centers text horizontally.

Creating Lists

A common typographical element used to break up long streams of text is a *list*. Lists are used quite extensively in books and magazines. For instance, the following list is called a *numbered list*:

1. This is the first item in the list.
2. This is the second item in the list.
3. This is the third item in the list.
4. This is the fourth item in the list.

In the world of HTML, a numbered list is referred to as an *ordered list*. Two tag pairs designate an ordered list. The <OL> and </OL> pair designate the beginning and ending of the list. The <LI> and </LI> pair mark each individual item in the list. We could use a numbered list in our Web page, as shown here:

```
<HTML>
<HEAD>
<TITLE>Discovery Computing Inc.</TITLE>
<META NAME="description" CONTENT="Home page for Discovery
Computing Inc., a company specializing in providing
information services.">
<META NAME="keywords" CONTENT="computer books consulting
programming technical editing Sundance Wyoming WY
Web Advertising fulfillment distribution writing authoring">
</HEAD>

<BODY>

<CENTER><H1>Welcome to Discovery Computing Inc.</H1></CENTER>

Discovery Computing Inc. (DCI) is a multi-faceted company providing
a host of services to many different companies and individuals. As
a corporation, we have been in business for just under ten years,
helping many companies solve problems, increase sales, and improve
productivity.

<P>In essence, our services can be boiled down to the following:<BR>
<OL>
<LI>Authoring</LI>
<LI>Consulting</LI>
<LI>Publishing Services</LI>
<LI>Order Fulfillment</LI>
</OL>

</BODY>
</HTML>
```

Notice that the <BR> tags, previously used to break the lines in the HTML code, were removed from the ordered list. Your browser knows that each item within the list should begin on a new line. Figure 8–6 shows the results of viewing this page.

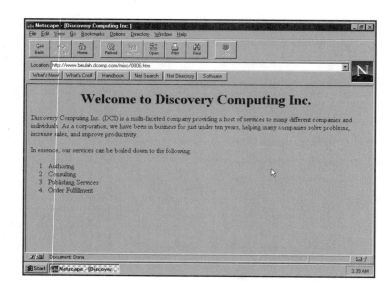

FIGURE 8–6

*An ordered list, using the
<OL> tag, includes
consecutive numbers
at the beginning of each
list item.*

Nesting Lists

You can also *nest* lists, in effect creating an outline. You do this by enclosing each level of
the list within the <OL> and </OL> tag pairs. The following sample text shows a three-
level list used within a document:

```
<HTML>
<HEAD>
<TITLE>Sample of nested lists</TITLE>
</HEAD>
<BODY>
The following is a sample of a nested list:

<OL>
<LI>Introduction</LI>
<OL>
<LI>Grateful for opportunity to speak</LI>
<LI>Come up with ice-breaker joke</LI>
<LI>Show overhead of presentation outline</LI>
</OL>
<LI>Traditional sales at our company</LI>
```

```
<OL>
<LI>Discuss overhead of sales force structure</LI>
<OL>
<LI>Greatest numbers in Eastern US</LI>
<LI>Weak representation in South</LI>
</OL>
<LI>Strengths of traditional approach</LI>
<LI>Changes in marketplace</LI>
<LI>Weaknesses in traditional approach</LI>
<LI>Issue challenge for change</LI>
</OL>
<LI>Proposed sales changes</LI>
<OL>
<LI>Discuss overhead of proposed sales force structure</LI>
<LI>Discuss how weaknesses are met</LI>
<LI>Show results of market testing</LI>
</OL>
<LI>Bottom-line modifications</LI>
<OL>
<LI>Greater flexibility</LI>
<LI>Greater cash flow</LI>
<LI>Better sales representative motivation</LI>
</OL>
</OL>

</BODY>
</HTML>
```

> **NOTE:** Adding nested lists can greatly expand your HTML code, because so many tags are associated with the list.

Figure 8–7 shows how the nested lists look.

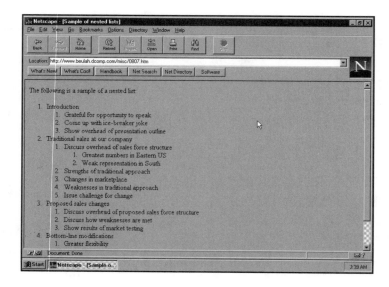

FIGURE 8-7

You can nest lists to create an outline appearance for your document.

Using Unordered Lists

Ordered lists aren't the only type of lists you can use in your document. The other type of list is known as an *unordered list*. In the typographical world, this type of list is called a *bulleted list*. For example, the following is a bulleted list:

- This is the first item in the list.
- This is the second item in the list.
- This is the third item in the list.
- This is the fourth item in the list.

To use an unordered list in your Web page, you simply replace the <OL> and </OL> tag pair with the <UL> and </UL> tag pair. You still use the <LI> and </LI> pair to specify the individual items in the list. The results are shown in Figure 8-8.

> **TIP:** Whether you use an ordered or unordered list is entirely up to you. In general, you should let the nature of your text make the determination of which you use. If your material represents steps that must be followed in order, or if it is similar to an outline, use the ordered list. In all other instances you are better off using the unordered list.

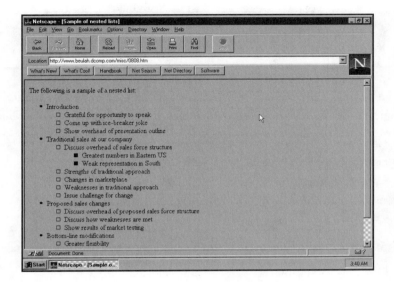

FIGURE 8–8

An unordered list has bullets (special characters, such as dots) at the beginning of each item.

Formatting Characters

Paragraphs aren't the only part of your document you can format with HTML tags. Some tags can format individual characters. These tags are broken into two categories: physical styles and logical styles.

Physical Styles

Physical styles are implemented by tags that force a particular attribute to be used by a browser. For example, *italic text* can be forced by using an <I> and </I> tag pair. Not many physical styles are available, as shown in Table 8–1.

Table 8–1   Physical style tags.

Tag Pair	Purpose
<B></B>	Bold text
<I></I>	Italic text
<TT></TT>	Fixed-width (monospace) text
<U></U>	Underlined text

> **CAUTION:** Some browsers don't support all the physical tags. Generally, you can count on at least < B > and < I > being supported.

Physical tags can be used collectively, as well. If you want text to be both ***bold and italic***, for example, you can use the <B> and <I> tags together, as in the following sample lines:

```
Discovery Computing Inc. (DCI) is a <B><I>multi-faceted company</I></B> providing
a host of services to many different companies and individuals. As
a corporation, <B>we have been in business for just under ten years,</B>
helping many companies solve problems, <I>increase sales,</I> and improve
productivity.
```

In this example, the words ***multi-faceted company*** would appear in both bold and italics.

> **TIP:** Don't overdo the use of physical styles. If you use too much of a special type characteristic, it loses its desired effect. Use these effects sparingly.

Logical Styles

The preceding section mentioned physical styles, which force the browser to use a specific text effect. Many designers prefer, instead, to use *logical styles*. These style tags focus on defining the effect desired, and then leave it up to whoever programmed the browser to decide how that effect should be implemented. Table 8–2 lists the various logical styles you can use.

Again, the logical style tags can be used cumulatively to achieve any effect you desire. You should understand, however, that because the effect used to implement a logical style is entirely up to the browser's programmer, you may not get the effect you want by combining logical style tags. Also, some logical style tags may not be implemented in all browsers.

Table 8–2   Logical style tags.

Tag Pair	Effect
<CITE></CITE>	Used for citations, usually displayed in italics.
<CODE></CODE>	Used for program code, usually displayed in a monospace typeface.
<DFN></DFN>	The first instance of a term, where it is being defined. Typically displayed as bold or bold and italics.
<EM></EM>	Used for emphasis, usually displayed in italics.
<KBD></KBD>	Used to designated keystrokes a user should type.
<SAMP></SAMP>	Used to specify a sequence of literal characters.
<STRONG></STRONG>	Used for strong text, usually displayed in bold.
<VAR></VAR>	Used to define a variable, as in programming code.

Special Characters

There are some characters that cannot (or should not) be used directly within your text. These characters, when received by some browsers, may not be able to be formatted and displayed correctly. To compensate for this, there is a set of *escape codes* you can use in your text.

Escape codes begin with an ampersand, and are followed immediately by a keyword. When received by a browser, the ampersand and keyword are automatically replaced by the proper special characters. The escape codes you should use are shown in Table 8–3.

Table 8–3   Escape codes for use in text.

Escape Code	Character
&amp	&
&copy	©
&gt	>
&lt	<
&quot	"

Including Graphics in a Document

Because the Web is the multimedia portion of the Internet, it makes sense that you are able to include graphics in your HTML documents. To do so, you use the <IMG> tag. No ending tag is needed to pair with <IMG>, as it designates the place where a single graphic should be inserted.

To use <IMG>, you must use an attribute with the tag. *Attributes* are modifiers that can be included in an HTML tag. They affect the way in which the tag is interpreted by the browser. The sample Web document includes attributes in the <META> tag, used in the document head.

To specify a file name to be loaded as an image, you use the SRC attribute. The HTML code to load an image could appear as follows:

```
<IMG SRC = "/dcilogo.gif">
```

Notice that the attribute name (SRC, which stands for *source*) is separated from the keyword for the tag (IMG) by a space, and then followed by an equal sign (=). After the equal sign is the *value* for the attribute, enclosed within quotation marks (" ").

Notice, as well, that the file reference (which is the value for the SRC attribute) is to dcilogo.gif. There is also a slash (/) before the file name. This signifies the path to the file, the same as specifying a path within DOS or UNIX. In this case, the leading slash signifies that searching for the file should begin at the root directory. Note that this means the root directory for the FastTrack server, not for the hard drive on which the server is located. If the slash had been left out, the graphic file would have been looked for in the same directory as the HTML document that referenced it. You will see many examples of using directory paths used throughout the rest of this chapter.

The sample now shows the HTML document with the proper code to load a logo at the beginning of the document:

```
<HTML>
<HEAD>
<TITLE>Discovery Computing Inc.</TITLE>
<META NAME="description" CONTENT="Home page for Discovery
Computing Inc., a company specializing in providing
information services.">
```

```
<META NAME="keywords" CONTENT="computer books consulting
programming technical editing Sundance Wyoming WY
Web Advertising fulfillment distribution writing authoring">
</HEAD>

<BODY>

<CENTER>
<IMG SRC = "/dcilogo.gif">
<H1>Welcome to Discovery Computing Inc.</H1>
</CENTER>

Discovery Computing Inc. (DCI) is a multi-faceted company providing
a host of services to many different companies and individuals. As
a corporation, we have been in business for just under ten years,
helping many companies solve problems, increase sales, and improve
productivity.

<P>In essence, our services can be boiled down to the following:<BR>
<UL>
<LI>Authoring</LI>
<LI>Consulting</LI>
<LI>Publishing Services</LI>
<LI>Order Fulfillment</LI>
</UL>

</BODY>
</HTML>
```

Notice that the <IMG> tag appears within the <CENTER> and </CENTER> pair of tags, just before the heading. This placement insures that the graphic will be centered horizontally within the browser window. The results of this use of the <IMG> tag can be seen in Figure 8–9.

CAUTION: You can include any type of graphics format you want in your documents, but you should know that the *de facto* standard on the Web is the GIF format. An understanding of this format, initially popularized by CompuServe, is built into each browser on the market. Other graphics formats can be used, but can only be viewed by browsers if the proper viewer is loaded.

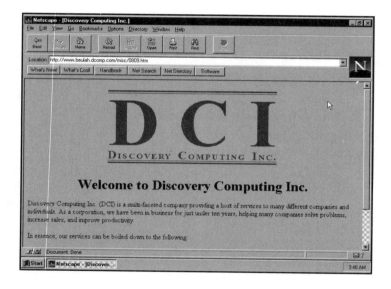

FIGURE 8–9

The <IMG> tag instructs the browser to insert a graphic at that location.

Notice that the entire HTML document can no longer be seen all at one time, because the graphics take up so much vertical space. The person using the browser must scroll through the document. (The browser adds the scroll bars automatically, as necessary for your HTML document.)

NOTE: Remember that graphics, depending on the type, resolution, and size, can take considerable space on your server's hard disk. The larger or more complicated the graphic, the longer it takes to transfer from your Internet site. If your graphics are too big, you may alienate the people visiting your site.

Adding Links

Links are at the heart of the Web. You can include links on your Web page to wherever you would like, whether at your site or around the world. To include a link, you use the <A> and </A> tag pair, which stands for *anchor*. In conjunction with the tag, you use the HREF attribute to specify the URL of the related information. You can include effectively two types of URLs in the HREF attribute:

♦ *Local.* You specify a local URL in much the same way that you provided a graphic file name using the SRC attribute in the preceding section.

♦ *External.* An external reference is the entire, formal URL. You specify the URL by using the same syntax discussed in Chapter 4, "Installing Your Web Server."

The following text shows both local and external links added within the sample Web document:

```
<HTML>
<HEAD>
<TITLE>Discovery Computing Inc.</TITLE>
<META NAME="description" CONTENT="Home page for Discovery
Computing Inc., a company specializing in providing
information services.">
<META NAME="keywords" CONTENT="computer books consulting
programming technical editing Sundance Wyoming WY
Web Advertising fulfillment distribution writing authoring">
</HEAD>

<BODY>

<CENTER>
<IMG SRC = "/dcilogo.gif">
<H1>Welcome to Discovery Computing Inc.</H1>
</CENTER>

Discovery Computing Inc. (DCI) is a multi-faceted company providing
a host of services to many different companies and individuals. As
```

a corporation, we have been in business for just under ten years,
helping many companies solve problems, increase sales, and improve
productivity.

```
<P>In essence, our services can be boiled down to the following:<BR>
<UL>
<LI><A HREF="/DCI/Authoring.Htm">Authoring</A></LI>
<LI><A HREF="/DCI/Consulting.Htm">Consulting</A></LI>
<LI><A HREF="/DCI/PubServices.Htm">Publishing Services</A></LI>
<LI><A HREF="/DCI/Fulfillment.Htm">Order Fulfillment</A></LI>
</UL>

<CENTER>
<STRONG>Check out our on-line
<A HREF="/DCI/MfgList/MfgList.Htm">guide to equipment manufacturers</A>!
</STRONG>
</CENTER>

<P>Thanks for stopping by our page. While you are at it, check
out some of the communities around our area, including
<A HREF="/Sundance/Sundance.Htm">Sundance</A>,
Hulett,
Moorcroft, and
<A HREF="/Aladdin/Aladdin.Htm">Aladdin</A>.
Each of these are in beautiful Crook County, Wyoming. (If you would
like to understand one of the big reasons DCI is located in this
area, click <A HREF="/Sundance/Business.Htm">here</A>.)

<P>You might also like to see some of our
<A HREF="/DCI/FavoriteWeb.Htm">favorite web sites</A>.

<P>
<CENTER>
<P>Send comments to:
<A HREF = "mailto:Webmaster@dcomp.com"><EM>Webmaster@dcomp.com</EM></A>
```

```
<P>Copyright &copy 1996 Discovery Computing Inc. All rights reserved.
</CENTER>

</BODY>
</HTML>
```

When you view this document, the center of the document looks like Figure 8–10. The links appear in a different color than the rest of the text, and they are underlined. This is the universal Web indication that clicking on the text leads to related information.

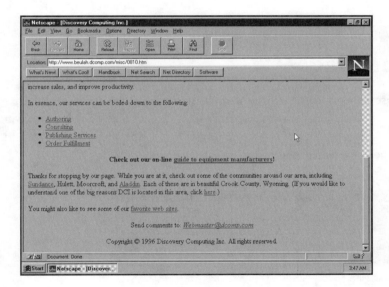

FIGURE 8–10

The anchor tag specifies links from your page to other pages.

TIP: If you specify links in your Web documents, test them from a browser immediately after publishing the page. You should actually view the page and then click the link to make sure that it works. Web users are very frustrated by running across something that looks interesting, only to find out that the URL it links to is invalid.

Notice that the bottom of the Web page includes a link to an e-mail address. The <A> reference looks like this:

```
<A HREF = "mailto:Webmaster@dcomp.com"><EM>Webmaster@dcomp.com</EM></A>
```

Here the HREF attribute points to an e-mail address, rather than another URL. The code at the beginning of the reference, mailto, is the key word needed by the browser. When you click the link and the browser sees this reference, it opens your e-mail program and allows you to create an e-mail message. The message then is sent to the specified address.

> **TIP:** Include an e-mail address at the bottom of your pages. This plan allows readers to send you messages automatically—many of which may help you improve your pages.

Miscellaneous Tags

A couple of miscellaneous tags can help "jazz up" your pages. The <HR> tag adds a horizontal rule to your document. This rule automatically extends across the browser window, regardless of its width. Figure 8–11 shows an example of a document with a rule added (immediately above the e-mail address).

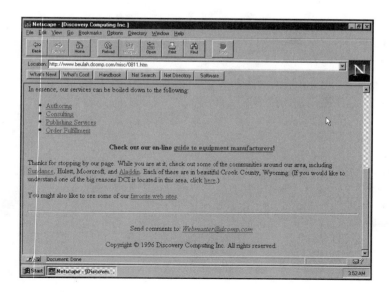

FIGURE 8–11

Horizontal rules can be used to break up sections of your document.

The <HR> tag is a lone tag; it doesn't require a closing tag. You can add these types of rules wherever you like in your documents.

Another useful tag is the <ADDRESS> and </ADDRESS> tag pair, which has two effects on your document:

- It identifies the address of the organization or individual responsible for the page.
- It causes the information between the tags to be presented in a special font, typically italics.

The following lines show the completed HTML sample Web page, with the <ADDRESS> tag in place (near the bottom of the code):

```
<HTML>
<HEAD>
<TITLE>Discovery Computing Inc.</TITLE>
<META NAME="description" CONTENT="Home page for Discovery
Computing Inc., a company specializing in providing
information services.">
<META NAME="keywords" CONTENT="computer books consulting
programming technical editing Sundance Wyoming WY
Web Advertising fulfillment distribution writing authoring">
</HEAD>


<BODY>


<CENTER>
<IMG SRC = "/dcilogo.gif">
<H1>Welcome to Discovery Computing Inc.</H1>
</CENTER>


Discovery Computing Inc. (DCI) is a multi-faceted company providing
a host of services to many different companies and individuals. As
a corporation, we have been in business for just under ten years,
helping many companies solve problems, increase sales, and improve
productivity.
```

```
<P>In essence, our services can be boiled down to the following:<BR>
<UL>
<LI><A HREF="/DCI/Authoring.Htm">Authoring</A></LI>
<LI><A HREF="/DCI/Consulting.Htm">Consulting</A></LI>
<LI><A HREF="/DCI/PubServices.Htm">Publishing Services</A></LI>
<LI><A HREF="/DCI/Fulfillment.Htm">Order Fulfillment</A></LI>
</UL>

<CENTER>
<STRONG>Check out our on-line
<A HREF="/DCI/MfgList/MfgList.Htm">guide to equipment manufacturers</A>!
</STRONG>
</CENTER>

<P>Thanks for stopping by our page. While you are at it, check
out some of the communities around our area, including
<A HREF="/Sundance/Sundance.Htm">Sundance</A>,
Hulett,
Moorcroft, and
<A HREF="/Aladdin/Aladdin.Htm">Aladdin</A>.
Each of these are in beautiful Crook County, Wyoming. (If you would
like to understand one of the big reasons DCI is located in this
area, click <A HREF="/Sundance/Business.Htm">here</A>.)

<P>You might also like to see some of our
<A HREF="/DCI/FavoriteWeb.Htm">favorite web sites</A>.

<P>
<HR>
<CENTER>
<ADDRESS>
Discovery Computing Inc.<BR>
20101 US Highway 14<BR>
PO Box 738<BR>
Sundance, WY  82729<BR>
```

```
800-628-8280<BR>
307-283-2714 (fax)

<P>Send comments to:
<A HREF = "mailto:Webmaster@dcomp.com"><EM>Webmaster@dcomp.com</EM></A>
<P>Copyright &copy 1996 Discovery Computing Inc. All rights reserved.
</ADDRESS>
</CENTER>

</BODY>
</HTML>
```

Notice that the <ADDRESS> and </ADDRESS> tags surround a great deal of text in this page. In your page, it can surround as much or as little as you want. The finished page, with the address area visible, is shown in Figure 8–12.

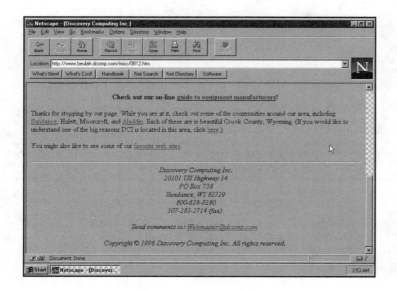

FIGURE 8–12

The <ADDRESS> tag causes address information to be displayed in italics.

Understanding Image Maps

If you have spent any time on the Web, you've seen image maps. An *image map* is a graphic that has different clickable regions. When the user clicks the image, your server looks up the coordinates of the click in a map file. These coordinates have a URL assigned to them, which is then transferred by the server. The following sections describe each part of the image map.

The HTML Tags

Because an image map has two parts (the image and the map file), you need to specify both of these elements in the HTML document that uses the image map. Consider the image map in Figure 8–13. This map enables the user to click a letter of the alphabet, and then information beginning with that letter is displayed.

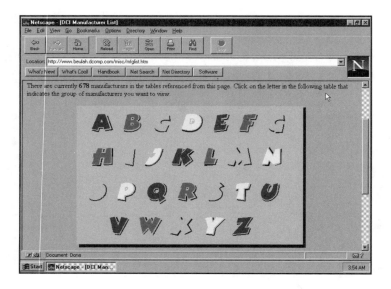

FIGURE 8–13

An image map initially looks like any other graphic, until you move the mouse pointer over it.

The HTML commands to implement this image map are as follows:

```
<A HREF = "/DCI/MfgList/Alphabet.Map">
<IMG SRC = "Alphabet.gif" ISMAP></A>
```

These statements appear in the body section of the document. The actual statements should appear familiar; earlier sections of this chapter discuss the tags. Notice, however, that the reference for the anchor points not to a URL, but to a special file called a *map file*. (Map files are discussed in the following section.) The <IMG> tag immediately following the anchor points to the image which is used for the image map. The special attribute that must be included is the *ISMAP* attribute, which informs the server and browser that an image map has been displayed.

The Map File

A map file is an ASCII file that essentially contains a series of coordinates, and URLs associated with those coordinates. The coordinates refer to different pixel ranges within the graphic file. Coordinates are specified in an X,Y system, with the upper-left corner of the graphic being 0,0.

As you learned in Chapter 5, "Converting from Another Server," there are two types of map file formats: CERN and NCSA. The FastTrack server uses the CERN format. Under this map format you can define three types of regions within a map file: rectangles, circles, and polygons:

♦ Rectangles are defined by two sets of coordinates that define the corners of the rectangle.

♦ Circles are defined by a coordinate pair for the centerpoint and a radius for the circle.

♦ Polygons are defined as a series of coordinates that define the outline of the shape.

As an example, following is the first couple of lines of the map file used for the image map shown in Figure 8–13:

```
default /DCI/MfgList/MfgList.Htm
poly 34,56 48,21 65,21 69,25 80,56 65,60 48,62
➡/dci/mfglist/a.htm
poly 104,59 113,21 131,19 145,27 140,37 145,42 145,50 134,58 118,63   /dci/mfglist/b.htm
poly 203,62 181,59 174,40 180,25 194,19 209,21 212,25 213,36 209,48   /dci/mfglist/c.htm
```

Notice that the map file defines coordinates for polygons, as indicated by starting each line with the keyword *poly*. At the beginning of the file is a default specification in case the user clicks outside any other region defined in the map file. The server uses the coordinates from the file to see whether the user clicked a defined region. If so, the URL at the end of the line is sent to the user.

Creating an Image Map

To create an image map, you simply create your graphic as you normally would, and then create the map file. Tools are available on the Internet that you will find invaluable in creating the map file. One such tool that is very popular is MapEdit, which is available at http://www.boutell.com/mapedit/.

MapEdit enables you to load the graphic to be used for the image map, and then use the mouse to trace regions on the map. After a region is defined, you can specify a URL to be associated with that region. If you later change the image map, you can reload both the graphic and the map file to make your changes.

MapEdit can save map files in both the CERN and NCSA formats. (Again, you will want to use the CERN format, which is understood by the FastTrack server.)

Creating Tables

Another common element in an HTML document is a table. Tables allow you to organize information so that it looks much more structured on-screen. Tables are quite flexible in nature; they can have as many rows or columns as you like.

Because tables are a special element in documents, a special tag pair (<TABLE> and </TABLE>) encloses the entire table. Within the table, you define rows by use of the <TR> tag. Within each row, you define the beginning and end of each *cell* with the <TD> and </TD> tag pair, or with the <TH> and </TH> tag pair. (A cell is created by the intersection of a column and row.) The difference between these two pairs is the way that the text in each of the cells is displayed. If you use the <TH> tag, the cell is considered to contain some sort of heading for the table, and the text is displayed in a bold typeface.

You can have as many cells in a row as desired. From a design standpoint, however, you probably want to only have a couple. If you have too many cells, the result is a table that is wider than your display area. In this instance, the remote browser will display what it can and then provide a horizontal scroll bar so the user can move their screen left and right.

With these elements (table, rows, and cells), you have all you need to create a simple table in your Web document. Consider the following simple HTML document:

```
<HTML>
<HEAD>
<TITLE>Sample of creating a table</TITLE>
</HEAD>
<BODY>
The following is a sample of a table.

<TABLE>
<TR><TH>One</TH><TH>Two</TH><TH>Three</TH><TH>Four</TH>
<TR><TD>A1</TD><TD>A2</TD><TD>A3</TD><TD>A4</TD>
<TR><TD>B1</TD><TD>B2</TD><TD>B3</TD><TD>B4</TD>
<TR><TD>C1</TD><TD>C2</TD><TD>C3</TD><TD>C4</TD>
<TR><TD>D1</TD><TD>D2</TD><TD>D3</TD><TD>D4</TD>
</TABLE>

</BODY>
</HTML>
```

This code creates a table that has four columns and five rows. Notice the use of the <TH> tag for the first row of the table. This indicates that the row contains headings for each column. You can see the results of this code in Figure 8–14.

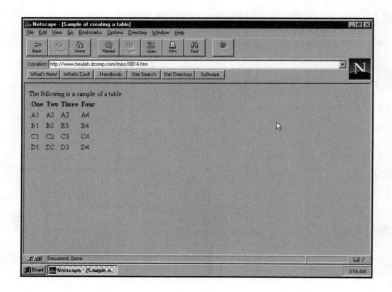

FIGURE 8–14

A simple table can organize information on a Web page.

The table, when created this way, enables you to organize information so that it appears in columns. The browser takes care of determining the width of each column, generally based on the widest contents of any cell within a column.

Borders and Other Table Attributes

If you prefer, you can change the HTML code slightly so that the table has borders. This is done with the BORDER attribute, used within the <TABLE> tag. If you simply want to include a border, use the BORDER attribute as follows:

```
<TABLE BORDER>
```

This designation includes a standard border. HTML also allows you to specify a border width, as in the following example:

```
<TABLE BORDER="4">
```

The border width can be anywhere from 0 (no border, which is the same as leaving out the BORDER attribute) to virtually any number you can figure out. The default border value (if you don't specify a value) is 1. Figure 8–15 shows an example of two tables, the first with a border set to the default, and the second with the border set to 5.

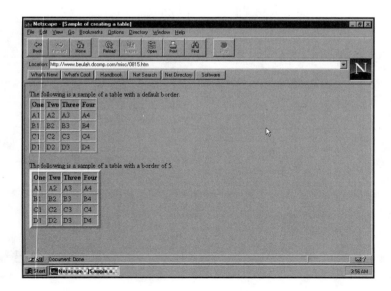

FIGURE 8–15

The BORDER attribute specifies the width of the outside border of a table.

Remember that the BORDER attribute affects only the outside of the table, not the spacing within the cells. If you want to affect the inside cell dividers, you use the CELLSPACING attribute. This attribute accepts values just like the BORDER attribute, but is used to define the thickness of the cell walls. For instance, the following code would define a table with a border of 5 and interior dividers with a thickness of 4:

```
<TABLE CELLSPACING="4" BORDER="5">
```

A table with these attributes is shown in Figure 8–16. Compare this table with the second sample table in Figure 8–15, and you can see the effects of the CELLSPACING attribute; it's the only difference between the two tables.

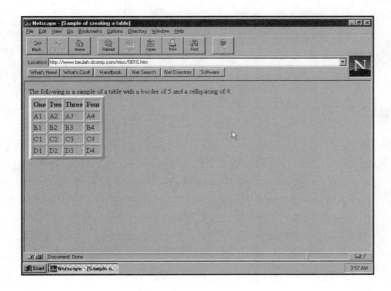

FIGURE 8–16

The CELLSPACING attribute specifies the width of the dividers between the cells in a table.

The final common attribute that affects an entire table is the CELLPADDING attribute, which defines the space between the contents of the cell and the cell dividers. By default, the value for this attribute is 1, but you can set it to any value you like, just as you did with the other table attributes. The larger the value you set, the more space within your cells. Figure 8–17 shows an example of two tables, one with CELLPADDING set to 2 and the other set to 15.

By experimenting with the BORDER, CELLPADDING, and CELLSPACING attributes, you can create just the right appearance for your table.

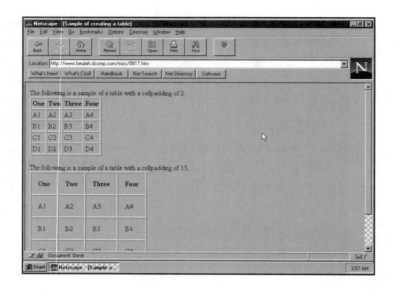

FIGURE 8–17

The CELLPADDING attribute defines the distance between cell contents and the cell dividers.

Skipping Cells

Information in a table can't always be presented in a simple grid format. You may need to create complex headings, or leave out the contents of some cells. Leaving out information is easy. All you need to do, basically, is define a cell with no text in it. Look at the sample table again, this time without the text for cells B2 and C4:

```
<HTML>
<HEAD>
<TITLE>Sample of creating a table</TITLE>
</HEAD>
<BODY>
The following is a sample table with some cells left empty.

<TABLE CELLSPACING="4" BORDER="5">
<TR><TH>One</TH><TH>Two</TH><TH>Three</TH><TH>Four</TH>
<TR><TD>A1</TD><TD>A2</TD><TD>A3</TD><TD>A4</TD>
<TR><TD>B1</TD><TD></TD><TD>B3</TD><TD>B4</TD>
<TR><TD>C1</TD><TD>C2</TD><TD>C3</TD>
<TR><TD>D1</TD><TD>D2</TD><TD>D3</TD><TD>D4</TD>
```

```
</TABLE>

</BODY>
</HTML>
```

Notice that B2 was simply left out, but the <TD> and </TD> tag pair for the cell is still there. In the case of C4, the text and the cell definition tags were both deleted. The reason you can do this for C4, but not B2, is that C4 appears at the end of a row. When the browser sees this, it still fills out the table appearance, as shown in Figure 8–18.

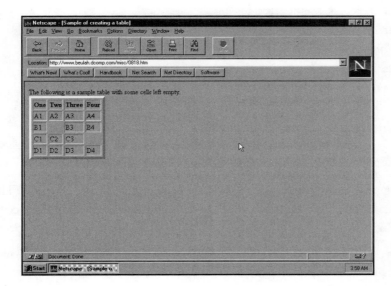

FIGURE 8–18

When you leave information out of cells in a table, the appearance of the table changes quite a bit.

TIP: If you don't like the way that tables appear when you skip cells, you can always place a filler in a cell, such as a dash or period. Again, the appearance of your information is entirely up to you.

Spanning Columns

Now take a look at a more common table. This one is simple in concept, but it takes a bit of planning to present effectively. It has only three columns, but some of the data in the body of the table needs to span more than one column.

```
<HTML>
<HEAD>
<TITLE>Sample of creating a table</TITLE>
</HEAD>
<BODY>
The following table uses the COLSPAN attribute.

<H4>Elementary & Secondary Education</H4>
<TABLE CELLSPACING="4" BORDER="5">
<TR><TH></TH><TH>Schools</TH><TH>Students</TH>
<TR><TD>Elementary</TD><TD>1</TD><TD>267</TD>
<TR><TD>Junior HS</TD><TD COLSPAN="2">included in HS</TD>
<TR><TD>High School</TD><TD>2</TD><TD>235</TD>
<TR><TD>Private</TD><TD>1</TD><TD>22</TD>
</TABLE>

</BODY>
</HTML>
```

The new attribute used here is the COLSPAN attribute, in the row for the Junior HS. Notice that this attribute is used with the <TD> tag, and it causes the number of cells specified (in this case, two cells) to be merged. This effect is shown in Figure 8–19.

COLSPAN is particularly useful in the headings of some tables. It's common to have tables that require multiple rows for headings, as shown in the following example:

```
<HTML>
<HEAD>
<TITLE>Sample of creating a table</TITLE>
</HEAD>
<BODY>
The following table uses the COLSPAN attribute in
the table heads.

<H2>Results of 1996 Widget Sales</H2>
<TABLE BORDER>
<TR><TH></TH><TH COLSPAN="2">Units Sold</TH><TH COLSPAN="2">Revenue Generated</TH>
```

```
<TR><TH>Product</TH><TH>Eastern US</TH><TH>Western US</TH><TH>Eastern US</TH><TH>
➥Western US</TH>
<TR><TD>Red Widgets</TD><TD>3,241</TD><TD>2,981</TD><TD>164,766</TD><TD>152,821</TD>
<TR><TD>Blue Widgets</TD><TD>2,917</TD><TD>3,614</TD><TD>149,540</TD><TD>185,272</TD>
<TR><TD>White Widgets</TD><TD>4,084</TD><TD>4,756</TD><TD>209,366</TD><TD>243,816</TD>
<TR><TD>Black Widgets</TD><TD>5,123</TD><TD>4,874</TD><TD>262,631</TD><TD>249,866</TD>
<TR><TD>Pink Widgets</TD><TD>1,962</TD><TD>2,288</TD><TD>100,582</TD><TD>117,294</TD>
<TR><TD>Yellow Widgets</TD><TD>2,112</TD><TD>2,693</TD><TD>108,272</TD><TD>138,057</TD>
<TR><TD>Invisible Widgets</TD><TD>314</TD><TD>567</TD><TD>16,097</TD><TD>29,067</TD>
<TR><TH>Totals</TH><TH>19,753</TH><TH>21,773</TH><TH>1,011,254</TH><TH>1,116,193</TH>
<TR><TH>Company Totals</TH><TH COLSPAN="2">41,526</TH><TH COLSPAN="2">2,127,447</TH>
</TABLE>

</BODY>
</HTML>
```

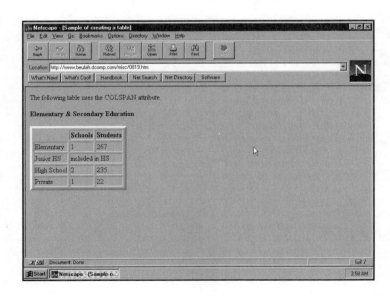

FIGURE 8–19

The COLSPAN attribute merges adjacent cells.

This code creates a table that has two header rows at the beginning of the table and two at the end of the table. Both of them utilize the COLSPAN attribute to create the desired effect in relation to the data being presented. The results are shown in Figure 8–20.

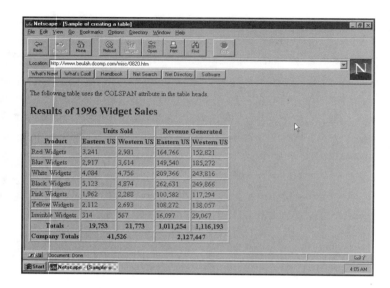

FIGURE 8–20

The COLSPAN attribute is commonly used in table headings.

Notice that the headings are automatically centered by the browser. This isn't desirable in all instances; later in this chapter you learn how to control the alignment of information within the cells.

Spanning Rows

Just as you can span columns in tables, you can also span rows. This method is commonly used for the same reasons as spanning columns—to make the information in the table more meaningful. For example, you may have a table where you want to present enrollment figures over the course of several years, as in the following code:

```
<HTML>
<HEAD>
<TITLE>Sample of creating a table</TITLE>
</HEAD>
<BODY>
The following table uses the ROWSPAN attribute.

<H2>Results of Three-Year Enrollment Study</H2>
<TABLE BORDER>
<TR><TH></TH><TH></TH><TH>1993</TH><TH>1994</TH><TH>1995</TH>
```

```
<TR><TH ROWSPAN="3">Junior</TH><TH>School 1</TH><TD>257</TD><TD>315</TD><TD>389</TD>
<TR><TH>School 2</TH><TD>542</TD><TD>563</TD><TD>535</TD>
<TR><TH>School 3</TH><TD>475</TD><TD>452</TD><TD>421</TD>
<TR><TH ROWSPAN="3">Senior</TH><TH>School 1</TH><TD>897</TD><TD>954</TD><TD>1,016</TD>
<TR><TH>School 2</TH><TD>1,234</TD><TD>1,312</TD><TD>1,278</TD>
<TR><TH>School 3</TH><TD>942</TD><TD>1,003</TD><TD>988</TD>
</TABLE>

</BODY>
</HTML>
```

Notice that when you use the ROWSPAN attribute, the rows immediately below that row don't need a cell defined in the space that will be occupied by the spanning cell. Thus, the rows for schools 2 and 3 in this example don't have a first cell defined. Figure 8–21 shows the results of this code.

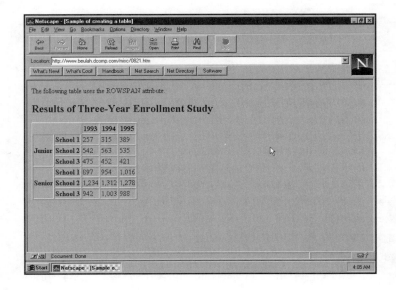

FIGURE 8–21

The ROWSPAN attribute spreads cell contents over the specified number of rows.

Aligning Cell Contents

You may have noticed that the cell contents in the last couple of examples didn't look as good as they could, because the information in the cells wasn't aligned properly. Aligning the contents of cells can make them more readable; you use the ALIGN attribute for this purpose.

You can use the ALIGN attribute in two places. Used with the <TR> tag, the specified alignment is used for every cell in the row. Used with the <TD> or <TH> tags, it affects only the contents of that one cell.

Three types of alignment are available: LEFT, CENTER, and RIGHT. By default, the LEFT alignment is used. To specify some other alignment, do it as follows (substituting "RIGHT" or "LEFT" as appropriate):

```
<TD ALIGN="CENTER">
```

Judicious use of the ALIGN attribute can make your table much more readable, particularly when displaying numbers. The following code shows the widget sales table presented earlier, but this time with the ALIGN attribute:

```
<HTML>
<HEAD>
<TITLE>Sample of creating a table</TITLE>
</HEAD>
<BODY>
The following table uses the ALIGN attribute
to make information more readable.

<H2>Results of 1996 Widget Sales</H2>
<TABLE BORDER>
<TR><TH></TH><TH COLSPAN="2">Units Sold</TH><TH COLSPAN="2">Revenue Generated</TH>
<TR><TH ALIGN="LEFT">Product</TH><TH>Eastern US</TH><TH>Western US</TH><TH>Eastern
➥US</TH><TH>Western US</TH>
<TR ALIGN="RIGHT"><TD ALIGN="LEFT">Red Widgets</TD><TD>3,241</TD><TD>2,981</TD>
➥<TD>164,766</TD><TD>152,821</TD>
<TR ALIGN="RIGHT"><TD ALIGN="LEFT">Blue Widgets</TD><TD>2,917</TD><TD>3,614</TD>
➥<TD>149,540</TD><TD>185,272</TD>
<TR ALIGN="RIGHT"><TD ALIGN="LEFT">White Widgets</TD><TD>4,084</TD><TD>4,756</TD><TD>
➥209,366</TD><TD>243,816</TD>
<TR ALIGN="RIGHT"><TD ALIGN="LEFT">Black Widgets</TD><TD>5,123</TD><TD>4,874</TD><TD>
➥262,631</TD><TD>249,866</TD>
```

```
<TR ALIGN="RIGHT"><TD ALIGN="LEFT">Pink
Widgets</TD><TD>1,962</TD><TD>2,288</TD><TD>100,582</TD><TD>117,294</TD>
<TR ALIGN="RIGHT"><TD ALIGN="LEFT">Yellow Widgets</TD><TD>2,112</TD><TD>2,693</TD><TD>
➥08,272</TD><TD>138,057</TD>
<TR ALIGN="RIGHT"><TD ALIGN="LEFT">Invisible Widgets</TD><TD>314</TD><TD>567</TD><TD>
➥16,097</TD><TD>29,067</TD>
<TR ALIGN="RIGHT"><TH ALIGN="LEFT">Totals</TH><TH>19,753</TH><TH>21,773</TH><TH>1,011,254
➥</TH><TH>1,116,193</TH>
<TR><TH ALIGN="LEFT">Company Totals</TH><TH COLSPAN="2">41,526</TH><TH COLSPAN="2">
➥2,127,447</TH>
</TABLE>

</BODY>
</HTML>
```

Notice the use of ALIGN in many places. In the main body of the table, the attribute is used in the <TR> tag, and then overridden in the first cell of each of those rows. This is the easiest way to apply the attribute for this data, although I also could have simply used right alignment in each of the cells containing numbers. The results of this code are shown in Figure 8–22. (You may want to compare this with Figure 8–20 for readability.)

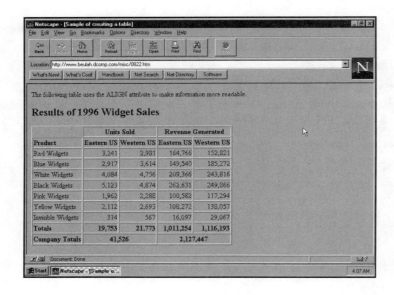

FIGURE 8–22

The ALIGN attribute adjusts how text appears within a cell.

Graphics in Tables

You may have realized after working through the graphics section earlier in this chapter that HTML really has no provisions for displaying text and graphics side by side. The way around this is to use a table to display the text and graphics. Typically this is done with simple two- or three-cell tables. The following code is a simplified version of one of DCI's Web pages for a popular natural attraction in our area. (If you want to see the real page, it's at http://www.dcomp.com/sundance/dtower.htm.)

```
<HTML>
<HEAD>
<TITLE>Devils Tower National Monument</TITLE>
</HEAD>

<CENTER>
<TABLE CELLPADDING="25">
<TR>
<TD><IMG SRC = "/sundance/pictures/DevilsTower.gif"></TD>
<TD><CENTER><H1>Devils Tower<BR>National Monument</H1></CENTER></TD>
</TABLE>
</CENTER>


<P>Devils Tower National Monument is located in northeastern Wyoming and was designated
as our nation's first National Monument by President Teddy Roosevelt in 1906.
Scientists believe that Devils Tower is the core of a volcano exposed after millions
of years of erosion caused by the Belle Fourche River and weather. The 865-foot tower,
featured in the movie "Close Encounters of the Third Kind," is a favorite destination
for skilled rock climbers from around the globe. Devils Tower is also a favorite
family destination.  Kids and adults alike can enjoy deer and antelope in their natural
habitat and kids of all ages will like the prairie dog town. Miles of walking trails
offer ever-changing views of the Tower and flora and fauna that abound at the Tower.

</P>
<CENTER>
<IMG SRC="/Aart/rainban.gif">
```

```
</P>
Send comments to: <A HREF = "mailto:Webmaster@dcomp.com"><EM>Webmaster@dcomp.com</EM>
➥</A><BR>
Copyright &copy 1996 <A HREF="/DCI/DCI.Htm">Discovery Computing Inc.</A> All rights
➥reserved.
</CENTER>


</BODY>
</HTML>
```

Notice how we handled the beginning of the page: a centered table, with two cells. The left cell has the graphic in it, and the right cell has the heading (with the <H1> tag) centered within it. Also notice that the <BR> tag is used in the middle of the heading to break it to two lines. The result of this code is shown in Figure 8–23.

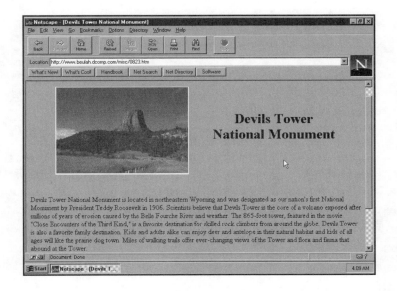

FIGURE 8–23

Graphics can be inserted into table cells to create a more professional look.

Because you can put graphics into tables, you can also combine the other table attributes to make the graphic look any way you desire. I have seen one effect which I thought was a nice touch, and a unique use of the BORDER attribute for tables. The following code shows the Devils Tower page with the change in how the graphic is handled:

```
<HTML>
<HEAD>
<TITLE>Devils Tower National Monument</TITLE>
</HEAD>

<CENTER>
<TABLE BORDER="8">
<TR><TD>
    <TABLE BORDER="4">
    <TR><TD>
       <TABLE BORDER="2">
       <TR>
       <TD><IMG SRC = "http://www.dcomp.com/sundance/pictures/DevilsTower.gif"></TD>
       </TR>
       </TABLE>
    </TD></TR>
    </TABLE>
</TD></TR>
</TABLE>
<H1>Devils Tower<BR>National Monument</H1>
</CENTER>

<P>Devils Tower National Monument is located in northeastern Wyoming and was designated
as our nation's first National Monument by President Teddy Roosevelt in 1906.
Scientists believe that Devils Tower is the core of a volcano exposed after millions
of years of erosion caused by the Belle Fourche River and weather. The 865-foot tower,
featured in the movie "Close Encounters of the Third Kind," is a favorite destination
for skilled rock climbers from around the globe. Devils Tower is also a favorite
family destination.  Kids and adults alike can enjoy deer and antelope in their natural
habitat and kids of all ages will like the prairie dog town. Miles of walking trails
offer ever-changing views of the Tower and flora and fauna that abound at the Tower.

</P>
<CENTER>
<IMG SRC="/Aart/rainban.gif">
```

```
</P>
Send comments to: <A HREF = "mailto:Webmaster@dcomp.com"><EM>Webmaster@dcomp.com</EM>
➥</A><BR>
Copyright &copy 1996 <A HREF="/DCI/DCI.Htm">Discovery Computing Inc.</A> All rights
➥reserved.
</CENTER>

</BODY>
</HTML>
```

Here the graphic has been enclosed in a nested table, with the two outer tables being included only for the effect of the border. The border of each table layer is progressively narrower, producing the effect of a compound border. In addition, the heading for the page (using the <H1> tag) has been moved outside the table and placed just beneath it.

Often with HTML code, it is easy to lose your place when nesting items. For this reason, I indented the various lines for the table layers in this code. This has no effect on the page produced; it is included solely to help me understand what I did in the HTML code. The resulting page, showing the special border effect, is shown in Figure 8–24.

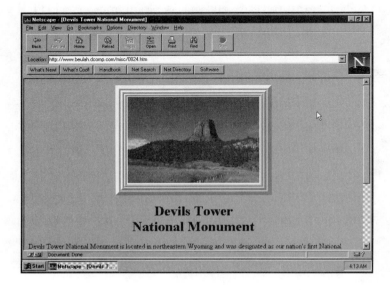

FIGURE 8–24

Graphics and tables can be used together to create special effects.

The way in which you combine HTML tags to create special effects is up to you entirely. The tags provided in the HTML specifications give you the building blocks you need to create most of the effects you need. Remember, however, that the exact implementation of HTML is up to the browser, not the server. With this in mind, you should test any pages that use strange combinations of tags. Test them on several browsers to make sure you get the exact effect you desire. In this way you can be sure your pages are viewed favorably by whoever visits your site.

Summary

Writing HTML documents isn't particularly difficult; it just takes practice and time. You can code your documents "by hand," or you can use one of the HTML document-creation tools springing up on the Web. (Personally, I think these tools haven't quite developed far enough to make them preferable to coding the old-fashioned way—by hand.)

This chapter has focused on the basics of putting together your HTML documents, exploring document structure, tags you can use, and how you should use them. Don't take this as the complete story, however. Remember that this chapter only introduces the basics; there is still quite a bit that you can—and should—learn from a good HTML reference book.

In the next chapter, you learn a bit more about running your Web server. There you gain the skills you need to start creating your own scripts.

Chapter | 9

Creating Pages with
Netscape Navigator Gold

There are many ways you can create documents for the Internet. Some of those ways are easy, others are more difficult, but none of them are terribly hard. In this chapter you will learn how you can use Netscape Navigator Gold, a tool provided with FastTrack, to create your Web documents. Here you will learn how to effectively (and simply) create Web pages without the need to learn as much HTML code.

What Is Netscape Navigator Gold?

Anyone who has been around the Web for any length of time already knows what Netscape Navigator is. This product is one of the forerunners in the Web browser market. In fact, some statistics indicate that Navigator has actually captured about 70% of the browser market, with all other browsers possessing the other 30%.

Netscape Navigator Gold is a special version of Navigator that allows you to not only browse the Web, but to create your own Web pages very simply. You can use special editing commands and familiar Windows features, such as drag-and-drop, to create pages in a fraction of the time necessary for creating pages manually.

> **NOTE:** It is not the purpose of this chapter to discuss how you use Netscape Navigator Gold as a browser. Instead, the focus is on creating your own Web pages. If you want to know how to browse with the product, you should either experiment (Navigator is very easy to use) or read the product documentation.

The Navigator Gold Interface

When you start Navigator Gold, the first thing you see is the Browser Window, as shown in Figure 9-1. If you have had experience with Navigator before, this window looks very similar to what you see when you are browsing the Web.

Although it may not appear that way at first glance, there are interface differences between Navigator and Navigator Gold. The following two sections detail the differences; first in the Browser Window, and then the Editor Window.

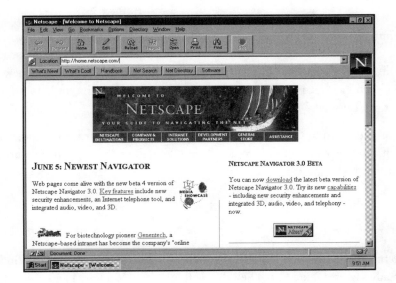

FIGURE 9-1

At first appearance, Navigator Gold looks just like Netscape Navigator.

Browser Window Differences

As far as the Browser Window is concerned, there are very few differences between Navigator and Navigator Gold. The biggest differences are in the menu structure, although there is a difference in the toolbar.

As far as the menus are concerned, Netscape Gold has added a couple new menu items. While each of these will be discussed during the course of this chapter, it is helpful to understand the differences right up front. The biggest additions are to the File menu. If you compare the File menus from Navigator and Navigator Gold, you will find the following new items available:

- ◆ *New Document.* Allows you to open (create) a new Web page.
- ◆ *Edit Document.* Allows you to edit an existing Web page.
- ◆ *Open File in Browser.* Allows you to view an HTML document from your disk drive in the Browser Window.
- ◆ *Open File in Editor.* Allows you to open an HTML document from your disk drive and view it in the Editor Window.

There is only one additional item on the Go menu—Default Publish Location. This item allows you to jump to the place where you normally publish the Web documents you create. Under the Options menu is a new item called Editor Preferences. How you use this menu item is discussed a little later in this chapter. Finally, the Help menu has a new option entitled Web Page Starter. This jumps to the Netscape Web site for help information about starting your own Web pages.

There is only one addition to the toolbar—the Edit tool. It is the fourth tool from the left; the one with the pencil on it. This tool will come in quite handy as you are editing documents later in this chapter.

The Editor Window

There are two major windows used in Navigator Gold. The first is the Browser Window, which you already saw in Figure 9-1. The other is the Editor Window. These two windows are used exactly for what they sound like—the Browser Window is for browsing the Web, and the Editor Window is for editing a Web document. The Editor Window appears as shown in Figure 9-2. (This is the Editor Window with no file loaded; it is ready for you to begin designing your page.)

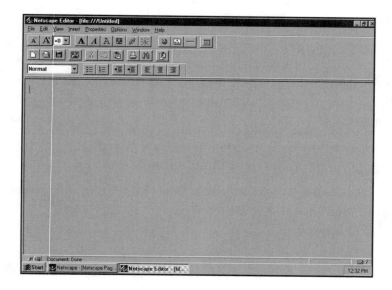

FIGURE 9-2

The Editor Window is used to edit Web documents.

Notice that the Editor Window includes quite a few tools, and the menus are completely different from the Browser Window. There are several different ways you can access commands in the Editor Window, including the following:

♦ Toolbars

♦ Menus

♦ Pop-Up Menus

Each of these items is discussed in the following sections.

> **NOTE:** Most of the tools and many of the menu options actually generate the HTML codes discussed in Chapter 8, "Basic Web Publishing." Although you don't need to know HTML in order to use Navigator Gold, it is helpful so you can understand exactly what the program is doing.

Toolbars

As you notice from Figure 9-2, the Editor Window includes three toolbars. Each toolbar includes tools designed to accomplish related groups of tasks. The Editor Window toolbars are, from top to bottom:

♦ *Character Format Toolbar.* This toolbar includes tools that allow you to adjust the size and style of characters in your document. Also included are tools to establish links, insert images, and add horizontal lines.

♦ *File/Edit Toolbar.* This toolbar features tools that allow you to save, open, view, edit, and publish your Web document.

♦ *Paragraph Format Toolbar.* The tools on this toolbar are useful in applying styles or adjusting alignment of paragraphs.

When you first open the Editor Window, all three toolbars are visible. If you decide that you don't need a particular toolbar, you can turn it off (or back on) by using the Options menu. Select the menu, and then select the toolbar you want hidden or displayed.

Menus

At the top of the Editor Window are a series of menus, similar to menus in other Windows programs. The options on these menus accomplish many of the same tasks for which you can use the toolbars. The Editor Window contains eight menus, as listed here:

◆ *File.* This menu contains options that are similar to any other File menu in other Windows programs. The options allow you to create new documents, load existing documents, save or print your current document, and exit the Editor Window.

◆ *Edit.* This menu contains options that allow you to cut, copy, paste, delete, and undo. You can also use the <u>F</u>ind option to locate text within the current document.

◆ *View.* This menu contains options that allow you to view or edit the HTML source document which you are viewing in the Editor Window.

◆ *Insert.* This menu contains options that allow you to insert non-text items in your document. For instance, you can insert links, images, or breaks.

◆ *Properties.* This menu contains options that allow you to modify how Navigator Gold treats the various objects in your document. For instance, you can modify how a horizontal rule or an image appears.

◆ *Options.* This menu contains options that allow you to configure Netscape Gold and the Editor Window itself. Some of these options are the same as what is in the <u>O</u>ptions menu of the Browser Window.

◆ *Window.* This menu contains options that allow you to control which Netscape windows are displayed and how those windows appear.

◆ *Help.* This menu contains options that allow you to receive help on using Navigator Gold. (Many of the options in the <u>H</u>elp menu actual connect with the Netscape Web site for additional information.)

Pop-Up Menus

If you have used Windows NT 4.0 for any length of time, or even Windows 95, you already know about context menus. These are the menus that appear when you right-click on an object. Navigator Gold also includes menus that appear when you right click, but Netscape refers to them as pop-up menus. These menus display a series of options that are appropriate to the item on which you right-clicked. For instance, Figure 9-3 shows what a pop-up menu for a graphic image looks like.

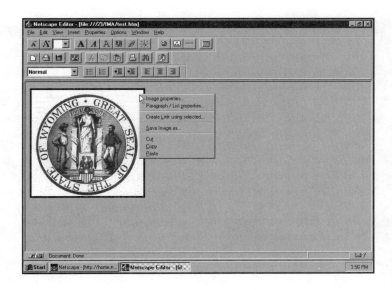

FIGURE 9-3

Pop-up menus present options applicable to different document objects.

Again, the exact type of pop-up menu you see depends on the type of object being selected. Navigator Gold allows you to use pop-up menus with any of the following items:

◆ Selected text

◆ Links

◆ Images

◆ Horizontal lines

◆ HTML tag markers

Setting the Editor Preferences

Before you can start to effectively use the Editor Window, you must set the editor preferences. These are nothing but your indications of how you want the Editor Window to function. To set the editor preferences, select Editor Preferences from the Options menu. The Editor Preferences dialog box appears, as shown in Figure 9-4.

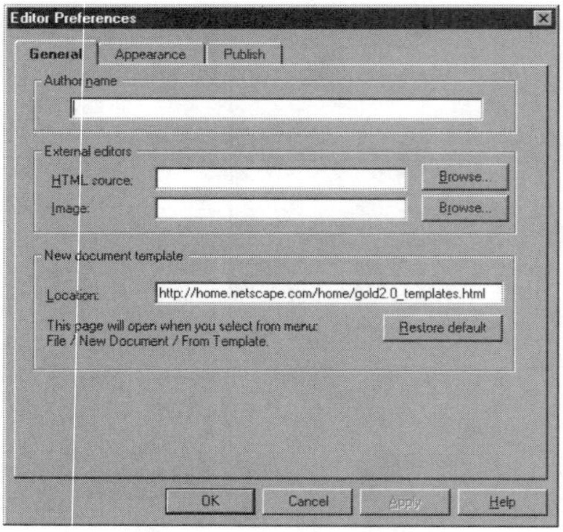

FIGURE 9-4

The Editor Preferences dialog box is used to specify how you want the Editor Window to work.

There are three tabs in the Editor Preferences dialog box. The General tab is the first tab to appear; here you can set the following information:

◆ *Author name.* This is where you can put the name you want to use when authoring Web documents. The name appears in the header information at the beginning of your documents. The exact HTML tag used is a <META> tag, with the NAME attribute set to "Author".

◆ *HTML source.* This is where you can specify which program you want to use as your HTML source code editor. This should be a regular text editor, although you can use a specialized HTML editor. A good candidate (as a text editor) is c:\winnt\system32\notepad.exe, which runs the Notepad accessory.

◆ *Image.* This is where you can specify the program you want used as an image editor. Everyone seems to have their favorites, and you can specify yours here. For example, you might like Paint Shop Pro. In this case you would supply the name of the executable file for Navigator Gold to use.

◆ *Location.* This is where you specify which Web document you want to use as a template. Notice that the default here is located on the Netscape Web server. Later in this chapter you will learn how you can use this site as your template. If you have a different template you want to use, you can supply the name here.

If you expect to use source code and image editors with the Editor Window, then you should at least supply the names of the programs you want to use here. Providing the other information on the General tab is optional.

If you click on the Appearance tab, you have the opportunity to control the appearance of colors in your new documents. The Editor Preferences dialog box, with the Appearance tab selected, appears as shown in Figure 9-5.

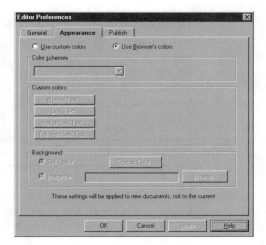

FIGURE 9-5

The Appearance tab is used to set document colors.

As you can tell, most of the items in the Appearance tab are turned off by default. This is because the Use Browser's colors option is selected. For many users, the browser defaults will be more than acceptable; leaving control up to the browser also allows your visitors to control what their pages look like. If you don't want to leave anything to chance, however, you can click on the Use custom colors option, and the entire Appearance tab comes to life, as shown in Figure 9-6.

There are 11 color schemes you can pick (in the Color schemes pull-down), or you can set your own custom colors. You can pick from any of 64 colors for normal text, link text, active link text, and followed link text. These four text colors are set in the <BODY> tag, along with the background color or wallpaper, using the attributes shown in Table 9-1.

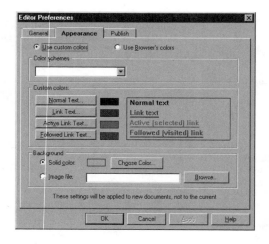

FIGURE 9-6

You can create your Web documents so the entire appearance is under your control.

Table 9-1 Color translation to HTML code.

Editor Preference	HTML <BODY> Attribute
Normal Text	TEXT
Link Text	LINK
Active Link Text	ALINK
Followed Link Text	VLINK
Solid Color Background	BGCOLOR
Image File Background	BACKGROUND

NOTE: The values you set on the Appearance tab affect all future Web documents, not any currently open.

The final tab in the Editor Preferences dialog box is Publish. This tab allows you to define how you want to save information to your hard disk when copying from the Web, as well as how information should be published by you. If you click on the Publish tab, the Editor Preferences dialog box appears as shown in Figure 9-7.

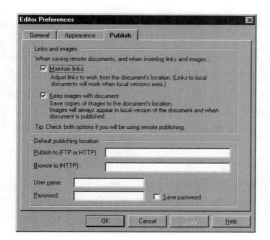

FIGURE 9-7

Navigator Gold gives you control on how your documents are published.

The top half of the Publish tab controls how information is references and images are handled when you publish or copy a Web document. Selecting the first check box causes links in the file to be adjusted to automatically point to wherever the document is stored. Thus, if it is on your hard drive, the links point to your hard drive; if you publish on a remote Web site, then the links point to the remote site. The second check box controls the same sort of translation for images. With the check box selected, images referenced by a page are copied when you publish or coy the page.

The bottom portion of the Publish tab is used to indicate how information should be transferred from your local system to a remote site. You can publish to either an HTTP site or an FTP site, but you need to provide the URL for that site. You also need to indicate your user name and password for logging in to that site. The information in this area is used when you click on the Publish tool on the toolbar, as discussed later in the chapter.

Creating a Page

Navigator Gold provides at least five different ways you can create a new Web document. The method you choose is up to you, and depends on what you want to do. The following sections describe the different ways to create a page.

Blank Pages

If you want to start a new document from scratch, you can do so by choosing <u>N</u>ew Document from the <u>F</u>ile menu, and then choosing <u>B</u>lank. This displays an empty Editor Window, as shown earlier in Figure 9-2. Once you have a new, blank page displayed, you can start to add text, images, and other objects as desired.

When you create a new document in this way, it is similar to starting with a blank sheet of paper. The only thing that Navigator Gold takes into account when creating a blank document is your settings in Editor Preferences, as detailed earlier in the chapter.

From a Template

Earlier in the chapter you learned about setting the general Editor Preferences for Navigator Gold. You learned that you can specify a URL for the template used to create a new document. This template URL is used when you choose <u>N</u>ew Document from the <u>F</u>ile menu, and then choose From <u>T</u>emplate. If you left this URL setting at its default, the result is shown in Figure 9-8.

FIGURE 9-8

The default document template is located at the Netscape Web site.

> **NOTE:** In order to create a page from a template (assuming you are using the default template URL), you must have an active Internet link.

If you read through the information on this Web page, you will find a way to use any of 14 different templates in the following six categories:

- Personal/Family
- Company/Small Business
- Department
- Product/Service
- Special Interest Group
- Interesting and Fun

To use one of the templates, simply click on the link, and the template appears on your browser as a regular page. (For instance, the Travel Club template, from the Special Interest Group category, is shown in Figure 9-9.) To then make the file editable, as a basis for your own pages, you follow the directions provided a little later in this chapter, in the section entitled "From the Web."

FIGURE 9-9

There are numerous templates available on the Netscape Web site.

If you are developing a large Web site, you might want to create your own template. If you do, you can simply save the template as an HTML file, and then configure Navigator Gold so it loads your file as the default template. To change the template URL, refer to the section earlier in this chapter on setting editor preferences.

Using a Wizard

Wizards seem to have been very popular since the introduction of Windows 95 and Windows NT 4.0. A Wizard is a series of steps that walk you through what might otherwise be a complicated task. In this case, a Wizard is a series of Web pages, from the Netscape Web server, that lead you through creating a Web page.

> **NOTE:** In order to create a page with a Wizard, you must have an active Internet link while using the Wizard.

To create a page using a Wizard, choose <u>N</u>ew Document from the <u>F</u>ile menu, and then choose From <u>W</u>izard. Shortly you will see the page shown in Figure 9-10.

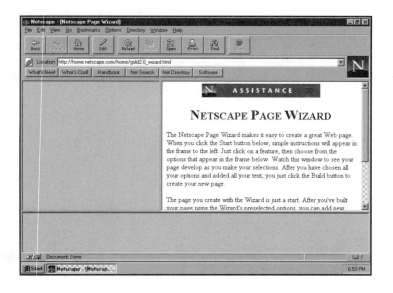

FIGURE 9-10

The Netscape Page Wizard helps you create your own Web pages.

Notice that the Wizard uses frames in the browser window. When you first access the Wizard, only one of the three frames are active. To continue, you must scroll down through the frame, and click on the Start button. This changes the browser display and fills in additional information, as shown in Figure 9-11.

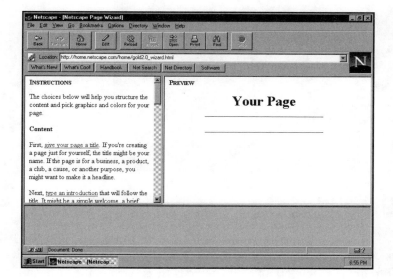

FIGURE 9-11

The purpose of the Wizard is to walk you through the steps of creating a Web page.

To use the Wizard, work through the choices in the top left frame. For instance, if you wanted to provide a title for your page, you would enter it by clicking on the "give your page a title" link. This displays an input box in the bottom frame of the page, into which you can enter the title. When you click on the Apply button (also in the bottom frame), then your preview page is updated and you can continue to the next choice for your page.

This iterative process of choosing an item to add, providing the information for the item, and then clicking on Apply can continue until you are satisfied with your Web page. When you are done, click on the Build button at the bottom of the top left frame. Your page then appears in your browser window (a sample page is shown in Figure 9-12).

At this point the page is still not in the Editor Window, it is still in the browser. To continue editing the page you must save it as described later in this chapter, in the section entitled "From the Web."

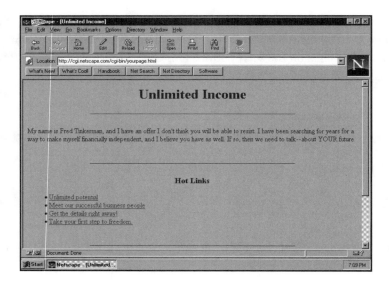

FIGURE 9-12

When you are done with the Wizard, your finished page appears in the browser window.

An Existing Page

Navigator Gold would not be much help if it didn't provide a way for you to save pages and later work on them. There are two ways you can edit an existing page—load it from disk or grab it from the Web. Both of these methods are covered in the following sections.

From Disk

Loading a Web page from disk is quite easy. In fact, it is just as easy as loading a document into your word processor. You can load a file into the Editor Window, with the Browser Window visible, by selecting Open File in Editor from the File menu. This displays a regular file dialog box, from which you can select a drive, directory, and file name. When you then click on the Open button, the file is opened in the Editor Window.

From the Web

As you are browsing around the Web, you may see a page that really tickles your fancy. The design may be unique, and you like the color balance used in the document. If you desire, you can use Navigator Gold to grab the page and edit it on your system. This is particularly helpful in collaborative situations where you and someone else across the country are working on the same Web site.

> **CAUTION:** Remember that US copyright protection extends to much of what is available on the Web. Taking what you find there, without regard to who it belongs to, is infringing on the intellectual property of others. Make sure you have permission to use someone else's page before doing so.

Grabbing a Web page from off the Web is also at the heart of the templates and Wizard provided by Netscape at their site. Once the page you want is visible on your browser, click on the Edit tool on the toolbar. You will then see the Save Remote Document dialog box, as shown in Figure 9-13.

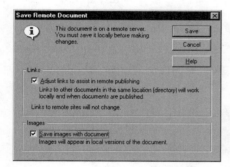

FIGURE 9-13

Before editing a Web page, it must be saved to disk.

The defaults in this dialog box are those you specified when you set your Editor Preferences earlier in the chapter. You can make your changes, and then click on the Save button. This displays a quick dialog box informing you that you should get permission before downloading. When you then click on the OK button, you will see a standard file dialog box, asking you to indicate a name under which this file should be saved. Once you supply the name and click on Save, the file is saved, and you can edit the file in the Editor Window.

Editing a Page

Once you have a Web document loaded in the Editor Window, you are ready to start working with it. Editing a page is quite easy, once you learn how to use the menus and tools offered in the Editor Window.

The idea behind Navigator Gold is that you can enter your text and graphics by using traditional Windows methods. Thus, you can use the mouse to move information or selection commands. In the following sections you learn how to edit pages so they appear the way you want them to.

Working with Text

Text is the basis of most Web documents. You can enter text in the editor window as you would in any other text-related program; for instance, a word processor. All you need to do is position the cursor and start typing. The text is entered in a plain fashion, without any special formatting. Figure 9-14 shows an example of how text appears when first entered.

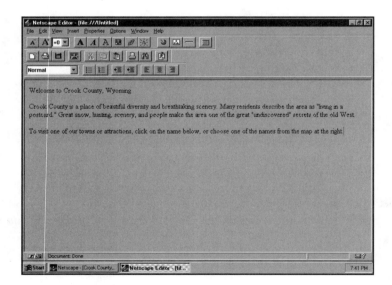

FIGURE 9-14

Entering text in the Editor Window is quick and easy.

You can enter as much text as you want, pressing Enter only at the end of each paragraph. The idea is to get all your text in at once, and then start using the Editor Window to make it look the way you want.

Changing Text Attributes

As you learned in Chapter 8, "Basic Web Publishing," there are a variety of ways you can change attributes of text. For instance, you can change the color, type (bold or italic), or size of text. In addition, there are several pre-defined styles you can apply to your text.

When you first put text into the Editor Window, it is plain text. This means it is formatted as normal paragraphs, without the font being enlarged or reduced, and using a regular type. The easiest way to change the format of your text is to start using the tools on the toolbar. For instance, take a look back at Figure 9-14. The first line of this text is the heading for the page. You can change this to a first-level heading (HTML tag <H1>) by positioning the cursor somewhere on the text line and then choosing Heading 1 from the pull-down list at the left side of the paragraph toolbar. The result of this point, pick, and click operation is shown in Figure 9-15.

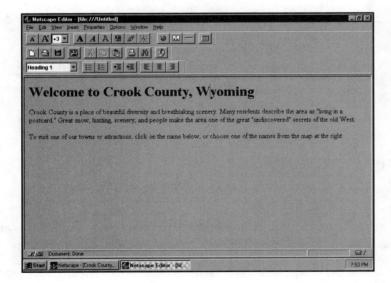

FIGURE 9-15

Changing text attributes is a simple task in Navigator Gold.

Notice that you didn't need to know the HTML codes, and you didn't need to place the opening and closing tags. (Navigator Gold takes care of all this behind the scenes for you.) When you placed the cursor on the first line of text, Navigator Gold assumed you wanted the whole paragraph formatted with the style you selected (Heading 1). If you wanted to only format a selection of characters (not a whole paragraph), you would first select the characters and then choose what you want to do.

As an example, let's suppose you wanted to emphasize the first letter of each paragraph in the body of the page. You can do this by selecting the letter and then clicking on the Bold tool, and then increase the font size by two notches. The result, after formatting both letters, is shown in Figure 9-16. (Notice that the first letter of the second paragraph is still selected.)

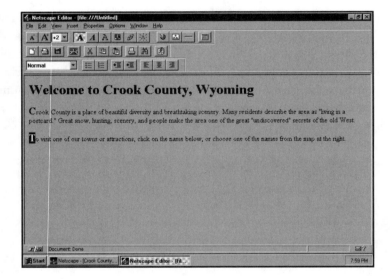

FIGURE 9-16

You can select characters and then apply formatting to your selection.

Formatting Paragraphs

In the last section you learned how to format characters, but you also learned how to apply pre-defined styles to entire paragraphs. There are other ways you can format your paragraphs, as well. The paragraph toolbar provides seven other tools (besides the style list) you can use to indent, align, and apply lists to your paragraphs.

As an example, one of the most common paragraph formats is to align the paragraph so it is centered. This is particularly helpful with headings, as in the heading at the top of our page. To center this paragraph, simply position the cursor within the paragraph, and then click on the Center tool. The paragraph is centered, as shown in Figure 9-17.

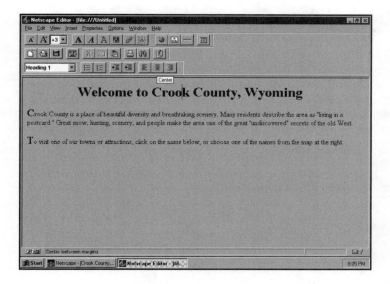

FIGURE 9-17

Paragraphs are easily formatted in Navigator Gold.

You can also format information as lists. As an example, I added some text to the page; text which I intend to make a list. Each item was entered as a paragraph, pressing Enter after the item. Once the items were entered, all I did was select all the paragraphs (the items to be in the list), and then clicked on the Bulleted List tool. The result, with the text still selected, is shown in Figure 9-18.

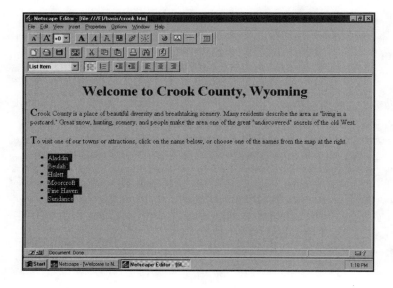

FIGURE 9-18

Adding lists is easy in Navigator Gold.

Adding Graphics

Graphics are one of the great advantages of the Web. Navigator Gold allows you to easily add graphics to your documents. To insert an graphic image, simply position the cursor where you want the image initially placed, and then click the Image tool on the Character Format toolbar. This displays the Properties dialog box shown in Figure 9-19.

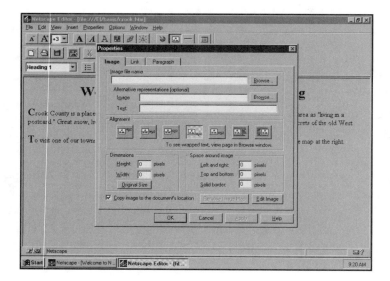

FIGURE 9-19

Inserting an image involves specifying a file and setting properties.

In the Image file name field, specify the path to the image. (You can also click on the Browse button to search for the image file.) You can then set the other properties for the image, as indicated below:

- ◆ *Alternative representations.* These fields control alternative information sent to the remote browser if it cannot display your image. For instance, if you place something in the Text field, then that information is displayed in the remote browser if it cannot handle graphics or if the user has their graphics turned off.

- ◆ *Alignment.* Pick one of the alignment options that best indicates how you want the image to be associated with text in you page. There are seven alignment options, each selectable from the buttons in the middle of the dialog box.

◆ *Dimensions.* This allows you to specify how large the image should be when displayed in the page. You pick the height and width, or you can choose for it to be displayed in the original size.

◆ *Space around image.* This controls the area to be left between the image and text, or as a border around the image. You specify the settings in pixels.

When you are done setting the properties for your image, click on the OK button. The image appears in the Editing window, using your specifications. The only difference is that the display does not show exactly how text wrapping occurs. If you want to see text wrapping, you must look at your page in the Browser window by choosing the Netscape Browser option from the Window menu. Figure 9-20 shows what our page looks like with a graphic inserted, and then viewed in the Browser window.

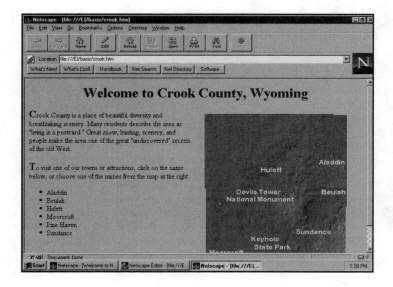

FIGURE 9-20

Text wrapping is only visible in the Browser window.

TIP: You can change the image properties at any time you desire. You do this by right-clicking on the image and then choosing the Image properties option from the pop-up menu.

Adding Links

As you might expect, Navigator Gold also allows you to add links to your pages. Adding links is simply a matter of selecting the text you want to be the link (what the user would click on) and then clicking on the Make Link tool on the Character Format toolbar. For instance, if you look back at Figure 9-20, you can see a bulleted list on the left side of the screen. To make Aladdin an active link, all I need to do is return to the Editor window, select the text Aladdin, and then click on the Make Link tool. The resulting dialog box is shown in Figure 9-21.

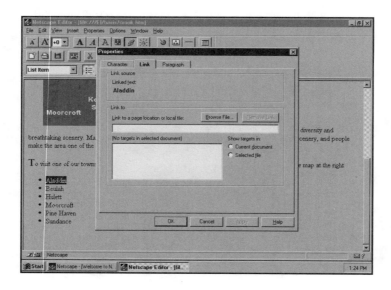

FIGURE 9-21

Adding a link involves picking text and the target for the link.

It so happens that the Aladdin link will be to a target within another HTML file, not another HTML file as a whole. All that needs to be done is to specify the file name in the Link field, and the targets in the other HTML file are automatically listed in the dialog box (see Figure 9-22).

At this point I can pick the target (aladdin) within the other HTML file (CrookCounty.htm), and then click on the OK button. The result is that a link is established, and the text in the Editor window appears underlined. This same process of adding links can be repeated for each link you want to establish.

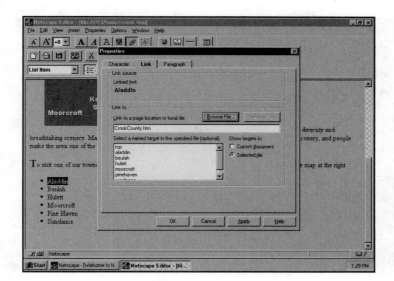

FIGURE 9-22

If the HTML file to which you are linking contains targets, they are displayed in the Properties dialog box.

Saving Your Work

Navigator Gold allows you to automate quite a bit of Web-page creation. As you are working in the Editor window, you will undoubtedly want to save your work periodically. As with any other application, this is a good idea so you don't lose your work in case of an error or other problem.

To save the page on which you are working, you can either click on the Save tool on the File/Edit toolbar, or you can choose Save or Save As from the File menu. (The Save command stores your information in the same file, while Save As saves it in a new file.)

If you use the Save As command, or if you use either of the Save commands without having saved before, you are presented with a standard Windows saving dialog box (see Figure 9-23). This dialog box allows you to pick the location where you want your page saved.

TIP: If you plan on making your HTML page available to others, make sure you place it in a directory accessible from your Web site.

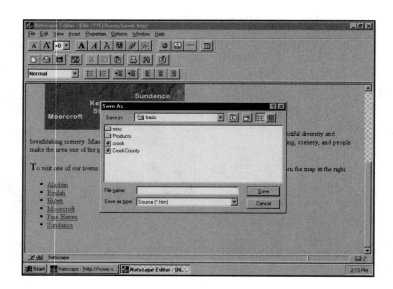

FIGURE 9-23

*Information created in the
Editor window is saved as
a standard HTML file.*

Hand Crafting

In Chapter 8, "Basic Web Publishing," you learned how to create HTML code. When
you use the Editor window of Navigator Gold, you are using a program to help you create your HTML code. Even though this is a great time-saving feature, there are some
things that Navigator Gold cannot do well, or which you can do easier and quicker by
working directly with the HTML code. For instance, the following two areas are easier to
create by hand:

♦ *Tables.* Tables are used extensively and often creatively in some pages. Table
   creation is not supported in Navigator Gold. If you want to add tables, you
   will need to edit your HTML source directly.

♦ *Image Maps.* Image maps add interactive graphics to your pages. These
   allow a user to click on an image area and have the server treat it as a link to
   another resource.

For more information on each of these areas, refer to Chapter 8, "Basic Web Publishing."

Summary

Navigator Gold is more than a traditional Web browser, and it is significant that this product is being provided with the FastTrack server. The most exciting thing about Navigator Gold is that you can use it to create your own Web pages. Much of the actual work of creating pages can be streamlined or handled entirely by Navigator Gold. This chapter has taught you the basics of how to use Navigator Gold to create your own Web pages. When coupled with the information presented in Chapter 8, "Basic Web Publishing," you are armed with the information you need to create professional-looking Web pages.

In the next chapter, you learn how to interface your Web pages (and your Web site) with other Internet services.

Chapter | 10

Interfacing with
Other Services

Chapter 8, "Basic Web Publishing," describes how you can create your Web site content by using HTML files. Most Web browsers have become rather adept at accessing many different kinds of information besides simply HTML files. In this chapter, you learn how you can create content pages (using HTML) that allow your Web site visitors to access information you may have available on either your FTP or Gopher server, or on servers maintained by others.

Access Basics

You are already aware that the basis for accessing information on the Web is the URL. The Uniform Resource Locator got its name because it provides a way to designate not only the address of a resource, but the type of resource at the address. For instance, the following is a simple URL that designates a Web site:

```
http://www.beulah.dcomp.com
```

You know that this is a Web site because it starts with the letters http. This indicator designates the server at the address www.beulah.dcomp.com as an http server (a Web server). If you want to access a different type of resource, you simply provide the resource type at the beginning of the URL, along with the address of the server. Most Web browsers can understand and handle the various resource types indicated in Table 10-1.

Table 10-1   URL Resource Types.

Type	Meaning
ftp://	FTP server
gopher://	Gopher server
http://	http (Web) server
https://	secure Web server
mailto:	e-mail location
news:	news server
telnet://	telnet
wais://	wide area information server

Because you can place the resource type at the beginning of the URL, this means that you can provide links from your Web site to resources located on different types of servers. These may be servers that you maintain, or they may be servers located in a different department of your company or located around the world.

The biggest benefit to providing links to these other types of resources is that it expands the value of your Web site. By providing a common starting point for resources, people will want to visit your site more often. In addition, if the information is located somewhere else, you won't need to maintain the information[—only the link.

Besides the Web, the three most popular resources you can provide links to are FTP, Gopher and e-mail.

Accessing FTP Files from Your Web Site

FTP is an acronym for *file transfer protocol*. It's one of the most common methods of transferring information over a TCP/IP network—including the Internet. Literally thousands of FTP sites exist around the world, and you can easily set up your own FTP site using software available for free through the Internet.

It's not uncommon to run into FTP files that are accessible from the Web. Providing Web-to-FTP access can be done in one of two ways. I refer to the first method as a *directory link*, and the other as a *file link*.

Establishing a Directory Link

Establishing a directory link to your FTP site doesn't take a lot of work. All you need to do is provide a link from one of your Web pages to the home directory of an FTP site. For example, the following code could be used to provide such a link:

```
<HTML>
<HEAD>
<TITLE>Ajax Software Company</TITLE>
<META NAME="description" CONTENT="Home page for Ajax Software Company.">
<META NAME="keywords" CONTENT="software computers PC productivity
cleaning janitor janitorial">
</HEAD>

<BODY>
```

```
<CENTER>
<IMG SRC="logo.gif">
<H1>Welcome to Ajax Software Company</H1>
</CENTER>

Ajax Software is the premier supplier of software for the janitorial
and cleaning industries. We provide the software you need to manage
your company in an efficient, cost-effective manner. Browse through
our site and try one of our demonstration software products. We are
sure you will like the value inherent in our software.

<P>To get one of our demonstration programs, visit
our <A HREF="ftp://ftp.ajax.com">ftp site</A>.

<P><HR><P>
<ADDRESS>
Ajax Software Company<BR>
2714 Fenderman Circle<BR>
Nashville, TN  55555<BR>
606-555-1212
</ADDRESS>


</BODY>
</HTML>
```

This Web page is fairly straightforward; it probably looks similar to some pages you have created. The line of interest is about halfway through the code. Notice that this link to the FTP page is a simple, descriptive link, using the familiar <A> tag to establish the link. The URL reference in the tag points to the FTP server, which means that the FTP home directory is referenced. When the user clicks this link, what he sees on his Web browser screen appears similar to Figure 10-1.

The information displayed by this type of link is similar to what the user sees if he uses FTP to visit the FTP site—basically, just a listing of files and directories. He can navigate the directories by double-clicking folders, or he can download a file by double-clicking the file name.

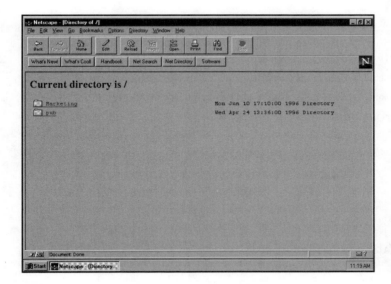

FIGURE 10-1

You can access an FTP directory with your Web browser.

NOTE: Browsing through an FTP site in this way is very similar to browsing through directories at a Web site. In order to accomplish the same thing at a Web site, you must have directory indexing enabled, as described in Chapter 4, "Installing Your Web Server."

Establishing directory links has several advantages:

- It's easy to do—much easier than the file links discussed in the next section.
- It gives the user full access to everything at your FTP site.
- If the contents of your FTP site change quite often, directory links provide the most stable way to link from your Web site. On the negative side, not much descriptive information is provided with a directory link; the user needs to figure out the purpose of the files. (This can be quite frustrating to some users.)

Another way to establish a directory link is to bypass your home directory and jump directly to your individual directories. Look back at Figure 10-1. Notice that three directories are listed. From the names of the folders, you can't exactly tell their purpose. Someone familiar with Ajax Software's products might be able to figure it out, but first-time visitors would definitely be at a loss. The following change to the previous Web page would be a bit more helpful in leading your visitor to exactly what he wants:

```
<HTML>
<HEAD>
<TITLE>Ajax Software Company</TITLE>
<META NAME="description" CONTENT="Home page for Ajax Software Company.">
<META NAME="keywords" CONTENT="software computers PC productivity
cleaning janitor janitorial">
</HEAD>

<BODY>

<CENTER>
<IMG SRC="logo.gif">
<H1>Welcome to Ajax Software Company</H1>
</CENTER>

Ajax Software is the premier supplier of software for the janitorial
and cleaning industries. We provide the software you need to manage
your company in an efficient, cost-efficient manner. Browse through
our site and try one of our demonstration software products. We are
sure you will like the value inherent in our software.

<P>We have developed software for three types of needs. Take a
moment to browse through the following links to our ftp site, where
you will locate something of interest.
<UL>
<LI><A HREF="ftp://ftp.ajax.com/commercial/">Commercial cleaning</A></LI>
<LI><A HREF="ftp://ftp.ajax.com/residential/">Residential cleaning</A></LI>
<LI><A HREF="ftp://ftp.ajax.com/management/">Company management</A></LI>
</UL>

<P><HR><P>
<ADDRESS>
Ajax Software Company<BR>
2714 Fenderman Circle<BR>
Nashville, TN  55555<BR>
```

```
606-555-1212
</ADDRESS>


</BODY>
</HTML>
```

Now the URLs provided in the links are just a bit more complex, but not overly so. Instead of simply pointing to the home directory of your FTP server, they point to individual directories at your site. When people click these links, they see the contents of the appropriate directory on your FTP server. Basically, there is one less directory level for users to navigate on your site. This makes your site much more friendly to first-time visitors or people not exactly familiar with computers.

Establishing a File Link

Many Web sites utilize the files at their FTP site by establishing direct file links. This strategy provides the most user-friendly method of accessing your FTP files. In this type of link, the reference is directly to a file name on the FTP site, rather than to a directory. Perhaps the simplest example of this scheme would be the following code:

```
<HTML>
<HEAD>
<TITLE>Ajax Software Company</TITLE>
<META NAME="description" CONTENT="Home page for Ajax Software Company.">
<META NAME="keywords" CONTENT="software computers PC productivity
cleaning janitor janitorial">
</HEAD>


<BODY>


<CENTER>
<IMG SRC="logo.gif">
<H1>Welcome to Ajax Software Company</H1>
</CENTER>


Ajax Software is the premier supplier of software for the janitorial
```

```
and cleaning industries. We provide the software you need to manage
your company in an efficient, cost-efficient manner. Browse through
our site and try one of our demonstration software products. We are
sure you will like the value inherent in our software.

<P>To download our latest multimedia catalog,
click <A HREF="ftp://ftp.ajax.com/marketing/catalog.zip">here</A>.

<P><HR><P>
<ADDRESS>
Ajax Software Company<BR>
2714 Fenderman Circle<BR>
Nashville, TN  55555<BR>
606-555-1212
</ADDRESS>

</BODY>
</HTML>
```

Notice that the FTP link used in this example points directly to a ZIP file on the FTP server. When the user clicks the link, the file is accessed, and she has the opportunity to download the file to her drive. Exactly how this is handled on the user's part is up to the browser being used, but the process is all pretty much the same—the user is prompted as to whether to download the file, as shown in the Navigator dialog box shown in Figure 10-2.

Using file links in this manner requires no navigation on the user's part, and she can directly access the file she needs. How elaborate you get with this method of access is up to you. The following variation on previous examples in this chapter provides a great deal of information on products available at the Ajax Software Company:

```
<HTML>
<HEAD>
<TITLE>Ajax Software Company</TITLE>
<META NAME="description" CONTENT="Home page for Ajax Software Company.">
<META NAME="keywords" CONTENT="software computers PC productivity
cleaning janitor janitorial">
</HEAD>
```

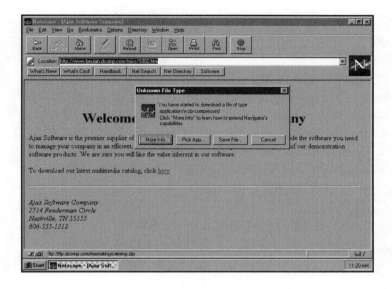

FIGURE 10-2

When jumping to a file, the browser allows you to download it to your hard drive.

```
<BODY>

<CENTER>
<IMG SRC="logo.gif">
<H1>Welcome to Ajax Software Company</H1>
</CENTER>
```

Ajax Software is the premier supplier of software for the janitorial and cleaning industries. We provide the software you need to manage your company in an efficient, cost-efficient manner. Browse through our site and try one of our demonstration software products. We are sure you will like the value inherent in our software.

```
<P>All of our software runs on IBM PC compatible systems, using the
```
Windows 95 operating system. We have developed three products which can help you in all areas of your cleaning or janitorial business. Select the demonstration file that is right for you.

```
<TABLE>
<TR ALIGN="Left"><TH>Software</TH><TH>Description</TH>
```

```
<TR VALIGN="Top"><TD><A
HREF="ftp://ftp.ajax.com/commercial/v46dcom.zip">Commercial</A></TD>
<TD>If you do commercial cleaning, you will love the job management features of
our commercial software. You can keep track of clients by job, by location, by
contact, or by responsible employee. Track work completed and scheduled work.
Provides links directly to our company management software, as well. This demo
version allows you to use the software for a limited time (30 days).</TD>
<TR VALIGN="Top"><TD><A
HREF="ftp://ftp.ajax.com/residential/v22dres.zip">Residential</A></TD>
<TD>Residential cleaning jobs can be particularly difficult to keep track of.
Because of the sheer volume of clients and the differences from one client to
another, residential job management presents special needs. Our residential
software provides the same time-saving features of our commercial version, but
slanted toward the special needs of residential customers. This demo version
allows you to use the software for a limited time (30 days).</TD>
<TR VALIGN="Top"><TD><A HREF="ftp://ftp.ajax.com/management/v51dman.zip">Company</A></TD>
<TD>When it comes time to manage your company as a whole, our management
software allows you to keep a tight rein on every aspect of your business.
This superb product interfaces with both our commercial and residential
software, plus you can keep track of receivables, payables, payroll, and
your general ledger. Also provides profitability reporting by job. This demo
version allows you to use the software for a limited time (30 days).</TD>
</TABLE>

<P><HR><P>
<ADDRESS>
Ajax Software Company<BR>
2714 Fenderman Circle<BR>
Nashville, TN  55555<BR>
606-555-1212
</ADDRESS>

</BODY>
</HTML>
```

In this example, the user clicks the choice appropriate to him, and he can directly download the file he needs. This page is shown in Figure 10-3.

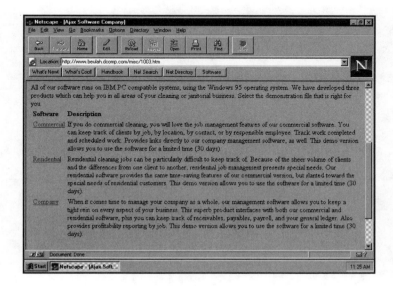

FIGURE 10-3

FTP file linking enables you to create pages that contain quite a bit of descriptive text.

Although establishing file links is definitely the most user-friendly approach to sharing FTP content, it does have a drawback. Let's say that your company runs both a Web site and an FTP site. You are in charge of the Web site, and another department is in charge of the FTP site. In this type of arrangement, it's possible for the contents of the FTP site to change often or without warning. This fact means you may need to update your Web pages quite often to point to the right files, or to provide complete links to the FTP files. If you instead establish a directory link, the contents can change all they want and you won't need to change the Web link. This setup shifts the burden to your site visitor to figure out what he needs from the FTP site.

That being said, I've seen some very elaborate Web-to-FTP connections, using the file link approach. For instance, use your browser to visit the site at `http://www.humberc.on.ca/~coleman/cw-media.html`. As shown in Figure 10-4, this site has quite a few links.

Some of these links point to other Web servers, but most of them point to files on various FTP sites. Someone not using a Web browser could access the files, but if she's using a Web browser she gets the added advantage of complete descriptions of what the files are for.

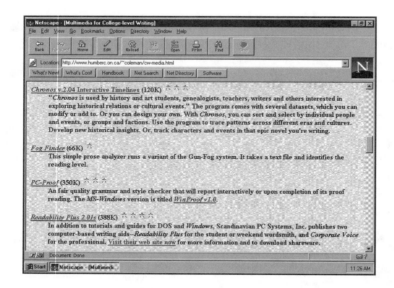

FIGURE 10-4

FTP file linking can be as elaborate as you like.

Accessing Gopher Files from Your Web Site

Before the advent of the World Wide Web, Gopher was the hottest method of accessing widely distributed information. If you have established a Gopher site, or if you know of unique information available through a remote Gopher site, you can make the content directly available to your Web visitors. This goal is accomplished by establishing a link from a Web page to the Gopher server, as in the following code line:

```
For more info, visit the Electronic Frontier Foundation <A
HREF="gopher://gopher.eff.org">Gopher site</A>.
```

This simple link provides a way to access your Gopher server from the Web browser. When your site visitor clicks on the link, she sees the page in Figure 10-5.

Exactly what the user sees depends, of course, on the content of the Gopher site and how well it has been designed. Using the Web browser, the visitor can click a folder to work through directories (this is similar to an FTP site or to a Web site using directory indexing), or click a document to view it or download it.

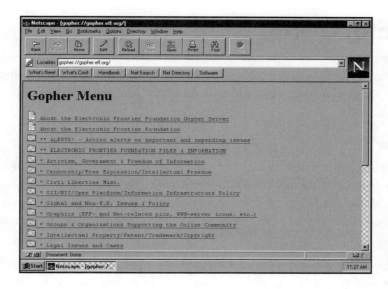

FIGURE 10-5

You can use a Web browser to access a Gopher site.

Typically, Gopher access is handled as just that—access to a Gopher server. Links are sometimes established to directories within a Gopher server, but seldom are links established to specific files at Gopher sites, as they are for FTP sites. The example shown in Figure 10-5 enters the Gopher site at the highest level. If you want to provide links to lower directories, you could do so as shown here:

```
There are some documents available on our Gopher server which may be appropriate
for your needs. Feel free to check out one of the following links to see if the
information contained there is helpful:
<UL>
<LI><A HREF="gopher://dcomp.com/western/">Western United States</A></LI>
<LI><A HREF="gopher://dcomp.com/missouri/">Information specific to Missouri</A></LI>
<LI><A HREF="gopher://dcomp.com/michigan/">Information specific to Michigan</A></LI>
</UL>
```

Notice that each link simply provides a different directory at the Gopher site. When the user clicks a link, he's still within the Gopher environment, but hopefully closer to the end information he wants to view.

Sending Electronic Mail

Perhaps the most common type of external resource referenced in Web pages is e-mail accounts. Chapter 8, "Basic Web Publishing," explains that you can place a link in your Web pages that allows mail to be sent to an e-mail account. In many Web pages, this sort of link appears like this:

```
<A HREF = "mailto:Webmaster@dcomp.com">Send us Feedback</A>
```

To the user, this link appears just like any other link. The difference (as far as the browser is concerned) is denoted by the `mailto:` resource type at the beginning of the URL. When someone clicks on this type of link, the e-mail program used by the browser is opened and the user can enter an e-mail message. The message is then sent to the address specified in the link.

This ability to link references to e-mail addresses can come in handy. One unique application could be developing an in-house e-mail directory. This could then be accessed by people to help them make sending messages easier and faster. The following sample script shows how such a directory could be coded:

```
<HTML>
<HEAD>
<TITLE>DCI E-Mail Directory</TITLE>
</HEAD>

<BODY>

<CENTER>
<H1>Discovery Computing Inc.<BR>E-Mail Directory</H1>
</CENTER>

<CENTER><TABLE>
<TR ALIGN="LEFT"><TH WIDTH=150>Name</TH><TH WIDTH=175>Title/Comments</TH><TH>Address</TH>
<TR><TD>Hlavka, Maryann</TD><TD>Support</TD><TD><A HREF="mailto:mhlavka@dcomp.com">
➥mhlavka@dcomp.com</A></TD>
```

```
<TR><TD>Mackey, Scott</TD><TD>Sales Rep</TD><TD><A HREF="mailto:smackey@dcomp.com">
➥smackey@dcomp.com</A></TD>
<TR><TD>Pease, Garrett</TD><TD>Tech Specialist</TD><TD><A
HREF="mailto:gpease@dcomp.com">gpease@dcomp.com</A></TD>
<TR><TD>Peters, Roxie</TD><TD>Sales Rep</TD><TD><A
➥HREF="mailto:rpeters@dcomp.com">rpeters@dcomp.com</A></TD>
<TR><TD>Sales</TD><TD></TD><TD><A HREF="mailto:sales@dcomp.com">sales@dcomp.com</A></TD>
<TR><TD>Tech Support</TD><TD></TD><TD><A
➥HREF="mailto:support@dcomp.com">support@dcomp.com</A></TD>
<TR><TD>Webmaster</TD><TD></TD><TD><A
➥HREF="mailto:webmaster@dcomp.com">webmaster@dcomp.com</A></TD>
<TR><TD>Worthington, Vic</TD><TD>Sales Rep</TD><TD><A
➥HREF="mailto:vic@dcomp.com">vic@dcomp.com</A></TD>
<TR><TD>Wyatt, Allen</TD><TD>President</TD><TD><A
➥HREF="mailto:awyatt@dcomp.com">awyatt@dcomp.com</A></TD>
<TR><TD>Wyatt, Debra</TD><TD>Secretary/Treasurer</TD><TD><A
➥HREF="mailto:dwyatt@dcomp.com">dwyatt@dcomp.com</A></TD>
<TR><TD>Wyatt, Eric</TD><TD>Designer</TD><TD><A
➥HREF="mailto:ewyatt@dcomp.com">ewyatt@dcomp.com</A></TD>
</TABLE></CENTER>

<P><HR><P>
<CENTER>
<P>Send comments to:
<A HREF = "mailto:Webmaster@dcomp.com"><EM>Webmaster@dcomp.com</EM></A>
<P>Copyright © 1996 Discovery Computing Inc. All rights reserved.
</CENTER>

</BODY>
</HTML>
```

This page provides a simple way to list your e-mail accounts so others know how to contact members of your organization. Look at Figure 10-6 for the results.

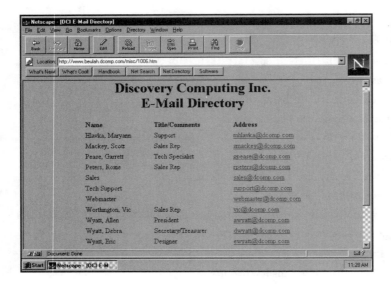

FIGURE 10-6

The mailto: *resource type can be used to put together a directory of e-mail accounts at your organization.*

Summary

The World Wide Web has become a very valuable and versatile tool on the Internet. In fact, some people who use the Internet may never venture any further into Internet tools than what their Web browser provides for them. In this chapter, you have learned how you can provide Web links to resources other than those at a Web site.

In the next chapter, you begin the process of learning about advanced content development by learning about CGI scripting.

PART IV

Advanced Content Development

Chapter | 11

Working with Scripts

Scripting enables you to provide a degree of interaction between the user and your server. The user can provide information that's processed by the script. The response returned to the user is based on the user's input. This chapter introduces scripting, and you will learn more about scripting in several later chapters as well. The information presented here, however, provides the basis for everything about scripting that follows.

This chapter isn't meant to be the final word in scripting, nor should you accept it as such. Indeed, entire books have been written on how you can use scripts effectively in Web documents. By the end of this chapter, however, you will know the fundamentals, which can get you up and running right away.

Scripting Basics

To understand how scripting works, you need to understand a few basics, such as what scripts are, and how forms enter into the picture. These issues are covered in the following sections.

Understanding Scripts

If you've been around computers for some time, when you hear the word *script* you may think of a macro command as used in an application program, such as a spreadsheet or word processor. In the HTML world, however, the only similarity between a script and a macro is that they both accomplish a task. In HTML, a script is a full-fledged program that receives information from the server, processes it, and passes information back. This program can be written in virtually any programming language you like. The only requirement is that the program must be able to receive information via either the standard input or environment variables, and return information via the standard output stream. In reality, these requirements aren't much of a limit. Virtually every programming language allows you to do this.

The earliest standard developed for writing scripts is called *CGI*, which stands for *common gateway interface*. CGI isn't a programming language for writing scripts; it's a specification of how scripts should be developed. Scripts that conform to this standard are referred to as *CGI scripts*. The actual programming language used to implement the script is beside the point.

> **Tip:** If you want more information about the CGI specification, check out the information at `http://hoohoo.ncsa.uiuc.edu/cgi/overview.html`.

Understanding Forms

It's hard to use the Web these days without running into forms. If you've used common search engines such as Yahoo or Alta Vista, you've seen simple forms. Forms such as this allow you, the user, to enter information in a Web document displayed on your browser. This information is then transmitted to the Web server, where it's passed to a specified script. The script can then use the information to do whatever is required.

Forms are created entirely with HTML statements, in much the same way that you create lists or tables (see Chapter 8, "Basic Web Publishing"). In the next section, you learn how to create a simple form.

Keep in mind that forms are only one part of scripting. The form lets the user enter information. Without a script, properly implemented at your server, the form does no good at all. The trick is to make sure that you develop a meaningful form and an efficient script.

Creating a Form

The basic HTML tags used to create a form are the <FORM> and </FORM> pair, as well as the <INPUT> tag. Although there are other tags related to forms, these simple tags allow you to create a functioning form. The first two tags establish the boundaries of your form. In many ways they're similar to the <TABLE> and </TABLE> tags, which define the limits of a table.

The <INPUT> tag is used, along with various attributes, to actually get input from a user. For instance, consider the following HTML code:

```
<HTML>
<HEAD>
<TITLE>DCI Mailing List</TITLE>
<META NAME="description" CONTENT="Sign-up page for the DCI mailing
list. Participants receive our quarterly e-mail newsletter.">
```

```
<META NAME="keywords" CONTENT="mail newsletter software computers
information knowledge">
</HEAD>

<BODY>

<CENTER>
<IMG SRC = "/smdcilogo.gif">
<H1>DCI Mailing List</H1>
</CENTER>

Sign up for the DCI mailing list, and we will keep you informed of
late-breaking news about our company. You also will receive our
quarterly newsletter which provides helpful information you can
use to improve your computing skills.

<HR>
<FORM>
Your name: <INPUT TYPE="text" NAME="UserName"><BR>
E-mail address: <INPUT TYPE="text" NAME="UserAddress">
</FORM>

<P>
<CENTER>
<IMG SRC="/Aart/rainban.gif">
<P>
Send comments to: <A HREF =
"mailto:Webmaster@dcomp.com"><EM>Webmaster@dcomp.com</EM></A><BR>
Copyright &copy 1996 <A HREF="/DCI/DCI.Htm">Discovery Computing Inc.</A> All rights
reserved.
</CENTER>

</BODY>
</HTML>
```

Notice that two attributes are used with the <INPUT> tag. The first, TYPE, identifies the type of input that the user can enter. The CGI specification identifies many different types, each of which is introduced at the appropriate place in this chapter. The second attribute is NAME. This attribute identifies a label by which this piece of input is to be known. For those with a programming background, this is analogous to a program variable. At a minimum, both the TYPE and NAME attributes must be used with <INPUT>.

The result of this code is a simple form in which two pieces of information are requested from the user—her name and her e-mail address. Figure 11-1 shows what the user sees on her browser.

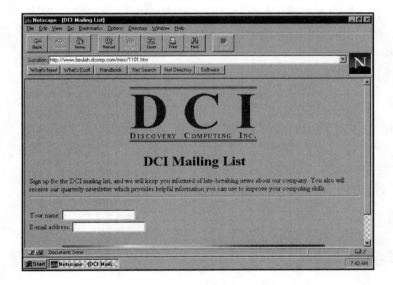

FIGURE 11-1

A simple HTML form to request information from a user.

Submitting a Form

Notice that the form developed in the preceding section doesn't allow any way for the user to signify that she has completed and is ready to submit her information; it only allows her to enter information. In this case, the user's Web browser makes the assumption that when the second field (E-mail address) has been filled in and the user presses Enter, the information should be submitted. That might not be a good assumption, however. It's much better to include a submit button that allows the user to indicate when she's ready to proceed:

```
<HTML>
<HEAD>
<TITLE>DCI Mailing List</TITLE>
<META NAME="description" CONTENT="Sign-up page for the DCI mailing
list. Participants receive our quarterly e-mail newsletter.">
<META NAME="keywords" CONTENT="mail newsletter software computers
information knowledge">
</HEAD>

<BODY>

<CENTER>
<IMG SRC = "/smdcilogo.gif">
<H1>DCI Mailing List</H1>
</CENTER>

Sign up for the DCI mailing list, and we will keep you informed of
late-breaking news about our company. You also will receive our
quarterly newsletter which provides helpful information you can
use to improve your computing skills.

<HR>
<FORM>
Your name: <INPUT TYPE="text" NAME="UserName"><BR>
E-mail address: <INPUT TYPE="text" NAME="UserAddress">
<P><INPUT TYPE="submit"><INPUT TYPE="reset">
</FORM>

<P>
<CENTER>
<IMG SRC="/Aart/rainban.gif">
<P>
Send comments to: <A HREF =
```

```
"mailto:Webmaster@dcomp.com"><EM>Webmaster@dcomp.com</EM></A><BR>
Copyright &copy 1996 <A HREF="/DCI/DCI.Htm">Discovery Computing Inc.</A> All rights
reserved.
</CENTER>

</BODY>
</HTML>
```

The addition of one line of code results in quite a big change to the actual form. Notice that two new <INPUT> fields have been added, but each uses a new input type. The first instance, which uses the submit type, displays a button on the screen, as does the reset type. Both of these are shown in Figure 11-2.

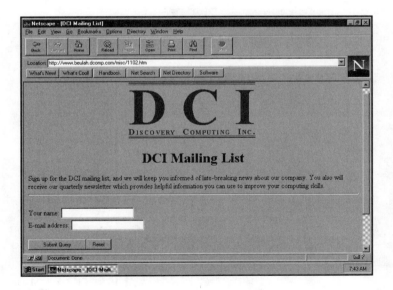

FIGURE 11-2

The addition of buttons lets your user control when information is submitted from your form.

The appearance of the buttons is handled exclusively by the user's browser. In Figure 11-2, the submit input type results in a Submit Query button, while the reset input type results in a Reset button. When the user clicks the Submit Query button, the information entered in the form is sent to the server. If she instead clicks the Reset button, the contents of the <INPUT> fields are cleared. The form is essentially renewed and the user can start over again.

TIP: The Reset button is similar in purpose to the Reload button located on the toolbar of many browsers. The difference is that the Reset button is faster because all processing occurs at the browser itself; there is no need to request the entire Web page again from the server.

What happens if you don't like the default names supplied by a browser? Worse still, what if they just don't make sense? After all, Submit Query doesn't particularly make sense when you're asking the user for information instead of putting together a search query. The answer is to use the VALUE attribute with the submit or reset type. Whatever you assign to VALUE is used as the text in the button. If you want the Submit Query button to instead say *Add My Name*, you would change the single code line as follows:

```
<P><INPUT TYPE="submit" VALUE="Add My Name"><INPUT TYPE="reset">
```

Now the button appears as shown in Figure 11-3.

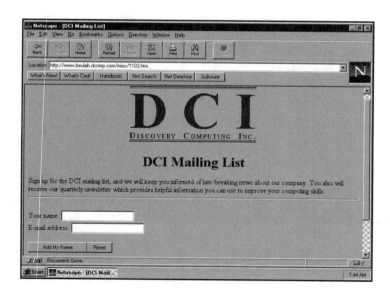

FIGURE 11-3

You can use the VALUE *attribute to rename buttons as desired.*

Regardless of what you rename the buttons, the common accepted name for them is still the Submit Button or the Reset Button. This is simply a recognition of what the buttons do—one submits information to the server, and the other resets the form.

Limiting Input

You can do two things to limit the way in which the <INPUT> tag works. The first is to limit the width of the input box displayed by the browser. This is done with the SIZE attribute. You can specify any width (size) between 1 and whatever limit you desire. The default width is 20, which means 20 characters. (It's unclear exactly how the browser can calculate width based on characters, because each character can be a different width, but nonetheless, this is the meaning provided in the specification.) In the Windows environment, it may be better to think of the value specified in SIZE as a relative value. For instance, a SIZE setting of 10 would be a certain width, 20 would be twice that size, and 40 would again be twice as large.

The second attribute that limits your input is the MAXLENGTH attribute, which limits the length of the input that the user can enter. Thus, if MAXLENGTH is specified as 40, the user can enter only 40 characters.

> **TIP:** Always include the MAXLENGTH attribute. Forgetting to include it could result in scripting errors if the information provided by the user is too long.

The relationship between SIZE and MAXLENGTH is independent. If SIZE is smaller than MAXLENGTH, as the user enters information, it is scrolled in the on-screen field until MAXLENGTH is reached. If MAXLENGTH is larger than SIZE, the user will never be able to reach the right side of the input field.

As an example of how these attributes work, take a look at the following code:

```
<HTML>
<HEAD>
<TITLE>DCI Mailing List</TITLE>
<META NAME="description" CONTENT="Sign-up page for the DCI mailing
list. Participants receive our quarterly e-mail newsletter.">
<META NAME="keywords" CONTENT="mail newsletter software computers
information knowledge">
</HEAD>

<BODY>
```

```
<CENTER>
<IMG SRC = "/smdcilogo.gif">
<H1>DCI Mailing List</H1>
</CENTER>

Sign up for the DCI mailing list, and we will keep you informed of
late-breaking news about our company. You also will receive our
quarterly newsletter which provides helpful information you can
use to improve your computing skills.

<HR>
<FORM>
Your name: <INPUT TYPE="text" NAME="UserName" SIZE=45 MAXLENGTH=50><BR>
E-mail address: <INPUT TYPE="text" NAME="UserAddress" SIZE=40 MAXLENGTH=60>
<P><INPUT TYPE="submit" VALUE="Add My Name"><INPUT TYPE="reset">
</FORM>

<P>
<CENTER>
<IMG SRC="/Aart/rainban.gif">
<P>
Send comments to: <A HREF =
"mailto:Webmaster@dcomp.com"><EM>Webmaster@dcomp.com</EM></A><BR>
Copyright &copy 1996 <A HREF="/DCI/DCI.Htm">Discovery Computing Inc.</A> All rights
reserved.
</CENTER>

</BODY>
</HTML>
```

When this form is displayed, the only visible difference is the size of the input fields, as shown in Figure 11-4. Compare the widths with those in Figure 11-3.

From an operational standpoint, the user won't be able to enter more than the number of characters specified in MAXLENGTH. Outside of this, the only way you can limit input is through your actual script. For instance, if you require input that's at least a certain length, or you only want numbers, you'll need to handle that with your script.

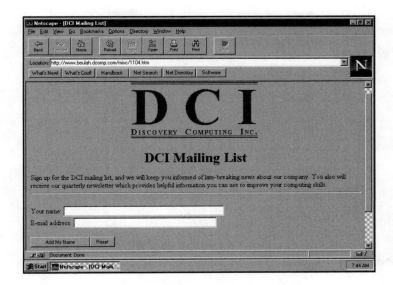

FIGURE 11-4

The SIZE *attribute specifies the width of an input
field, while* MAXLENGTH
*specifies how long the
input can be.*

Using Check Boxes and Radio Buttons

Another type of input you can get in a form is with a check box or a radio button. Both
types of controls should be familiar to any Windows user. A check box allows you to
select or deselect an option; a radio button allows you to select one (and only one) option
from a group.

Check boxes are implemented by using a different <INPUT> attribute, as shown in the following script:

```
<HTML>
<HEAD>
<TITLE>DCI Mailing List</TITLE>
<META NAME="description" CONTENT="Sign-up page for the DCI mailing
list. Participants receive our quarterly e-mail newsletter.">
<META NAME="keywords" CONTENT="mail newsletter software computers
information knowledge">
</HEAD>


<BODY>
```

```
<CENTER>
<IMG SRC = "/smdcilogo.gif">
<H1>DCI Mailing List</H1>
</CENTER>

Sign up for the DCI mailing list to receive the latest information
about our company and services. You can select to receive press
releases or our quarterly newsletter.

<HR>
<FORM>
Your name: <INPUT TYPE="text" NAME="UserName" SIZE=45 MAXLENGTH=50><BR>
E-mail address: <INPUT TYPE="text" NAME="UserAddress" SIZE=40 MAXLENGTH=60>
<P>Please indicate which type of e-mail you want:<BR>
<INPUT TYPE="checkbox" NAME="Newsletter" CHECKED> Newsletter<BR>
<INPUT TYPE="checkbox" NAME="PressRelease"> Press releases
<P><INPUT TYPE="submit" VALUE="Add My Name"><INPUT TYPE="reset">
</FORM>

<P>
<CENTER>
<IMG SRC="/Aart/rainban.gif">
<P>
Send comments to: <A HREF =
"mailto:Webmaster@dcomp.com"><EM>Webmaster@dcomp.com</EM></A><BR>
Copyright &copy 1996 <A HREF="/DCI/DCI.Htm">Discovery Computing Inc.</A> All rights
reserved.
</CENTER>

</BODY>
</HTML>
```

Notice that the input type of checkbox is used. Also, the implementation of the two check
boxes differs. The first check box, for the newsletter, also uses the CHECKED attribute, which
results in that check box being selected as the default when the form is first displayed.
The results of these changes to the form are shown in Figure 11-5.

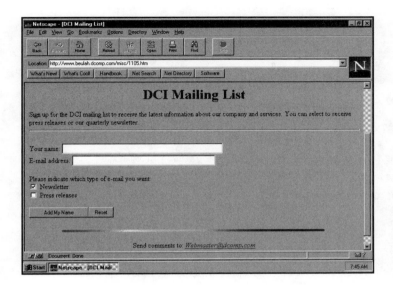

FIGURE 11-5

You can use check boxes in your forms so users can select options.

When a user clicks a check box, its state is changed. If it was previously checked, it becomes unchecked, and vice versa. When the user clicks the Submit Query button, the value of the variable associated with the check box is set to *on* if it was selected. If it wasn't selected, your script will never know about it, because only information about variables (check boxes) that were selected are passed to the script. Your script can then take the appropriate action based on the settings it receives.

Radio buttons are a bit different. When you use radio buttons in your form, only one button per group can be selected. You specify the group to which a radio button belongs by use of the NAME attribute. All radio buttons belonging to the same group have their NAME attribute set the same. The following script shows how radio buttons are used:

```
<HTML>

<HEAD>

<TITLE>DCI Mailing List</TITLE>

<META NAME="description" CONTENT="Sign-up page for the DCI mailing

list. Participants receive our quarterly e-mail newsletter.">

<META NAME="keywords" CONTENT="mail newsletter software computers

information knowledge">

</HEAD>
```

```
<BODY>

<CENTER>
<IMG SRC = "/smdcilogo.gif">
<H1>DCI Mailing List</H1>
</CENTER>

Sign up for the DCI mailing list to receive the latest information
about our company and services. You can select to receive press
releases or our quarterly newsletter.

<HR>
<FORM>
Your name: <INPUT TYPE="text" NAME="UserName" SIZE=45 MAXLENGTH=50><BR>
E-mail address: <INPUT TYPE="text" NAME="UserAddress" SIZE=40 MAXLENGTH=60>
<P>Please indicate which type of e-mail you want:<BR>
<INPUT TYPE="checkbox" NAME="Newsletter" CHECKED> Newsletter<BR>
<INPUT TYPE="checkbox" NAME="PressRelease"> Press releases
<P>How would you best describe your position in your company:<BR>
<INPUT TYPE="radio" NAME="Position" VALUE="President">President<BR>
<INPUT TYPE="radio" NAME="Position" VALUE="Officer">Officer<BR>
<INPUT TYPE="radio" NAME="Position" VALUE="Manager">Manager<BR>
<INPUT TYPE="radio" NAME="Position" VALUE="Employee" CHECKED>Regular employee<BR>
<INPUT TYPE="radio" NAME="Position" VALUE="None">None of the above
<P>Please select the statement which best describes your
decision-making authority:<BR>
<INPUT TYPE="radio" NAME="Power" VALUE="Full">I can make any decision
necessary to further the needs of my company or department.<BR>
<INPUT TYPE="radio" NAME="Power" VALUE="Partial">I must clear my
decisions with my boss.<BR>
<INPUT TYPE="radio" NAME="Power" VALUE="None">I provide input to the
appropriate committees or individuals, and they make the final decisions.
<P><INPUT TYPE="submit" VALUE="Add My Name"><INPUT TYPE="reset">
</FORM>
```

```
<P>
<CENTER>
<IMG SRC="/Aart/rainban.gif">
<P>
Send comments to: <A HREF =
"mailto:Webmaster@dcomp.com"><EM>Webmaster@dcomp.com</EM></A><BR>
Copyright &copy 1996 <A HREF="/DCI/DCI.Htm">Discovery Computing Inc.</A> All rights
reserved.
</CENTER>


</BODY>
</HTML>
```

This code implements two groups of radio buttons. The first group is named Position, and the second is named Power. Remember that when radio button groups have the same name selecting one radio button unselects the others of the same name. The first group has a default radio button selected, as indicated by the CHECKED attribute. If the user selects a different option in the same Position group, then the default is deselected. The second group, which does not have a default option set, functions in the same way—the user can pick one (and only one) option from the group, but is not required to do so. The results of this form are shown in Figure 11-6.

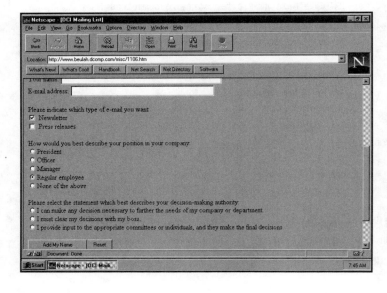

FIGURE 11-6

Radio buttons are used to select one option out of a group.

From your script's perspective, only one variable exists for each radio button group, and that variable can have varying values. When the user clicks on the Submit Query button, the value specified by the VALUE attribute of the selected radio button is assigned to the variable name for the radio button group. This may sound confusing, but it isn't really. As an example, in the form shown in Figure 11-6, if the user clicks President as his position, the variable named Position will have the value of President assigned to it. If, instead, he clicks Manager as his position, the Position variable will have the value Manager assigned to it.

Using Pull-Down Lists

In the Windows environment, pull-down lists are used all the time. You can also create pull-down lists in your forms. In forms, however, pull-down lists are called *option menus.* You can include a pull-down list by using the <SELECT>, <OPTION>, and </SELECT> tags. Let's say that you want to replace the first radio button group in the previous form with a pull-down list. You could do that with the following code:

```
<HTML>
<HEAD>
<TITLE>DCI Mailing List</TITLE>
<META NAME="description" CONTENT="Sign-up page for the DCI mailing
list. Participants receive our quarterly e-mail newsletter.">
<META NAME="keywords" CONTENT="mail newsletter software computers
information knowledge">
</HEAD>

<BODY>

<CENTER>
<IMG SRC = "/smdcilogo.gif">
<H1>DCI Mailing List</H1>
</CENTER>

Sign up for the DCI mailing list to receive the latest information
about our company and services. You can select to receive press
releases or our quarterly newsletter.
```

```
<HR>
<FORM>
Your name: <INPUT TYPE="text" NAME="UserName" SIZE=45 MAXLENGTH=50><BR>
E-mail address: <INPUT TYPE="text" NAME="UserAddress" SIZE=40 MAXLENGTH=60>
<P>Please indicate which type of e-mail you want:<BR>
<INPUT TYPE="checkbox" NAME="Newsletter" CHECKED> Newsletter<BR>
<INPUT TYPE="checkbox" NAME="PressRelease"> Press releases
<P>How would you best describe your position in your company:
<SELECT NAME="Position">
<OPTION>President
<OPTION>Officer
<OPTION>Manager
<OPTION SELECTED>Regular employee
<OPTION>None of the above
</SELECT>
<P>Please select the statement which best describes your
decision-making authority:<BR>
<INPUT TYPE="radio" NAME="Power" VALUE="Full">I can make any decision
necessary to further the needs of my company or department.<BR>
<INPUT TYPE="radio" NAME="Power" VALUE="Partial">I must clear my
decisions with my boss.<BR>
<INPUT TYPE="radio" NAME="Power" VALUE="None">I provide input to the
appropriate committees or individuals, and they make the final decisions.
<P><INPUT TYPE="submit" VALUE="Add My Name"><INPUT TYPE="reset">
</FORM>


<P>
<CENTER>
<IMG SRC="/Aart/rainban.gif">
<P>
Send comments to: <A HREF =
"mailto:Webmaster@dcomp.com"><EM>Webmaster@dcomp.com</EM></A><BR>
Copyright &copy 1996 <A HREF="/DCI/DCI.Htm">Discovery Computing Inc.</A> All rights
reserved.
</CENTER>
```

```
</BODY>
</HTML>
```

In this example, the <SELECT> and </SELECT> tags surround the options to be included in the pull-down list. Each option begins with the <OPTION> tag. The default option also includes the SELECTED attribute. The form appears as in Figure 11-7.

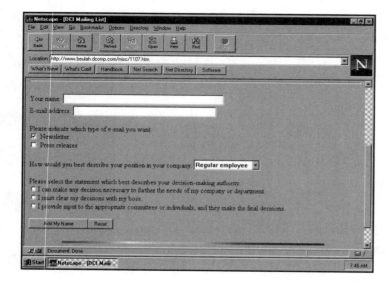

FIGURE 11-7

Pull-down lists are easy to create in your forms.

Using pull-down lists allows your form to take less space, vertically, but it also means that the user can't see all the options at once. Pull-down lists are particularly useful if you have lots of different options. On the Web, they're used quite frequently on forms where the user must select a state or a country.

From the standpoint of your script, there's no difference between what's returned by a pull-down list and what's returned by a radio button group. In either case, the value selected from the list or the group is assigned to the variable specified by the NAME attribute.

Using Text Boxes

While the <INPUT> tag is useful for getting limited information from a user, it isn't necessarily good for getting large amounts of information. In these instances, you can use the <TEXTAREA> and </TEXTAREA> tags to specify an input box in which large amounts of text can be placed. This tag pair is particularly useful for comment fields, as shown in this script:

```
<HTML>
<HEAD>
<TITLE>DCI Mailing List</TITLE>
<META NAME="description" CONTENT="Sign-up page for the DCI mailing
list. Participants receive our quarterly e-mail newsletter.">
<META NAME="keywords" CONTENT="mail newsletter software computers
information knowledge">
</HEAD>

<BODY>

<CENTER>
<IMG SRC = "/smdcilogo.gif">
<H1>DCI Mailing List</H1>
</CENTER>

Sign up for the DCI mailing list to receive the latest information
about our company and services. You can select to receive press
releases or our quarterly newsletter.

<HR>
<FORM>
Your name: <INPUT TYPE="text" NAME="UserName" SIZE=45 MAXLENGTH=50><BR>
E-mail address: <INPUT TYPE="text" NAME="UserAddress" SIZE=40 MAXLENGTH=60>
<P>Please indicate which type of e-mail you want:<BR>
<INPUT TYPE="checkbox" NAME="Newsletter" CHECKED> Newsletter<BR>
<INPUT TYPE="checkbox" NAME="PressRelease"> Press releases
<P>How would you best describe your position in your company:
<SELECT NAME="Position">
<OPTION>President
<OPTION>Officer
<OPTION>Manager
<OPTION SELECTED>Regular employee
<OPTION>None of the above
</SELECT>
```

```
<P>Please select the statement which best describes your
decision-making authority:<BR>
<INPUT TYPE="radio" NAME="Power" VALUE="Full">I can make any decision
necessary to further the needs of my company or department.<BR>
<INPUT TYPE="radio" NAME="Power" VALUE="Partial">I must clear my
decisions with my boss.<BR>
<INPUT TYPE="radio" NAME="Power" VALUE="None">I provide input to the
appropriate committees or individuals, and they make the final decisions.
<P>What sort of topics would you like covered in our newsletter?<BR>
<TEXTAREA NAME="Ideas" ROWS=4 COLS=50></TEXTAREA><BR>
<P><INPUT TYPE="submit" VALUE="Add My Name"><INPUT TYPE="reset">
</FORM>

<P>
<CENTER>
<IMG SRC="/Aart/rainban.gif">
<P>
Send comments to: <A HREF =
"mailto:Webmaster@dcomp.com"><EM>Webmaster@dcomp.com</EM></A><BR>
Copyright &copy 1996 <A HREF="/DCI/DCI.Htm">Discovery Computing Inc.</A> All rights
reserved.
</CENTER>

</BODY>
</HTML>
```

Notice that three attributes are used with the <TEXTAREA> tag. The purpose of the first, NAME, should be obvious—this is the variable name used by your script for what the user enters in the text box. The second, ROWS, indicates the number of vertical rows the text box should occupy. Similarly, COLS indicates the width of the text box (this is similar to the SIZE attribute for the <INPUT> tag). The result of including a text box in the form is shown in Figure 11-8.

The biggest drawback to using a text box is that you can't limit the length of what's put in the box. Your user could type a novel in the box, and it would be passed to your script. (Later in this chapter, however, you learn of a way to handle this situation in your script.)

Thus, unless you have a real need to allow the user to enter lots of text, you may want to stay away from the `<TEXTAREA>` tag.

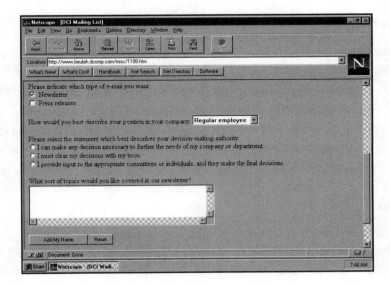

FIGURE 11-8

A text box allows input of unlimited length in your form.

Creating a Script

What happens after a user submits his input from a form? The response is sent from the browser to the server, which then acts on that response. Exactly what the server does with the information depends on the submission method used in your form, as discussed in the following section.

Submission Methods

There are two ways in which data can be passed from a form back to the script at the server. The submission method is actually a directive to your Web browser as to how it should formulate the response to your server. The server then acts on that response.

The default submission method is the GET method. In this method, information passed back to the Web server is stuffed into an environment variable, where it can then be accessed by your script. The other method is the POST method. When the FastTrack server sees that your form wants this method to be used, it passes the information to the script through the standard input channel.

You specify the submission method to be used through the METHOD attribute, which is used with the <FORM> tag. For instance, the following single line of HTML code could be used at the beginning of your form:

```
<FORM METHOD="GET">
```

Even if you want to use the GET method (the default), it's a good idea to explicitly specify which submission method you want used. The reason is that the submission method is up to the browser. You never know when you may run across a browser that doesn't follow the standard of using GET as the default.

Another item should be mentioned about submission methods. If you use the <TEXTAREA> tag in your forms, you shouldn't use the GET method, because the <TEXTAREA> tag lets the user put in infinite amounts of text. The GET method then tries to stuff all that data into an environment variable. This is a sure recipe for disaster, and a way to crash your server. In these instances you should explicitly use the POST method.

The submission method being used by your form is always available to your script in the REQUEST_METHOD environment variable. The contents of this environment variable will either be GET or POST, depending on your specification. Your program can then check for the method being used and react accordingly.

The *ACTION* Attribute

In order for your server to know what to do with information received from a form, you need to specify the name of the script to which the server should pass the information. This is done with the ACTION attribute, which appears in the <FORM> tag. For example, a fully specified <FORM> tag would appear this way:

```
<FORM METHOD="GET" ACTION="/cgi-bin/domail.pl">
```

The value assigned to the ACTION attribute is the URL of the executable script file. In this example, the URL is a relative path, meaning that it's on your server. The program is called domail.pl, which is a Perl script. (Perl is discussed in the following section.) You should provide a complete specification for the program name. Thus, if your program has an .exe extension, you should include it in the specification; don't assume that a default extension will be used by the server.

> **CAUTION:** The majority of scripts you execute will be located on your server. You also can specify a fully qualified URL on a different server. Unless you have established a relationship with the Webmaster at the remote server, however, this isn't a good idea. Scripts have a tendency to change periodically, and whatever is passed from the form to the script needs to match what the script expects. If it doesn't, errors can occur. To visitors at your site, the errors appear to be problems with your site, not with the remote script.

Choosing a Scripting Language

In broad terms, you can use almost any programming language your want for your scripts. The programming language should include the following capabilities, however:

- ◆ Capacity to access information in environment variables
- ◆ Capacity to access the standard input (STDIN)
- ◆ Capacity to create 32-bit programs or run in a 32-bit environment
- ◆ Propensity toward linear execution of program code

The first two items are the ways in which information can be passed to your script, based on the submission method specified in the form's METHOD attribute. If it isn't easy to do either of these from your language, steer clear of it and use another language instead.

The third item refers to the fact that the FastTrack server will work only with 32-bit CGI programs. This restriction has to do with memory usage in Windows NT. 16-bit programs are stored in their own virtual machine, separate from 32-bit programs. Thus, if you will be using a compiled language, you need to use a compiler that produces 32-bit executable files in order for them to work with your forms. Likewise, if you will be using an interpreted language, you need to use one that was developed for a 32-bit environment.

The final capability refers to the design intent of the language. The language you select should be designed for linear execution of your program code. This can best be explained with an example. Let's say that your favorite language is Visual Basic. You could use this language for your scripting, but that goes against the original purpose of the language and the way in which scripts are executed. In the first place, Visual Basic's primary use is meant to be just that—visual—using forms and the like. But scripts aren't meant to be visual; they do their work behind the scenes and interface only with your Web server.

Visual Basic is also an event-driven language. When an event happens while the program is running, the code associated with that event is executed. Scripts used in an HTML environment aren't event-driven. Instead, they are typically very short and are executed sequentially—in a linear manner. They typically accomplish a specific task (such as processing a few pieces of data) and return information to the server; the info is then passed to the remote browser. For these reasons, a language such as Visual Basic isn't a good choice for your scripting needs.

> **NOTE:** If you want to use Visual Basic to process your scripts, take a look at the WinCGI method discussed in Chapter 12, "Working with WinCGI."

The two most common languages used for scripting are C (not C++) and Perl. Perl is an acronym for *practical extraction and reporting language*, and was developed primarily for use in scripting. It's reminiscent of C in some of its constructs, although there are some similarities to the old DOS batch files. The examples provided in this book use the Perl programming language.

You can get a copy of Perl from several places on the Internet. One such location is `http://www.perl.hip.com`. You should look around and find the version of Perl you want to use at your site.

> **NOTE:** Don't assume that this chapter or this book provides everything you need to know about Perl. Other books are on the market for that, or you can find on-line information at `http://bones.eandm.co.il/perl/pl-exp-io.html`, or any number of other locations. As you become more adept at writing scripts and your needs become more complex, you will want to invest in a good Perl reference.

What the Script Sees

Before you write your script, it's helpful to understand exactly what your script sees when it is passed information by the server. Regardless of the type of METHOD you designated for use in your forms, your script is passed a single string of characters that contain the user input from the form. The length of the string depends on the type of information requested in the form.

Suppose that your form consists of the following code, as developed earlier in this chapter:

```
<HTML>
<HEAD>
<TITLE>DCI Mailing List</TITLE>
<META NAME="description" CONTENT="Sign-up page for the DCI mailing
list. Participants receive our quarterly e-mail newsletter.">
<META NAME="keywords" CONTENT="mail newsletter software computers
information knowledge">
</HEAD>

<BODY>

<CENTER>
<IMG SRC = "/smdcilogo.gif">
<H1>DCI Mailing List</H1>
</CENTER>

Sign up for the DCI mailing list to receive the latest information
about our company and services. You can select to receive press
releases or our quarterly newsletter.

<HR>
<FORM METHOD="GET" ACTION="/cgi-bin/domail.pl">
Your name: <INPUT TYPE="text" NAME="UserName" SIZE=45 MAXLENGTH=50><BR>
E-mail address: <INPUT TYPE="text" NAME="UserAddress" SIZE=40 MAXLENGTH=60>
<P>Please indicate which type of e-mail you want:<BR>
<INPUT TYPE="checkbox" NAME="Newsletter" CHECKED> Newsletter<BR>
<INPUT TYPE="checkbox" NAME="PressRelease"> Press releases
<P>How would you best describe your position in your company:
<SELECT NAME="Position">
<OPTION>President
<OPTION>Officer
<OPTION>Manager
```

```
<OPTION SELECTED>Regular employee
<OPTION>None of the above
</SELECT>
<P>Please select the statement which best describes your
decision-making authority:<BR>
<INPUT TYPE="radio" NAME="Power" VALUE="Full">I can make any decision
necessary to further the needs of my company or department.<BR>
<INPUT TYPE="radio" NAME="Power" VALUE="Partial">I must clear my
decisions with my boss.<BR>
<INPUT TYPE="radio" NAME="Power" VALUE="None">I provide input to the
appropriate committees or individuals, and they make the final decisions.
<P><INPUT TYPE="submit" VALUE="Add My Name"><INPUT TYPE="reset">
</FORM>

<P>
<CENTER>
<IMG SRC="/Aart/rainban.gif">
<P>
Send comments to: <A HREF =
"mailto:Webmaster@dcomp.com"><EM>Webmaster@dcomp.com</EM></A><BR>
Copyright &copy 1996 <A HREF="/DCI/DCI.Htm">Discovery Computing Inc.</A> All rights
reserved.
</CENTER>

</BODY>
</HTML>
```

When you run this code, the resulting form appears as shown in Figure 11-9.

When the user clicks on the Add My Name button, the information from the form is compiled by the server and sent as an environment variable (QUERY_STRING) to the script. When this environment variable is retrieved by the program, it may appear as follows:

```
UserName=John+Doe&UserAddress=jdoe@widget.com&Newsletter=on&Position=Regular+employee&
➥Power=Partial
```

Notice that I said *may* appear—the exact contents of the string will vary, depending on the form choices made by the user. The structure of the information returned, however, is always the same. The information your program has to work with will follow these general guidelines:

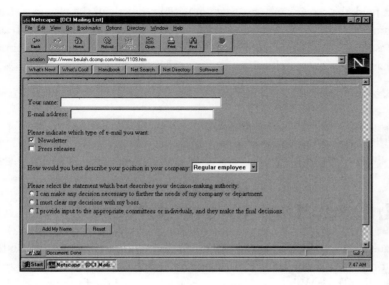

FIGURE 11-9

This form contains several standard controls that allow user input.

◆ Responses are separated by ampersands (&).

◆ Responses appear in the same order in which they appear in your form.

◆ The variable name you specified in your form is the first part of any response.

◆ The second part of any response is an equal sign.

◆ The final part of any response is the value specified by the user.

◆ In any "on/off" form control such as check boxes or radio buttons, only variables turned on are returned to the script. (This means that the default setting for all controls is off.)

◆ All spaces are replaced by plus signs (+).

◆ Responses include escape codes.

These guidelines are pretty straightforward, except perhaps the last one. *Escape codes* are a standard way of treating nonstandard characters. The server, when it detects certain non-standard characters in a response string, replaces them with escape sequences that define the hexadecimal value of the character. Escape codes come into play predominantly when the user is entering input directly into your form. For instance, if the user types an ampersand into a text field, the server can't pass that ampersand directly in the response string. If it did, your program would think the end of the response had been reached. Instead, the ampersand is replaced with a percent sign (%) followed by a two-digit hexadecimal value for the character, as in the following:

```
UserName=John+%26+Mary+Doe&UserAddress=jdoe@widget.com&Newsletter=on&Position=Regular+
➥employee&Power=Partial
```

Notice the `UserName` response. The user entered a name of `John & Mary Doe`. Thus, your program must allow for this and convert the escape codes back to their regular values.

Returning Information to the Server

You can also cause your program to return dynamic information from your script to the user. Thus, your program can create HTML pages on-the-fly, and feed them back to the user through the FastTrack Web server. For example, if you used the form presented in the preceding section, you might want to create a confirmation page for the user.

You create dynamic HTML pages by simply adding `PRINT` statements to your program. Any printed output is captured by the FastTrack server and passed along to your user. The only requirement is that you preface the output with two lines. The first contains the following code:

```
Content-type: text/html
```

This line is referred to as the MIME header, which indicates the type of information being transmitted to the remote browser. Normally the MIME header is added by the server (in the case of your normal HTML documents). However, the information created by your script program is passed directly to the remote browser, without interference by the server. The second line required is simply a blank line. Then you send information exactly as it would appear in a regular Web page.

Writing the Script

Once you understand what you receive from the server, and how you can create output to send back to the server, you are ready to put your script program together. The following sample program, written in Perl, processes the mailing list request form presented earlier in this chapter:

```perl
# Get the input from the server

if ($ENV{'REQUEST_METHOD'} eq "POST") {
    $Length = $ENV{'CONTENT_LENGTH'};                    # Environment variable contains
length of input
    while ($Length) {
        $FORM_DATA .= getc(STDIN);                       # Get characters from standard
input
        $Length-;
    }
} else {
    $FORM_DATA = $ENV{'QUERY_STRING'};
}


# Set initial values for array elements

$MailData{'Newsletter'} = "off";
$MailData{'PressRelease'} = "off";


# Parse the data, saving it into an array

foreach (split(/&/, $FORM_DATA)) {                       # Responses separated by amper-
sands
    ($VarName, $Value) = split(/=/, $_);                 # Divide at equal signs
    $VarName =~ s/\+/ /g;                                # Replace plus signs with
spaces
    $VarName =~ s/%([0-9|A-F]{2})/pack(C,hex($1))/eg;    # Replace escape codes
```

```perl
    $Value =~ s/\+/ /g;                                 # Replace plus signs with
spaces
    $Value =~ s/%([0-9|A-F]{2})/pack(C,hex($1))/eg;   # Replace escape codes
    $MailData{$VarName} = $Value;
}


# Append parsed data to a text file
# Text file needs to be later processed for inclusion
# in e-mail distribution lists

$Flag = "yes";
if ($MailData{'UserName'} eq "") {$Flag = "no"}
if ($MailData{'UserAddress'} eq "") {$Flag = "no"}
if ($Flag eq "yes") {
    open(OutFile, '>>/maillist.raw');
    print OutFile "$MailData{'UserName'}\n";
    print OutFile "$MailData{'UserAddress'}\n";
    print OutFile "$MailData{'Newsletter'}\n";
    print OutFile "$MailData{'PressRelease'}\n";
    print OutFile "$MailData{'Position'}\n";
    print OutFile "$MailData{'Power'}\n";
    print OutFile "\n";
    close(OutFile);
}


# Create confirmation page

print "Content-type: text/html\n\n";
print "<HTML>";
print "<HEAD>";
print "<TITLE>Mailing List Confirmation</TITLE>";
print "<HEAD>";
print "<BODY>";
```

```
print "<CENTER>";
print "<IMG SRC = \"http://www.dcomp.com/smdcilogo.gif\">";
print "<H1>DCI Mailing List</H1>";
print "</CENTER>";

if ($Flag eq "no") {
    print "We're sorry; your request cannot be processed because";
    print "you have not supplied both a name and an e-mail";
    print "address. Please return to the previous page and try";
    print "again.";
} else {
    print "Name: $MailData{'UserName'}<BR>";
    print "E-mail address: $MailData{'UserAddress'}<P>";
    print "<HR>";
    print "<P>Thank you for registering for the DCI mailing list.";
    print "This is to confirm that you have requested ";
    $Getting = "";
    if ($MailData{'Newsletter'} eq "on") {$Getting = "newsletters "}

    if ($MailData{'PressRelease'} eq "on") {
        if ($Getting ne "") {$Getting = "both " & $Getting & "and "}
        $Getting = $Getting & "press releases ";
    }
    if ($Getting eq "") {$Getting = "none of our information "}
    print $Getting;
    print "to be sent to you.";
    print "<P>";
    print "Thank you for your interest in DCI, and watch your upcoming";
    print "mail for more information.";
}
print "<P>";
print "<CENTER>";
print "<IMG SRC=\"http://www.dcomp.com/Aart/rainban.gif\">";
```

```
print "<P>";
print "Send comments to: <A HREF =
\"mailto:Webmaster\@dcomp.com\"><EM>Webmaster\@dcomp.com</EM></A><BR>";
print "Copyright &copy 1996 <A HREF=\"http://www.dcomp.com/DCI/DCI.Htm\">Discovery
Computing Inc.</A> All rights reserved.";
print "</CENTER>";

print "</BODY>";
print "</HTML>";
```

If you have programmed before, you may notice some similarities between Perl and C. They aren't the same, however, and if you are well-versed in C you may find it difficult to watch out for the sometimes subtle differences.

This sample program is quite straightforward. Basically, it parses the information passed from the server, writes it to a text file, and then creates a response to the user. At some later point, a different program will need to process the text file created by your script program. The reason for doing this is to save time. Remember that you want to provide the response to the user as quickly as possible.

It isn't the purpose of this section or chapter to explain how to use Perl, but you can gather a few pieces of information just from examining this sample program:

- Comments begin with the pound sign (#)
- Program variables begin with a dollar sign ($)
- Variable arrays (such as $MailData) are associative in nature, meaning that the elements of the array can be referenced with text or variable names between the braces ({})
- Information following a print statement is returned to the server (and passed on to the remote browser)

Outside of this, programming in Perl is fairly similar to programming in any of the other popular programming languages. You may want to study the program as presented here to get a good idea of what it does, and then try to make your own script program. The results of running this script (the Web page returned to the user) is shown in Figure 11-10.

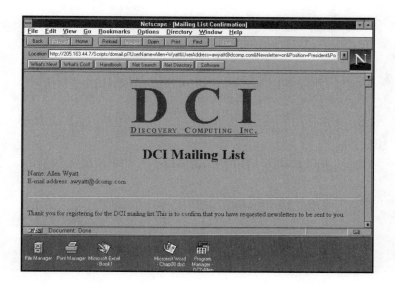

FIGURE 11-10

CGI scripts can be used to create dynamic documents that are created based on user input.

Allowing Your Script to Run

To run scripts on the system containing your FastTrack server, you first need to make sure that you have configured FastTrack properly and that under Windows NT you have set the proper permissions on the directory that contains your scripts. Follow these steps to make sure that both of these steps are completed properly:

1. Choose the Programs option from the Start menu. This displays the Programs menu.

2. Choose the Netscape option from the Programs menu. This displays the Netscape menu.

3. Click on the Administer Netscape Servers option. This starts Netscape Navigator, and shortly you will see a security dialog box asking for your user name and password.

4. Enter your user name and password, then click on OK. This displays the Server Selector page.

5. Scroll through the Server Selector page and click on the name of the server on which you want to set permissions. This displays the Netscape Server Manager, as shown in Figure 11-11.

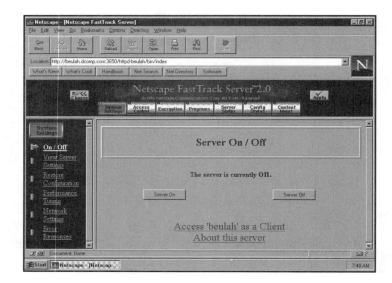

FIGURE 11-11

The Netscape Server Manager is used to configure your Web server.

6. On the toolbar in the top frame, click on the Programs button. This changes the information displayed in the lower frames. In the lower-left frame, the CGI Directory option should be selected, as shown in Figure 11-12.

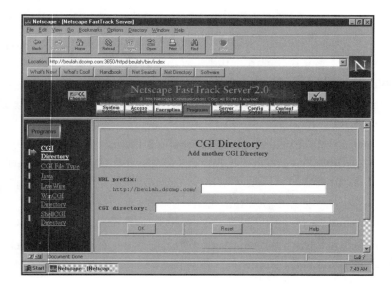

FIGURE 11-12

Netscape keeps track of where your CGI scripts are stored.

7. In the CGI directory field, enter the full path of the directory that will contain your CGI scripts.

8. In the URL prefix field, enter the name by which the directory you specified in step 7 will be known. Thus, if your domain is www.widgets.com, and you enter a URL prefix of cgi-scripts, then all references to www.widgets.com/cgi-scripts will actually be directed to the directory from step 7.

9. Scroll through the lower-right frame until you find the OK button, then click on it. This sends your information to the server and changes the page displayed in the lower-right frame.

10. Scroll through the lower-right frame and click on the Save and Apply button. Shortly you will see a dialog box indicating the completion of your request.

11. Click on OK to close the dialog box.

12. Close the Navigator browser.

13. From your desktop, browse until you find the directory you specified as your CGI scripts directory. Similarly, you can use the Explorer to locate the same directory.

14. Right-click on the directory. This displays a context menu.

15. Select the Properties option. This displays the Properties dialog box for the directory.

16. Click on the Security tab.

17. Click on the Permissions button. The Directory Permissions dialog box now appears as shown in Figure 11-13.

At this point, you can see the permissions that have been granted for this directory. (Directory permissions are covered in depth in Chapter 15, "Basics of Security.") By default, the only user with permissions is the Everyone group, which has full access to the directory. This *must* be changed to secure your site. Use the controls in the dialog box to change the permissions for the directory, its files, and all subdirectories, so that the Everyone group has only Read permission. Also, you can add the Administrators group and give that group Full Control permission.

When you're finished, click the OK button to save your changes, and then close the dialog boxes and windows you opened earlier.

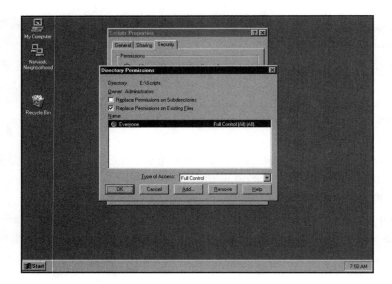

FIGURE 11-13

The Directory Permissions dialog box is used to set permissions on a directory.

Summary

Creating static HTML documents is easy, and FastTrack makes it very easy to publish them to the world. Creating dynamic documents, however, leads to user interaction and possibly more interest in your pages. As with any computer service that allows user interaction, things always get a bit more complicated than you may like.

CGI scripts aren't particularly complicated. The CGI standard offers a way for you to easily provide the interactivity you need. In this chapter, you've learned how CGI works both from an HTML perspective (the forms you create) and from a script perspective (the programs you design).

In the next chapter, you learn how to use a different type of scripting, this time following a standard known as WinCGI.

YOUR COMMENTS
Send Us

Dear Reader:

Thank you for buying this book. In order to offer you more quality books on the topics *you* would like to see, we need your input. At Prima Publishing, we pride ourselves on timely responsiveness to our readers' needs. If you complete and return this brief questionnaire, *we will listen!*

Name (First) _____ (M.I.) _____ (Last) _____

Company _____ Type of business _____

Address _____ City _____ State _____ ZIP _____

Phone _____ Fax _____ E-mail address: _____

May we contact you for research purposes? ❑ Yes ❑ No

(If you participate in a research project, we will supply you with the Prima computer book of your choice.)

❶ How would you rate this book, overall?

❑ Excellent   ❑ Fair
❑ Very good   ❑ Below average
❑ Good   ❑ Poor

❷ Why did you buy this book?

❑ Price of book   ❑ Content
❑ Author's reputation   ❑ Prima's reputation
❑ CD-ROM/disk included with book
❑ Information highlighted on cover
❑ Other (please specify):_____

❸ How did you discover this book?

❑ Found it on bookstore shelf
❑ Saw it in Prima Publishing catalog
❑ Recommended by store personnel
❑ Recommended by friend or colleague
❑ Saw an advertisement in:_____
❑ Read book review in:_____
❑ Saw it on Web site:_____
❑ Other (please specify):_____

❹ Where did you buy this book?

❑ Bookstore (name):_____
❑ Computer store (name):_____
❑ Electronics store (name):_____
❑ Wholesale club (name):_____
❑ Mail order (name):_____
❑ Direct from Prima Publishing
❑ Other (please specify):_____

❺ Which computer periodicals do you read regularly?_____

_____
_____
_____

❻ Would you like to see your name in print?

May we use your name and quote you in future Prima Publishing books or promotional materials?

❑ Yes   ❑ No

❼ Comments & suggestions: _____

_____
_____

TAPE HERE

❽ I am interested in seeing more computer books on these topics

- ❏ Word processing
- ❏ Desktop publishing
- ❏ Databases/spreadsheets
- ❏ Web site development
- ❏ Networking
- ❏ Internetworking
- ❏ Programming
- ❏ Intranetworking

❾ How do you rate your level of computer skills?

- ❏ Beginner
- ❏ Intermediate
- ❏ Advanced

❿ What is your age?

- ❏ Under 18
- ❏ 18–29
- ❏ 30–39
- ❏ 40–49
- ❏ 50–59
- ❏ 60–over

SAVE A STAMP

Visit our Web site at **http://www.primapublishing.com**

and simply fill out one of our online response forms.

PRIMA PUBLISHING
Computer Products Division
701 Congressional Blvd., Suite 350
Carmel, IN 46032

PLEASE
PLACE
STAMP
HERE

Chapter | 12

Working with WinCGI

In Chapter 11, "Working with Scripts," you learned the basics of how to develop CGI scripts that work with your FastTrack server. This chapter is essentially an extension of that chapter. Here you learn how to develop programs that follow the WinCGI standard.

To understand the information in this chapter, it is helpful if you know how to program in Visual Basic. The WinCGI specification was developed to primarily aid Visual Basic programmers, although you can use it from virtually any programming language.

What Is WinCGI?

WinCGI is short for Windows CGI, which is an interface specification developed by Robert Denny for use with Windows-based Web servers. It was first implemented for use with the WebSite server developed by O'Rielly & Associates, but has since been implemented by other Web servers, including Netscape FastTrack.

> **NOTE:** As of this writing, the latest version of the WinCGI specification is 1.3a, but FastTrack supports only WinCGI 1.1. If you want detailed information on the WinCGI specification, you can visit http://website.ora.com/wsdocs/32demo/windows-cgi.html.

From a developer's perspective (that's you), WinCGI is implemented in much the same was as a normal CGI program. Thus, it is important that you understand the information presented in Chapter 11, "Working with Scripts." You can still use forms to develop your interface to the WinCGI script, but your program is handled differently.

Using WinCGI, your program is expected to be an executable (EXE) file. This means you can easily use programs developed in languages such as Visual Basic, C, C++, or Delphi. This differs from regular CGI, in which the program used is expected to be a script program, such as a Perl script. Thus, people often refer to CGI scripts (because scripts are used) and WinCGI programs (because compiled, executable programs are used). Even if you see reference to a WinCGI script, you should still expect that the "back-end" program is just that—a program.

The most popular language to use with WinCGI is Visual Basic. This is because you can, on the Internet, find a Visual Basic WinCGI framework which you can use as a starting point for your programs. This framework is introduced a bit later in this chapter.

HTML Links to WinCGI

The first place to start is how you can access a WinCGI program from your Web page. There are two ways, really: you can create a form or you can access the program directly through a URL. Both methods are covered in the following sections.

Using a Form

When you learned how to use CGI scripts in Chapter 11, "Working with Scripts," you learned that you can develop forms to access the scripts. The WinCGI specification is no different. You can develop forms in exactly the same way as you did for CGI scripts, and they can work with WinCGI programs with no problem.

The forms you create can use either the POST or GET methods of invoking the program. You specify the submission method through the METHOD attribute, which is used with the <FORM> tag. For instance, the following single line of HTML code could be used at the beginning of your form:

```
<FORM METHOD="GET">
```

The GET method is the default submission method, but even so, you should be explicit about the submission method in your forms. As with regular CGI scripts, the <FORM> tag is expanded to include the ACTION attribute, which specifies which program should be run with the information from your form. For instance, the following is a valid way to use the ACTION attribute:

```
<FORM METHOD="GET" ACTION="/cgi-win/addname.exe">
```

The value assigned to the ACTION attribute is the URL of the executable program file. In this example, the URL is a relative path, meaning it's on your server. The program is called addname.exe. Notice that a full program name was used. This is always a good idea, since you cannot assume that any default file extension will be used.

> **NOTE:** By tradition, most WinCGI programs are stored in a directory named cgi-win. This is a play on the traditional CGI script directory, which is cgi-bin.

Using a URL

You can also access a WinCGI program using a URL link in your Web page. This is handy in instances where the link is expected to return the same type of information each time, but the details of what is returned must be created on the fly. For instance, take a look at the following Web page code:

```
<HTML>
<HEAD>
<TITLE>DCI Publication Listing</TITLE>
<META NAME="description" CONTENT="A comprehensive list of bookswritten by Allen L.
Wyatt, president of Discovery Computing Inc.">
<META NAME="keywords" CONTENT="DCI books allen wyatt">
</HEAD>

<BODY>

<CENTER>
<IMG SRC = "/smdcilogo.gif">
<H1>DCI Publication Listing</H1>
</CENTER>

Allen L. Wyatt, president of Discovery Computing Inc., has written
many books for a wide variety of publishers. If you would like to
see listings of the books or publishers, click on one of the
selections below.

<HR>
<A HREF="/cgi-win/bl.exe?titles">Click here for a list of book titles</A><BR>
<A HREF="/cgi-win/bl.exe?publishers">Click here for a list of publishers</A>
<HR>

<P>
<CENTER>
```

```
<IMG SRC="/Aart/rainban.gif">
<P>
Send comments to: <A HREF =
"mailto:Webmaster@dcomp.com"><EM>Webmaster@dcomp.com</EM></A><BR>
Copyright &copy 1996 <A HREF="http://www.dcomp.com/DCI/">Discovery Computing Inc.</A>
All rights reserved.
</CENTER>

</BODY>
</HTML>
```

As shown in Figure 12-1, this Web page provides two links on which the visitor can click. If you look at the code, you can see that both links go to the exact same program: in this case, a WinCGI program. The information after the question mark in each reference is passed to the program as a parameter. In this way, the program can make a decision about what information is passed back to the visitor.

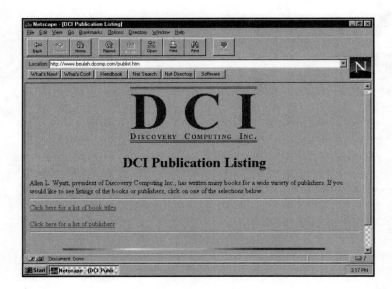

FIGURE 12-1

Links can be used to access information from a WinCGI program.

Remember that the usefulness of using URL links to WinCGI programs depends on the type of information you are publishing. The benefit of this approach to your visitor is that they don't need to fill in a form, they simply need to point and click.

How Information Is Passed

Even though you invoke a WinCGI program the same as a CGI script (from your HTML page), information is not passed to the program in the same way. Even though you use the GET or POST methods, information is passed through an intermediary file. This file is created by the server, and is what is termed a *private profile file*. The file is constructed in much the same way as a regular Windows INI file. For instance, the following is an example of such a file, as created by FastTrack:

```
[CGI]
Request Protocol=HTTP/1.0
Request Method=GET
Executable Path=/cgi-win/bl.exe
Document Root=c:/netscape/scripts/cgi-win
Query String=publishers
Referer=http://www.beulah.dcomp.com/publist.htm
User Agent=Mozilla/2.0 (WinNT; I)
Content File=\temp\7\7.con
Server Software=Netscape-FastTrack/2.0
Server Name=beulah.dcomp.com
Server Port=80
CGI Version=CGI/1.3a (Win)
Remote Address=205.163.44.3
HTTPS=off
[Accept]
image/gif=yes
image/x-xbitmap=yes
image/jpeg=yes
image/pjpeg=yes
*/*=yes
[System]
GMT Offset=-25200
Debug Mode=Yes
Output File=\temp\7\7.out
Content File=\temp\7\7.con
[Extra Headers]
```

```
host=www.beulah.dcomp.com
referer=http://www.beulah.dcomp.com/publist.htm
user-agent=Mozilla/2.0 (WinNT; I)
connection=Keep-Alive
```

Notice that the file consists of major sections within brackets (such as [CGI] and [System]). These sections then contain values which can be accessed by your program. If you want to know the full range of possible sections and values within sections, then you should refer to the specification at http://website.ora.com/wsdocs/32demo/windows-cgi.html.

The intermediary file is given a name by FastTrack based on the name of the WinCGI program you are calling. For instance, if your WinCGI program is called addname.exe, then the first intermediary file created is called addname1.dat, the second is addname2.dat, and so on. The files are created in a folder in the TEMP directory for your system (normally C:\TEMP). The intermediary file name (and its path) is actually passed to your WinCGI program as a parameter when it is invoked.

If you use the framework file discussed a little later in this chapter, you won't need to worry about picking apart the intermediary file. Instead, you can use functions within the file to automatically initialize variables with the passed information.

Creating the Program

If you are converting to the FastTrack server from a different Web server that supported the WinCGI interface, you may already have some WinCGI programs developed. If so, there should be no problem in using your existing WinCGI programs with FastTrack. If you do not fall in this category, then you need to develop your own programs from scratch. The easiest way to do this is to use the Visual Basic WinCGI framework file, and then add your own code.

The Framework File

The Visual Basic WinCGI framework file provides a starting point for your own WinCGI program. The file is actually the source code for a Visual Basic program which provides the common functions you need to take advantage of the WinCGI specification. There are several places you can get this file from the Internet, including the following:

- **Netscape.** Download the file at http://home.netscape.com/assist/ support/downloads/WinCGI.zip. This file includes a sample program, but the framework file is called CGI.BAS. This file works with Visual Basic 3.0.

- **O'Rielly.** Download the file at http://website.ora.com/software/cgi32.zip. This includes the framework file named CGI32.BAS, which works with Visual Basic 4.0.

- **Intermedia.** Download the file at http://www.intermedia.net/intermedia/ files/cgi32.zip. This, again, includes the CGI32.BAS file.

- **DCI.** Download the file at ftp://dcomp.com/pub/Utilities/WinCGI/ cgi32.zip or /cgi32.bas. These are compressed and non-compressed versions of the CGI32.BAS files.

- **RadWare.** Download the file at http://www.radware.net/ftp/WinNT/ cgi32.bas. This is a non-compressed version of the CGI32.BAS file.

When you download the file and decompress it (if necessary), you should copy it to the directory in which you do your Visual Basic development. Remember that this framework file is a starting point for your WinCGI program. Don't make changes to the original file (CGI.BAS or CGI32.BAS); instead, copy the file to a new name, and then make changes in the copy.

When you examine the program code, you notice that the first procedure run is Main():

```
'_ _ _ _ _ _ _ _ _ _ _ _ _ _ _ _ _ _ _ _ _ _ _ _ _ _ _ _ _ _ _ _
'
'   main() - CGI script back-end main procedure
'
' This is the main() for the VB back end. Note carefully how the error
' handling is set up, and how program cleanup is done. If no command
' line args are present, call Inter_Main() and exit.
'
'_ _ _ _ _ _ _ _ _ _ _ _ _ _ _ _ _ _ _ _ _ _ _ _ _ _ _ _ _ _ _ _
Sub Main()
    On Error GoTo ErrorHandler

    If Trim$(Command$) = "" Then    ' Interactive start
        Inter_Main                      ' Call interactive main
        Exit Sub                        ' Exit the program
    End If
```

```
    InitializeCGI          ' Create the CGI environment


    '===========

    CGI_Main               ' Execute the actual "script"

    '===========


Cleanup:

    Close #CGI_OutputFN

    Exit Sub                           ' End the program
' _ _ _ _ _

ErrorHandler:

    Select Case Err                    ' Decode our "user defined" errors

        Case ERR_NO_FIELD:

            ErrorString = "Unknown form field"

        Case Else:

            ErrorString = Error$       ' Must be VB error

    End Select


    ErrorString = ErrorString & " (error #" & Err & ")"

    On Error GoTo 0                    ' Prevent recursion

    ErrorHandler (Err)                 ' Generate HTTP error result

    Resume Cleanup

' _ _ _ _ _

End Sub
```

There are three important things to note about this code. First of all, if the program is called with nothing on the command line, then the "interactive" portion of the program is called. Realize that if this program is started by FastTrack, there will always be something on the command line—the name of the intermediary file, as described earlier in the chapter. The only way there would not be a file name is if you started the program from the command prompt, outside of the FastTrack environment.

If you want to create an interactive interface, then you need to add a subroutine called Inter_Main, and create the interface yourself. If you don't want an interactive interface, then you should add the following subroutine to your program:

```
Sub Inter_Main()
    Dim Message As String, OK As Integer


    Message = "Sorry, this program cannot be run interactively."
    OK = MsgBox(Message, 0)
End Sub
```

If there is something on the command line, then the initialization routine is called (InitializeCGI), which parses the contents of the intermediary file and places everything in the file into system variables which you can access from your program. The list of potential variables is quite lengthy, but you can review it in the declarations section of CGI.BAS or CGI32.BAS, if you desire.

The initialization routine calls several other procedures which are included in the framework file:

- **GetArgs.** This function returns the number of command line arguments on passed by FastTrack.

- **GetAcceptTypes.** This subroutine parses key pairs from the [Accept] section of the intermediary file. (Refer back to Chapter 11, "Working with Scripts," to understand key pairs.)

- **GetExtraHeaders.** This subroutine parses any extra header information from the [Extra Headers] section of the intermediary file.

- **GetFormTupples.** This subroutine parses key pairs from the four different form sections of the intermediary file.

- **GetProfile.** This function actually pulls the requested information from the intermediary file and returns it to the caller.

- **ParseFileValue.** This subroutine is used in parsing the [Form File] section of the intermediary file.

Notice that after InitializeCGI is called, a routine called CGI_Main is called. This is your entry point to the WinCGI program. This routine is not included with the framework file; instead, you must create it and do your processing either in CGI_Main or from other procedures called from CGI_Main.

The final item to note in the Main() subroutine is how error handling is done. Errors in your program are passed back to the server and passed on to the visitor (hopefully this is you) as an HTML message. This is a great help in debugging your WinCGI forms.

Adding Your Code

As you learned in the previous section, you need to add your code in the CGI_Main procedure. Your code can be any Visual Basic code you desire, but should be procedural in nature. In other words, the code should not be interactive, as traditional Visual Basic programs are. Remember that there are no forms, buttons, or other Visual Basic controls to use in your programs. The entire purpose of your code should be to process a request passed from the FastTrack server, and then return HTML code that the server can pass on to the remote browser.

As you write your code, there are several procedures you will want to use. These procedures, which are built into CGI.BAS or CGI32.BAS, are listed in Table 12-1. Each of the routines you can call is discussed in the following sections.

Table 12-1   Procedures You Can Use in Your WinCGI Program.

Procedure	Meaning
FieldPresent	Checks to see if a form field is present in the information passed by FastTrack
FindExtraHeader	Returns the value associated with an extra header name
GetSmallField	Returns the value of a form field
Send	Send information to the output file
PlusToSpace	Replaces plus marks in a string with spaces
SendNoOp	Sends an HTTP message to the remote browser telling it to do nothing
Unescape	Replaces escape codes in a string with the characters represented by the codes
WebDate	Formats a date in the format expected for HTTP commands

The FieldPresent Function

This function is used to check if a value for a particular form field was passed to your program by the server. Typically this is used for check boxes, but can be used for any form field. When you call the function you should use the name of the variable as used in your HTML file. (Remember, information is passed to your program in much the same manner as a regular CGI script—using key pairs.) When the function is completed, it returns either TRUE or FALSE, depending on whether the variable was passed.

As an example, let's say you use an HTML form to invoke your WinCGI program. This form contains several different items, but one if particular is an e-mail account field, and you named it EACCT. If the user of the form filled in the e-mail account field, then the value will be passed to your program; if not, then nothing will be passed for EACCT. If you wanted to see if a value for this variable exists, you could use the following code:

```
If FieldPresent("EACCT") Then

    '

    ' Code to process e-mail account

    '

End If
```

The FindExtraHeader Function

This function is used to return the value assigned to an extra header name. Extra headers are those added to the intermediary file by the server. FastTrack uses this area to save information about the host on which the server is running, the URL from which the WinCGI program was called, and the system on which FastTrack is running.

You use the function by passing it with the name of the header whose value you want, and then the function returns the value as a string. If there was no value for the header you requested, then an empty string (length of zero) is returned.

The GetSmallField Function

This function is used to retrieve the value associated with a form field. These values are passed in either the [Form Literal] or [Form External] sections of the intermediary file. To use the function, simply supply the name of the field.

If there is no value associated with the name you supply, then the function generates an error and your WinCGI program won't function as you desire. For example, let's say you create an HTML form, and there is a phone number field in the form, and that field is named PHONE. If the user doesn't provide a phone number, then there is no PHONE variable passed to your program. If you try to use GetSmallField to get PHONE, an error is generated.

To get around the potential error problem, make sure you always use the FieldPresent function before you try to retrieve a value. For instance, the following would prohibit any errors when processing the phone number:

```
If FieldPresent("PHONE") Then
    PhoneNum = GetSmallField("PHONE")
Else
    PhoneNum = ""
End If
'
' Code to process phone number
```

The Send Subroutine

This subroutine is used to send output to the file which is sent back to the server. You would use this subroutine to send any HTML output you want sent back to the remote browser. All you need to do is make sure you send your information as a string, as in the following:

```
Send("<P>Thank you for registering for the DCI mailing list.")
Send("We appreciate your interest in our company, and hope")
Send("to hear from you soon!")
Send("<P><HR><P>")
```

All the Send subroutine does is write your string to an output file. Although you could do this quite easily yourself, using Send makes for much more readable code.

The PlusToSpace Subroutine

This subroutine is used to convert all plus signs within a string into spaces. When you are working with raw information that has been encoded for HTTP, you may need to convert it to something more "normal." When text is encoded for HTTP, all the spaces are converted to plus signs (for instance, in a URL). This subroutine converts the string back.

Since this is a subroutine, nothing is returned. You should pass the string to be converted as a pointer to a real string, as in the following:

```
PlusToSpace(ByRef myHTTP)
```

This example uses the ByRef keyword to explicitly ensure that the reference to myHTTP is passed, rather than a copy of the value. According to the Visual Basic documentation, ByRef is the default way of passing values, but you should feel free to use the keyword so there is no confusion on your part later.

> **TIP:** To ensure that raw data is converted properly, make sure you use the PlusToSpace subroutine *after* the Unescape function.

The SendNoOp Subroutine

This subroutine formats and sends an HTTP response code 204 to the remote browser. This is used to indicate that your program had no response for the information passed to it.

> **TIP:** Most browsers can handle a 204 response code, but not all do it in the same way. So there is no confusion on the part of your visitor, it would make more sense to format an HTML document that expresses your inability to process their request.

The Unescape Function

This function is used to remove escape codes from raw HTTP text. (Escape codes were discussed in Chapter 11, "Working with Scripts.") You pass the function a string, and it returns a string in which the escape codes have been converted to the characters that they actually represent. The following would convert the rawHTTP string to myHTTP:

```
myHTTP = Unescape(rawHTTP)
```

The Unescape function relies on the x2c function, which is also provided in the framework file.

The WebDate Function

This function is used to properly format a date and time as required for HTTP commands. Typically you won't use this function; it is used by the error handling routine. You would use this function, however, if you are sending back raw HTTP commands to the remote browser rather than let FastTrack package them for you.

When you call the WebDate function, pass it a date & time variant variable. The function returns the date and time formatted as a string. The following example illustrates how the WebDate can be used with the built-in Visual Basic Now() function:

```
fmtDate = WebDate(Now)
```

Compiling Your Program

Once you have written the code for the CGI_Main procedure, and any other procedures you want to create, you can compile your program. There is nothing special about compilation; you simply need to make sure you create an EXE file. In Visual Basic you do this by choosing Make EXE File from the File menu. Once the executable is created, you will need to do the following:

- ◆ Make sure the EXE file has the name referenced in your HTML file.
- ◆ Move the EXE to the directory from which it is to be run.
- ◆ Use the Explorer to change the permissions on the EXE file so it can only be read and executed.

One of the other big things you will need to do is make sure that the machine on which you have FastTrack installed also has all the necessary DLL files required to run your compiled WinCGI program. For simple programs, this may mean you only need to copy the VB40032.DLL (for Visual Basic 4.0) or VBRUN300.DLL (for Visual Basic 3.0) files to the server. If your program is more complex, it is very difficult to determine exactly which DLLs are needed by the program.

Believe it or not, the easiest way to ensure that you have all the DLLs you need is to install Visual Basic on the server! This may seem dramatic, and I would not suggest that you use your Web server system as your Visual Basic development system, but it is a way to make sure that all your DLLs are installed and the Registry is updated the way it should be.

A Simple Sample Program

A very simple program is one that does no real processing on data sent to it, and accesses no external databases. For instance, using Visual Basic you can create a WinCGI program that returns the current date and time of where your server is located. The following is the code that would need to be added to the framework file to implement this:

```
Sub CGI_Main()
    Dim TimeHere As String


    Send ("Content-type: text/html")
    Send ("")
```

```
        Send ("<HTML>")
        Send ("<HEAD>")
        Send ("<TITLE>A Simple WinCGI Program</TITLE>")
        Send ("<HEAD>")
        Send ("<BODY>")

        Send ("Hi there. Thanks for trying this WinCGI program.")
        Send ("<P>Today is")
        TimeHere = Format(Now(), "dddd, mmmm d, yyyy,")
        Send (TimeHere)
        Send ("and it is currently")
        TimeHere = Format(Now(), "h:mm:ss am/pm.")
        Send (TimeHere)
        Send ("<P>Come again soon!")

        Send ("</BODY>")
        Send ("</HTML>")
End Sub
```

When you compile the program and access the WinCGI program from an HTML form, the resulting dynamic page is shown in Figure 12-2.

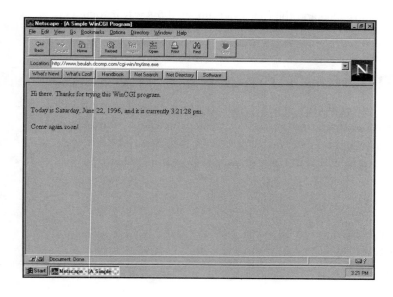

FIGURE 12-2

A simple WinCGI program to return the current date and time.

One thing you may notice about WinCGI programs is that they work much faster than regular CGI scripts. This is because the WinCGI programs are already compiled to executable files. There is no need to convert them from the scripting language to something the PC can understand.

A More Complex Sample Program

More complex programs are those that must perform quite a bit of processing, or those that access additional files, such as database files. Visual Basic, through DAO (data access objects) allows you to reach out and easily access data stored in separate databases, such as Microsoft Access. This sample program uses DAO to access information stored in such a database file.

The main procedure for the program (CGI_Main) looks like this:

```
Sub CGI_Main()
    Set MyDb = OpenDatabase("d:\BookList.mdb")

    Send ("Content-type: text/html")
    Send ("")
    Send ("<HTML>")
    Send ("<HEAD>")
    Send ("<TITLE>A More Complex WinCGI Program</TITLE>")
    Send ("<HEAD>")
    Send ("<BODY>")

    Select Case UCase$(CGI_QueryString)
        Case "TITLES"
            DoTitles
        Case "PUBLISHERS"
            DoPublishers
        Case Else
            Send ("Sorry, I cannot do """ & CGI_QueryString)
    End Select

    Send ("</BODY>")
```

```
    Send ("</HTML>")
End Sub
```

This program is meant to work with the HTML code presented earlier in the chapter (near Figure 12-1). The user clicks on one of the URL links, and this program (BL.EXE) is initiated. The main module does three things:

- ◆ Create the first part of the dynamic HTML file to be returned to the visitor.
- ◆ Check the CGI_QueryString variable to see which parameter was passed (TITLES or PUBLISHERS), and then call the subroutines to handle each instance.
- ◆ Create the end part of the dynamic HTML file.

In order for the program to work (as well as the subroutines, which are discussed shortly), you need to define some global variables for your program, as well. These globals include the following:

```
Global MyDb as Database
Global MyQuery as QueryDef
Global MySet as Recordset
```

The other subroutines, DoTitles and DoPublishers, each handle the actual processing. DoTitles consists of the following code:

```
Sub DoTitles()
    Set MyQuery = MyDb.QueryDefs!TitleOrder
    Set MySet = MyQuery.OpenRecordset(dbOpenDynaset)

    Send ("<TABLE BORDER>")
    Send ("<TR><TH>Title</TH><TH>Year</TH><TH>Publisher</TH>")
    While Not MySet.EOF
        Send ("<TR><TD>" & MySet("Title") & "</TD><TD>" & MySet("Year") & "</TD><TD>" &
MySet("Publisher") & "</TD>")
        MySet.MoveNext
    Wend
    Send ("</TABLE>")

    MySet.Close
    MyQuery.Close
End Sub
```

This code creates an HTML table that displays the title, publishing year, and publisher for a series of books. The output is shown in Figure 12-3.

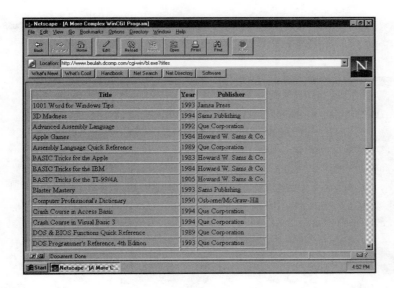

FIGURE 12-3

Dynamic HTML pages created with WinCGI can be as complex or as simple as you desire.

The other subroutine, DoPublishers, is much simpler. The code for this routine is as follows:

```
Sub DoPublishers()
    Dim SQLStmt As String


    SQLStmt = "SELECT DISTINCTROW * FROM Publishers "
    SQLStmt = SQLStmt & "ORDER BY [Publisher] "
    Set MySet = MyDb.OpenRecordset(SQLStmt, dbOpenDynaset)


    Send ("Allen L. Wyatt has written for the following publishers:")
    Send ("<P>")
    MySet.MoveFirst
    While Not MySet.EOF
        Send (MySet("Publisher") & "<BR>")
        MySet.MoveNext
    Wend
```

```
        MySet.Close
End Sub
```

This only creates a short page that lists the various publishers contained in the Access database. The result of this page is shown in Figure 12-4.

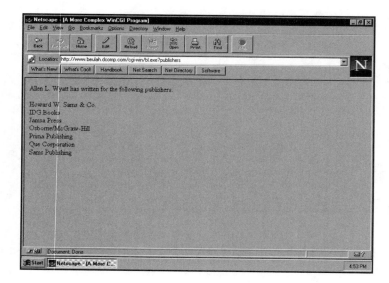

FIGURE 12-4

Short amounts of information can be returned very quickly by a WinCGI program.

Creating working WinCGI programs for your server may take some time, talent, and debugging, but the end result is pretty slick when you think how easy it is to interface with your existing Visual Basic expertise.

Allowing Your Script to Run

To run scripts on the system containing your FastTrack server, you first need to make sure you have configured FastTrack properly and that under Windows NT you have set the proper permissions on the directory that contains your scripts. The following sections describe how to accomplish these two tasks.

Configuring FastTrack Server

The easiest way to configure FastTrack to run your WinCGI programs is to designate a directory that will contain those programs. You then inform FastTrack that all the files in that directory are WinCGI programs, and you can then run them.

Earlier in this chapter, you learned that the traditional directory in which WinCGI programs are stored is cgi-win. You can create this directory anywhere you want, as long as it is on the disk drive where your FastTrack server is installed. Thus, if FastTrack is installed on drive C:, then you should also create the cgi-win directory on that drive.

CAUTION: FastTrack has this small problem, that when it creates the intermediate file that is passed to your WinCGI program, it doesn't include disk drive designations on all file references contained in that file. Thus, if your WinCGI programs are on a different drive than your server, you will always get an error.

To configure FastTrack to recognize your WinCGI directory, follow these steps:

1. Choose the Programs option from the Start menu. This displays the Programs menu.
2. Choose the Netscape option from the Programs menu. This displays the Netscape menu.
3. Click on the Administer Netscape Servers option. This starts Netscape Navigator, and shortly you will see a security dialog box asking for your user name and password.
4. Enter your user name and password, then click on OK. This displays the Server Selector page.
5. Scroll through the Server Selector page and click on the name of the server you want to configure. This displays the Netscape Server Manager, as shown in Figure 12-5.
6. On the toolbar in the top frame, click on the Programs button. This changes the information displayed in the lower frames.
7. In the lower-left frame, click on the WinCGI Directory option. The information in the lower-right frame changes, and your screen should now appear as shown in Figure 12-6.

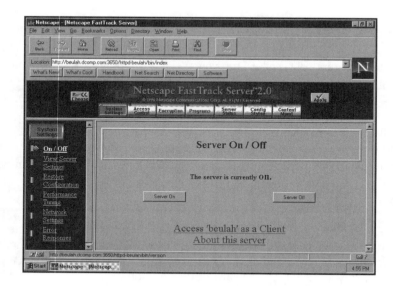

FIGURE 12-5

The Netscape Server Manager is used to config-ure your Web server.

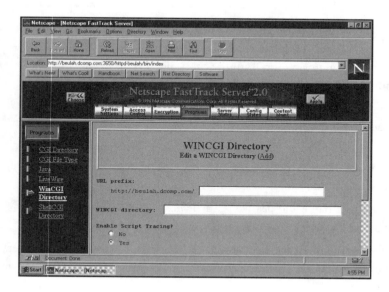

FIGURE 12-6

Netscape keeps track of where your CGI scripts are stored.

8. In the WINCGI directory field, enter the full path of the directory that will contain your CGI scripts.

9. In the URL prefix field, enter the name by which the directory you specified in step 8 will be known. Thus, if your domain is www.widgets.com, and you

enter a URL prefix of cgi-win, then all references to www.widgets.com/cgi-win will actually be directed to the directory from step 8.

10. Scroll through the lower-right frame until you find the OK button, then click on it. This sends your information to the server and changes the page displayed in the lower-right frame.

11. Scroll through the lower-right frame and click on the Save and Apply button. Shortly you will see a dialog box indicating the completion of your request.

12. Click on OK to close the dialog box.

13. Close the Navigator browser.

Setting Your Directory Permissions

The final step is to make sure that the proper permissions are set on your WinCGI program directory. You do this by following these steps:

1. From your desktop, browse until you find the directory you specified as your WinCGI scripts directory. Similarly, you can use the Explorer to locate the same directory.

2. Right-click on the directory. This displays a context menu.

3. Select the Properties option. This displays the Properties dialog box for the directory.

4. Click on the Security tab.

5. Click on the Permissions button. The Directory Permissions dialog box now appears as shown in Figure 12-7.

At this point, you can see the permissions that have been granted for this directory. (Directory permissions are covered in depth in Chapter 15, "Basics of Security.") As you can see from Figure 12-7, quite a few people have access to the directory. This *must* be changed to secure your site. Use the controls in the dialog box to change the permissions for the directory, its files, and all subdirectories, so that the Everyone group has only Read permission. Also, you can add the Administrators group and give that group Full Control permission. All other users or groups should be removed.

When you're finished, click the OK button to save your changes, and then close the dialog boxes and windows you opened earlier.

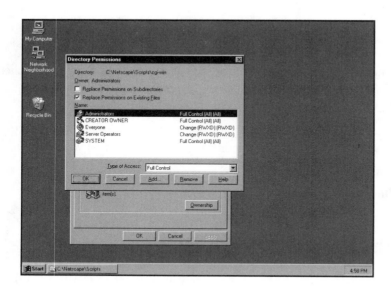

Summary

WinCGI is an interface specification developed strictly for use in the Windows environment. Although originally developed for a different server environment, WinCGI is now just as much at home under FastTrack server. In this chapter you have learned how WinCGI works, how your programs can take advantage of the WinCGI specification, and how to enable FastTrack to work with your WinCGI programs.

In the next chapter, you learn to use server-side scripting, as embodied in JavaScript.

Chapter | 13

Working with
JavaScript

In the last couple of chapters you have learned how you can provide a degree of interactivity at your Web site by adding scripting to your pages. These scripts, however, were external to the actual Web pages themselves. This is fine and good, but external scripts can slow down interaction with others—particularly if your site is quite busy.

In this chapter you learn about JavaScript, a scripting language that is not external to your Web pages. JavaScript is a recently new development in the world of the Web, but it is catching on quickly. This chapter presents the basics of the language, which means you will be able to create simple, useful scripts. For more in-depth information, you should definitely refer to a book dedicated to JavaScript.

What Is JavaScript?

For lack of a better term, JavaScript is a scripting language that was developed by Netscape and Sun Microsystems in late 1995. Since Sun was involved in the development, you might be tempted to think that that JavaScript and Java are related to each other. (For more information on Java, refer to Chapter 14, "Working with Java.") This is not true; even though the names are similar, they are not related to each other.

Remember that JavaScript is a scripting language, and in many ways can be viewed as an extension to HTML. Java, on the other hand, is a full-blown programming language, separate from HTML. In order for JavaScript to work properly, both the server and the browser must be capable of understanding the scripting language.

> **NOTE:** If you include JavaScript in your Web pages, not all browsers may be able to take advantage of your enhancements. This is because not all browsers understand JavaScript, but it seems it is being added to the latest versions of the most popular browsers. It may be a year or so, however, before the majority of the browsers graduate to JavaScript capability.

Earlier it was mentioned that using JavaScript was quicker than using other forms of scripting such as CGI or WinCGI. The reason for this is quite simple—much of the burden of interpreting the script has been transferred to the browser, rather than relying on the server. When using CGI scripts, the browser displays the form, but processing of the form information remains the duty of the server. This means the data must be transferred to the server, verified, processed, and information returned to the browser. Under

JavaScript, your programs can do at least verification on the browser, before transmitting back to the server for final processing. Depending on the script, this can have a dramatic effect on the dynamic nature of your Web site.

Adding JavaScript to Your Pages

You can easily add JavaScript code to your current HTML pages. This is done by using the <SCRIPT> and </SCRIPT> tag pair. Everything between these two tags is assumed to be JavaScript. For example, the following is a simple HTML page, with an even simpler script embedded in it:

```
<HTML>
<HEAD>
<TITLE>Sample Page Using JavaScript</TITLE>
</HEAD>

<BODY>

The following line is created by a JavaScript script:

<SCRIPT LANGUAGE="JavaScript">
    document.write("<P>Welcome to JavaScript")
</SCRIPT>

<P>Now we are back at regular HTML.

</BODY>
</HTML>
```

Notice that the script consists of a single line within the <SCRIPT> and </SCRIPT> tags. The script uses the document.write function, which is used to write information to the document being viewed.

When you view this page, the output is very simple, and should appear as three lines (see Figure 13-1). Granted, this is a very simple example, and it would be much easier to have created the three lines in straight HTML. However, the construction of the Web page shows how a script can be embedded in a document.

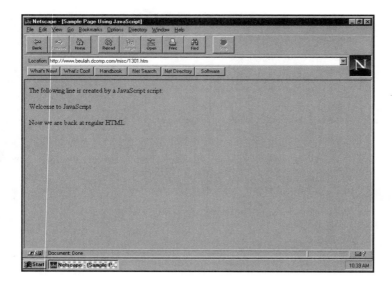

FIGURE 13-1

*JavaScript scripts are
interpreted by the browser
after the page is loaded.*

If you look back at the code for this page, you may notice something else. Notice that the <SCRIPT> tag uses the LANGUAGE attribute. This attribute, while optional, is a good idea to use. It implies that the <SCRIPT> tag can be used for other purposes (other scripting languages) in the future. While JavaScript is the only use right now, use of the LANGUAGE attribute is good form that guarantees compatibility when and if another embedded scripting language is developed.

Hiding the JavaScript Code

Earlier it was noted that not all browsers understand JavaScript. As an example, Microsoft Explorer 2.0 does not understand JavaScript, and if you tried to view the page developed in the previous section, the result would be unsatisfactory. (See Figure 13-2.)

To get around this, JavaScript allows you to embed the entire script in an HTML comment tag. This is handy, because it means that older browsers will ignore the embedded script, but newer browsers will still pick it up. For instance, the following is our sample page, but this time the script is placed within a comment tag:

```
<HTML>
<HEAD>
<TITLE>Sample Page Using JavaScript</TITLE>
```

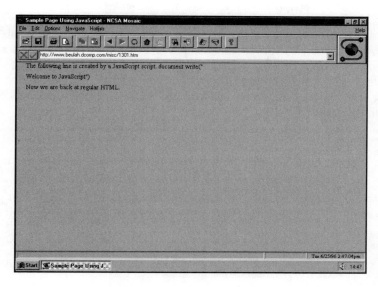

FIGURE 13-2

JavaScript is not support-ed by all browsers.

```
</HEAD>

<BODY>

The following line is created by a JavaScript script:

<SCRIPT LANGUAGE="JavaScript">
<!— Begin JavaScript
    document.write("<P>Welcome to JavaScript")
// End JavaScript —>
</SCRIPT>

<P>Now we are back at regular HTML.

</BODY>
</HTML>
```

The information placed at the beginning of the comment (in this case, Begin JavaScript) or at the end of the comment (End JavaScript) is not important. What is important is the inclusion on the comment start (<!—) and end (—>). You could use the lead-in information to help document your script, if desired.

> **CAUTION:** Make sure you place your < SCRIPT > tag before you start the HTML comment block, and the < /SCRIPT > tag after you end the HTML comment block. The HTML parsers in older browsers will ignore the < SCRIPT > tag pair, but the JavaScript interpreter in newer browsers needs to find the start of the script before it sees the start of the HTML comment block. If you don't place the lines in this order, JavaScript will never see your script.

When this page is displayed in an older browser, the information in the comment tag (the script) is ignored, as shown in Figure 13-3. While this may not be the best of all worlds, it is better than displaying "garbage" in the old browsers, which makes your pages look like they contain errors. In browsers that understand JavaScript, the embedded script is displayed as intended.

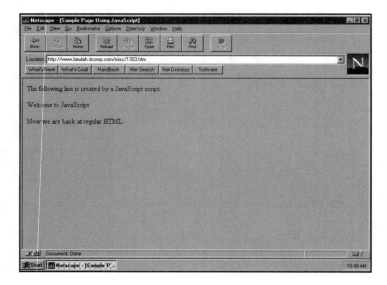

FIGURE 13-3

Placing your script within a comment tag means it is not displayed in older browsers.

Using Functions

The thing which gives JavaScript real power is the ability to define functions and to use them within a page. Implementing functions consists of two phases: defining the function and then actually using it. The following code shows both phases:

```
<HTML>

<HEAD>
```

```
<TITLE>Sample Page Using JavaScript</TITLE>
<SCRIPT LANGUAGE="JavaScript">
<!— Begin JavaScript
    function dosimple() {
        document.write("Now in the function<BR>")
    }
// End JavaScript —>
</SCRIPT>
</HEAD>

<BODY>

The following line is created by a JavaScript script:

<SCRIPT LANGUAGE="JavaScript">
<!— Begin JavaScript
    document.write("<P>In JavaScript<BR>")
    dosimple()
    document.write("Back in JavaScript")
// End JavaScript —>
</SCRIPT>

<P>Now we are back at regular HTML.

</BODY>
</HTML>
```

This code shows that functions are defined in much the same way as they are in other
languages. The definition begins with a function statement, followed by the name of the
function, and then the entire function is placed within curly braces ({}). Since JavaScript
is parsed and stored in memory after a page is completely loaded, many people place the
function definitions in the <HEAD> section of a page. This ensures that the functions
are defined before they have a chance to be called in the <BODY> section. This is particularly important for functions that take advantage of user feedback, as you will discover
later in this chapter.

Notice that the function defined in this code (dosimple) does not require any parameters to be passed, nor is it designed to return anything useful—it simply prints some text. The results of viewing this page are shown in Figure 13-4.

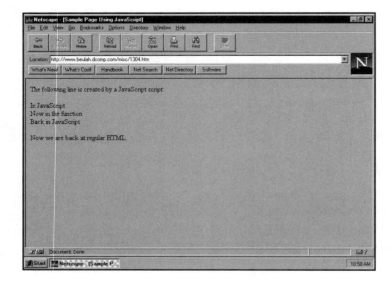

FIGURE 13-4

Functions must be both defined and used separately.

You can define as many functions in your program as you desire, and you can call them as many times. For instance, you might define a function that is used over and over again to display a standard part of a page, such as divisions between named sections of the page. In this way, the code is defined once, and it is called multiple times with a single line. You can examine your current pages for repetitious sections, and these become natural candidates for conversion to functions.

Understanding Objects

In some ways, JavaScript is similar to other modern programming languages. For instance, if you are already familiar with Visual Basic, you know that you can access objects. These objects can possess methods and properties. JavaScript is the same, in that it allows you to access objects, and these objects can have other methods and properties.

While this may sound a bit confusing to those not already familiar with the concept, you have already seen this in action in this chapter. Consider the following JavaScript line, taken from earlier in this chapter:

```
document.write("<P>Now in the function")
```

This line uses both an object (document) and a method (write). Notice that the object and its method are separated by a period. Document is just one possible object in an HTML page. At a minimum, the following objects exist in any page:

- ◆ *window.* This is the window in which the page is being displayed.
- ◆ *location.* This is the current URL for the page.
- ◆ *history.* This is a history of URLs previously visited by the user.
- ◆ *document.* This is the document represented by the page.

Remember that these four objects are only a beginning point. Most pages have many more objects, depending on the content of the page. Figure 13-5 shows the relationship of objects in any given page.

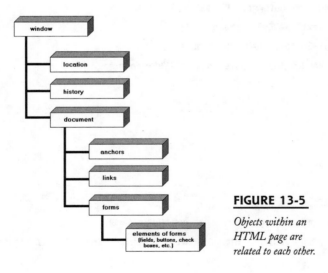

FIGURE 13-5

Objects within an HTML page are related to each other.

When you refer to an object in JavaScript code, you must provided the full "lineage" of the object, with the exception of the window object. For instance, let's say you created the following HTML page, which includes some links and a simple form:

```
<HTML>
<HEAD>
<TITLE>DCI Mailing List</TITLE>
</HEAD>
```

```
<BODY>

<CENTER>
<IMG SRC = "/smdcilogo.gif">
<H1>DCI Mailing List</H1>
</CENTER>

Sign up for the DCI mailing list, and we will keep you informed of
late-breaking news about our company. You also will receive our
quarterly newsletter which provides helpful information you can
use to improve your computing skills.

<HR>
<FORM NAME="UserInput" ACTION="doform()" METHOD="GET">
Your name: <INPUT TYPE="text" NAME="UserName"><BR>
E-mail address: <INPUT TYPE="text" NAME="UserAddress">
<P><INPUT TYPE="submit" VALUE="Add My Name"><INPUT TYPE="reset">
</FORM>

<P>
<CENTER>
<IMG SRC="/Aart/rainban.gif">
<P>
Send comments to: <A HREF =
"mailto:Webmaster@dcomp.com"><EM>Webmaster@dcomp.com</EM></A><BR>
Copyright &copy 1996 <A HREF="/DCI/DCI.Htm">Discovery Computing Inc.</A> All rights
reserved.
</CENTER>

</BODY>
</HTML>
```

When this page is displayed, in addition to the four standard objects (already discussed), the browser creates the following objects, each of which can be referenced as shown:

- *document.UserInput.* This is the form in the document. (Notice how the form's name, as defined by you, is used as the object name.)
- *document.UserInput.UserName.* A text input field in the form.
- *document.UserInput.UserAddress.* Another text input field in the form.
- *document.UserInput.elements[2].* This is the submit button on the form. It must be referenced with the elements array because it is not named.
- *document.links[0].* This is the first link established in the form, which is the pointer to the mailto: address. This link must be referenced with the links array because it is not named.
- *document.links[1].* This is the second link established in the form, which is the Discovery Computing link.

> **NOTE:** The full range of objects created by JavaScript actually depends on how the browser implements the language. If you want to see the full range of objects created when using a Netscape browser, check out http://home.netscape.com/eng/mozilla/Gold/handbook/javascript/index.html.

The Window Object

The window object is the currently active window within the browser. Every other object within JavaScript is subservient to the window object.

If the browser supports frames, each frame represents a new window. If you are working with more than one window under script control, each window should have a name so you can keep them separate. A window's name is defined when the window is created. To create a window, use the open method (as described shortly) in the following manner:

```
LowerRight = window.open("http://www.dcomp.com/dci/", "NewWin")
```

In this example, the name of the created window is LowerRight. There are multiple synonyms for the window object name. These include the following:

- self
- top
- parent

Of course, if you are working with named windows, you can always refer to a specific window by its defined name. Window object synonyms can be used at any time in place of the window object. You would use them when it makes sense from a readability stand-point. In addition, you can leave off the window object from a reference when you are referring to an object in the current window. As an example, all of the following refer to the exact same object:

```
window.document.title
document.title
self.document.title
top.document.title
```

Properties

You typically use the properties of a window to change items associated with the window. In practice, there are only four properties you can use with the window object:

- **defaultStatus.** This property is used to set the default message in the window's status bar.

- **frames.** This property refers to an array of frames defined within the current window.

- **length.** This property represents the number of frames defined within the current window.

- **status.** This property is used to set a temporary message to be displayed in the window's status bar.

The two status bar-related properties are the ones most often used. For instance, you would use the following code to define the default status bar message, and then (in con-junction with the onMouseover event) define how you want the status bar to appear when the user moves the mouse over a defined link:

```
self.defaultStatus = "Welcome to Discovery Computing Inc."
    .
    .
    .
<A HREF="http://www.dcomp.com/dci/mfglist/mfglist.htm" onMouseover="self.Status='Really
cool place!; return true'">Computer Manufacturer's Contact List</A>
```

Methods

Many of the methods available for windows are used for user interaction, as well as actually opening and closing windows. User interaction is done through dialog boxes, while opening and closing windows is typically done only when managing frames. Remember that the browser must understand JavaScript and support frames to utilize many of these methods. Table 13-1 shows the different methods available for the window object.

Table 13-1   Methods for the window object.

Method	Meaning
clearTimeout	Clears a timeout condition previously set with the setTimeout method. Requires, as a parameter, the timeout ID returned by setTimeout.
alert	Displays an alert dialog box, with an OK button at the bottom of the dialog box. Requires a single parameter, which is the message to be displayed in the dialog box.
close	Closes a window. You must use a valid window object reference with this method.
confirm	Displays a confirmation dialog box, with an OK button and a Cancel button at the bottom of the dialog box. Requires a single parameter, which is the message to be displayed in the dialog box. Returns TRUE if the user clicked on OK; FALSE if they clicked on Cancel.
open	Opens a new window. Can use up to three parameters, each enclosed in quotes and separated by commas. The first is the URL of the document to be displayed in the new window, the second is the target name for the window, and the third (optional) is a list of features for the new window (see below).
prompt	Displays a prompt dialog box which the user must fill in. Can use two parameters. The first, which is required, is the message to be displayed in the dialog box. The second, which is optional, is the default string value for the input field. Returns the string value of the user's input.
setTimeout	Evaluates an expression after a specified number of milliseconds. The first parameter is the expression to be evaluated, the second is the number of milliseconds. Returns a timeout ID which can subsequently be used in the clearTimeout method.

When you open a window, you can specify the features that the window should utilize. If you don't specify any features, then all optional features are present. If you specify any features, then only those features an no others are present. The following are the features you can use:

- toolbar
- location
- directories
- status
- menubar
- scrollbars
- resizeable
- width
- height

You specify features in a list by separating them with commas. All features (except width and height) can be specified with yes/no or 1/0. Width and height are specified as a number of pixels. The following is an example of using the features list in an open method:

```
DetailWin = window.open("", "details", "status=yes,scrollbars=yes,width=75,height=50")
```

The Document Object

The document object is perhaps the most used object in JavaScript. This object refers to the current HTML page, regardless of whether the page is complete or not. This means that you can use the document object to output information that will end up in the current page, or to read values that reference the page currently displayed.

Properties

The properties used with the document object are those which define how a page looks on the screen. Table 13-2 shows the different properties for the document object.

Table 13-2   Properties for the document object.

Property	Action	Meaning
alinkColor	R/W	The color used for links in the current document which are in the process of being clicked.
anchors	R	An array of anchors in the document.
BgColor	R/W	The background color used for the entire document.

Property	Action	Meaning
Cookie	R/W	Used to manipulate the cookie file. (For information on cookies, refer to http://home.netscape.com/newsref/std/cookie_spec.html.)
fgColor	R/W	The foreground (text) color used in the document.
forms	R	An array of forms in the document.
LastModified	R	The date on which the current document was last modified. This date is taken from the file date of the HTML file for the document.
linkColor	R/W	The color used for the links in the current document that have not been visited.
links	R	An array of links in the document.
Location	R	The complete URL of the current document. (This is not the same as the location object, as discussed shortly.)
Referrer	R	The complete URL of the document from which this document was linked. (If the user typed the URL directly into the browser, then this property is empty.)
Title	R/W	The title of the current document.
VlinkColor	R/W	The color used for the links in the current document that have already been visited.

The Action column in Table 13-2 indicates what actions you can take using a certain property. If there is an R in the column, then the property can be read; if there is a W, then it can be written to. You should understand, however, that many of the writeable properties can only be written before the HTML page has been completely laid out by the browser.

To use a document property, simply separate the document object from the property by a period. The following is an example of JavaScript code used to display the properties of a document:

```
document.write("This document (", document.Title, ") is located at ")
document.write(document.Location, ", and was called from ", document.Referrer)
document.write("This document was last modified on ", document.LastModified)
document.write("<P>The following are the colors used in the current document:")
document.write("<UL>")
document.write("<LI>BgColor=", document.BgColor, "</LI>")
document.write("<LI>fgColor=", document.fgColor, "</LI>")
document.write("<LI>alinkColor=", document.alinkColor, "</LI>")
```

```
document.write("<LI>VlinkColor=", document.VlinkColor, "</LI>")
document.write("<LI>linkColor=", document.linkColor, "</LI>")
document.write("</UL>")
Count = document.anchors.length
if (Count > 0) {
    document.write("<P>The following are the anchors defined in the current document:")
    document.write("<UL>")
    for (j=0; j < Count; j++) {
        document.write("<LI>", document.anchors[j], "</LI>")}
    document.write("</UL>")}
    else {document.write("<P>There are no anchors defined in the current document.")}


Count = document.forms.length
if (Count > 0) {
    document.write("<P>The following are the forms defined in the current document:")
    document.write("<UL>")
    for (j=0; j < Count; j++) {
        document.write("<LI>", document.forms[j], "</LI>")}
    document.write("</UL>")}
    else {document.write("<P>There are no forms defined in the current document.")}


Count = document.links.length
if (Count > 0) {
    document.write("<P>The following are the links defined in the current document:")
    document.write("<UL>")
    for (j=0; j < Count; j++) {
        document.write("<LI>", document.links[j], "</LI>")}
    document.write("</UL>")}
    else {document.write("<P>There are no links defined in the current document.")}
```

Methods

The methods used with the document object are those used to manage the page on the screen. Table 13-3 shows the different methods for the document object.

Table 13-3   Methods for the document object.

Method	Meaning
clear	Clears the current document.
close	Informs the browser that the document being constructed is completed.
open	Opens a document stream, n preparation for constructing a new document. The open method requires one parameter—mimeType. This can be any normal MIME type which the browser understands, such as text/html, text/plain, image/gif, or image/jpeg.
write	Writes information to the current document. You can include any number of expressions as parameters to the write method, as long as each of them are separated by commas.
writeln	The same as the write method, except a carriage return is printed at the end of the line. (Since most browsers ignore carriage returns in HTML code, this method is all but worthless.)

Of all the methods available to be used with the document object, the write method is probably the most often used. It has been used numerous times in this chapter already; it creates text that is added to the HTML file being displayed.

The Location Object

The location object is the complete URL of the current window. The URL is considered to be constructed as follows:

protocol//hostname:port/pathname?search#hash

In this construct, the *protocol* is any valid URL protocol, such as http:, ftp:, or gopher:. Notice that the *protocol* includes the colon. The *hostname* is the DNS host address for the server or an IP address, and *port* is the explicit port to be used at that address. The *pathname* is the path (and possibly file name) to be used at the server. The *search* item is optional, and it represents anything appearing after a question mark in the URL. The *hash* item is also optional, and represents a target within the *pathname*.

Properties

The properties of the location object represent the various parts of the URL, as previously described. The properties you can use with the location object are shown in Table 13-4.

Table 13-4   Properties for the location object.

Method	Meaning
hash	A target within the HTML file specified by the URL. In a standard URL, the hash is the portion after a pound sign (#).
host	The DNS or IP address of the server, along with the port at that address. The two items are separated by a colon. This property is equivalent to the hostname property, followed by a colon, followed by the port property.
hostname	The DNS or IP address of the server.
href	The entire URL.
pathname	The path and possibly file name (if present) of the URL.
port	The port number to use at the server.
protocol	The protocol specified in the URL, including the trailing comma.
search	The query string, if any, included with the URL. In standard construct, the search property is any portion after a question mark.

Methods

There are no methods applicable to the location object.

The History Object

The history object is a list of the user's most recently visited sites. In the Navigator browser, it is the same as the information appearing at the bottom of the Go menu.

Properties

There is only a single property of the history object—length. This property indicates the number of items (URLs) contained in the history list.

Methods

There are three methods provided with the history object. Each method provides a different way to navigate the history list:

- **back.** This method is the same as clicking on the back button in the browser.
- **forward.** This method is the same as clicking on the forward button in the browser.

♦ **go.** This method uses a single parameter which represents the relative offset in the history list, or a search string to be applied to the history list. If the offset provided is negative, the movement through the history list is backward, while positive is forward. If a search string is supplied, then the URL from the history list that contains the search string is reloaded.

Working with Events

So far the JavaScript examples have been rather static in nature—they have been used to display routine information. The dynamic nature of JavaScript is evidenced when you start defining functions that can be used when certain events occur. Events typically occur as a result of something done by the user, but some objects also include methods which can simulate events.

User Events

User events, strangely enough, are those events which are caused by actions of the user. For instance, if the user moves the mouse over a link, over a button, or selects a text input field, then these are all events. JavaScript allows you to identify these events and take an action—such as running code or a function—when the event occurs. JavaScript supports the events listed in Table 13-5.

Table 13-5   Events supported in JavaScript.

Event	Meaning
Blur	User leaves a form element such as a text field or textarea
Click	User clicks on form element (button, radio button, check box, etc.) or a link
Change	User changes the value of a form element such as a text field or textarea
Focus	User enters a form element such as a text field or textarea
Load	User loads the page
Mouseover	User moves the mouse pointer over a link
Select	User selects a form element such as a text field or textarea
Submit	User submits a form
Unload	User exits the page

You set up an event handler by adding the proper JavaScript command, as an attribute, to the HTML tag that defines the element on which the event can occur. For instance, consider the following code:

```
<A HREF="http://www.dcomp.com" OnMouseover="CoolPage('dcomp')">Visit DCI's Home Page</A>
```

This looks like a normal anchor for a link, with the exception of the OnMouseover attribute. This tells JavaScript what to do when the mouse is moved over the link. In this case, a JavaScript function, named CoolPage, is initiated with a parameter called dcomp.

> **NOTE:** Notice that single quotes (') are used in place of double quotes (") when using double quotes would mess up the command line. There should only be one set of double quotes around a complete string. Within that string, you use single quotes in place of double quotes.

All event handlers are coded in this manner; the proper attribute is added to the HTML tag. The name of the attribute is derived by adding the word "on" to the beginning of the event for which you are trapping.

Simulated Events

Many objects within JavaScript include methods which are used to simulate user events. These are used to allow your program to trigger actions which you have already coded for the user events. Table 13-6 shows the different simulated events and the types of objects to which they can apply.

Table 13-6   Simulated events supported in JavaScript.

Method	Applicable Objects
Blur	password, select, text, textarea
Click	button, checkbox, radio, reset, submit
Focus	password, select, text, textarea
Select	password, text, textarea
Submit	form

Data Types and Variables

If you have used a programming language before, you know that any language needs a way to specify different types of data, as well as a way to define variables. JavaScript is no different; it includes ways to do both of these items as well.

Unlike more complex or structured programming languages, there are only four data types defined within JavaScript:

- **numbers.** These can be any numeric value. JavaScript makes no distinction between integers and real numbers, as some languages do. To JavaScript, they are all in one group—numbers.
- **logicals.** There are two possible values for this data type—true or false.
- **strings.** A string is anything between two quote marks.
- **null.** This is a special value which simply means the absence of a value.

Variables can be used wherever and whenever you want. You don't need to explicitly declare them; you simply need to assign them a value. For instance, the following assigns a value to a variable name:

```
MyVar = 14
```

This results in MyVar being set to the numeric value of 14. Notice that the variable did not need to be declared as a certain type; JavaScript made the assumption based on what was on the right side of the equal sign.

You can also assign hexadecimal or octal values to numeric variables. To indicate that a number is hexadecimal, simply precede it with 0x; to indicate it is octal, include a leading zero. For instance, all three to the following assign the same value to the variable BigNum:

```
BigNum = 6701
BigNum = 015055
BigNum = 0x1A2D
```

Variable names are case sensitive, meaning that MyVar is different from mYvAR. In addition, your variable names must begin with either a letter or an underscore. All the rest of the characters in a variable name can either be a letter, number, or the underscore. No other characters can be used in variable names.

All variables are available anywhere within a page, unless you use the var keyword when assigning a variable, as in the following:

```
var MyVar = 14
```

In this case, the variable MyVar only has meaning within the function in which it is defined.

As you assign names to variables, you should understand that there are some names you cannot use. This is not unusual for any programming language. These names are referred to as reserved words. They are reserved because they are either used as JavaScript key words or they are planned to possibly have meaning in future versions of JavaScript. The reserved words are the following:

abstract	float	public
boolean	for	return
break	function	short
byte	goto	static
case	if	super
catch	implements	switch
char	import	synchronized
class	in	this
const	instanceof	throw
continue	int	throws
default	interface	transient
do	long	true
double	native	try
else	new	var
extends	null	void
false	package	while
final	private	with
finally	protected	

When working with strings, JavaScript recognizes certain special character sequences in the character stream. Table 13-7 shows the different special codes, which are reminiscent of the C language.

Table 13-7   String characters with special meaning.

Code	Meaning
\b	backspace
\f	form feed
\n	new line
\r	carriage return
\t	tab
\"	quote mark

Conversion Functions

JavaScript is very loose in switching between data types. This means it will easily convert variables from numeric to string and back again. For instance, the following three lines of code will not cause an error:

```
MyStuff = 45.678
MyStuff = "This used to be a number"
MyStuff = 123
```

In each instance, JavaScript blithely switches the type of information stored in the variable, and simply does what you instruct it. There are, however, some explicit conversion functions you can use with JavaScript. These are necessary, for instance, if you have string data you need to convert to a number for a subsequent math operation. There are only three such functions:

- ◆ eval
- ◆ parseInt
- ◆ parseFloat

The eval function is used to convert a string to a number, as in the following examples:

```
result = eval("123")
result = eval("4 * (60 / 2) + 12 - 9")
result = eval("123 is the result")
```

In all three cases, the result variable will be assigned the numeric value of 123. Notice how useful eval is in the second case, where it doesn't just blindly convert to a number, but actually performs the math. Likewise, if the parameter used with eval had contained JavaScript expressions, those expressions would have been evaluated as well. In all cases, however, the results of the eval function are expressed as a number.

The parseInt and parseFloat functions are closely related. They blindly convert strings to numbers, without doing the complete evaluation that eval does. The parseInt function converts to a whole number, while parseFloat converts to a real number. This does not mean, however, that JavaScript differentiates between real numbers and integers; remember that there is only one numeric data type. The difference is in how parseInt and parseFloat arrive at their results. For instance, take a look at the following:

```
result = parseInt("123.456")
result = parseFloat("123 is a great number")
```

In both cases, the result is exactly the same—the result variable is equal to the numeric value 123. Had the usage been reversed, as in the following, then the results would not have been the same:

```
result = parseFloat("123.456")
result = parseInt("123 is a great number")
```

In this case, after the first expression the result variable would have been equal to the numeric value 123.456. After the second expression, the result variable would have been equal to 123.

More About Strings

Whenever you create a string in JavaScript, you are actually creating an object that represents that string. For instance, let's assume that you use the following in a script:

```
filename = "artis.jpg"
```

In this instance, you have created a string object named filename. As with other objects in JavaScript, string objects can have both properties and methods. There is only a single property, which returns the length of the string:

```
HowLong = filename.length
```

In this case, the variable HowLong would be set to the numeric value of 9.

When working with strings, there are quite a few different methods you can use. These methods provide an entire range of what would be considered functions in other languages. Table 13-8 lists the various methods applicable to any string object.

Table 13-8 Methods you can use with string objects.

Method	Example	Meaning
anchor	MainDish.anchor("dinner")	Creates an HTML anchor statement using the MainDish string as the text and the required parameter ("dinner") as the anchor name.
big	Shout.big()	Creates an HTML statement that encloses the Shout string within a <BIG> and </BIG> tag pair.
blink	Obnoxious.blink()	Creates an HTML statement that displays the string (Obnoxious) within a <BLINK> and </BLINK> tag pair.
bold	BoldText.bold()	Creates an HTML statement that displays the string (BoldText) within a <B> and </B> tag pair.
charAt	OneChar = Full.charAt(12)	Returns the character at the offset (12) of the string (Full). String offsets start at zero. In this case, the 11th character is assigned to OneChar.
fixed	FixedFont.fixed()	Creates an HTML statement that displays the string (FixedFont) as if it were within a <TT> and </TT> tag pair.
fontcolor	Bright.fontcolor("00FFFF")	Creates an HTML statement that sets the font color to the specified parameter (4), displays the string (Bright) and then sets the font color back to normal.
fontsize	BigText.fontsize(4)	Creates an HTML statement that sets the font size to the specified parameter (4), displays the string (BigText) and then sets the font size back to normal.

continued

Table 13-8   continued

Method	Example	Meaning
indexOf	J = Full.indexOf("xy", 5)	Returns the offset of the first parameter ("xy") within the string (Full). Searching begins at the offset specified in the second parameter (5). If the second parameter is omitted, searching starts at the beginning of the string. All offsets begin at zero. In this case, the result is assigned to J.
italics	ItalicsText.italics()	Creates an HTML statement that displays the string (ItalicsText) within an <I> and </I> tag pair.
lastIndexOf	K = Long.lastIndexOf("q", 5)	Returns the offset of the first parameter ("q") within the string (Long). Searching is done backwards, and begins at the offset specified in the second parameter (5). If the second parameter is omitted, searching begins at the end of the string. All offsets begin at zero. In this case, the result is assigned to K.
link	Cool.link(URL)	Creates an HTML link statement using the string (Cool) as the text and the required parameter (URL) as the destination for the link.
small	Whisper.small()	Creates an HTML statement that encloses the Whisper string within a <SMALL> and </SMALL> tag pair.
strike	StrikeOut.strike()	Creates an HTML statement that displays the string (StrikeOut) within a <STRIKE> and </STRIKE> tag pair.
sub	GoDown.sub()	Creates an HTML statement that displays the string (GoDown) as subscript text within a _{and} tag pair.
substring	Two = One.substring(2, 5)	Returns a portion of the original string (One) beginning at an offset of the first parameter (2) and concluding with the character before the second parameter (5). All offsets begin with zero. In this case, three characters are assigned to the variable Two.

Method	Example	Meaning
sup	GoUp.sup()	Creates an HTML statement that displays the string (GoUp) as superscript text within a ^{and} tag pair.
toLowerCase	down = Mix.toLowerCase	Returns the original string (Mix) converted to lowercase. In this example, the result is assigned to the variable down.
toUpperCase	UP = Mix.toUpperCase	Returns the original string (Mix) converted to uppercase. In this example, the result is assigned to the variable UP.

Arrays

Most programming languages allow you to define arrays, but not JavaScript. There is, unfortunately, no outward mechanism for creating an array as a data type. Instead, you need to define objects which contain the information normally stored in an array. This may sound confusing, but after a little experience, it is simply different from other languages.

As an example, let's say you wanted to create an array to hold the name of the members of your softball team. The first thing you need to do is to add the following function to your code:

```
function MakeArray(max) {
   this.length = max;
   for (var j = 1; j <= max; j++) {
     this[j] = "" }
   return this
   }
}
```

This function creates an array as an object, and stores the maximum number of array elements in the length property of the object. (The special *this* object, as in this.length, automatically refers to the current object. It is essential to use this syntax, since the function does not know the explicit name for the object it is creating.) For your softball team, you would invoke the function as follows:

```
TeamNames = new MakeArray(12)
```

In this case, TeamNames is a brand new object with a length property of 12 and each element of the object set to an empty string. To later assign values to the elements, the following code will suffice:

```
TeamNames[1] = "Fred Myers"
TeamNames[2] = "Aaron Jacoby"
TeamNames[3] = "Brian Davis"
```

Other Scripting Considerations

In most other ways, JavaScript is similar to the C language. For instance, operators (shown in Table 13-9) are based on C. In addition, the construction of conditional statements, loop statements, and the like are all based on C.

Table 13-9 JavaScript operators.

Operator	Meaning
=	Assignment
+	Addition (for numbers) or concatenation (for strings)
-	Subtraction (as in 1+2) or negation (as in -3)
*	Multiplication
/	Division
%	Modulus (the remainder after an integer division
++	Increment
—	Decrement
&&	Logical AND
||	Logical OR
!	Logical NOT
<	Logical less than
>	Logical greater than
==	Logical equal
>=	Logical greater than or equal
<=	Logical less than or equal
!=	Logical not equal
&	Bitwise AND
|	Bitwise OR

Operator	Meaning
^	Bitwise XOR
<<	Bitwise left shift
>>	Bitwise right shift with sign propagation
>>>	Bitwise right shift with zero propagation

If you want to add comments to your scripts, you use the // characters if the comment is the balance of a line. For example, everything after the // in the following is considered a comment:

```
x = (x + 17) / 2              //Figure the new result
```

If your comments are more extensive, then you can add a comment block. Comment blocks are begun with the /* characters and ended with */, as in the following:

```
/* The following code is used to figure
   the current interest rate based on
   the prime rate and a limited set of
   overhead variables. */
```

Example Scripts

Now that you know all the major pieces of JavaScript, and how they fit into your current HTML pages, you are ready to begin putting them all together. The following sections provide some samples of JavaScript and how it can be used in your Web pages.

A Changed Link Page

When you are running an active Web site, there are many times that a page many be no longer available. In these instances, you might want to add a page that provides a forward reference to the new site. Granted, there are ways you can make the user skip to the new site automatically, but this does not provide them the information they need to update their own links.

The following program is quite simple in concept. It displays a welcome message, let's the user know that the page location has changed, and then shows two links that connect the visitor either to the new location or to their previous page (where they came from).

```
<HTML>
<HEAD>
<TITLE>Changed Page Location</TITLE>
</HEAD>

<BODY>

<CENTER><H1>Notice</H1></CENTER>
Thank you for visiting this page. The location of this page has changed.
Please make note of the new location, which is
http://www.dcomp.com/Sundance/JustKids.htm.
Click on one of the links below to either visit the new site or return to your previous
location.
<P>(If your previous location URL is not visible, then your browser does not support
JavaScript.
If this is the case you should click on the Back button on your browser to return to
your
previous site.)

<P><A HREF="http://www.dcomp.com/Sundance/JustKids.htm">New Location</A>
<SCRIPT LANGUAGE="JavaScript">
<!— Begin JavaScript
    document.write("<P>")
    OldPlace = document.referrer
    if (OldPlace.length > 0) {
        document.write("<A HREF='" + OldPlace + "'>" + OldPlace + "</A>")}
        else {
            if (history.length > 1) {
                document.write("<A HREF='' onClick='history.go(-1)' onMouseOver='win-
dow.status='Return to previous page'; return true'>Previous Page</A>")}
                    else {document.write("Sorry, there are no entries in the history
file from which to select.")}}

</BODY>
</HTML>
```

This example does not use any JavaScript functions, but places some JavaScript within the body of the document. It checks to see what the address for the referring document is, and then uses that as a link on the page. The results of the page are shown in Figure 13-6.

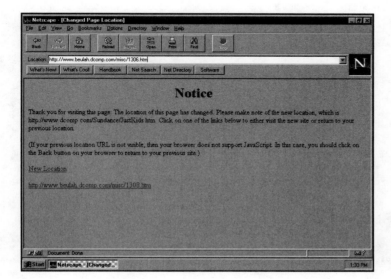

Formatting Input

Many times you need to have input formatted correctly so that it will work properly with a CGI script you may be running. As an example, you may need to format phone numbers so they appear in a certain way. The following page includes JavaScript that will take a user's phone number, format it correctly, and display it on the screen.

```
<HTML>
<HEAD>
<TITLE>Changed Page Location</TITLE>
<SCRIPT LANGUAGE="JavaScript">
<!— Begin JavaScript
    function DoPhone(Raw) {
        FmtPhone = "["
        for (j=0; j < Raw.length; j++) {
            Digit = Raw.substring(j, j+1)
```

```
              if (Digit >= "0") {
                      if (Digit <= "9") {FmtPhone += Digit}}}
       Raw = FmtPhone.substring(1, FmtPhone.length)
       FmtPhone = ""
       j = Raw.length
       if ((j != 7) && (j != 10)) {
               alert("The phone number must be 7 or 10 digits")}
               else{
                 Count = 0
                 for (k=j-1; k >=0; k—) {
                     FmtPhone = Raw.substring(k, k+1) + FmtPhone
                     Count++
                     if (Count == 4) {FmtPhone = "-" + FmtPhone}
                     if (Count == 7) {
                         if (k > 0) {FmtPhone = "-" + FmtPhone}}}}
       return FmtPhone
   }
// End JavaScript —>
</SCRIPT>
</HEAD>


<BODY>


<CENTER><H1>Enter Phone Number</H1></CENTER>


<FORM NAME="GetPhone" METHOD="POST">
Enter your phone number: <INPUT NAME="RawPhone" TYPE="TEXT"><BR>
<INPUT TYPE="BUTTON" VALUE="Format"
OnClick="document.GetPhone.DonePhone.value=DoPhone(document.GetPhone.RawPhone.value)">
<HR><P>Formatted output: <INPUT NAME="DonePhone" TYPE="TEXT"><HR>


</BODY>
</HTML>
```

When you display this page, there is a text input box and a submission button. (This button is labeled Format on the form.) When you enter a phone number in the text box, then click on the button, the formatted phone number appears further down the page. Figure 13-7 shows how this output appears.

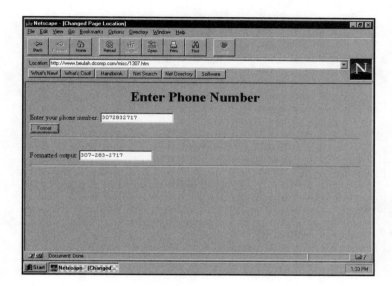

FIGURE 13-7

You can use JavaScript to check and format information before returning to your server.

This program could easily be modified so that the formatted phone number is sent to a different location, such as your server for processing by a CGI script. You can also add additional formatting routines by using the same techniques demonstrated in this code.

Summary

JavaScript is a big step forward in creating dynamic content pages for your Web site. The reason is that you can "offload" quite a bit of the processing from your server to the remote browser. This also allows faster response times to your site's visitors.

In this chapter, you have learned the basics of JavaScript. Entire books could (and have) been written on this subject, so the information provided here is just enough to whet your appetite for more. If you find you want to know more, this chapter provided references to some on-line sources of information, or you can visit your local bookstore.

In the next chapter, you are introduced to yet another potential development environment for your Web server—Java.

Chapter | 14

Working with Java

If you have been browsing the Web for a while, or you have been keeping tabs on the Internet in the popular media, you have probably heard Java mentioned at least in passing. Java seems to be very popular among Internet developers. In this chapter you will learn how you can start to use Java to develop your own programs.

Remember that this chapter provides only an introduction to Java. If, after reading through this chapter, you decide you want more detailed information about what Java is and how it can be used, there are many books on the market where you can get more information. In addition, there are many on-line resources available, such as the Website at http://java.sun.com.

In addition, this chapter must assume that you are at least a bit familiar with object-oriented programming concepts, and perhaps with C++ in particular. Were this assumption not made, this chapter could indeed occupy way too much space, up to the better part of this entire book.

What Is Java?

Java is a programming language that was first developed by Sun Microsystems in 1990 under the name of Oak. The language was originally intended for use in embedded systems. (Embedded systems are applications stored on computer chips in devices such as automobiles, home electronics, appliances, etc.) When that use of the language did not pan out, Java was released on the Internet, and the excitement and spread of the language has been phenomenal.

The Java language is a simplified version of C++, so many programmers will feel right at home using it. It is object-oriented, interpreted, secure, portable, and multithreaded. Programs written in Java are stored on the server, downloaded to the browser on demand, and executed within a "virtual machine" on the remote system. The benefit to the developer is that you only need to develop a single time. The virtual machine on each platform takes care of running your program, so you don't need to develop a version for disparate systems, such as Windows, UNIX, Macintosh, etc.

In Chapter 13, "Working with JavaScript," you learned how to develop programs using the JavaScript language. JavaScript is a scripting language developed by Netscape and Sun, and originally called LiveWire. The name was changed to JavaScript, however, when the popularity of Java became evident. While much of the syntax and programming procedure in JavaScript is similar to Java, the two languages are not the same.

The Virtual Machine Concept

As was mentioned in the previous section, Java relies on a concept referred to as a virtual machine. This means that an environment suitable for running Java programs must be created on the host machine where the program will be executed. These days, the virtual Java machine is created by the browser which you are using. For instance, you may have heard that Netscape Navigator 2.0 (or greater) understands Java. This simply means that Navigator creates an environment (a virtual machine) in which a Java program can be executed.

To a programmer, the biggest advantage of this virtual machine concept is that they only need to develop a single version of the program; one designed to run on the virtual machine. This single version can then be executed on a universal virtual machine, even though that virtual machine may be contained within widely different hardware platforms. This means that Java is platform-independent.

If you have used a programming language before, you may be familiar with the traditional write/compile/link/execute cycle. As you develop a program, you must first write it, then compile it, then link it, and finally you can execute it. Each step in the cycle is necessary to produce a program that can be used on the target machine. As illustrated in Figure 14-1, Java changes this development cycle slightly. Now the cycle is write/compile/download/execute. The download and execute phases are handled by the server and browser, while the programmer only needs to write and compile the program (there is no linking necessary).

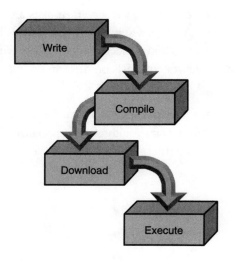

FIGURE 14-1

The Java development cycle is a bit different from the traditional cycle.

Another advantage of the virtual machine is that it means it is harder for unruly programs and viruses to be transmitted to a host system. Since everything runs within a virtual machine, created by software, the added buffer between application and hardware makes spreading viruses much more difficult.

The virtual machine used as a basis for Java allows quite a bit of flexibility, but does have a few drawbacks. The biggest drawback is that programs downloaded from the Internet are not executed directly on the hardware. This means that Java is stored in an intermediate code format that must be translated by the virtual machine into something that can be run on the host system. This translation phase means that Java programs run slower— much slower— than programs compiled and linked to the native format of the host. While this may make huge, monolithic programs impractical in Java, it should not present an insurmountable barrier for most of the smaller programs now beginning to surface on the Net.

Applications vs. Applets

There are two types of programs you can develop using Java. The first is called an application, and the second is called an applet. Applications are full-blown, Internet-aware programs that run within the virtual machine on your system. For instance, you might develop a Java application that is used as a word processor or as a spreadsheet program.

Applets are smaller programs, designed to perform limited tasks or to add flavor to a Web page. For instance, a Java applet might be used to add animation to a Web page or to check information before it is transmitted back to your server. Applets are stored at your Web site the same as any other resource, such as a graphic file or a sound clip. When the applet is referenced in an HTML page, it is downloaded to the browser without intervention by the Web server. If a Java environment exists on the remote system, then the applet is executed.

This chapter focuses on how to use Java to create applets. If you want to know how to create larger, more demanding applications, you should refer to specialized books or to programming resources available on the Internet.

Server-Side vs. Client-Side

As you read about Java programs, you may also see reference to server-side and client-side programs. Server-side simply means that the Java program is executed on the server, with some amount of interfacing going on with the client. A client-side program is the opposite, with all processing taking place on the client's machine. In today's Internet environment, most Java programs are applets, and all applets are client-based. Most Webmasters want to off-load processing from their server, and thus choose Java programs that will place the computing burden on the client.

The exception to this is when developing intranets. In an intranet, where the community of users is smaller and more homogenous, there are advantages in creating server-side applications. These allow a certain amount of centralized control over processing.

The Building Blocks

Java has many features which can be considered building blocks of the language. These features will be familiar to those acquainted with C or C++, and very similar to the features of JavaScript, discussed in Chapter 13, "Working with JavaScript."

Data Types

There are three data types which can be used in Java: numerics, characters, and booleans. A numeric is any value treated as a number. Numerics include four types of integers and two types of real numbers, as detailed in Table 14-1.

Table 14-1 Numeric data types in Java.

Type	Category	Size
byte	integer	8 bits
short	integer	16 bits
int	integer	32 bits
long	integer	64 bits
float	real	16 bits
double	real	64 bits

Characters are not a category of data types (as were numerics), but a single data type. In traditional C or C++, the char data type was used for 8-bit unsigned values which represented ASCII characters. In Java, the char data type represents a 16-bit Unicode character. This is the same character representation code used in many operating systems, including Windows NT and Windows 95.

The boolean data type is used for logical operations. A boolean value can have either the value true or the value false; there are no other values.

Operators

The operator set utilized in Java is virtually identical to what is used in C and C++. Table 14-2 shows the various operators you can use, along with their meanings.

Table 14-2   Java operators.

Operator	Meaning
=	Assignment
+	Addition (for numbers) or concatenation (for strings)
-	Subtraction (as in 1+2) or negation (as in -3)
*	Multiplication
/	Division
%	Modulus (the remainder after an integer division)
++	Increment
—	Decrement
&&	Logical AND
||	Logical OR
!	Logical NOT
<	Logical less than
>	Logical greater than
==	Logical equal
>=	Logical greater than or equal
<=	Logical less than or equal
!=	Logical not equal
&	Bitwise AND
|	Bitwise OR

Operator	Meaning
^	Bitwise XOR
<<	Bitwise left shift
>>	Bitwise right shift with sign propagation
>>>	Bitwise right shift with zero propagation

Arrays and Strings

Arrays and strings are handled in the same manner as under JavaScript. Both arrays and strings are objects in Java, and are handled as such by the language. This is a departure from the treatment of these items in both C and C++.

Objects, Objects, Objects

Everything in the world of Java is object oriented; that point cannot be stressed enough. In fact, the only thing that is not an object is the primitive data types discussed earlier in the chapter. Everything else is treated as an object, so you (as a programmer) must be familiar with how objects work. If you are familiar with procedural programming (starting at point A, proceeding to point B, on the way to a result C), but have not learned object-oriented programming (OOP), you may be in for a shock. Learning OOP is like stepping into an alien world in which there are some things that look familiar, but they don't act like they did in your previous world.

While such a transition can be disorienting, it is not necessarily fatal. More often than not, it simply means becoming familiar with the new world and adapting your mindset to the environment. Many texts that teach object-oriented concepts refer to a "steep learning curve" when learning an OOP language. For many people, this may be an understatement. If you are already familiar with an OOP language, then you may not have as many problems adapting to Java. On the other hand, if you are not familiar with OOP, then you may find it a small consolation that Java is not as ambiguous, complex, or overwhelming as some OOP languages (such as C++). Thus, you may find it easier to learn.

In order to understand OOP in relation to Java, you need to understand some of the terminology which Java uses. The following sections discuss classes, objects, instance variables, methods, interfaces, and packages.

Classes and Objects

An integral concept of OOP, classes can best be thought of as templates for objects. Looked at hierarchically, objects inherit all the design attributes of the class to which they belong. If you change the class definition, you automatically change the objects which belong to the class.

Objects are instances of a class. This concept can perhaps be better understood by saying that you are an instance of a human. Humans, as a class, have many characteristics. For instance, a head, hair, nose, mouth, torso, arms, legs, toes, fingers, and so on. You, as an instance of a human, are assumed to have all the general characteristics of the class (human), but may have your own variations on the model. For example, you may have a nose, but it may be a flat nose, curly hair, stubby arms, and long legs. Rather than being created from scratch, you are an object created from parents, much as you can create Java objects from the template known as a class.

Java also allows you to create subclasses, which are new classes derived from existing classes. For example, let's say you created a class known as buildings. This class might define characteristics such as dimensions, number of windows, building material, and the like. You could create an object from this class, and the object instance would define a particular building. However, you might want to create a new class to describe a house. Understanding that houses are buildings, you can define the house class as being derived from the buildings class. It would inherit all the characteristics of the original, or base, class, plus any new characteristics you wanted to add. For instance, you might define characteristics of chimney, shrubs, utility room, kitchen, etc.

Instance Variables and Methods

Objects consist of two things: instance variables and methods. Instance variables are the data intrinsic to an object; these define the state of the object. If desired, you can think of instance variables as properties or characteristics of the object. In the previous section, you learned that you are an object of the human class. Your characteristics are described by your instance variables, which describe your condition at any given point.

The other part of objects are known as methods. These describe actions which define an object's behavior. This is the part of the object that is defined by programming code. It makes sense that different objects would necessarily have different methods. For example, if you created an object that represented a car, it would have different methods (accelerate, turn, stop, etc.) than an object representing a telephone (ring, dial, flash, etc.).

To bring the example begun in the previous section full circle, we started with the human class. Your parents represent an instance of that class, and are objects in their own right. Your parents have many instance variables associated with them, such as hair color, eye color, height, weight, temperament, etc. In addition, they also have many methods associated with them. To be simplistic, these might include eat, sleep, age, stand, sit, and conceive. When the conceive method was utilized, a new object of the human class (you) was created. You inherited many of the attributes (instance variables) of your parents, and pretty much the same methods. An OOP language such as Java works in much the same way as this analogy.

Interfaces

Java does not allow multiple inheritance, as does C++. (Multiple inheritance means that an object can inherit instance variables and methods from more than one class.) This exclusion actually makes programming in Java much less esoteric, much easier, and less potentially confusing.

There may be times, however, when you need to use methods across a number of objects. This can be done with what Java refers to as an interface. An interface is a collection of methods and constants that one or more classes can use. The method cannot contain any instance variables, only constants, or actual program code to implement a method. It only contains the declaration of a method which is later implemented by the instance object of the class that uses the interface.

Packages

Packages can best be viewed as collections of classes. In this way, they are very similar to libraries in other computer languages. Java comes with seven built-in packages:

- *java.applet.* This package consists of classes needed to create applets that can be executed under Java-compatible browsers.
- *java.awt.* This package consists of classes used to create GUI applications.
- *java.io.* This package consists of classes used for I/O operations.
- *java.lang.* This package consists of the base classes common to implementing the Java language. (If you use Java, you automatically use this package.)
- *java.net.* This package consists of the classes used for making network connections.

- ◆ *java.util.* This package consists of miscellaneous classes not contained in the other packages.

Memory Management

Unlike C, C++, and many other languages, Java takes care of all memory management for you. This is a great time-saving feature for programmers. Traditionally, quite a bit of a programmer's time was spent allocating memory, tracking it to make sure it was still being used, and then freeing that memory when it was no longer needed. Under Java, memory management is handled by the virtual machine environment.

Since everything in Java is considered an object (except for primitive data types), and you must create objects using the new keyword, Java keeps tabs on the objects for you. When you are no longer using the object, the memory previously allocated to the object is reclaimed and made available for other uses. This automatic memory management has been referred to as garbage collection in other languages (such as the original interpreted BASIC), and is touted as a feature in Java. The difference is that when garbage collection occurred in these older languages, the performance of the program suffered. Because Java is multithreaded, the garbage collection routines are always running as a low-priority background thread. In other words, Java is always collecting unused memory and adding it to the memory pool. This allows for better overall performance and a higher degree of system optimization.

Developing Java Programs

In order to develop Java programs, you need a compiler that will translate your source code into Java bytecode. This bytecode is what is interpreted, at run time, by the virtual machine environment discussed earlier in the chapter.

There are several Java compilers on the market, with more becoming available every day. For instance, Borland provides a Java compiler with the Development Suite of their latest C++ compiler. In addition, Microsoft has stated that they will provide Java compatibility with future versions of their programming products. Perhaps the best, easiest, and least-expensive place to get a compiler, however, is from the Sun web site. The Java Developers Kit (JDK) is available by connecting to http://java.sun.com/java.sun.com/general-binary-license.html. As described at the site, you need to accomplish the following steps to use the JDK (assuming you have no previous version of the JDK on your system):

1. Download the file JDK file (approximately 3.8 MB).
2. Unpack the JDK.
3. Update your environment variables.

The first two items are easy; you simply need to connect to the Web site, download the file with your browser, and run the file from within the directory where you want it to be located. (The JDK is stored in a self-extracting archive file. When fully unpacked, it consumes about 5.5 MB of disk space.)

The final item involves adding the /java/bin directory to your system path. Assuming you are using Windows NT 4.0, you do this by right-clicking on the My Computer icon on your desktop. This displays the System Properties dialog box, and you should click on the Environment tab. The System Properties dialog box now appears as shown in Figure 14-2.

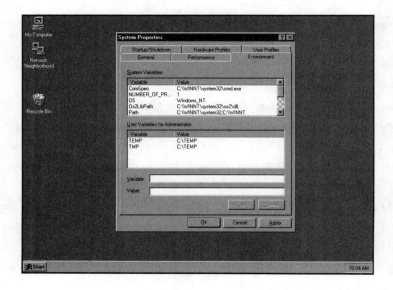

FIGURE 14-2

The Environment tab of the System Properties dialog box allows you to change Windows NT operating parameters.

At the bottom of the <u>S</u>ystem Variables list is the system path. Click on the word Path, in the <u>V</u>ariable column. This changes both the <u>V</u>ariable and Va<u>l</u>ue fields at the bottom of the dialog box. Modify the Va<u>l</u>ue field by adding the following to the end of the information in the field:

```
;d:\java\bin
```

If you are using a different directory for your \java directory, then you should substitute it for this example. When you have made this change, click on the S<u>e</u>t button. The path information in the <u>S</u>ystem Variables list should now reflect your modification. You can click on the OK button to save your changes.

The Java Developers Kit does not use a graphical interface, instead it is used from the command line. (Those who have been programming for some time may remember when all development tools used the command line instead of a GUI.) The JDK includes the following elements:

- *Compiler.* This program (javac.exe) allows you to create Java bytecode from your source code.

- *Interpreter.* This program (java.exe) allows you to test your Java programs. (It creates the virtual machine described earlier in the chapter.)

- *Debugger.* This program (jdb.exe) allows you to track and isolate errors in your programs.

- *Disassembler.* This program (javap.exe) allows you to disassemble previously compiled Java bytecode.

- *Documenter.* This program (javadoc.exe) allows you to create summary documentation files from the comments in your source code.

- *Header and Stub Creator.* This program (javah.exe) uses your source files to create C header files and stub files necessary for interfacing Java with C programs.

- *Applet Viewer.* This program (appletviewer.exe) allows you to view applets, which are normally only viewable through browsers such as Netscape Navigator.

To test whether you have installed the JDK correctly, change to the \java\demo\tictactoe directory and enter the following at the command line:

```
appletviewer example1.html
```

You should see a window containing a copyright notice (this notice won't appear on subsequent uses of the Applet Viewer). When you click on the Accept button, you will see the Applet Viewer window, as shown in Figure 14-3.

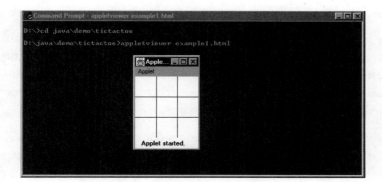

FIGURE 14-3

If the JDK is installed correctly, you should be able to use the Applet Viewer.

This applet allows you to play tic-tac-toe against the program. Click on a position on the board, and continue to play by using the mouse. This type of applet could just as easily be available from your own Web pages. Remember that the applet would be a program running on the user's browser, not on your server. Thus, you have provided a new level of interactivity by providing applets at your site.

Creating Your First Java Applet

Now that you have all the building blocks of a Java program, you are ready to dive into the deep end of the pool and create your first Java applet. For this example, we will create an applet that displays a simple text message. This applet is created as follows:

```
// Simple Java applet

import java.awt.*;
import java.applet.*;

public class NewApplet extends Applet {
    Font BigFont = new Font("Ariel", Font.BOLD, 24);
    public void paint(Graphics Out) {
```

```
        Out.setColor(Color.red);
        Out.setFont(BigFont);
        Out.drawString("Here We Are!", 15, 50);
    }
}
```

This applet may be very short, but it illustrates the way in which the vast majority of applets are created. The applet begins with a comment, indicating the purpose of the applet (single-line comments begin with the // convention). Immediately after that is two commands to include two Java packages in our code. These commands use the import keyword, followed by the name of the packages to include.

Next is the definition of the public class to be used for our applet. This class name, NewApplet, must match the name of the file in which this code appears. Thus, the NewApplet class must be stored in the file called NewApplet.java. When the file is compiled, the file NewApplet.class is created.

The next line is used to create an object:

```
Font BigFont = new Font("Ariel", Font.BOLD, 24);
```

This line effectively tells the compiler to create a new Font object, named BigFont. When creating the object, some of the font attributes (instance variables of the object) are set by using the parameters used in the command line. When this command is complete, you are left with a 24-point bold Ariel font, all contained within an object named BigFont. This object will be used just a bit later in the applet.

Next, the applet includes its only method:

```
public void paint(Graphics Out) {
        Out.setColor(Color.red);
        Out.setFont(BigFont);
        Out.drawString("Here We Are!", 15, 50);
    }
```

This method, which belongs to the NewApplet class, creates a Graphics object, in this case named Out, and then uses that object in the completion of the method. The first line of the method sets the color of Out, using SetColor, which is a method of the Out object. The next line uses the SetFont method (again, a method of the Out object) to set the font equal to the BigFont object which was created earlier. The final line uses the drawString method to actually write the text. The text is within the applet window at a horizontal offset of 15 pixels and a vertical offset of 50 pixels. This location defines the point where the lower-left corner of the text appears.

Compiling the Applet

To compile the applet, make sure it is saved in a file called NewApplet.java, as described in the previous section. Then, open a Windows command-line window, change to the directory where the source code file is located, and enter the following at the command prompt:

```
javac NewApplet.java
```

Make sure you enter the command line exactly as it appears here. If you don't, you will get an error message. For instance, Figure 14-4 shows what happens if you even use improper capitalization on the command line.

FIGURE 14-4

The Java compiler is very picky about spelling, punctuation, and capitalization.

If you get an error after using the javac command, then you should check to make sure everything in the source code file is spelled correctly and that you have entered the command line properly.

When the compiler is completed, a new file appears in the directory. This file has the same root name as the original file (NewApplet), but a different extension (class). This is the Java bytecode file which is used by the browser to display the Java program.

Adding the Applet to a Web Page

Including applets in your Web pages is a simple process, using much the same steps you use to include graphics, audio, or video files. For this example, the Web page can be very simple, as shown here:

```
<HTML>
<HEAD>
<TITLE>First Java Try</TITLE>
</HEAD>

<BODY>
<HR>
<APPLET CODE="NewApplet.class" WIDTH=175 HEIGHT=50>
Can you see this Java applet?
</APPLET>
<HR>
</BODY>
</HTML>
```

There isn't much in the body of this document, other than the <APPLET> and </APPLET> tag pair. Everything between this pair is assumed to be used for the Java applet which it identifies. In the <APPLET> tag, the CODE attribute is used to define the name of the applet's bytecode file. The WIDTH and HEIGHT attributes define the size of the window, in pixels, where the applet will be displayed.

Another interesting thing to note here is the addition of the following line within the applet definition:

```
Can you see this Java applet?
```

Remember that when a browser encounters tags it cannot understand, it ignores them. Thus, if the browser doesn't understand Java, it will ignore the <APPLET> and </APPLET> tags. It will, however, display the text in between. Thus, the message is only seen if the browser does not understand Java. If it does understand Java, then the browser assumes that the message is to be parsed by the Java interpreter. The interpreter, however, effectively ignores everything except a very limited number of keywords. Thus, the Java interpreter ignores the message and does not display it.

In order to make the Java applet run properly, you need to place the class file (in this case, NewApplet.class) in the location specified by the CODE attribute in the <APPLET> tag. Since this example does not indicate any different path for the file (or a different URL), then NewApplet.class should reside in the same directory as the HTML file from which it is called. When someone access this small HTML file, the see a Web page that has the Java file included (as shown in Figure 14-5).

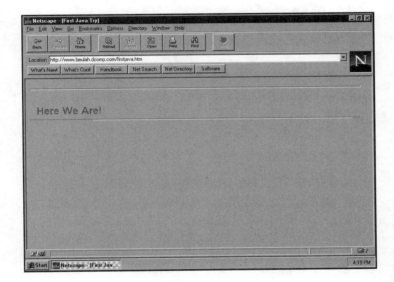

FIGURE 14-5

The results of a Java applet are displayed by a Java-enabled browser.

A More Elaborate Java Applet

You can get as elaborate with your Java applets as you want, and you probably will get much more elaborate as your needs and skills increase. For the next example here, let's look at an applet that loads a company logo and plays an audio file. The applet appears as follows:

```
/* Java applet to display the DCI
   logo and play a sound */


import java.awt.*;
import java.applet.*;


public class DCILogo1 extends Applet {
```

```java
// Panels and canvases that the applet uses
Canvas c_north = null;

// Images and sounds the applet uses
Image img = null;
AudioClip sound = null;

// MediaTracker class ID numbers
static final int STARTUP_ID    = 0;
static final int BACKGROUND_ID = 1;
static final int ANIMATION_ID  = 2;

// The background color
Color bkgnd;

// Initialize the applet
public void init() {
    // Set up the display
    setLayout(new BorderLayout());
    c_north = new Canvas();
    add("North", c_north);

    // Load image and sound
    MediaTracker tracker = new MediaTracker(this);
    showStatus("Loading image from SmDCILogo.gif");
    img = getImage(getCodeBase(), "SmDCILogo.gif");
    tracker.addImage(img, STARTUP_ID);
    showStatus("");
    try {tracker.waitForID(STARTUP_ID);}
    catch (InterruptedException e) {System.out.println("Could not load image!");}
    showStatus("Loading sound from DCIAudio.au");
    sound = getAudioClip(getCodeBase(), "DCIAudio.au");
    showStatus("");
}
```

```
    public void start() {
        sound.play();
    }

    public void stop() {
        sound.stop();
    }

    public void paint(Graphics g) {
        if (img != null) {
            g.drawImage(img, 0, 0, getBackground(), c_north);
        }
    }
}
```

Right off the bat you can tell that this applet is a bit more complex. For one thing, it is quite a bit longer than the previous applet. Regardless of this, the applet has the same general construction as the previous applet.

Applet Methods

The biggest difference is that this applet defines additional methods for use by the DCILogo1 class. These include the following:

- init()
- start()
- stop()
- paint()

The final method should look familiar; it was used in the earlier applet. The other methods may require some explanation, however. When a Java applet is first loaded by a browser, it runs the init() method. This method, if not defined in your applet, is defined in the Applet class from which your new class is derived. Normally the init() method does nothing, but you can override the default init() by including your own version of init(), as is done in this example.

What should you do in the init() method? Typically, you should set your initial values which you need for the balance of your applet. In this example, the display is set up, the MediaTrack object (provided with Java) is initialized, the image and sound files are loaded.

The other methods, start() and stop(), are called when the page is loaded and discarded, respectively. This means that you can control exactly what happens when the page containing the reference to the applet is loaded simply by changing the contents of the start() method. Conversely, this means you should close down anything that the applet was doing by using the stop() method.

There is one other method that is common to all applets, but is not used in this particular example. The destroy() method can also be used to perform any last-minute clean-up prior to the applet being cleared from memory. This is different than the stop() applet, which is called when the page is left.

The HTML Document

After compiling the DCILogo1.java file and moving it to the directory from where it will be referenced, you are ready to insert it into a Web document. The Web document used for this invocation is as follows:

```
<HTML>
<HEAD>
<TITLE>Discovery Computing Inc.</TITLE>
<META NAME="description" CONTENT="Home page for Discovery Computing, Inc., a company
specializing in providing information services.">
<META NAME="keywords" CONTENT="computer books consulting programming technical editing
Sundance Wyoming WY Web Advertising fulfillment distribution writing authoring">
</HEAD>

<BODY>
<CENTER>
<APPLET CODE="DCILogo1.class" WIDTH=301 HEIGHT=139>
<IMG SRC="SmDCILOGO.gif">
</APPLET>
<H1>Welcome to Discovery Computing Inc.</H1>
```

```
</CENTER>

Discovery Computing Inc. (DCI) is a multi-faceted company providing a host of services
to many different companies and individuals. As a corporation, we have been in business
for just under ten years, helping many companies solve problems, increase sales, and
improve productivity.

<P>In essence, our services can be boiled down to the following:
<UL>
<LI><A HREF="/DCI/Authoring.Htm">Authoring</A>
<LI><A HREF="/DCI/Consulting.Htm">Consulting</A>
<LI><A HREF="/DCI/PubServices.Htm">Publishing Services</A>
<LI><A HREF="/DCI/Fulfillment.Htm">Order Fulfillment</A>
<LI><A HREF="/DCI/WebAdvertising.Htm">Internet Advertising</A>
</UL>

<P>If you want to contact us, check out our <A HREF="/DCI/mail.htm">e-mail
directory</A>.

<P>
<CENTER>
<IMG ALIGN="MIDDLE" SRC="/DCI/Art/NEW02.gif"><STRONG>Check out our on-line <A
HREF="/DCI/MfgList/MfgList.Htm">guide to equipment manufacturers</A>!</STRONG>
</CENTER>

<P><P>Thanks for stopping by our page. While you are at it, check out some of the commu-
nities around our area, including
<A HREF="/Sundance/Sundance.Htm">Sundance</A>,
Hulett,
Moorcroft, and
<A HREF="/Aladdin/Aladdin.Htm">Aladdin</A>.
Each of these are in beautiful
<A HREF="/CrookCounty/Crook.htm">Crook County</A>, Wyoming.
(If you would like to understand one of the big reasons DCI is located in this
area, click <A HREF="/Sundance/Business.Htm">here</A>.)
```

```
<P>You might also like to see some of our <A HREF="/DCI/FavoriteWeb.Htm">favorite web
sites</A>.

<P>
<CENTER>
<IMG SRC = "/DCI/Art/rainban.gif">
<ADDRESS>
Discovery Computing Inc.<BR>
20101 US Highway 14<BR>
PO Box 738<BR>
Sundance, WY  82729<BR>
800-628-8280<BR>
307-283-2714 (fax)
<P>Send comments to: <A HREF =
"mailto:Webmaster@dcomp.com"><EM>Webmaster@dcomp.com</EM></A>
<P>Copyright © 1996 Discovery Computing Inc. All rights reserved.
</ADDRESS>
</CENTER>

</BODY>
</HTML>
```

This document may look familiar, particularly if you recently read through Chapter 8, "Basic Web Publishing." The difference is that a Java applet was used for the masthead of the page, rather than a simply in-line image. The result for the end user is the same either way, as you can see from Figure 14-6. The difference is that the Java applet not only loads the logo, but automatically plays a little jingle when the page is first loaded.

An important thing to notice in this Web document is that the HEIGHT and WIDTH attributes of the <APPLET> tag have been changed to reflect the exact size of the graphic to be displayed. This may not be obvious from looking at the code, but the size was determined by using a graphics program to see what the dimensions of the graphic were, and then these numbers were used in the <APPLET> tag. Had this not been done, then the logo might have appeared cut off or odd sized.

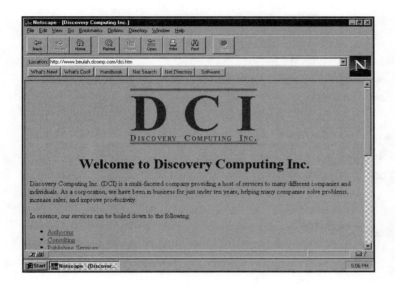

FIGURE 14-6

Java applets need not do anything terribly fancy to be useful.

Passing Parameters to Applets

It is not uncommon to develop applets that are meant to work in a wide variety of situations. For instance, in the previous section you examined an applet that was created to load a logo and play a sound clip. By making the applet a bit more generic, you could easily use it to load any graphic and play any tune. The following shows the modified applet source code to achieve this:

```java
/* Java applet to display a graphic
   file and play a sound file */


import java.awt.*;
import java.applet.*;


public class DCILogo2 extends Applet {
    // URLs
    private String img_url = null;
    private String sound_url = null;


    // Panels and canvases that the applet uses
```

```
Canvas c_north = null;

// Images and sounds the applet uses
Image img = null;
AudioClip sound = null;

// MediaTracker class ID numbers
static final int STARTUP_ID    = 0;
static final int BACKGROUND_ID = 1;
static final int ANIMATION_ID  = 2;

// The background color
Color bkgnd;

// Initialize the applet
public void init() {
    // Set up the display
    setLayout(new BorderLayout());
    c_north = new Canvas();
    add("North", c_north);

    // Read in the parameters from the Web page
    img_url = getParameter("picture");
    sound_url = getParameter("sound");

    // Load image and sound
    MediaTracker tracker = new MediaTracker(this);
    showStatus("Loading image from " + img_url);
    img = getImage(getCodeBase(), img_url);
    tracker.addImage(img, STARTUP_ID);
    showStatus("");
    try {tracker.waitForID(STARTUP_ID);}
    catch (InterruptedException e) {System.out.println("Could not load image!");}
    showStatus("Loading sound from " + sound_url);
```

```
        sound = getAudioClip(getCodeBase(), sound_url);
        showStatus("");
    }

    public void start() {
        sound.play();
    }

    public void stop() {
        sound.stop();
    }

    public void paint(Graphics g) {
        if (img != null) {
            g.drawImage(img, 0, 0, getBackground(), c_north);
        }
    }
}
```

The only real differences between this example and the previous applet is in the init() method. Here the crux of the example can be seen:

```
// Read in the parameters from the Web page
        img_url = getParameter("picture");
        sound_url = getParameter("sound");
```

In these lines, the getParameter method is used to retrieve parameters from the HTML file used to invoke the applet. In the case of the first use of the method, a parameter with the name of picture is stored in the img_url object, and the sound parameter is stored in the sound_url object. These are then used as variables in the lines to load the requested files.

On the Web document side of the fence, the applicable lines of the document look like this:

```
<CENTER>
<APPLET CODE="DCILogo1.class" WIDTH=301 HEIGHT=139>
<PARAM NAME="picture" VALUE="smdcilogo.gif">
```

```
<PARAM NAME="sound" VALUE="haildci.au">
<IMG SRC="SmDCILOGO.gif">
</APPLET>
<H1>Welcome to Discovery Computing Inc.</H1>
</CENTER>
```

Notice the use of the addition of the <PARAM> tags. These tags allow you to define parameters you want passed to your Java applet. The NAME attribute is used to specify the name assigned to the parameter, and the VALUE attribute indicates the value you want assigned to the parameter. Within the applet, as you have already seen, you then use the getParameter() method to retrieve the individual parameters.

A Template for Applets

With the information you have under your belt so far, you are ready to generalize Java applets and make a template. This template can be used as a starting place for all your other applets. The template appears as follows:

```
// Name of Class (the file name and class name must be the same)

/* Description
   Insert a description of your applet here
 */

// Import Necessary Packages
// The java.applet package is always needed. Uncomment
// any other packages you need to include

import java.applet.*;
// import java.awt.*;
// import java.io.*;
// import java.lang.*;
// import java.net.*;
// import java.util.*
```

```
// Start the class definition for the applet
public class Template extends Applet {

    // Insert instance variable declarations

    // Insert methods unique to this new class

    // Methods you might need to override
    public void init() {

    }

    public void start() {

    }

    public void stop() {

    }

    public void destroy() {

    }

    public void paint(Graphics g) {

    }
}           // end the class
```

This template is handy in that it provides a quick outline for your applets. To use the template, you simply need to fill in the information specific to your applet, and in some cases delete information you don't need. For instance, if your applet doesn't need all the packages, then you can delete those you don't need instead of leaving them commented out.

Developing Your Skills

Believe it or not, you now know the basics of how to create Java applets. The best way to learn how to create your own is to simply jump right in and try it out. There are a wide variety of resources you can use to help you out, including the Java Developer's Kit, newsgroups, and additional Web sites.

Resources in the JDK

You learned about the Java Developer's Kit earlier in this chapter. One of the great things about the JDK is that it provides demonstration programs which you can either learn from or use as a basis for your own programs. These demos are included in the java\demo directory, and include the following:

- ◆ *Animator.* This demo animates a series of gif files (up to 10 files). You can control the speed at which each file is displayed, along with the sounds played. This demo is great to use in your own pages, if desired. It helps to examine the source code to see what parameters should be passed from your Web page. There are four examples in this demo (example1.html through example4.html).

- ◆ *ArcTest.* This demo allows user input to specify a starting and ending position for an arc drawn on a grid. Good examples of user input and converting math to drawings.

- ◆ *BarChart.* This demo draws a simple horizontal bar chart. Demonstrates how to draw different color graphics on the page.

- ◆ *Blink.* This is an annoying little demo that graphically displays some text and then sets about making it blink randomly. Illustrates how you can make your text blink, if desired.

- ◆ *CardTest.* This demo shows how to create active buttons and pull-down lists in your applets.

- ◆ *Clock.* This demo displays an analog clock on the screen. This is similar to the Windows clock accessory.

- ◆ *DitherTest.* This demo uses your input for the horizontal and vertical axes and then creates a dithered color pattern to display in the middle of the screen.

Depending on the speed of your machine, displaying the colors may take a while, but provides a good example of user interaction and color capabilities.

◆ *DrawTest.* This demo implements a very rudimentary drawing program in your browser. You can pick different colors to draw with, and then draw lines or points (freehand drawing). Excellent example of non-text interaction with the user.

◆ *Fractal.* This demo displays a simple fractal design on the screen and then proceeds to fill it out. Clicking on the design starts the process over again.

◆ *GraphicsTest.* This demo allows you to create five different types of multi-colored geometric shapes. Allows user input through buttons and a pull-down list. Also shows how to create graphic shapes.

◆ *GraphLayout.* This is a fascinating demo that randomly moves a relational graph around the screen. You can also use the mouse to grab and move elements of the graph, after which the program reacts accordingly. There are four examples in this demo (example1.html through example4.html).

◆ *ImageMap.* This demo shows how to create an image map using Java. Be forewarned that the links are back to the java.sun.com site, so it may take a while to work through them all.

◆ *JumpingBox.* This demo is an interactive game in which you try to click the mouse on a box that is moving around the screen. The game is harder than it sounds, since your mouse movement controls how the box jumps around. Every time you click the mouse button, a sound is played and your results are shown at the bottom of the screen.

◆ *MoleculeViewer.* This demo displays an interactive picture of a molecule. You can click on a part of the image and drag it, which results in the molecule rotating to follow the mouse. There are three examples in this demo (example1.html through example3.html). The rotational feature is easiest to see with example3.html.

◆ *NervousText.* This demo displays a string of neurotic text on the screen. (Looks like it had too much caffeine.)

◆ *SimpleGraph.* This demo is perhaps the simplest one of them all. It draws a line graph based on some trigonometric functions. Entire source code is only 13 lines long.

- ◆ *SortDemo.* This demo graphically demonstrates how three popular sorting algorithms function. It is fascinating to watch how the bubble sort, bi-directional bubble sort, and quick sort do their work. Simply click on a sort graph, and that example is shown.
- ◆ *SpreadSheet.* This demo implements a simple spreadsheet, all within Java.
- ◆ *TicTacToe.* This demo allows you to play tic-tac-toe, complete with sounds. This is the demo you ran earlier in this chapter to check whether the JDK was installed correctly.
- ◆ *WireFrame.* This demo displays wire-frame models of three-dimensional objects. You can turn and rotate the objects by clicking and dragging with the mouse. There are four examples in this demo (example1.html through example4.html).

Each of the demonstrations is in its own directory within the java\demo directory. For instance, the JumpingBox demo is in the java\demo\jumpingbox directory. You can use the Applet Viewer program to look at the examples, or you can make the java\demo directory available from your Web site and view them that way. Unless otherwise noted, each demo consists of a single HTML file named example1.html.

Newsgroups

If you are interested in continuing information and discussion about Java, then the comp.lang.java newsgroup is a great place to visit. You can access this newsgroup through most newsreaders and providers.

Web Sites

There are a number of Web sites which provide good information about Java, as well as numerous examples. Perhaps the two best sites are http://java.sun.com and http://www.gamelan.com. The first is the Sun Microsystems site dedicated to official Java-related documentation and news. The second is not a game site (despite the domain name), but is a site providing an extensive index to Java and JavaScript resources around the Web. The directory for the Gamelan site is shown in Figure 14-7.

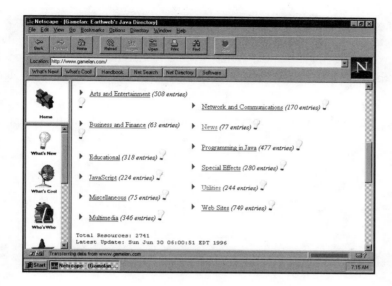

FIGURE 14-7

The Gamelan site provides a wide variety of resources for Java developers.

Additional Web sites you might want to check out include the following:

- http://www.vaxxine.com/candleweb/java/java.html
- http://www.acm.org/~ops/java.html
- http://www.javaworld.com
- http://www.jade.org
- http://www.hamline.edu/personal/matjohns/webdev/java/

Periodically you should also check in with index sites such as Yahoo to see what they have available for Java links, as well.

Summary

Java is a full-blown programming language that is based on C++ and several other languages. It provides a simpler way to implement object-oriented design and to create either full-blown programs or applets. Applets are particularly well suited to use on the Internet, and FastTrack server supports both client-side and server-side Java.

In this chapter, you have had a whirlwind introduction to Java and how you can create your own applets. As with any programming language, there is much more information than can be covered in a single chapter. While the information here provides a good starting place, there are numerous other sources which can be helpful in providing additional information.

In the next chapter, you learn the ways in which you can start to make your Web site secure.

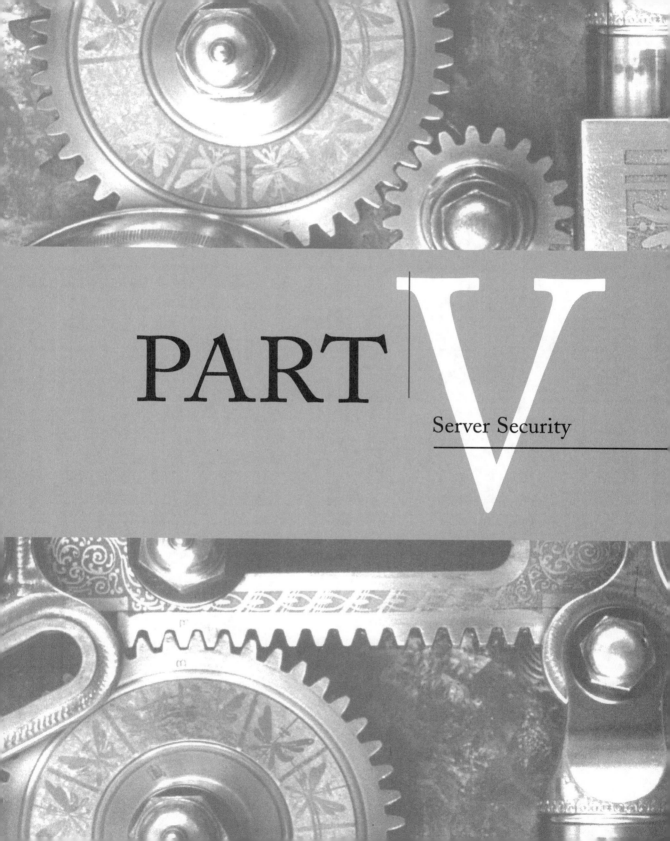

PART V

Server Security

Chapter | 15

Basics of Security

Whenever you make your system available to outside users, you also accept the risks that go along with such availability. Your job, as site administrator, is to ensure that your system is as secure as possible without being an inconvenience to legitimate users from the outside.

This chapter focuses on the basics of securing your system. Predominately, the discussion revolves around security features built into Windows NT and how you can use them effectively. In Chapter 16, "Internet Services and Security," you learn how to apply the concepts in this chapter to your FastTrack server environment.

Windows NT Security

Because Windows NT was designed from the ground up to be a secure system, it includes many intrinsic features that you can use to prevent unauthorized access to your system. These features range from the file system itself to various configuration settings you determine. The next several sections address each of the NT security areas.

The NTFS File System

The Windows NT file system (NTFS) provides additional security not available under other file systems, such as the FAT system used in other versions of Windows. Windows NT allows you to use either the FAT or NTFS system for your drives. If you have been using FAT drives for some time, you may wonder why you should consider NTFS. Here are three reasons:

- Greater security
- More flexible file attributes
- More efficient use of disk space

On the downside, if you convert to NTFS, you can't access the drive after booting to DOS. The only way to access the drive is with Windows NT.

You can create an NTFS drive in two ways. The first is to create the drive from scratch by using the FORMAT command from the command prompt. When you finish creating the drive in this manner, it's empty and ready to accept new information. To create a drive from scratch, enter the following command at the command prompt:

```
FORMAT D: /FS:NTFS
```

This particular example formats the D: drive. If you want to format some other drive, reference the appropriate drive letter. Notice the use of the /FS switch, which enables you to specify the file system to use when formatting.

The other method to create an NTFS drive is to convert an existing drive to NTFS. This option is appropriate if you already have a lot of data saved on a drive using the FAT file system. When you are done creating a drive in this manner, you not only have an NTFS volume, but you also have all your data stored on that volume. To create an NTFS drive, enter the following command from the command prompt:

```
CONVERT D: /FS:NTFS
```

As you can see, the syntax of this command is very similar to that used for the FORMAT command.

Setting Effective Account Policies

In the Windows NT environment, you can set policies that apply to all user accounts that you establish. Because these policies are used as the default values for any new accounts, they should represent the rules you want applied to most of your users.

> **NOTE:** You may wonder why I'm discussing account policies before discussing user accounts. The reason is that account policies affect all your accounts, and are therefore more fundamental than the accounts themselves.

Account policies are established (or changed) with the User Manager program. To display the Account Policy dialog box, follow these steps:

1. Choose the Programs option from the Start menu. This displays the Programs menu.

2. Choose the Administrative Tools (Common) option from the Programs menu. This displays a list of system administration tools installed on your system.

3. Click on the User Manager for Domains option. This opens the User Manager window (which is discussed fully later in this chapter).

4. Choose the Account option from the Policies menu. This action displays the Account Policy dialog box, as shown in Figure 15-1.

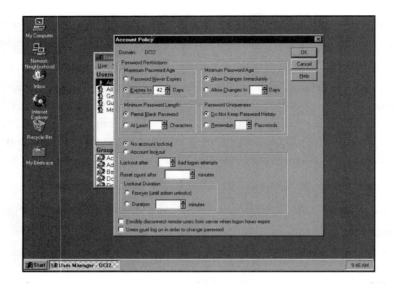

Using this dialog box, you can establish policies that govern the use of passwords, as well as how the system reacts to the passwords. Notice that the dialog box contains two parts; both parts are discussed in the following sections.

Password Restrictions

Passwords are the primary security feature for user accounts under Windows NT. Using the Account Policy dialog box, you can indicate the following information:

- ◆ *When and if passwords expire.* The related fields allow you to set a minimum and maximum age for passwords. Generally, the more often you force passwords to be changed, the more secure your system.

- ◆ *How long passwords must be.* You can indicate a minimum length for the passwords, and also indicate whether blank passwords are acceptable.

- ◆ *Whether passwords must be unique.* This area controls how often a user can reuse the same password. Thus, if you stipulate that the system remember four passwords, it will allow a user to reuse the same password only after she has used three other passwords.

If you want to make your system secure, consider the following settings as a starting point. Some systems may require that you become even more strict; it all depends on the sensitivity of your data and the perceived threat from outsiders.

◆ *Maximum Password Age.* In this area of the dialog box, set the age to no more than 28 days. You should never select Password <u>N</u>ever Expires. If passwords never expire, it provides a "stationary target" for people trying to break into your system.

◆ *Minimum Password Age.* In this area, select the <u>A</u>llow Changes Immediately radio button.

◆ *Minimum Password Length.* The longer your password, the more secure your system, but the harder it is to remember your password. A good compromise is to require a length of at least six characters.

◆ *Password Uniqueness.* Force a password history of at least four passwords; even better is six passwords.

At the very bottom of the Account Policy dialog box is a check box that controls how users change their passwords. In a secure system, you probably want users to log on before changing passwords, so this check box should be selected. If you don't select the check box, the user can change her password from the Windows NT logon screen, provided that her password has expired. The upshot of selecting this check box is that if a user's account expires, she must contact the network administrator to clear her account before she can log on and change her password.

Account Lockout

The bottom portion of the Account Policy dialog box is where you can set account lockout information. The settings in this area control how Windows NT reacts to unsuccessful logon attempts. If someone unauthorized is attempting to get into your system, he may try several passwords that he thinks are most likely for a given account. You can instruct the system to lock out any user after unsuccessful attempts.

Turning on the lockout feature is a good idea. A good compromise between human users (who can mistype entries) and security needs is to lock a workstation after three failed attempts. The lockout duration should also be of such a length that it discourages the user from waiting around; 15 or 20 minutes should do the trick.

Understanding User Accounts

If you have been using Windows NT for any length of time, you are probably familiar with user accounts. Users are the heart of any network, and you need to set up a user account for each person using your network on a regular basis. Some software (including FastTrack) may set up special user accounts so they can run on the system properly.

You already know that the User Manager is the tool with which you set up, change, and otherwise manage your user accounts. You also use it to do the same actions with group accounts, which are discussed in the next section. To start the User Manager, follow these steps:

1. Choose the <u>P</u>rograms option from the Start menu. This displays the Programs menu.

2. Choose the Administrative Tools (Common) option from the Programs menu.

3. Click on the User Manager for Domains option. Shortly the User Manager appears, as shown in Figure 15-2.

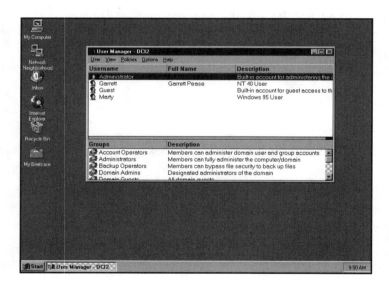

FIGURE 15-2

The User Manager enables you to control users who have access to your system.

NOTE: To get the full effect from User Manager, you need Administrator privileges. If you have lesser privileges, User Manager allows you to make changes only in accounts with fewer privileges than yours.

The User Manager itself reflects the fact that you can work with both users and groups. Users are shown in the top part of the window, and groups in the bottom. If you want to make changes to a user account, all you need to do is highlight the account name and then choose the action you want to perform.

If you need to set up a new user account, choose New Underline User from the Underline User menu. This action displays the New User dialog box, as shown in Figure 15-3.

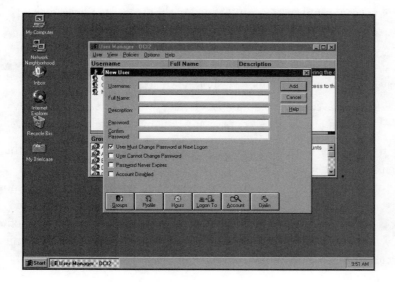

FIGURE 15-3

The New User dialog box is used to define a new system user.

The minimum amount of information you need to set up an account is a user ID and a password. (The user ID is placed in the Username field, and the password is placed in both the Password and Confirm Password fields.) To add a bit of security to your system, however, you will want to provide additional information for your new users. For example, you may want to set some of the following fields in the New User dialog box:

◆ *Full Name.* Use this field to note the user's full name, which is probably different from the user ID. This field isn't particularly critical to security.

◆ *Description.* This field can include any comments you want to note about the user or the account. This information isn't crucial to security.

◆ *User Must Change Password at Next Logon.* When selected, this option forces the user to change her password the next time she logs on. This is a good security feature, as it forces the user to choose her own password—one you don't even know.

♦ ***User Cannot Change Password.*** If the account is set up for a short duration or for the use of some software program, you probably don't want the user to change the password. Selecting this check box makes the password permanent.

♦ ***Password Never Expires.*** When this check box is selected, it overrides the length of account information you defined in the Account Policies dialog box (described earlier in this chapter). If you allow the password to expire, but the user can't change her password, you have made a limited-duration account that the user can't do anything about. This approach is very handy if you have users who need temporary, short-term access to your system.

♦ ***Account Disabled.*** When this option is selected, the account is temporarily disabled. You can enable the account at any time by clearing the check box.

Clicking the Groups button at the bottom of the dialog box allows you to specify the groups to which this user belongs. (Groups are described in the following section.) Clicking the Profile button enables you to define a log-in profile for the user. For those familiar with Novell or UNIX networking, this involves the use of log-in scripts and home directories. This feature is a valuable benefit when dealing with a collection of users that you don't want to have access to your entire system. Using profiles, you can limit access for those users to a smaller portion of your system.

When you are finished setting up the account, click the Add button. The user's name then appears in the User Manager window. If you later want to change anything for the user, simply double-click on the user's name.

Working with User Groups

As you have learned so far, each Windows NT user must have an account, and users must belong to at least one group. A group is used to define common rights and privileges that belong to a number of different users.

If you want to make changes to a group, you do it using the same methods as for users—you highlight the group name, and then choose the action you want to perform.

You may have two different types of groups defined on your system:

♦ A *local group* has rights only on your local computer.

♦   A *global group* has rights across all the computers in your workgroup (or
    domain).

Global groups are differentiated from local groups in the User Manager by the icon that
appears to the left of the group name. Windows NT comes with a wide array of groups
already defined. This setup can be a time-saver when working with a local area network.
From a security standpoint, however, it has a drawback. Because the groups are predefined, anyone can know what the groups are. If you want a very secure system, you should
change all the predefined user groups to group names that are unique to your site. You
can also remove any groups that you don't need or don't expect to need.

> **NOTE:** You need the Administrators group to run Windows NT properly. Don't try
> to delete it or change its name.

To add a new group, choose New Local Group from the User menu. This option displays
the dialog box shown in Figure 15-4.

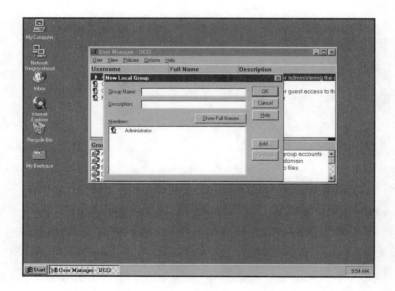

FIGURE 15-4

*Use the New Local Group
dialog box to define a new
group.*

All you need to do is supply the name of the new group in the Group Name field, and (if
desired) provide a Description of the group. Clicking the Add and Remove buttons
enables you to add and remove the initial users of the group. (Remember that you can

always change the group composition later, as well.) When you are satisfied with the composition of the group, click OK.

To grant rights to your groups, use the U̲ser Rights option from the P̲olicies menu, as discussed in the next section.

Understanding User Rights

The simplest definition of *user rights* is that they control who can do what on your network. Because you access user rights by using the P̲olicies menu, some people view user rights as being global in nature. In one sense they are, as the rights possessed by a user can be used anywhere within the network. But it's better to look at rights as being expansive. If a user starts with no rights, he can do very little in your system or network. As rights are added, however, his capacity to affect the environment and other accounts increases.

You define the rights assigned to a group or individual by selecting the U̲ser Rights option from the P̲olicies menu in the User Manager. This selection displays the small dialog box shown in Figure 15-5.

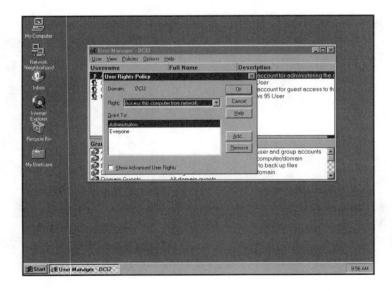

FIGURE 15-5

In the User Rights Policy dialog box, you can define how users can affect your system or network.

The User Rights Policy dialog box is quite simple to use; not much is available to change in the dialog box. Basically, setting user rights is a two-step process:

1. Select a right from the pull-down list at the top of the dialog box.
2. Decide whether the groups or users at the bottom of the dialog box should have that particular right.

If you don't like which users or groups possess a certain right, use the <u>A</u>dd and <u>R</u>emove buttons to adjust those shown in the list. When you click the <u>A</u>dd button, you see the dialog box shown in Figure 15.6.

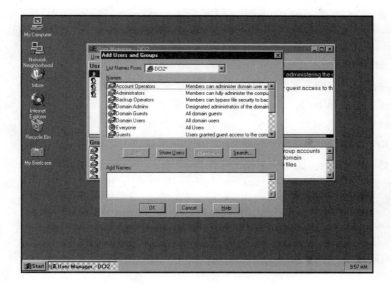

FIGURE 15-6

In the Add Users and Groups dialog box, you specify which users have a certain right.

The Add Users and Groups dialog box is very powerful. Using this dialog box, you can select which groups should be granted the particular right you selected. When you assign a right to a group, all the members of that group possess that right. However, you can add individual users to create exceptions to the group-rights approach. When you are satisfied with the groups or users you want added, clicking OK displays the new names at the bottom of the User Rights Policy dialog box.

Regular Rights

The pull-down list at the top of the User Rights Policy dialog box contains the rights you can grant to groups or users on your system. The rights defined within Windows NT are rather extensive. These rights give you quite a bit of control over your system, and if applied thoughtfully and properly can make your system very secure. The rights which you can normally set are the following:

- ◆ *Access this computer from network.* Allows access to resources on your system from other computers connected to the network. Normally, this right is assigned to a broad range of users, because resources are routinely shared over the network.

- ◆ *Add workstations to domain.* Enables the user to add new workstation definitions to an existing domain. By default, this right isn't granted to anyone.

- ◆ *Back up files and directories.* Enables the user to run the backup programs provided with Windows NT. Users with this right can back up information and do whatever they want with it, so the right shouldn't be granted to everyone.

- ◆ *Change the system time.* Lets the user change the date and time from the Control Panel. Whether this setting is critical depends on whether you have services that rely on the correct time in order to run. If you do, then you shouldn't grant this right to everyone.

- ◆ *Force shutdown from a remote system.* Allows the user, if logged on from a remote system, to shut down your computer. This right should be limited to only those people who might have a need to do this.

- ◆ *Load and unload device drivers.* Enables the user to manage system device drivers. Typically, this right is granted only to the Administrators group. Other users normally don't have a need to perform such nuts-and-bolts operations.

- ◆ *Log on locally.* Permits the user to log on to the computer when she is physically in front of it. This is a good right to restrict for your server. If only your administrators can log on, you can limit what can be done on the machine. (This setting deals with local log-on. Other users can still access server resources across the network.)

- ◆ *Manage auditing and security log.* Enables the user to modify the various access logs generated by Windows NT. This right should be granted only to administrators; people with access to the logs can delete the tracks of their actions.

- *Restore files and directories.* Users can restore files from backups previously made. (Users with this right don't have to be the same as those with backup rights.) This is a powerful right, because it allows the user to overwrite existing files on your system.

- *Shut down the system.* Allows the user to shut down your system at the local machine. This is different from the remote shutdown right discussed earlier. Normally those with this right are a subset of those who have local log-on rights.

- *Take ownership of files or other objects.* Permits the user to take complete control (ownership) of Windows NT objects. This right is quite powerful, as it means that the user can change who has access to your files.

Advanced Rights

The rights discussed in the preceding section may seem quite extensive, but they aren't the only rights possible under Windows NT—simply the most common. In addition to the rights in the preceding section, Windows NT provides a group of advanced rights. You access these rights by clicking the Show Advanced User Rights check box at the bottom of the User Rights Policy dialog box. These 16 rights are typically used by programmers or when setting up user accounts for specific programs.

This last use of advanced rights is the most typical—granting rights to programs. Thus, as you read through the following rights, remember that the term *user* is used loosely, and applies primarily to programs acting as users of your system. (Users utilize resources on a system; thus, programs can be users.) The advanced user rights are as follows:

- *Act as part of the operating system.* Allows the user (a program) to act as a secure, trusted part of the operating system. This right is typically granted to secure programs so that they can operate with the highest clearance possible. This right should be granted only if you are sure that you can trust the program, because improper use can seriously compromise your system. (Most administrators take several looks at programs that require this level of system access; it isn't to be granted lightly.)

- *Bypass traverse checking.* Permits the user to move through directory trees freely. Generally this right is granted to everyone, unless you want the user to stay within a particular directory. This option is helpful to limit the effect that a program can have on your system.

- ◆ *Create a pagefile.* Lets the user create page files. This setting is used primarily for programs that use page files (swap files) to do their work.

- ◆ *Create a token object.* Allows the user to create access tokens. These tokens are used within the operating system to represent users or groups of users. If a program has this right, it can masquerade as other users or groups, thereby bypassing normal security safeguards by circumventing absolute audit trails. It should go without saying that this right shouldn't be granted lightly or freely.

- ◆ *Create permanent shared objects.* Enables the user (a program) to create special permanent objects, such as \\Device, which are used elsewhere within the operating system. By default, this right isn't granted to anyone.

- ◆ *Debug programs.* Accepts low-level debugging of objects such as threads. This right is necessary when developing programs for Windows NT, but should not be granted to any other user. Some security features of Windows NT are automatically bypassed by users with this right.

- ◆ *Generate security audits.* Lets the user (a program) add entries to the security audit log. This right isn't granted to anyone, nor should it necessarily be granted. The use of this right is, itself, not audited. Thus, a user possessing this right can compromise security by changing the logs in which security events are recorded.

- ◆ *Increase quotas.* Permits the user to increase object quotas. This right isn't currently implemented in Windows NT, but may be in future versions.

- ◆ *Increase scheduling priority.* Allows the user to raise the priority level assigned to a program or process. Programs started normally usually share their time with other programs in the system. But a program run in "real time" gets a much larger share of the CPU's attention. This right is normally assigned to administrators and power users. If you find it's being abused, you can remove the right from some users.

- ◆ *Lock pages in memory.* Enables the user (a program) to lock memory pages so that they can't be paged out to the swap file. This option has the effect of limiting a valuable resource (memory) that you may need for other purposes.

- ◆ *Log on as a batch file.* Lets the user log on to Windows NT by using a batch queue facility. This right isn't implemented in this version of Windows NT, but may be in the future.

♦ *Log on as a service.* Permits the user (a program) to log on to Windows NT as a system service, which means that it has access to high-level security procedures. Many programs run as services, including the FastTrack programs that must be available all the time.

♦ *Modify firmware environment values.* On some systems, environment variables are kept in non-volatile RAM so that they are quickly available from one session to another. This right allows the user to modify those variables, provided that it's a feature of the hardware. Normally this right is granted only to administrators.

♦ *Profile single process.* Eventually, this right will allow the user to use the profiling (performance sampling) capabilities of Windows NT on a program or process. This right isn't implemented in the current version of Windows NT.

♦ *Profile system performance.* Enables the user to use the profiling (performance sampling) capabilities of Windows NT on the entire system. This right is required to use the Performance Monitor effectively, so it's granted to administrators by default.

♦ *Replace a process level token.* Lets the user (a program) modify the security access token for a process. This setting effectively gives the program complete run of your system and shouldn't be granted lightly. By default it isn't granted to any user.

Working with Permissions

All the security features discussed thus far involve what the user can do. You (and all users) can also grant permissions for who can access individual resources, such as files and directories. Making changes is very simple, and the concept behind it is very straightforward:

1. Select a directory or file whose access you want to limit in some way.
2. Select which groups or users can access that directory or file.

NOTE: Security permissions can be set for directories and files only on NTFS drives. If you're using FAT drives, skip the information in this section; it isn't applicable to you.

To make changes in the permissions for a directory or file, follow these steps:

1. Browse your desktop until you find the directory or file whose permissions you want to change. Similarly, you can use the Explorer to locate the object.

2. Right-click on the directory or file. This displays a context menu.

3. Select the Properties option. This displays the Properties dialog box for the object.

4. Click on the Security tab.

5. Click on the Permissions button. The Directory Permissions dialog box now appears as shown in Figure 15-7.

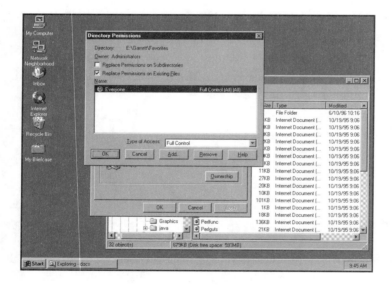

FIGURE 15-7

Using the Directory Permissions dialog box allows you to indicate who can have access to the selected directory.

The example in Figure 15-7 is shown when setting permissions for a directory. If you had first selected a file, essentially the same dialog box would be displayed, with a few minor differences. In particular, the first two check boxes in the dialog box aren't included (they don't have meaning for files).

If you worked through the User Manager discussion earlier in the chapter, the interface for the Permissions dialog box should seem familiar. In the middle of the dialog box is a list of users who have access to the file or directory. Immediately after each name is two sets of parentheses. The first set indicates the directory permissions granted to the user, and the second indicates the file permissions granted. You can add or remove users by using the <u>A</u>dd and <u>R</u>emove buttons at the bottom of the dialog box.

If you are working with directories, you can use the check boxes at the top of the dialog box to indicate whether the changes you are making should apply to subdirectories and to existing files in your directories.

It is interesting to note that Windows NT allows you two different ways to assign permissions. At the bottom of the Directory Permissions dialog box, you can see a pull-down list that indicates common groupings of permissions. The options are:

- ◆ *No Access.* This setting clears all permissions and prohibits access to the object.
- ◆ *List.* This option sets only the Read and Execute permissions for the directory, and the Not Specified permission for the files in the directory.
- ◆ *Read.* Use this option to set the Read and Execute permissions for both the directory and the files in the directory.
- ◆ *Add.* This selection sets the Write and Execute permissions for the directory, and the Not Specified permission for the files in the directory.
- ◆ *Add & Read.* This feature sets the Read, Write, and Execute permissions for the directory, and the Read and Execute permissions for files in the directory.
- ◆ *Change.* This choice sets the Read, Write, Execute, and Delete permissions for both the directory and the files it contains.
- ◆ *Full Control.* This option grants all six of the individual permissions.

In addition, there are two other options in the pull-down list. If you choose Special File Access or Special Directory Access, another dialog box appears which allows you to control individual permissions, as opposed to groupings of permissions. Both options present essentially the same dialog box; an example of the Special File Access dialog box is shown in Figure 15-8.

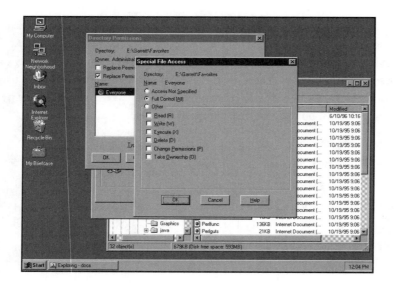

FIGURE 15-8

You can control individual permissions on files or directories.

Notice that the check boxes in this dialog box allow you to specify individual permissions. The following are the permissions and what they mean:

- ◆ *Read.* The user can read the file or directory.

- ◆ *Write.* The user can overwrite the file or save information in the directory.

- ◆ *Execute.* The user can run a program file.

- ◆ *Delete.* The user can delete the file or directory.

- ◆ *Change Permissions.* The user can change permissions on the file or directory.

- ◆ *Take Ownership.* The user can take complete control of the file or directory.

- ◆ *Not Specified.* This permission, unique to files, indicates that the directory permissions don't apply to the files in the directory. Instead, permissions must be granted on a file-by-file basis.

For your server to work properly, you need to make sure the proper users have the proper type of access to your files *and nothing more.* This requirement means that you need to look at the directories you are making available, and think through what access is necessary. Then, starting with the home directory for a service, change the permissions to reflect the access needed.

CAUTION: Write down the old permissions on a directory and make sure that you test out access to your site after you have made permission changes. If you encounter problems, you can change back to the old permission settings.

Understanding Auditing

Auditing is an NTFS security feature that enables you to track when a file or directory is accessed by a user or group of users. Auditing is very powerful, and you can control exactly what types of access are audited.

In some ways, setting up auditing is similar to setting permissions for a file or directory. All you need to do is display the Properties dialog box for the file or directory for which you want to create an audit trail, click on the Security tab, and then click on the Auditing button. The Properties dialog box then appears as shown in Figure 15-9.

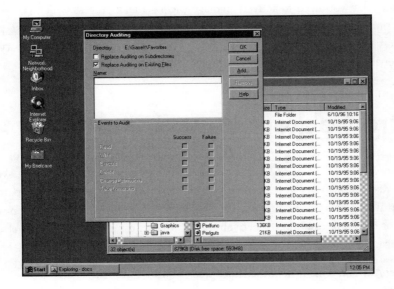

FIGURE 15-9

The Directory Auditing dialog box controls exactly what auditing is done on a file or directory.

This example shows the dialog box for setting up auditing on a directory. If you had first selected a file, essentially the same dialog box is displayed, with a few minor differences. For instance, the title bar is different, and the first two check boxes in the dialog box aren't included (because they don't have meaning for files).

If you are setting up auditing for a directory, the first two check boxes control how the audit should apply to files in the directory, as well as to subdirectories in the directory. The usage of these check boxes is very similar to the check boxes used when setting permissions.

The Directory Auditing dialog box contains two major areas. The first area is in the center of the dialog box, where you specify the users or groups whose actions you want to audit. You use the <u>A</u>dd and Re<u>m</u>ove buttons to control the list of accounts you want audited. If you want to audit all activity on a directory or file, select the Everyone group. (But note that this setting can make your audit trail quite large.)

At the bottom of the dialog box, you can specify what actions you want audited. Notice that the actions are the same as the permissions you can grant, but that you can audit both the success and failure of the action. The failure side is particularly helpful, as you can determine who has tried to get into a file and failed in their efforts.

Consider carefully what you are trying to achieve through auditing. When auditing is turned on and a recordable event is detected, a record is generated in the Security log file. This fact implies that you need to actively manage the log file, a process which is discussed in Chapter 16, "Internet Services and Security." On an active system, it's also possible to overflow the Security log file rather quickly. Judicious use of file and directory auditing also enables you to detect security problems more easily.

The Secure Sockets Layer

If you are interested in commerce on the Internet, you may have heard of a protocol known as *Secure Sockets Layer*, or *SSL*. This protocol, when implemented by both a Web server and browser, allows encrypted information to be transmitted between both parties. In the Internet world, this means that you can safely exchange sensitive information such as credit card or bank information. Effectively, SSL provides three functions for Web communications:

♦ *Authentication.* This function ensures that information for the intended server (your SSL-enabled server) is actually received and used by that server.

♦ *Encryption.* This function ensures that no other party can intercept and use the data intended for your server. (RSA encryption is very secure.)

◆ *Integrity.* This function ensures that the data contained in the transmission has not been altered from the time it left the sender until it arrived at the destination.

In order to use SSL, it must be implemented by both the Web server and the browser connecting to the server. As of this writing, only a few servers and browsers have incorporated SSL, but that is quickly changing as the latest versions of servers and browsers are all implementing SSL. One of the selling features of FastTrack is that it supports SSL 3.0, which is something that other servers cannot claim as of this writing.

Implementing SSL

From the server side of the fence, to implement SSL you need to accomplish several tasks. These include the following steps:

1. Generating a key pair file and a request file.
2. Enrolling your site.
3. Requesting an SSL certificate.
4. Installing the certificate in your FastTrack server.
5. Enabling SSL in the server itself.

These steps are covered in the following sections.

Generating Files

To set up SSL on your system, you need a registered encryption key (a certificate) that can be generated only by a registered Certification Authority. To get the certificate, you need to generate what is called a key file. This file is generated by a program called sec-key, and it is used to help identify the unique nature of your server.

The easiest way to generate the key file is to open a window showing the contents of the c:\netscape\server\bin\httpd\admin\bin directory. (The directory may be different if you installed FastTrack somewhere other than the default directory.) The sec-key program is located in this directory, and you can use it from this location. When you start sec-key, you will see the dialog box shown in Figure 15-10.

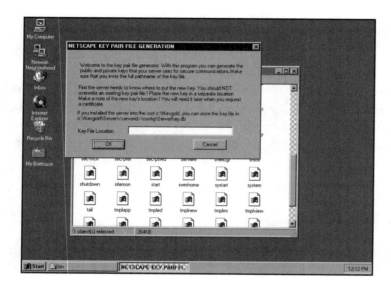

You need to indicate in this dialog box exactly where you want the file created. In the provided field you should place the full path name, along with the file name. Thus, if you wanted to the file to be in the c:\security directory, and you wanted the key file to be named myfile.sec, then you would enter c:\security\myfile.sec in the dialog box.

When you are done entering the information, click on the OK button. This displays the dialog box shown in Figure 15-11.

This dialog box is simply an explanation of what sec-key is doing while it generates your security key. Essentially, when you click on the OK button, the key is generated from your movement of the mouse and from other random items. To proceed, simply click on OK. You then see a progress dialog box that shows you how far along the completion process you have progressed. As this dialog box is displayed, you should be moving the mouse around the screen. There is no need for large, fast movements; small, leisurely movements are just fine. When the key is done being generated, you will see the dialog box shown in Figure 15-12.

Here you are asked to provide a password for your key file. The password can be anything you desire; the only requirements are that it be at least eight characters and have at least one non-alphabetic character. Go ahead and enter the password, then click on OK. You are again prompted to enter the password as a confirmation. When you are done doing that, click on OK again.

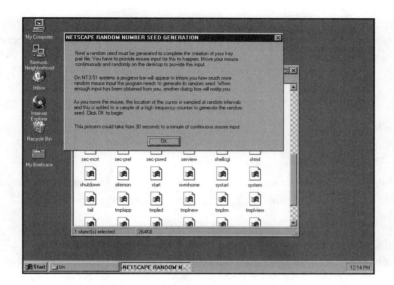

FIGURE 15-11

Sec-key explains how the key file will be generated.

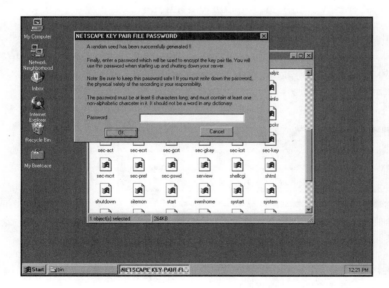

FIGURE 15-12

You need to provide a password for the key file.

CAUTION: Don't forget your key file password; you will need it at several points during implementing SSL.

At this point you are done creating the key file, and you will see a dialog box informing you of this fact. When you click on OK, the `sec-key` program ends and you can proceed with the next phase of implementing SSL.

Enrolling Your Site

To request a certificate, you need to work with an organization designated as a registered Certification Authority (CA). There are many different Certification Authorities springing up, and FastTrack can work with any CA you desire. When you purchased your copy of FastTrack, you should have received a list of CAs which Netscape suggests. You may want to spend some time visiting the Web sites of these Certification Authorities to make up your mind.

One such Certification Authority is VeriSign, Inc. (Their Web site is `http://www.verisign.com`.) So you can understand how working with a CA works, the information which follows is specific to getting a certificate from VeriSign; getting a certification from a different CA may require different information.

Before VeriSign will issue your certificate, you must document your Web site and your company. To do this, you must fill in an on-line questionnaire. You can start this process by connecting to the page at http://www.verisign.com/netscape. This page, shown in Figure 15-13, explains the process of getting a certificate.

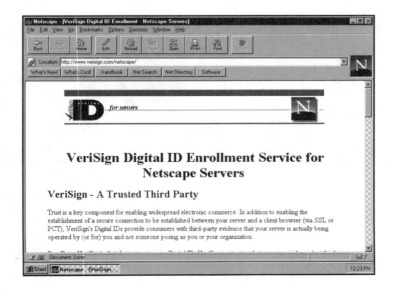

FIGURE 15-13

To get a VeriSign certificate, you start at their Web page.

Once you are ready to enroll your server (their wording for requesting a certificate), you simply scroll through the page and click on the Begin button at the bottom. You will then complete, on-line, the steps outlined on the beginning page. During the course of enrollment, you will be asked the following information:

+ The domain name of your server.

+ The legal name of the organization responsible for the server.

+ A division or department name, if any.

+ The city, state, and country in which your server is located.

+ The names and contact information for both technical and billing information.

+ How you will pay your fees. (Current VeriSign fees are $290 for the first year.)

Once you have this information, you are ready to enroll your server. Once you have enrolled, and you have sent in your request (covered in the next section), it generally takes three to five working days to verify your information (yes, VeriSign does check you out).

TIP: As you enroll your company, use your browser to make printouts of your enrollment pages with your information filled in. This way you will know what information you used and have a record of the steps you went through.

When you are through enrolling with the CA, you are provided with an e-mail address where you should send your certificate request. Make note of this address, as you will need it in the next section.

Requesting a Certificate

After you have documented your site by enrolling with the CA, you are ready to request your certificate. This request is done strictly via e-mail, and the e-mail message is generated by the Netscape Server Manager. To initiate the process, follow these steps:

1. Choose the Programs option from the Start menu. This displays the Programs menu.

2. Choose the Netscape option from the Programs menu. This displays the Netscape menu.

3. Click on the Administer Netscape Servers option. This starts Netscape Navigator, and shortly you will see a security dialog box asking for your user name and password.

4. Enter your user name and password, then click on OK. This displays the Server Selector page.

5. Scroll through the Server Selector page and click on the server name for which you want to request a certificate. This displays the Netscape Server Manager, as shown in Figure 15-14.

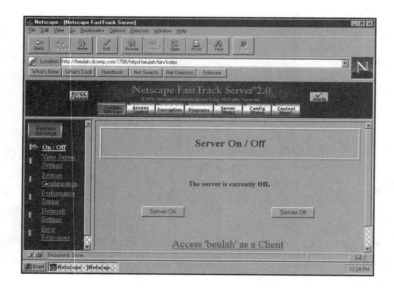

FIGURE 15-14

The Netscape Server Manager is used to configure your Web server.

6. On the toolbar in the top frame, click on the Encryption button. This changes the information displayed in the lower frames.

7. In the lower-left frame, click on the Request Certificate option. This changes the information displayed in the lower-right frame. Your screen should now look as shown in Figure 15-15.

8. In the Certificate authority field, enter the e-mail address for your certificate authority. (This address should have been provided when you enrolled with the CA.)

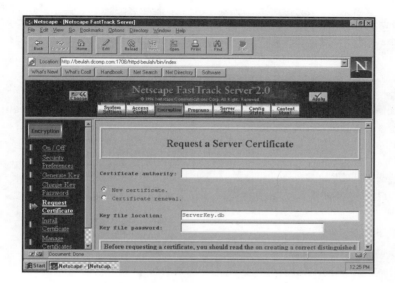

FIGURE 15-15

Requesting a certificate requires sending e-mail with specific information provided.

9. Indicate that this request is for a new certificate.

10. Enter the entire path to your key file (including the file name), along with the password you used when creating the key file.

11. Enter the identifying information for your server. This information is the same as what you supplied when you enrolled with the CA, in the last section. Make sure the information matches exactly, as the CA uses this information to match your e-mail request with your enrollment.

12. Double-check your information to ensure it is all correct.

13. Scroll through the lower-right frame until you find the OK button, then click on it. This sends your information to the server and changes the page displayed in the lower-right frame.

14. Scroll through the lower-right frame and click on the Save and Apply button. FastTrack composes the e-mail request and sends it to the CA. Shortly you will see a dialog box indicating the completion of your request.

15. Click on OK to close the dialog box.

After your request is e-mailed to the CA, and you have enrolled with the CA (as covered in the last section), it can take anywhere from three to five working days to receive your certificate. (This assumes, of course, that your information is in order.) The reason for the delay is not just the workload at the Certification Authority, but they also need time to verify that you are who you say you are. When the certificate comes back, it will be sent via e-mail to the technical contact you specified when you enrolled.

Installing the Certificate

When you receive your certificate from the Certification Authority (such as VeriSign), you need to install it. The certificate itself looks very similar to the request that you e-mailed to VeriSign in the first place. A typical certificate may look like this:

```
To:        jsmith@harryshats.com
Subject:   Certificate Request


— —-BEGIN CERTIFICATE— —·

IBCAFooCAQAB1YwXDQYJKoZIhvcNAECBQAJwczELMAkGA1UEMCVVNBMxIDAeBgNV
BAMTIDSX0QIQER1NA3VyDwzaQXR5LCBQbmMuMRwGgYDdVQQLExhQZXJzbhIENx21
cnRpZm1TJXCjSYhYFRYxNVNdPgVuINOXE01hcmt1wCBUZXNIFN1cFnZciA5M1TAw
MB4cA1UEChU1NBaMIER1GEhUiYdGpEjAIy9MwxW1D7aBgNV0VFBAsT1B1cnNvbmE
gQ2VydG1mXWNhdGUDAhBDxgNVjMTJ0AskW4Tu4j2HAlyrR1cN0NTTQU2VyAdpmVy
HEOGwzDMBEc5MjMygIMwWcQEwtc2DVBdTOGEwZEHBYDzMswCQY6DVQQGEwJVUzEg
IDExUThNMAsGSGSxINbJ3JQEBAQU0sAMFAEgCQQWU/gaygQvV0BhB3IqgGd4LSqA
GkD1iN3sEPfST0CqGXY5X3oZB4QnArA7mIfvpNi1tAgaYimvRbkP4XYeNy1MBmHL
AwD8QYJ+KoZIhvcNAQE8HJCDQQByps9EahjKKAefP+z+8NYNCqNfkhckggP2oL6s
pwhvEiP8m+bFy6HNDU1Fz8ZrVOu3WQapgLPV90kIskNKX3au
— —-END CERTIFICATE— —·
```

The easiest way to use this information in the installation process is to keep your e-mail window open, with the message displayed, during installation. Then, follow these steps:

1. Choose the <u>P</u>rograms option from the Start menu. This displays the Programs menu.

2. Choose the Netscape option from the Programs menu. This displays the Netscape menu.

3. Click on the Administer Netscape Servers option. This starts Netscape Navigator, and shortly you will see a security dialog box asking for your user name and password.

4. Enter your user name and password, then click on OK. This displays the Server Selector page.

5. Scroll through the Server Selector page and click on the server name in which the certificate is to be installed. This displays the Netscape Server Manager, as shown earlier in Figure 15-14.

6. On the toolbar in the top frame, click on the Encryption button. This changes the information displayed in the lower frames.

7. In the lower-left frame, click on the Install Certificate option. This changes the information displayed in the lower-right frame. Your screen should now look as shown in Figure 15-16.

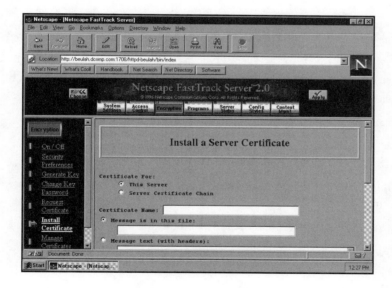

FIGURE 15-16

Installing a certificate involves filling out a simple form.

8. Switch to the e-mail window and copy the entire e-mail message containing your certificate.

9. Switch back to the Netscape Server Manager and paste the certificate in the Message text (with headers) field.

10. In the Certificate database field, enter the path in which the certificate is to be saved.

> **CAUTION:** Don't change the Certificate database field from the default unless you
> need to. (For instance, if this is a secondary certificate you are installing.) Remember
> the place where you installed your certificate, as you will need this information later.

11. Scroll through the lower-right frame until you find the OK button, then click
    on it. This sends your information to the server and changes the page displayed in the lower-right frame.

12. Scroll through the lower-right frame and click on the Save and Apply button.
    Shortly you will see a dialog box indicating the installation is complete.

13. Click on OK to close the dialog box.

Enabling SSL

The final step is to enable SSL in the Web server itself. This is done using the Netscape
Server Manager, which should still be on the screen after installing the certificate. To
enable SSL, follow these steps:

1. On the toolbar in the top frame, make sure the Encryption button is still
   selected.

2. In the lower-left frame, click on the On/Off option. This changes the information displayed in the lower-right frame. Your screen should now look as
   shown in Figure 15-17.

3. In the lower-right frame, click the On radio button.

4. Enter the Port Number you want used for secure communications. (The
   default, 443, is the accepted standard for secure communications.)

5. In the Key file field, enter the path to your key file (as generated earlier in
   this chapter).

6. In the Certificate file field, enter the path to your certificate file (as specified
   in the previous section).

7. Scroll through the lower-right frame until you find the OK button, then click
   on it. This sends your information to the server and changes the page displayed in the lower-right frame.

8. Scroll through the lower-right frame and click on the Save and Apply button.
   Shortly you will see a dialog box indicating the installation is complete.

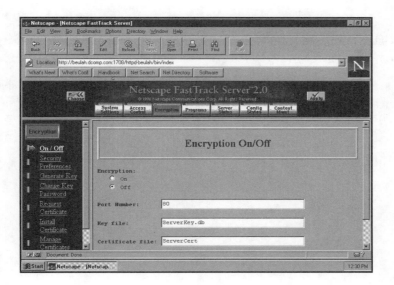

FIGURE 15-17

After your certificate is installed, you can enable SSL.

9. Click on OK to close the dialog box.

Usage Differences

After you have set up SSL in your server, there is very little difference from a Webmaster's perspective. You can continue to make files available, as you normally would. The only operational difference is for links to pages. If you establish a link to a document in a secure directory, you must preface the URL with `https://` instead of `http://`. Notice the addition of the `s`, which stands for *secure*.

When users try to access your secure documents, they also need to use the `https://` specification. If they don't, they can't access the documents; instead, they'll see an error message.

Summary

Part of the job of running Internet services is to make sure that your site is secure. This is particularly true if your Internet services are running on a server connected to your local network, or if you intend to conduct commerce over the Web. The information introduced in this chapter provides a good foundation for making your site secure. By learning this information and applying it wisely, you can give your site a good degree of security.

In the next chapter, you learn how you can use the information you gained in this chapter to plug any potential security leaks you developed when you started providing Internet services.

Chapter | 16

Internet Services
and Security

One of the tasks to be addressed by any MIS professional is making your Internet server as secure as possible. This task isn't eliminated with the FastTrack server, but is (in some respects) made a little simpler. The use of convenient interface for your server, along with some expanded FastTrack capabilities, have cut down on the amount of time necessary to secure your site.

In the preceding chapter, you learned how you can use the security features of Windows NT to enhance the security of the system on which your Web server is operating. This chapter focuses on putting those skills (and new ones) to work to make your system as secure as possible.

Developing Your Security Plan

The term *firewall* is very popular these days. Many people use it as if a firewall is a product that you can buy on the market. In reality, a firewall is any set of tools and procedures that, when carried out, act as a shield against unwanted intrusion in your system. The concept behind a very secure firewall is shown in Figure 16-1.

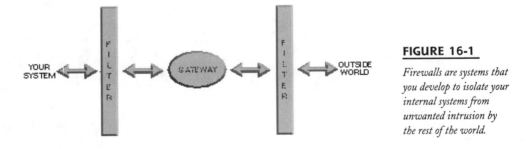

FIGURE 16-1

Firewalls are systems that you develop to isolate your internal systems from unwanted intrusion by the rest of the world.

Notice that the concept of a firewall is not limited to use on the Internet. Indeed, the concept applies just as well to an intranet. If you are in some fashion making your system available to others outside your organization (company or department), you need to be concerned with the security of that system. Your concerns, when analyzed, acted upon, and implemented, become your firewall.

In effect, your firewall can be viewed as your implemented plan for blocking intruders. With this in mind, you need to give thought to the following steps when considering your security:

- Developing a written plan
- Making backups
- Using log files
- Watching your directory structure
- Watching programs used
- Enforcing passwords
- Adding gateway machines
- Using secure machines

These issues are discussed in some depth in the following sections.

Developing a Written Plan

A wise person once said that a plan not written is not really a plan. This is true, because it's easy to forget, over time, what your plan was. If you have it written down, however, your plan becomes a set of written guidelines on which you can base all your subsequent actions.

To create an effective security plan, you should first understand how your system currently works, as well as how you want it to work. This knowledge isn't as easy to acquire as it sounds. Much of the information in this book can help you to understand how your system works, but only you can answer how you *want* it to work. How you want your system to work becomes, in effect, your vision of your service.

After you possess this knowledge, you can figure out how best to make your vision a reality. Understand that you may not get there overnight; you must make sure that each step you take along the way will not decrease your present security level or make your system harder for others to access or use.

When you start to write your plan, make sure that you include these two items:

- An indication of what you are doing for security
- An indication of what you will do if it doesn't work

These plan may seem odd to some people, but if you don't know what you are doing for security, it's doubtful that you have any security at all. In fact, your security may be just an illusion. Also, you should know what you are going to do if your security is breached.

Will you change passwords? Perhaps you might secure your system with SSL. Or you might cut off all outside connections until the security hole is plugged.

Exactly what you do is up to you, but you are basically setting checkpoints, along with a threshold that will trigger some remedial action on your part. If the checkpoints are breached, and the threshold is reached, you need to be prepared to carry out your remedial actions.

Making Backups

Most people don't think about backups as part of a security plan. Instead, they think of them as insurance in case of mechanical failure or human error. This is a good view, but perhaps not the best view.

Perhaps an example is in order here. Let's assume that you are running an Internet site, and you detect the fact that someone has broken into your system. Maybe they found an unprotected directory, or they found a way to execute a Trojan horse program on your system. If you detect it early enough, you can simply restore your earlier system from the backup, plug the security leaks, and continue business as usual. Without the backups, you couldn't do this. Thus, backups become critical not only from an insurance standpoint, but also from a security perspective.

When you make backups, make two types: a day zero backup, and routine backups. Routine backups are those you make as a matter of course. Most people back up their server every day or two, with a complete backup every week. The only problem with this system is that you may not detect a security problem for a week or a month. By that time, all your backups may also be compromised. What do you do then?

That's where the day zero backup comes into play. This level of backup earns its name from the fact that it's made when you first get your system up and running. At this point (day zero) you know that the security of your system hasn't been compromised because no one other than you has accessed the system.

Using your day zero backup is a serious decision, because it means that all your password files are erased and perhaps your "evolutionary system configuration" is lost. This situation can represent quite a bit of work to bring your system back up to its current status. More often than not, however, your security problems may be limited to a particular part of your server and you can restore just that part from the day zero backups. For example, if you think the server programs themselves have been corrupted, you can simply load those programs.

Using Log Files

You learned a bit about log files in Chapter 15, "Basics of Security." Log files are nothing more than journals indicating what happens on your system over time. Windows NT provides ways in which log files can be created automatically. You should take advantage of this capability. Why? Because figuring out how someone breached your security or compromised your system is virtually impossible if you can't follow some tracks. The best tracks you have are contained in your log files.

Later in this chapter, you learn how to use the Windows NT tools for analyzing log files. You should set up a regular schedule to analyze the log files, however. You should probably analyze them daily. Depending on the activity on your site, this process may take a while. Over time, however, you will be able to tell if something is wrong in the log files simply by quickly glancing over them. In addition, you may develop other programs that help you sift through the mountain of log file information you can create.

Finally, your log files should be kept for at least a week. Disk space is cheap enough that you should be able to afford this necessity. If you are analyzing your log files daily, keeping them for a week enables you to go back and examine longer-term activity taking place on your system.

Watching Your Directory Structure

You should create a directory structure that helps your security plans, rather than hindering them. I know of a company that installed a server with a 2GB drive because they wanted plenty of room for data files shared among all the nodes on their network. The problem was that they then configured the entire 2GB as one large drive. A much better approach would have been to partition the drive into three or four smaller drives. That way, they could keep the operating system on one drive and secure it against intruders. The data could then be kept on the other drives, which could then be made available to the general network population.

After your directory structure becomes manageable, you should learn what's in your directories. Unfortunately, very few people give much thought to what is in their directories—particularly the critical directories. For example, you should have a working knowledge of what's in your Windows NT system directories. Why? Because it allows you a reference point for determining whether someone has been messing with your critical files.

A good way to keep track of your files is to create a file (on paper, if desired) that lists the files in each critical directory. This can be done from the command prompt by using either of the following commands from within the critical directory:

```
dir > prn
dir > a:dirlist.txt
```

The first command sends the directory listing to the printer; the second sends it to a disk file called `dirlist.txt` on drive A:. Keep this file in a safe place, and then you can compare it to your current directory contents if a question ever arises.

> **TIP:** If you have a very active site, you may want to take the added precaution of examining your directories daily. This is easy enough to do if you use DIR /OD /TW at the command line, which sorts files in the order they were last written to. You can then examine the files to make sure that you agree that any new files should be there.

Watching Programs Used

Have you installed Internet services in the past which you no longer need or use? For instance, did you have a previous server installed which also provided ftp or Gopher service? Did you have these services operational at one time, but now they sit unused and unnoticed? If so, remove the components you no longer use. Every component you leave running is one more door into your system. If the component is a door you never check, it represents a grave security risk.

Since most Internet services—regardless of the vendor—are run as Windows NT services, you must at least stop the service using the Services applet in the Control Panel. Then, if there is an uninstall program provided with the software, you can remove the programs for the Internet service. If an uninstall program is not provided, then you will need to seek out the documentation provided with the software, contact the vendor, or "strong arm" your way into removing the software by deleting it and searching the Registry for any related entries.

Enforcing Passwords

In Chapter 15, "Basics of Security," you learned about Windows NT passwords. If you apply the information provided in that chapter, you will have a secure password system. The effectiveness of that security, however, depends on your willingness to enforce it for everyone.

It may be easy to institute password policies that require everyone to change their password every two weeks. But what if John, your closest and dearest friend, comes to you and says that he's tired of changing his password all the time? If you make an exception in his case and change his account so that his password never expires, you are starting to dismantle your security procedures. You may not think it's a big thing, but someone else may get hold of John's password and then have a permanent passkey into your system.

Another good idea is to get rid of default passwords in your system. A prime candidate is the Guest account that is included by default with Windows NT. Everyone knows that the Guest account is there, and that knowledge provides half the information needed to log in under that account. If you don't need Guest access, get rid of the account. Better yet, if you need Guest access, get rid of the Guest account and create a different guest account for your system—one that uses a different, unique name and password.

Adding Gateway Machines

The next highest level of security involves the use of dedicated hardware to act as gateways into your system. These gateways can be configured as stopping points between the outside world and the "inner sanctum" of your network. The primary purposes of a gateway include

- ◆ Authenticating messages
- ◆ Authenticating users

If a message or a user doesn't meet the requirements for entry into your network, that message or user is blocked by the gateway. In this way, your critical data and system programs are protected from intrusion.

Using Secure Machines

The final stage in a security plan—and the one offering the best security possible—is to use physically separate machines for the services you offer. In the case of FastTrack, this means arranging for a single Windows NT Server machine, running FastTrack, to be connected to the Internet. This machine doesn't serve as your LAN server at all; it's strictly for Internet access. While this setup may seem extreme, it does provide optimal security.

The drawback to this approach is that all published information must be used on the physical server. For instance, if you have a new Web document you want to create, you must create it on the server. You can't do it on a different workstation and then upload it; your workstations aren't connected to the Internet server. Thus, using a secure machine may involve changing some of your internal work habits. If this strategy is acceptable in light of the security gained, you should plan accordingly.

Security Issues for Your Site

As you work with the FastTrack server, you will find that various security issues crop up from time to time. A few issues, however, should be addressed up front, as you are first starting your site. The following sections describe issues that you need to understand to improve the security of your site.

The User Account

When you first install the FastTrack server, it logs on to your system as a system account. This means there is no user name or password required for the server to log on to the system. In most cases this does not present an overwhelming problem. You may, however, want to track (through auditing) how FastTrack accesses your system. The best way to do this is to force the server to log on using a specific user account and password.

To set up a user account specifically for FastTrack, you need to use the User Manager, the Netscape Server Manager, and the Control Panel. First, in the User Manager you will set up the account you want used. You do this by following these general steps (for specific steps to accomplish each item, refer to Chapter 15, "Basics of Security"):

1. Open the User Manager.

2. Create a new Global Group called Internet Users. This group should have no current users. (This means you will need to remove Guest as a user of the group.)

3. Create a new user account. Pick a descriptive name such as FastTrack or WebUser. Use a password that is relatively difficult, but not impossible for you to remember. (You will need this information again in a moment.)

4. Make sure the account selections (at the bottom of the New User dialog box) are specified as shown in Figure 16-2. *These are very important;* any other combination will result in problems later.

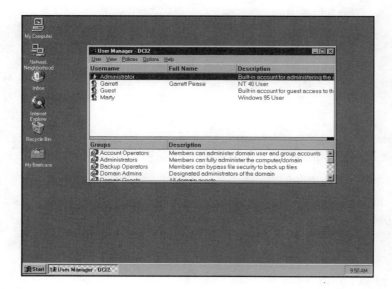

FIGURE 16-2

When setting up the new account, you can match these settings.

5. Click on the <u>G</u>roups button and make sure that the only group of which this user is a member is the new Internet Users group, which you just established. (You will need to set Internet Users as the primary group before removing the default group of Domain Users.)

6. Close the User Manager.

7. Open the Control Panel and double-click on the Services applet.

8. In the Services dialog box, select the Netscape FastTrack Server service and click on the Startup button. You should see the Service dialog box, as shown in Figure 16-3.

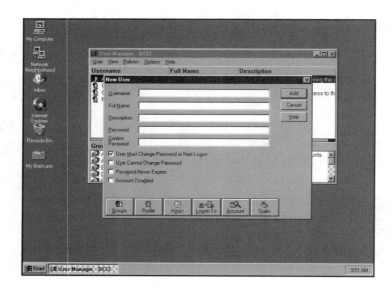

FIGURE 16-3

The Service dialog box allows you to control how a service is started by Windows NT.

9. In the bottom part of the dialog box, click on This Account and specify the account name and password you created in Step 3.

10. Close the Services dialog box.

11. Open the Netscape Server Manager for the server you are configuring. Click on the Network Settings option in the lower-left frame. Your screen should look similar to Figure 16-4.

12. In the lower-right frame, in the Server User field and the Password fields, enter the information you created in Step 3.

13. Click on OK, then choose Save and Apply.

14. Restart your entire system.

Once you have taken this action, you should keep the following items in mind, in reference to the new account you have created:

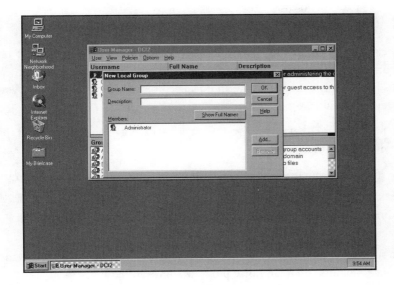

FIGURE 16-4

The Netscape Server Manager allows you to configure your server.

◆ You should make sure file and directory permissions are set properly for the new account, or for the new Internet Users group.

◆ You can set up auditing for the new user or group, in order to see the various ways in which the server is accessing files or directories.

◆ You may want to set up individual user accounts for each Internet service you offer. For instance, if you also maintain an FTP server, then you may want to set up an account for that server. (Individual accounts may make reading log files easier, as described later in this chapter.) To set up individual accounts, use the User Manager and assign them to your other Internet servers.

Document Files

Documents is a loose term that applies to everything you publish on your Internet servers. To secure the information in your server, you should make sure that all content directories are kept separate from executable files (discussed in the following section). In addition, you should make sure the directories containing your documents have only the Read permission set. This scheme protects the documents from being corrupted by users.

To set the Read permission on a directory, you use the Explorer or the browser in Windows NT. Follow the instructions provided in Chapter 15, "Basics of Security."

Executable Files

Consider very carefully whether you want to let users execute files on your system. This includes, of course, any CGI, WinCGI, JavaScript, or Java programs (as covered in earlier chapters of this book). Any time you allow an untrusted person to run a program, you make your system vulnerable.

If your service needs require that you allow at least some executable files, you need to keep the following points in mind:

- Make sure the executable file runs in a directory that has limited access to the rest of your system.

- The directory containing the executable file should have only the Execute privilege set.

- Make sure information uploaded by an executable is benign. (You don't want someone uploading a Trojan horse program, for example.)

In addition, if your site permits users to upload files, you should make sure that no way exists for them to immediately execute those files. You can ensure this by giving the upload directory only the Add permission.

Limiting Access to Your Server

The Netscape Server Manager enables you to limit access to your servers by any number of criteria. For instance, you can limit access by domain name, by user name, or by IP address. This feature is a great boon, particularly for intranet users. You can specify that only requests from specific users or addresses can access your system or, conversely, requests from specific users or addresses will be denied. All you need to do is perform the following steps:

1. Choose the Programs option from the Start menu. This displays the Programs menu.

2. Choose Netscape from the Programs menu.

3. Choose the Administer Netscape Servers option. This starts Netscape Navigator, and soon you are prompted for a user name and password.

4. Enter your user name and password, as required to configure your server, then click on OK. This displays the Server Selector page.

5. Click on the name of the server you want to configure. This displays the Netscape Server Manager.

6. On the toolbar in the top frame, click on the Access Control option. The information in the lower frames changes.

7. In the lower-left frame, click on the Restrict Access option. The information in the lower-right frame changes.

8. If the lower-right frame informs you that access control is turned off, click on the button labeled Turn on Access Control. Your screen should now look as shown in Figure 16-5.

9. For Read access, click on whether you want to Allow or Deny access to your server by default. (If you are limiting access to all but a few, you would click on

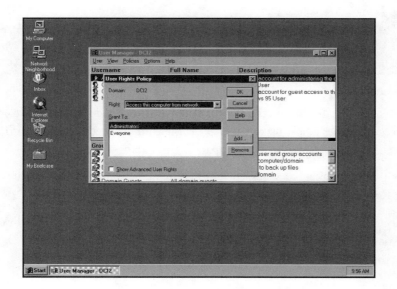

FIGURE 16-5

You must turn Access Control on before you can specify who can or cannot access your system.

Deny. If you are allowing access to all but a few, you would click on Allow.)

10. Click on the Permissions button to selectively grant or deny access. (If you clicked on the Allow radio button, then Permissions allows you to indicate who should be denied access. If you clicked on the Deny button, then Permissions allows you to specify who should be allowed access.)

At this point, exactly what you see depends on whether you selected Allow or Deny as your default approach to access. Figure 16-6 shows what you see if you had clicked on the Allow radio button.

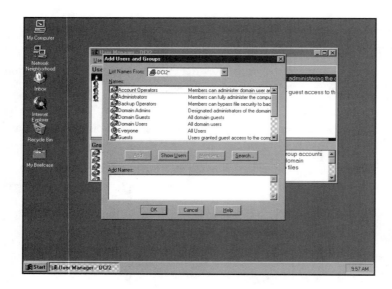

FIGURE 16-6

*The Netscape Server
Manager can limit access
based on your criteria.*

At this page you can specify who should not have access to your system. You can selectively limit access by either a host name (such as dcomp.com or hatethis.org) or an IP address. You can specify multiple entries by separating the items by commas.

When you are through making changes, click on the Done button. Your changes are saved and the Restrict Access page is again displayed.

If you had selected the Deny radio button on the Restrict Access page, and then clicked on the Permissions button you have quite a few more options. In this case, the Allow Access to a Resource page appears, as shown in Figure 16-7.

This page allows you to specify host names and IP addresses, the same as the page shown in Figure 16-06. However, if you scroll through this page, you will find other ways to allow access. When allowing access, Netscape Server Manager can utilize information from the user database. Thus, you can permit certain users or groups of users to access you site, while denying access to all others. (How you manage users and groups is covered in Chapter 18, "Day-to-Day Management."

When you have finished specifying who can have access to your system, click on the Done button. This returns you to the Restrict Access page. You should click on the OK button on this page, or else your changes won't be saved. You then see the Save and Apply page, where you should click on the Save and Apply button. You have now made your Web site more secure through allow or disallowing certain individuals.

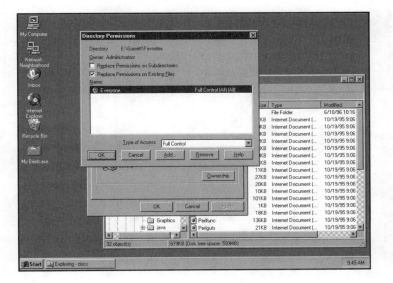

Reviewing Events

Windows NT offers the potential of tracking almost everything that happens on your server. This information is logged in one of three log files, and can be reviewed with the Event Viewer. Information on how to use the Event Viewer is detailed in the following sections.

Viewing Event Logs

You access the Event Viewer by following these steps:

1. Choose the Programs option from the Start menu. This displays the Programs menu.
2. Choose Administrative Tools (Common) from the Programs menu. This displays a menu of administrative tools.
3. Click on the Event Viewer option. This displays the Event viewer window, as shown in Figure 16-8.

There are three different types of logs maintained by Windows NT. You specify the log you want to view by selecting any of the following options from the Log menu:

◆ **System.** This log keeps track of events generated by Windows NT itself. Examples might be device drivers not loading, or messages about system memory usage.

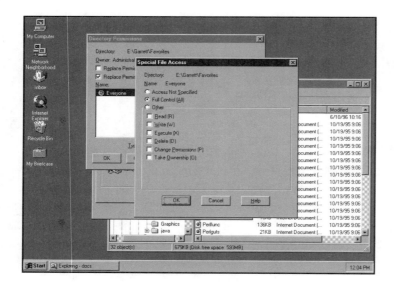

FIGURE 16-8

The Event Viewer enables you to manage the audit logs created by Windows NT.

- ◆ **Security.** This log tracks security violations. This includes all the permissions logging discussed in Chapter 15, "Basics of Security."

- ◆ **Application.** This log lists events generated by your applications programs. The exact types of events differ from program to program.

Obviously, the log that is most pertinent to the topic of this chapter is the security log. As mentioned earlier in this chapter, you should review the security log at least daily. Pay particular attention to the contents of the Category and User fields. Look for events that appear out of line with what you know should be happening. Pay special attention to repetitive events. For instance, you might notice several unsuccessful attempts at logging on to your system (events in the Logon/Logoff category). This either indicates someone is having difficulty (and perhaps needs some training), or else someone is trying to break into your system.

If you want additional information about an event, double-click the event to open a dialog box with details, as shown in Figure 16-9.

> **TIP:** If you have Administrator privileges, you can view the event log on your server from any workstation on the network. Choose Select Computer from the Log menu, and then select your server from the computer list.

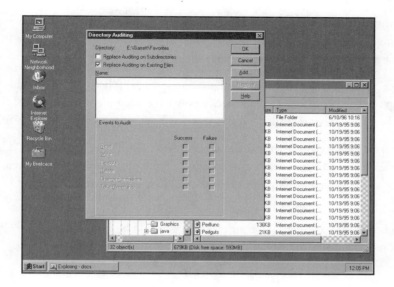

FIGURE 16-9

The security log keeps detailed information on each event.

Configuring Log File Settings

You can control how the logging system of Windows NT keeps the log files. Choose Log Settings from the Log menu. This option displays the dialog box shown in Figure 16-10.

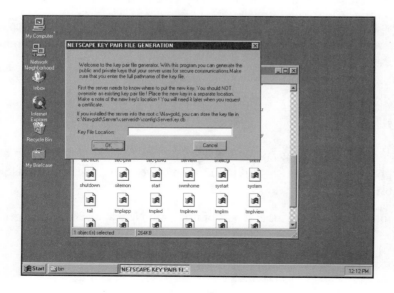

FIGURE 16-10

Windows NT allows you to configure how your log files are maintained.

The configuration settings you make in this dialog box are only for the log file you are currently viewing. To change a different log file, view that file first, or select the file from the pull-down list at the top of the Log Settings dialog box.

You should take some time to match the configuration settings to how you use the log files. At the top of the dialog box, you can specify how large a log file should be kept. This setting should be based on your available disk space and how many events you are logging.

Earlier, this chapter pointed out that you should keep your log files at least a week. The Log Settings dialog box lets you specify this setting in the Event Log Wrapping area. All you need to do is specify that events over seven days old are overwritten; Windows NT takes care of the rest.

When you are finished specifying how your event logs should be kept, click OK to close the dialog box and save your changes.

Managing Your Log Files

With the Event Viewer, you can easily manage your log files. For example, after reviewing your log file for a particular day, you may want to get rid of it. Just choose Clear All Events from the Log menu. Windows NT asks if you want to save the events in an archive before clearing the log file. If you do, specify a file name to use.

Archive files use the extension .evt. Thus, you could save the event log in a file such as April.evt. You can later review the events in the archive file by using the Open command from the Log menu.

Summary

Site security isn't a one-time thing. As you manage your site, pay constant attention to security. By applying the concepts covered in this chapter, you can make your site as secure as possible.

In the next chapter, you learn the ins and outs of using the Netscape Server Manager.

PART VI

Managing Your Site

Chapter | 17

The Netscape
Server Manager

Throughout this book you have used the Netscape Server Manager to configure the various sections of the FastTrack server. You may have the impression that this is the sole purpose for the Netscape Server Manager. If so, this is a mistaken impression.

As the name implies, you use the Netscape Server Manager for managing all aspects of your FastTrack server. This statement goes not only for servers running on your local system, but also for servers running on remote systems. This chapter focuses on how you can use the Netscape Server Manager in the everyday management of your sites.

Starting the Netscape Server Manager

You start the Netscape Server Manager by following the same steps you have followed elsewhere in this book:

1. Choose the <u>P</u>rograms option from the Start menu. This displays the Programs menu.

2. Choose the Netscape option from the Programs menu. This displays the Netscape menu.

3. Click on the Administer Netscape Servers option. This starts Netscape Navigator, and shortly you will see a security dialog box asking for your user name and password.

4. Enter your user name and password as you specified it when installing FastTrack, then click on OK. This displays the Server Selector page, as shown in Figure 17-1.

The Server Selector page displays the different servers installed on this system. As you scroll through the page, each server is listed by name. As the page name implies, you use this page to select which server you want to manage. This is not all you can do from this page, however. You can also:

♦ Turn a server off or on by clicking on the light switch to the left of the server name. (This is described in Chapter 6, "Troubleshooting Your Web Installation.")

♦ Install a new FastTrack server. (This is described in Chapter 4, "Installing Your Web Server.")

♦ Remove an existing server. When you click on the Remove a Server From This Machine button, you can remove any server you previously installed.

◆ Configure the Netscape Server Manager program. This allows you to change your user name and password, modify how the server logs on to Windows NT, and change the IP port used for the program.

FIGURE 17-1

The Server Selector page allows you to choose different servers to administer.

Most of these features are used only once or twice at any given site; some sites might not use them at all. The primary purpose of seeing the Server Selector page is to provide a way to get to the Netscape Server Manager for a particular server. You do this by simply clicking on the name of the server you want to manage.

The User Interface

When you have selected which server you want to manage, the Netscape Server Manager is displayed, as shown in Figure 17-2.

Notice that the Netscape Server Manager uses the Netscape Navigator as its user interface. If you look at the location field at the top of the browser, you can see that you are connected to a particular port (in this case, 3650) at the server. This port is used exclusively by the Netscape Server Manager. The port number is generated randomly when you first install FastTrack. Later, if you desire, you can change the port number, as mentioned in the previous section.

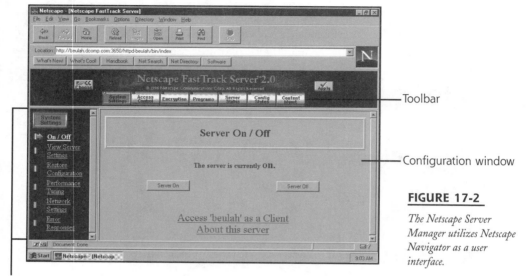

Toolbar

Configuration window

FIGURE 17-2

The Netscape Server Manager utilizes Netscape Navigator as a user interface.

Category choices

There are three frames used in the browser. Each frame has a specific purpose, as indicated in Figure 17-2. The upper frame contains the toolbar which you use to select the different categories of the manager which you want to use. The lower-left frame is used to select which choice you want made out of the current category. The lower-right frame is used to do your configuration work. Each of these areas of the Netscape Server Manager is discussed in the following sections.

The Toolbar

The upper frame in the browser contains what looks like a toolbar. This appearance is not really a toolbar, in the traditional sense of the word. For instance, clicking on an item on the toolbar does not accomplish a function. Instead, the buttons control in which configuration area you are working. The following are the choices on the toolbar:

♦ *System Settings.* This category controls items that affect the server as a whole. For instance, turning the server on or off, changing network settings, and specifying error responses.

♦ *Access Control.* This category is used to specify who can and cannot have access to the server.

- ◆ *Encryption.* This category is where you control general encryption and SSL settings for the server.
- ◆ *Programs.* This category is where you configure the server to handle different types of programs that can be run from your server.
- ◆ *Server Status.* This category is used to specify how access logs should be maintained and to generate reports based on those logs.
- ◆ *Config Styles.* This category allows you to define configuration styles that can be applied to different URL paths at your site.
- ◆ *Content Mgmt.* This category allows you to specify where information is stored at your site.

In addition there are two other buttons in the upper frame. The left-most button, Choose, is used to return to the Server Selector page. The right-most button, Apply, is used to apply your configuration changes before you leave the Netscape Server Manager.

The Category Choices

Once you select a configuration category from the toolbar, the information in the lower-left frame is changed to reflect the choices available for the category. The number and type of choices varies, depending on the category selected. Some categories have as few as five choices, while one has as many as 11.

The choice that is currently selected is shown in white, and there is an arrow to the left of the choice. If you want to select a different choice, simply point and click. The selection arrow moves to that choice, and the colors of the choices are updated.

The Configuration Window

The lower-right frame is the area where you actually configure the server. The information in the window changes, based on your choices in the other two frames. There are certain similarities between every configuration window, however:

- ◆ The window always starts with a heading that indicates what you are changing.
- ◆ The window always ends with three buttons: OK, Reset, and Help.

When you are done making changes in the main body of the configuration window, then you should click on the OK button to save your changes. If you don't click on the button, but instead exit Netscape Server Manager in some other way, then your changes are not saved. Whenever you click on the OK button, you are always shown the Save and Apply screen, as shown in Figure 17-3.

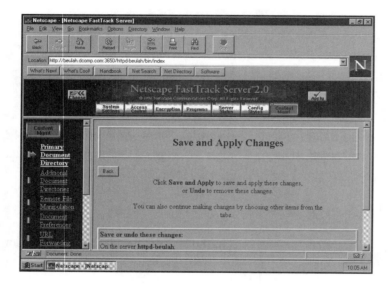

FIGURE 17-3

The Save and Apply screen allows you to undo your changes.

This screen is your "last chance" to undo your changes before the server is changed. If you scroll through the window, you will see three buttons: Save and Apply, Save, and Undo. The first two buttons are essentially the same, except that one applies your changes automatically, while the other does not. The Undo button is a way to change your mind and cancel your changes.

The Configuration Categories

When you use the Netscape Server Manager, you can select one of seven different categories that define your configuration options. As you learned earlier in this chapter, you select a category by using the toolbar in the upper frame. Each of the seven configuration categories are discussed in the following sections.

System Settings

The system settings category is what you first see when entering the Netscape Server Manager (see Figure 17-2). The options in this area include the following:

- ◆ *On/Off.* This option allows you to turn the server on or off. This procedure was covered in Chapter 6, "Troubleshooting Your Web Installation."

- ◆ *View Server Settings.* This option allows you to change many of the configuration settings for the server itself. Much of the information in this option is redundant, as most settings can also be changed by selecting options in other configuration categories.

- ◆ *Restore Configuration.* This option allows you to backup and restore configuration files for your server. This is handy if you want to transfer a configuration from one server to another. For general purpose backups, however, you should rely on the regular back you perform on your server.

- ◆ *Performance Tuning.* This option allows you to set DNS-related information. This option is discussed shortly.

- ◆ *Network Settings.* This option allows you to change the user name and password that the server uses in relation to the operating system. Using this option was covered in Chapter 16, "Internet Services and Security."

- ◆ *Error Responses.* This option allows you to create custom error messages that Netscape will use when it cannot fulfill a user's request. How you utilize these is covered in Chapter 18, "Day-to-Day Management."

If you choose the Performance Tuning option, your screen appears as shown in Figure 17-4.

This option allows you to configure how FastTrack works in relation to DNS names. Normally, when an HTTP request is received by the server, only the IP address of the requester is included. If you enable DNS on this screen, then FastTrack will do a reverse lookup on every IP address it receives. This means that instead of a name such as 205.163.44.2, a meaningful name such as alw.dcomp.com is written to the log files. This is a great help in administrative tasks, and particularly when you are creating reports.

If you enable DNS lookups, then you can also instruct FastTrack to cache DNS entries. This means that it keeps track of the IP address to DNS name correlations for a time. You specify the size of the cache (in number of entries) and how long an entry should be remembered (in seconds).

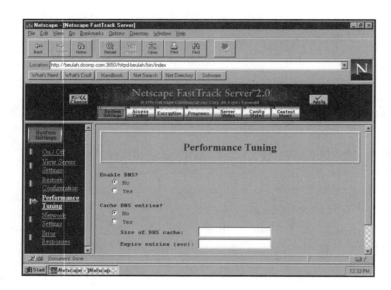

FIGURE 17-4

The Performance Tuning option allows you to control whether FastTrack does lookups on IP addresses.

The downside of this is that reverse lookups are costly in terms of time. If you have a busy site, and only an average computer, then you (and your visitors) will notice a definite slowdown in response time. You can mitigate this a bit by also turning on the DNS caching, but that only helps a bit. Remember that the initial lookup must still be done, and that takes time.

Access Control

The Access Control category has more options than any other category: 11. When you choose Access Control on the toolbar, your screen appears as shown in Figure 17-5.

The options available in this category are as follows:

- ◆ *Create User.* This option allows you to create a user definition for someone that should be allowed or denied access to your server.

- ◆ *Remove User.* This option allows you to delete a previously created user definition.

- ◆ *List Users.* This option lists the users you have defined for your server.

- ◆ *Edit User.* This option allows you to edit an existing user.

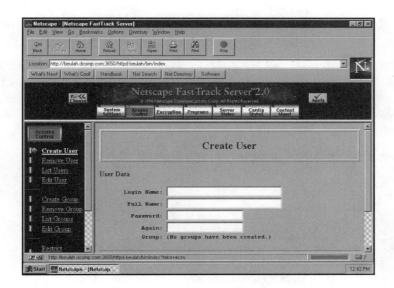

FIGURE 17-5

The Access Control category allows you to restrict access to your server.

- ◆ **Create Group.** This option allows you to create a group, to which users can belong.

- ◆ **Remove Group.** This option allows you to delete a previously defined group.

- ◆ **List Groups.** This option lists the groups you have defined for your server.

- ◆ **Edit Group.** This option allows you to edit an existing group.

- ◆ **Restrict Access.** This option allows you to limit who has access to your server. The use of this option was covered in Chapter 16, "Internet Services and Security."

- ◆ **Manage User Databases.** This option allows you to create or remove entire databases of users.

- ◆ **Import Users.** This option allows you to import a collection of users from a text file.

These options are used extensively if you are actively managing who has access to your system. FastTrack does not use the Windows NT security databases for tracking who can access your system; instead it relies on the information you create using these options. More information about managing server users is presented in Chapter 18, "Day-to-Day Management."

Encryption

Which users you allow to access your system (as discussed in the previous section) is only the first half of security. The other part has to do with the options presented in the Encryption category. When you click the Encryption button on the toolbar, your screen appears as shown in Figure 17-6.

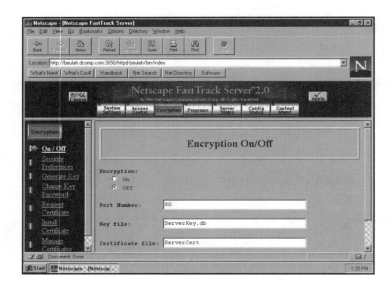

FIGURE 17-6

The Encryption category allows you to protect the information transferred by your server.

There are seven options in the Encryption category, as follows:

- ◆ *On/Off.* This option allows you to turn the entire encryption system on and off. The default is off, but if you intend on running a secure site (meaning, performing secure transactions using SSL), then you should turn encryption on.

- ◆ *Security Preferences.* This option allows you to specify which standards FastTrack should follow as it implements its security features. You use this option to configure both SSL versions 2 and 3 settings.

- ◆ *Generate Key.* This option is used to generate a key pair file, in preparation for getting a certificate from a Certification Authority. This is discussed in Chapter 15, "Basics of Security."

- *Change Key Password.* This option allows you to change the password you specified for your key pair file when you first created it. This is also discussed in Chapter 15, "Basics of Security."

- *Request Certificate.* This option is used to request a certificate from a Certification Authority. This option prepares e-mail that is sent to the CA, as discussed in Chapter 15, "Basics of Security."

- *Install Certificate.* After you receive your certificate from the CA, this option is used to install it in your server. This is part of the process discussed in Chapter 15, "Basics of Security."

- *Manage Certificates.* This option allows you to examine or remove the certificates installed in your system. FastTrack allows you to install multiple certificates in your system, but you probably won't spend much time using this option.

Programs

The Programs category is used to configure your server for various programming extensions to non-dynamic HTML pages. When you click on the Programs category on the toolbar, your screen appears as shown in Figure 17-7.

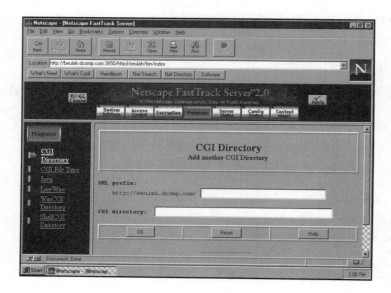

FIGURE 17-7

The Programs category is used to enable different types of Web programs.

There are six options available in the Programs category, as follows:

- ◆ *CGI Directory.* This option allows you to specify the directory from which you will run your CGI programs. Use of this option was discussed in Chapter 11, "Working with Scripts."

- ◆ *CGI File Type.* This option allows you to specify which types of files should be considered CGI files, in case you don't want to confine your programs to a single directory. CGI files were discussed in Chapter 11, "Working with Scripts."

- ◆ *Java.* This option allows you to specify whether you want FastTrack to be enabled for server-based Java programs. If you are using Java applets, then this option is not necessary. Java is discussed in Chapter 14, "Working with Java."

- ◆ *LiveWire.* This option allows you to interface with the LiveWire Application Manager, a separate Netscape program. LiveWire applications are developed using JavaScript, which is discussed in Chapter 13, "Working with JavaScript."

- ◆ *WinCGI Directory.* This option allows you to specify where your WinCGI programs will be stored. Setting up such a directory is discussed in Chapter 12, "Working with WinCGI."

- ◆ *ShellCGI Directory.* This option provides another way to configure FastTrack to work with CGI scripts. CGI is covered in Chapter 11, "Working with Scripts."

Server Status

The Server Status category allows you to work with the access logs generated by the FastTrack server. When you choose this category, your screen appears as shown in Figure 17-8.

The six options available in this category include the following:

- ◆ *View Access Log.* This option allows you to view either the current or an archived access log for your server.

- ◆ *View Error Log.* This option allows you to view the error log for your server. This log tracks errors and system events, such as starting and stopping the server.

◆ *Monitor Current Activity.* This option allows you to watch, in real time, exactly what is happening on any of your IP ports.

◆ *Archive Log.* This option allows you to specify how archive logs should be created.

◆ *Log Preferences.* This option allows you set the parameters that FastTrack uses when it creates log files.

◆ *Generate Report.* This option uses the log file analyzer to generate usage reports based on your log files.

Part of managing your server involves proper and effective use of the log files which your server can generate. Chapter 19, "Utilizing Log Files," discusses how to utilize log files.

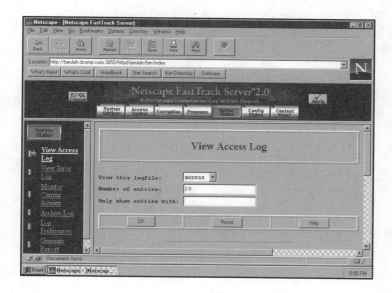

FIGURE 17-8

The Server Status category is used to control log files.

Config Styles

The Config Styles category allows you to create styles, or templates, that define how security and other common configuration options should be applied to a URL. When you choose this option, your screen appears as shown in Figure 17-9.

The five options available in the Config Styles category are:

◆ *New Style.* This option allows you to create a new configuration style.

- ◆ *Remove Style.* This option is used to delete a configuration style you previously created.
- ◆ *Edit Style.* This option is used to make changes to an existing configuration style.
- ◆ *Assign Style.* This option allows you to assign a configuration style to a URL on your server.
- ◆ *List Assignments.* This option is used to display the style assignments active on your server.

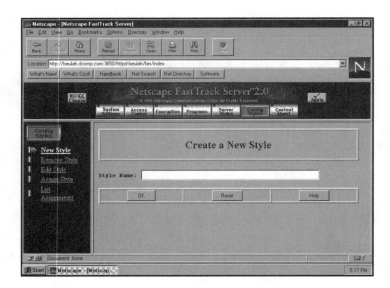

FIGURE 17-9

The Config Styles category allows you to define and manage configuration styles.

For more complex Web sites, configuration styles can be a big time saver. How to define and use configuration styles is discussed in more depth in Chapter 18, "Day-to-Day Management."

Content Mgmt

When you first set up your FastTrack server, you needed to define where your Web pages would be stored. The Content Mgmt category allows you to modify where information is located. When you choose the category from the toolbar, your screen appears as shown in Figure 17-10.

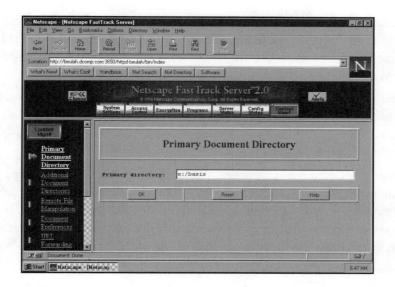

FIGURE 17-10

The Content Mgmt category allows you to specify where your Web pages are stored.

There are 10 options available in the Content Mgmt category, as follows:

◆ ***Primary Document Directory.*** This option allows you to indicate where your main URL is mapped to on your hard drive. This is the directory you set up when you installed FastTrack server. (Information on this directory is covered in Chapter 4, "Installing Your Web Server.")

◆ ***Additional Document Directories.*** This option allows you to make more directories available on your server. These directories are not directly accessible from your primary directory, but are elsewhere on your system.

◆ ***Remote File Manipulation.*** This option allows you to make the documents on your server available to others to manipulate. In order to protect your server, however, if you turn this option on, you should use the access control features of FastTrack to limit what specific access everyone has.

◆ ***Document Preferences.*** This option is where you specify what your default files are, and whether directory indexing is supported by the server. This is covered in Chapter 4, "Installing Your Web Server."

◆ ***URL Forwarding.*** This option is where you can configure FastTrack to automatically forward requests for certain URLs. This feature is discussed in Chapter 18, "Day-to-Day Management."

♦ *Hardware Virtual Servers.* This option allows you to establish another server at your location. Access to the server is determined by the domain used in the URL sent in the HTTP request. Virtual servers are discussed in Chapter 4, "Installing Your Web Server."

♦ *Software Virtual Servers.* This option also allows you to establish additional servers at your location. Access to the server is determined, however, by the IP address in the HTTP request. Virtual servers are discussed in Chapter 4, "Installing Your Web Server."

♦ *International Characters.* This option allows the server to associate a particular international character set with a URL. Once associated, the character set information is served to the browser every time the document is accessed. If the browser supports character set switching, then it automatically switches character sets based on the information provided by the server.

♦ *Document Footer.* This option is used to specify a short footer that is appended to all HTML documents within a particular area of your server. Primarily it is intended for adding information such as the last date a document was updated. The footer added with this option is limited to 765 characters.

♦ *Parse HTML.* This option controls whether the server modifies information it sends to the browser. Normally, HTML files are sent as-is, and the browser handles all interpretation. If parsing is turned on, then FastTrack can interpret either all your HTML files or those with a file name extension of .shtml.

Using Netscape Server Manager Over the Network

The Netscape Server Manager is most often used for controlling any FastTrack servers installed on the computer where you are running the Netscape Server Manager. However, because of the way in which the server manager works, you can also use it over a network. From the manager's perspective, remote management is transparent. This means that after you are connected to the Netscape Server Manager (either local or remote), all the features of the program function the same.

When you installed FastTrack, a random IP port was assigned to the Netscape Server Manager. Because the Netscape Server Manager relies on a browser for its interface, this port can be used to access the server manager program from anywhere in the network. All you need to do is remember the port number, and then use it in your connections.

For instance, let's say the port number used by your version of Netscape Server Manager is 3617. You can start a copy of Netscape Navigator anywhere in the world, enter the address to your server, append the port number, and have access to the Netscape Server Manager. This is not as big of a security risk as it sounds, however, because you need three pieces of information besides the server address:

- ◆ The port number
- ◆ The administrative user name
- ◆ The administrative password

Given these three pieces of information, remote management is a snap. To find the port number used for your system, you must have access to the machine on which FastTrack is installed. Then, follow these steps:

1. Choose the <u>P</u>rograms option from the Start menu. This displays the Programs menu.

2. Choose the Netscape option from the Programs menu. This displays the Netscape menu.

3. Click on the Administer Netscape Servers option. This starts Netscape Navigator, and shortly you will see a security dialog box asking for your user name and password, as shown in Figure 17-11.

At this point, take a look at the URL shown in the Location field at the top of the browser. Notice that the URL consists of an address for your server, followed by a colon and a port number. This port number is what you need to remember. Later, when you are at a remote browser, you can use the port number to access the Netscape Server Manager in the same way.

TIP: If, for some reason, you forget your user name and password, you can change them following the information presented in Chapter 6, "Trouble-shooting Your Web Installation."

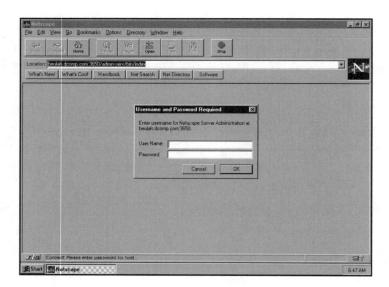

FIGURE 17-11

A user name and password is required before you can use the Netscape Server Manager.

As an example of how this works, shut down your session on the server, and move to another machine on which Navigator has been installed. The machine can be anywhere; it doesn't really matter. Let's say your server address is http://www.widget.com, and that the port number for your administrative use is 3281. Start Navigator at the remote machine, and once it is ready for your interaction, enter the following in the Location field:

```
http://www.widget.com:3281
```

When you press Enter, your server is accessed, on port 3281, and it responds with the administrative log-in dialog box you are so familiar with. Supply your user name and password, and you will then see the Server Selector page, as if you were working right at the server.

Summary

It seems that managing and administering an Internet site can be a full-time job. Fortunately, FastTrack includes the Netscape Server Manager, which makes the job somewhat easier. While you may have known how to use the Netscape Server Manager for configuration purposes prior to reading this chapter, hopefully you now have a fuller appreciation for the capabilities of the program. Regardless of the complexity of your network and the Web servers you are using, you can use the Netscape Server Manager to get a handle on your tasks.

In the next chapter, you learn how to perform some special types of management functions, as well as how to get into the routine of managing your site.

Chapter | 18

Day-to-Day Management

After you have installed your Web server, gotten through the hustle and hubbub associated with starting up, and standardized your content, you are faced with the challenge of fitting your site management tasks into your daily routine. This chapter focuses on some of the tasks you may face every day. Here you will find information on adding and removing pages, setting meaningful error messages, how to manage users, and how you can establish routines for your management tasks.

Before learning the information in this chapter, it would be helpful to understand the various functions available through the Netscape Server Manager. If you haven't done so yet, take this opportunity to read through Chapter 17, "The Netscape Server Manager," before proceeding.

Meaningful Error Messages

Let's face it: errors happen. Whether it be in a program you have written, a link you have created, or just in the general configuration of your server, they do happen. Part of your management responsibility is to do what you can to minimize the impact of errors on your site visitors.

Normally when an error occurs, FastTrack sends a rather generic error message. Some of the error messages, unfortunately, reflect poorly on you as a Webmaster. For instance, Figure 18-1 shows an example of the default error message that a visitor will see if there is a server error.

You may think that server errors are not that common, but they can be. This particular instance was generated when directory indexing was turned off and someone tried to access an existing directory that did not have a default page available within it. If the visitor had tried to access a non-existent directory, the error message shown in Figure 18-2 would have been displayed instead.

FastTrack allows you to change the messages displayed by the server whenever an error is encountered. There are four different errors for which you can customize messages:

- *Unauthorized.* This type of error occurs when the user attempts to access an existing document or directory for which they don't have clearance.
- *Forbidden.* This type of error occurs when the server is not permitted (by the operating system) to access a particular directory or file.
- *Not Found.* This type of error occurs when the URL entered by the user (or encountered in a link) is non-existent.

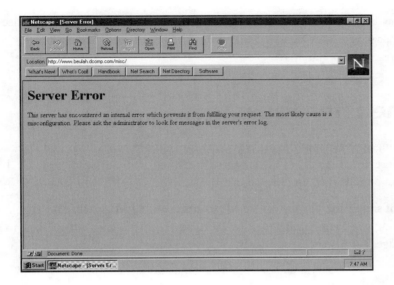

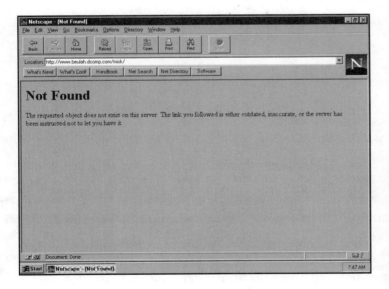

◆ *Server Error.* This type of error occurs in every other error case. Typically it happens when your content doesn't match your configuration (as in directory indexing not being turned on), or some other similar situation.

To change how FastTrack handles these error messages, there are two things you need to do: create the page you want displayed when the error occurs, and then configure FastTrack to react appropriately.

Creating the Error Pages

There is nothing special about the pages you use for your error handling. FastTrack allows you to use either regular HTML pages (the easiest method) or to create CGI scripts that can be run when an error occurs.

For the sake of simplicity, let's say you decide to create an HTML page. This page can contain anything you want, but it should at least give the visitor a way to get back to your main home page. For instance, consider the following code:

```
<HTML>
<HEAD>
<TITLE>Discovery Computing Inc.</TITLE>
</HEAD>

<BODY>
<CENTER>
<H1>Discovery Computing Inc.</H1>
</CENTER>

We're sorry, but the URL you have used does not refer to a valid page on oursite. Since
our Web site is a dynamic, exciting place, things are changing allthe time. This means
the page for which you are looking may actually beavailable elsewhere at this site.

<UL>
<LI>If you reached this page from an external site, please visit our home page.
We invite you to explore our site to make sure you don't miss out on the
information you are looking for.</LI>
<LI>If you reached this page by using a link elsewhere on our site, then we
want to fix it. Please make sure you leave a message for our Webmaster.</LI>
</UL>
```

```
<P>Visit our <A HREF="http://www.dcomp.com">home page</A> (a great place
to start).
<P>Leave a message for our <A HREF = "mailto:Webmaster@dcomp.com">Webmaster</A>.

<P>
<CENTER>
<IMG SRC = "http://www.dcomp.com/dci/art/rainban.gif">
<ADDRESS>
<A HREF="http://www.dcomp.com">Discovery Computing Inc.</A><BR>
20101 US Highway 14<BR>
PO Box 738<BR>
Sundance, WY   82729<BR>
800-628-8280<BR>
307-283-2714 (fax)
</ADDRESS>
<FONT SIZE=-1>
<P>Send comments to: <A HREF = "mailto:Webmaster@dcomp.com">
<EM>Webmaster@dcomp.com</EM></A><BR>
Copyright &copy 1996 <A HREF="http://www.dcomp.com">
Discovery Computing Inc.</A> All rights reserved.
</FONT>
</CENTER>


</BODY>
</HTML>
```

This is not a particularly complex page, it simply apologizes for any inconvenience and outlines the options for the visitor. Notice, however, that even though the page uses links and graphic images, it does not use any relative addressing. Thus, all addressing begins with the full http:// URL of the link. The reason for this is that the error message can be stored anywhere, and (as you will discover shortly) is typically stored outside of the normal site directory structure. If you used relative links, they would appear broken to whoever saw the page.

This error page is designed to be displayed when FastTrack generates a Not Found error. The page is much more descriptive (and friendly) than the default error message, as shown in Figure 18-3.

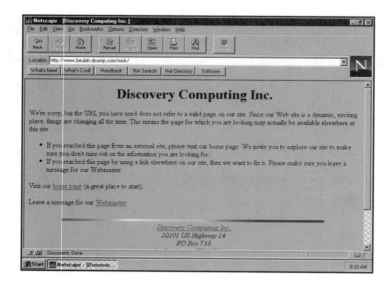

Remember that FastTrack allows custom responses to four different types of errors. While you don't need to create pages or CGI scripts for each one, you may want to for the sake of completeness. At a minimum, you should probably create custom messages for the Server Error Not Found error codes. These are the most common errors which visitors to your site could generate.

Once done, move the documents or scripts to their own directory on your hard drive. This directory does not need to be visible from your primary document directory. In fact, it is probably better if it is not accessible in this manner. That way, users cannot stumble across the error page files if you have directory indexing enabled at your site.

Configuring FastTrack

When you are done creating and storing the pages, you are ready to configure FastTrack to recognize your error messages. To do this, follow these steps:

1. Choose the Programs option from the Start menu. This displays the Programs menu.

2. Choose the Netscape option from the Programs menu. This displays the Netscape menu.

3. Click on the Administer Netscape Servers option. This starts Netscape Navigator, and shortly you will see a security dialog box asking for your user name and password.

4. Enter your user name and password as you specified it when installing FastTrack, then click on OK. This displays the Server Selector page.

5. Click on the name of the server whose error messages you want to configure. This displays the Netscape Server Manager, with the System Settings configuration category selected.

6. In the lower-left frame, click on the Error Responses option. Your screen should now look like what you see in Figure 18-4.

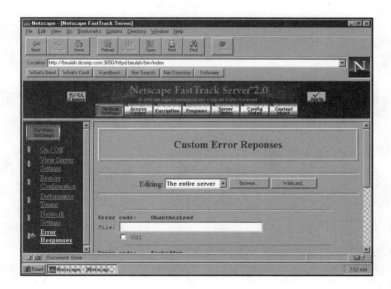

FIGURE 18-4

The Custom Error Responses page allows you to modify how FastTrack responds to error conditions.

All you need to do at this point is provide the file names for your custom error messages. Each of the four possible error conditions has their own File field in which you should place the full path name (not a URL) to the error message. If the file represents a CGI script, then you can click the CGI check box, as required.

When you are done, click on the OK button at the bottom of the page. Shortly you will see the Save and Apply page, where you can click on the Save and Apply button. Your changes are saved, and your custom error messages are enabled.

Testing Your Error Messages

Testing your error messages is a simple matter of generating the error condition that causes the error message to be displayed. Rather than wait for the user to generate an error, you should generate one so that you can check out the appearance of the message.

As an example, let's assume you want to test out the Not Found error message. You can do this by starting your browser and then entering a URL for a file you know does not exist at your site. You should then see the Not Found error message appear.

As another example, let's say you wanted to test the Server Error message. You can generate this error by first making sure directory indexing is turned off at your site. (You use the Netscape Server Manager to do this.) Then start your browser and enter a URL for a directory at your site that does not have a default Web page within it. This should result in FastTrack displaying the page associated with the Server Error code.

Managing Content Pages

A good portion of this book has been devoted to information concerning how you develop the content you make available on your Web site. You have learned how to create regular Web pages, as well as how to augment those pages with scripts and programs. No one every accused the Web of being placid or stagnant, and you will find that your pages will typically change frequently.

If you are adding pages to your Web site, it is typically no big deal. You simply add the page, link it to an existing page, and you have just made new content available to the world. Managing pages becomes much more complex, however, when you start deleting or moving pages at your site.

Moving or Removing Pages

You are already aware that there are companies that make it their job to index everything on the Web. While the growth of the Web may seem to make this an impossible job, companies such as Alta Vista, Yahoo, Inkatomi, and a multitude of others do an excellent job of keeping on top of the rising wave of the Web.

Many of these companies create their indexes through the use of robots. These special programs travel around the Web and examine different Web sites. They then dutifully catalog everything they find so that it can be retrieved by people visiting the index. For instance, the different Web sites we host have a total of perhaps 200 content pages. These pages are all linked together in one way or another. If a robot hits one of our pages, this means they can travel to them all. (See, a robot works through the maze of interconnected Web pages until all of them have been visited.) Once the visits have been made (and it happens at least weekly), then our pages are indexed, and others use those indexes to locate the content we have to offer.

The problem occurs if we decide to move a page (which changes its URL) or delete a page (which does away with its URL). When someone accesses our site through the index, all of a sudden they reach a roadblock—they cannot find the information they expected to find.

As you manage your Web site, you need to plan for these problems. (Don't be mistaken; they are problems which result from your actions.) As you manage your site, keep the following in mind:

- Only move or remove pages if you absolutely need to. Every time you move or remove pages you slam a door in the face of someone that wants to visit your site.
- If a page that has been removed from your site is now available elsewhere on the Web, create a forwarding page, or use the automatic URL forwarding feature of FastTrack. (This feature is discussed in the following section.)
- If a page has been moved elsewhere on your site, update the links at your site and create a forwarding page.
- Create pages for both the Server Error and Not Found error codes that may be generated by FastTrack. These pages should at least provide the user with a link to your main page or an index of available pages.

If you keep these items in mind, your visitors will have a smoother visit to your site. This means they will be more likely to come back again.

URL Forwarding

FastTrack allows you to implement URL forwarding, if you desire. This simply means that when one URL is requested by a browser, a second URL is automatically substituted for the first. For example, let's say that you used to have the following URL at your site:

```
http://www.beulah.dcomp.com/products/catalog.html
```

If this URL is available for any length of time, there are probably all sorts of links (which you may not even know about) established to this page. If your sales department later decides to change the catalog structure used by the company, or if the marketing department gets their own Web server, it might make more sense for the entire products directory (which includes the catalog page) to be stored elsewhere, as follows:

```
http://www.sales.dcomp.com/pubs/catalog.html
```

Rather than maintain two copies of the catalog (or the entire directory), or risk having "broken" links at your site, you can configure FastTrack to automatically forward requests for the first URL to the second. This is entirely transparent to the user, as well.

It is important, however, to remember that FastTrack allows you to transfer entire URL prefixes, not URLs that point to specific files. Thus, in the previous example, you could forward all references to http://www.beulah.dcomp.com/products to a different URL prefix or to a specific URL file. To forward a URL, follow these steps:

1. Choose the <u>P</u>rograms option from the Start menu. This displays the Programs menu.

2. Choose the Netscape option from the Programs menu. This displays the Netscape menu.

3. Click on the Administer Netscape Servers option. This starts Netscape Navigator, and shortly you will see a security dialog box asking for your user name and password.

4. Enter your user name and password as you specified it when installing FastTrack, then click on OK. This displays the Server Selector page.

5. Click on the name of the server you want to configure. This displays the Netscape Server Manager.

6. On the toolbar in the top frame, click on the Content Mgmt category. This changes the information in the lower frames.

7. In the lower-left frame, click on the URL Forwarding option. Your screen should now look like what you see in Figure 18-5.

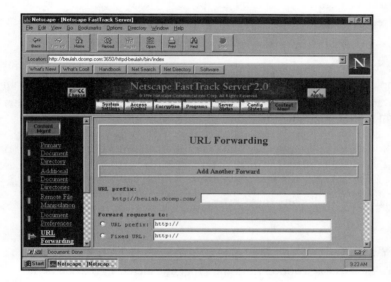

FIGURE 18-5

The URL Forwarding page is used to set up a forwarding condition.

All you need to do is enter the original URL prefix in the appropriate field. In the case of our example, you would enter products in the URL prefix field (the first part of the prefix is already supplied by Netscape Server Manager). Then, in the Forward Requests To area, you would specify how you wanted FastTrack to do the forwarding.

◆ If the entire directory has been transferred to a different area of your server or to a different server entirely, you would choose the URL Prefix option and then enter the new prefix. In our example, you would enter http://www.sales.dcomp.com/pubs as the new prefix.

◆ If the directory has been transferred off your server, and you want to display a notice indicating that people should update their links to the new site, then you should choose the Fixed URL option. This should then point to the informational page which you have set up on your server.

When you are done, click on the OK button to save your information. This displays the Save and Apply page, where you should click on the Save and Apply button.

Managing Server Users

In Chapter 15, "Basics of Security," you learned how you can set up users and groups of users under Windows NT. This is important information to know, because it can affect how you configure FastTrack to work with your operating system. The Windows NT security information (specifically users and groups) is not used to control who has access to your Web site. Instead, Netscape has decided to maintain their own user database for this purpose.

The user manager system used by Netscape is primarily used when you want to limit the number of people that have access to the information on your server. If you are running a free and public access site (meaning you want everyone to have access), then you don't need to worry about setting up users.

If you already understand how to manage users in the Windows NT environment, you will find it relatively easy to maintain users in the Netscape Server Manager. All management functions are done from the Access Control configuration area. You get to this part of the server manager by following these steps:

1. Choose the Programs option from the Start menu. This displays the Programs menu.

2. Choose the Netscape option from the Programs menu. This displays the Netscape menu.

3. Click on the Administer Netscape Servers option. This starts Netscape Navigator, and shortly you will see a security dialog box asking for your user name and password.

4. Enter your user name and password as you specified it when installing FastTrack, then click on OK. This displays the Server Selector page.

5. Click on the name of the server you want to configure. This displays the Netscape Server Manager.

6. On the toolbar in the top frame, click on the Access Control category. This changes the information in the lower frames. Your screen should now look like what you see in Figure 18-6.

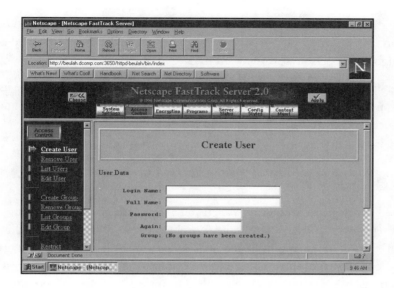

FIGURE 18-6

Netscape Server Manager allows you to control which users access your system.

Controlling Users

The first four options available in the Access Control configuration category allow you to manage user definitions. These are nothing more than a record of a potential user of your Web site. When you set up a user definition, you specify the following information:

- ◆ *Login Name.* This is the user name to be assigned to your visitor. The name can be up to 254 characters long.

- ◆ *Full Name.* This is the real name of the user (such as John Doe).

- ◆ *Password.* This is the password associated with the user name, up to eight characters in length. (You will need to enter the password twice.)

- ◆ *Group.* This is the user group to which you want the individual assigned. If there are no groups defined, then you cannot pick a group. (Groups are covered in the next section.)

That's it; there is no other information necessary in order to give someone access to your site. (You may remember that the Windows NT User Manager allows you to specify quite a bit more information about a user.) The information you supply here is entered by the user when they attempt to connect to your Web site. This process of logging in is very similar to the process you follow in gaining access to the Netscape Server Manager.

When you are through adding the individual, click on the OK button, and then on Save. The information is saved and you can continue adding users, as desired. You should add a user definition for every person who you want to have access to your Web site.

The other user-related choices in the Access Control category allow you to remove users, list the users you have defined, and edit users. All of these options function in essentially the same manner as when you added the user in the first place.

Controlling Groups

Groups are used to categorize your users. When you assign a user to a group, the user assumes all the rights and permissions of other members of that group (see the following section). As an example, members of the Production department in your company may need access to certain parts of the Web server, while those in Accounting need access to a different part. It makes sense, then, to create a Production group and an Accounting group. Each individual in those departments is than defined as a user (see the previous section) and included in the appropriate group.

To define groups, you click on the Create Group option of the Access Control configuration category. The Create Group page appears as shown in Figure 18-7.

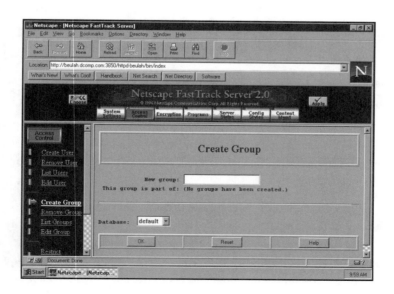

FIGURE 18-7

Groups are an organizational tool for your users.

To create a group, you simply need to supply the group name in the New Group field. For instance, you would enter the name Production or Accounting in the field. When you click on the OK button, your new group is saved in the user database.

The Access Control configuration category includes four options for managing your groups. These options parallel the options for users, allowing you to create, remove, list, and edit groups. You can select any of the options desired, and organize your groups in any manner desired.

Putting Users and Groups to Work

Users and groups are much more than a simple means to organize your Web site. In order for your users and groups to be useful, you need to restrict the access to your Web site. If you don't plan on restricting access, then it makes very little sense to create users and groups.

To restrict access according to your user database, you need to select the Restrict Access option of the Access Control configuration category. When you do, you can view the Restrict Access page. If access control is not turned on, you should click on the button labeled Turn On Access Control. The Restrict Access page then appears as shown in Figure 18-8.

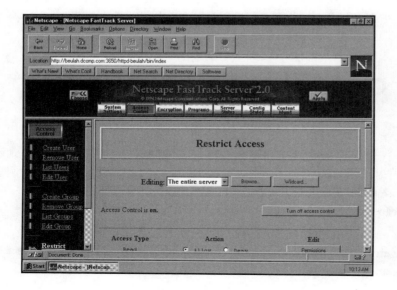

FIGURE 18-8

The Restrict Access page is used to specify who can have access to your Web site.

If you scroll through this page, you will see that FastTrack supports two types of access: read and write. You can, by default, either allow or deny either of these types of access. If you want to limit access to your site, you should make sure that the Deny action is selected. This means that everyone is denied access to your site. You can then click on the Permissions button to start allowing access to individual users as defined in your database.

For full information on how to use the Restrict Access page, refer to Chapter 16, "Internet Services and Security.")

Using Configuration Styles

With everything you have already learned in this book, you have probably come to the conclusion that there are quite a few ways in which you can configure your FastTrack server. Along with such flexibility comes the huge potential for confusion or mismanagement. To provide a way to possibly avoid such a problem, Netscape developed configuration styles. These styles are similar to style sheets in your word processor or spreadsheet program; they allow you to define common configuration characteristics, assign a name to that definition, and then apply the entire group of characteristics to specific directories or files in one fell swoop.

The advantage to using styles is that it allows you to apply the same configuration settings to different areas of your server. Thus, the styles help you save time because you don't need to "redesign the wheel" every time you want to similarly configure parts of your server.

Defining a Configuration Style

To create a new configuration style, follow these steps:

1. Choose the Programs option from the Start menu. This displays the Programs menu.

2. Choose the Netscape option from the Programs menu. This displays the Netscape menu.

3. Click on the Administer Netscape Servers option. This starts Netscape Navigator, and shortly you will see a security dialog box asking for your user name and password.

4. Enter your user name and password as you specified it when installing FastTrack, then click on OK. This displays the Server Selector page.

5. Click on the name of the server you want to configure. This displays the Netscape Server Manager.

6. On the toolbar in the top frame, click on the Config Styles button. Your screen should now look like what you see in Figure 18-9.

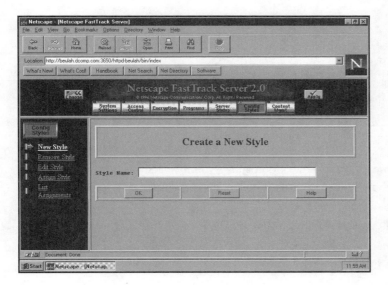

FIGURE 18-9

Netscape Server Manager makes it easy to create configuration styles.

7. In the Style Name field, enter the name you want used for this style, then click on the OK button. This automatically displays the Edit a Style page, as shown in Figure 18-10.

At this point you can specify different settings for this style. There are nine different areas in which you can make specifications, as follows:

- ◆ *CGI File Type.* This option allows you to specify different file name extensions for CGI scripts. CGI is covered in Chapter 11, "Working with Scripts."

- ◆ *Character Set.* This option allows you to set which international character set is applied to a directory. How this affects your documents is covered in Chapter 17, "The Netscape Server Manager."

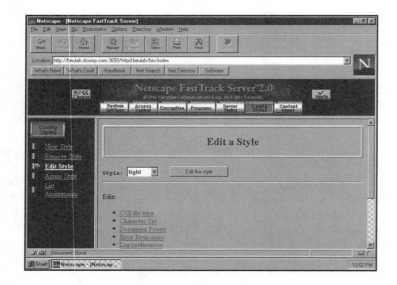

FIGURE 18-10

When you edit a configuration style, you can make changes in many areas.

- ◆ *Document Footer.* This option allows you to specify a short footer that is tacked onto all your pages. This option is discussed in Chapter 17, "The Netscape Server Manager."

- ◆ *Error Responses.* This option allows you to specify error message files to be used in conjunction with this style. These special message files were covered earlier in this chapter.

- ◆ *Log Preferences.* This option allows you to specify how information is written to the log files maintained by FastTrack. Server log files are discussed in Chapter 19, "Utilizing Log Files."

- ◆ *Remote File Manipulation.* This option allows you to control whether remote users have access to your document files.

- ◆ *Require Stronger Security.* This option allows you to specify how encryption should be handled for this style.

- ◆ *Restrict Access.* This option allows you to control who has access to the directories to which the style is applied.

- ◆ *Server Parsed HTML.* This option is used to specify how the server should handle parsing of Web pages in the affected directories.

Remember that as you make changes to each of these areas, you are not actually changing the server as a whole. Instead, you are defining parameters to be saved in your configuration style. These can later be applied to URLs, as required.

When you are done making changes, click on the OK button. This displays the Save and Apply page, where you should click on the Save and Apply button. Your changes are then committed to the server and you can start to use the style.

Editing Styles

Once a style is created, you can edit it at any time you desire. When you edit a style, you effectively go through the same configuration steps you did when you created it. (Remember, when you create a style the Edit a Style page is automatically displayed.)

If you ever get to the point where you no longer need a style, you should use the Remove Style option of the Config Styles configuration category to get rid of it. This frees up space on your server, and it also keeps clutter to a minimum. Once you delete a style, you cannot recover it; you must recreate the style from scratch.

Using Your Styles

After you have defined a style, you can associate it with a URL directory by clicking on the Assign Style option. This displays the Assign a Style page, as shown in Figure 18-11.

To assign the style to a URL prefix, simply enter the prefix into the field at the top of the page. For instance, if I wanted a style applied to the http://www.beulah.dcomp.com/general/info prefix, I only need to enter general/info into the field; the first part of the prefix is already there.

Next, pick the style you want applied by using the pull-down list. All of your defined styles are listed, along with the NONE option. (Picking NONE removes a style from a URL.) When you are done, click on the OK button, and you will see the Save and Apply page. When you click on the Save and Apply button, your changes are saved and you can continue assigning styles, if desired.

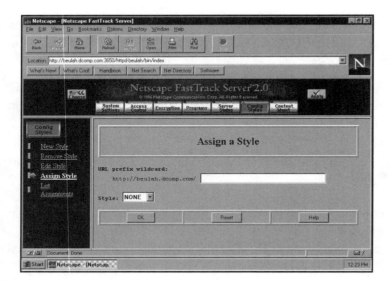

FIGURE 18-11

You can assign styles to any URL in your server.

Establishing Management Checklists

As you work with your Web site, over time you will setting into a routine of how you handle your management tasks. While it is true that the exact steps you follow will depend, in large part, on your site and your organization, there are some things which are common to all Web sites.

I have found it helpful to develop a management checklist that helps me remember what I need to do each day. The list is also helpful for training new people at my site, and as a reminder for those doing my duties when I am gone. The checklist is broken down based on frequency: items I must do daily, weekly, monthly, and as needed:

Web Site Management Checklist

Daily

☐ Add new content

☐ Review related sites on the Web

☐ Establish new external links

☐ Register with indexing services

☐ Review operating system security logs

☐ Back up Web site

Weekly

☐ Review server access logs

☐ Review error logs

☐ Check indexing services for proper links to our site

Monthly

☐ Print access reports

☐ Check pages and links

☐ Back up access logs

As Needed

☐ Change directory structure

☐ Add new users and groups

☐ Modify access control

☐ Renew encryption certificates

☐ Review system performance

Remember that this checklist is only a starting point. You should use it as such, and modify it to fit your needs. The important thing is that you quickly get a handle on what you need to do to effectively and efficiently fulfill your responsibilities.

Summary

The FastTrack server provides quite a bit of flexibility when it comes to configuring and managing your server. In this chapter you have learned about some of the tasks which you must do, from time to time, as a Webmanager. When combined with the information in the other chapters of this book, the information here can help make you very effective in your position.

In the next chapter, you learn how to utilize the log files generated by your FastTrack server.

Chapter | 19

Utilizing Log Files

The log files used in Web servers are similar to the log files you learned about in Chapter 16, "Internet Services and Security." The purpose of these log files is definitely the same—to provide an audit trail of what happens at your site.

The FastTrack server allows you to create two main types of log files: error logs and access logs. Exactly how much detail those files contain and how you use them is up to you. This chapter focuses on how those log files are put together and how you can use them to help manage your site.

> **NOTE:** Even though FastTrack maintains different types of log files, when people refer to just a plain log file (without any adjectives), they are typically referring to what FastTrack calls an access log.

Accessing the Error Log

FastTrack keeps track of all the errors that it encounters during operation, as well as any system-specific events, such as starting up and shutting down. This information is saved in a special log file referred to as the *error log*. This log file is particularly useful for finding "broken" URLs and other bad links.

You can view the error log through the Netscape Server Manager by following these steps:

1. Choose the Programs option from the Start menu. This displays the Programs menu.

2. Choose the Netscape option from the Programs menu. This displays the Netscape menu.

3. Click on the Administer Netscape Servers option. This starts Netscape Navigator, and shortly you will see a security dialog box asking for your user name and password.

4. Enter your user name and password as you specified it when installing FastTrack, then click on OK. This displays the Server Selector page.

5. Click on the name of the server whose error log you want to view. This displays the Netscape Server Manager.

6. In the toolbar in the upper frame, click on the Server Status button. This changes the information displayed in the lower frames.

7. In the lower-left frame, click on the View Error Log option. Your screen should now look like what you see in Figure 19-1.

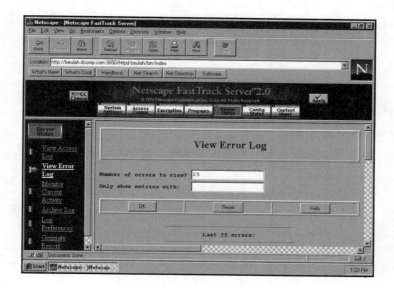

At this point you can enter the number of errors you wish to view (where each error represents an entry in the log file), as well as a filter word to use for displaying records. (If you supply a filter word, then only records containing that word will be displayed.) If you scroll through the View Error Log page, you can see the error log records that fulfill your request. The following is an example of what the error log entries look like:

```
[01/Jul/1996:06:56:45] info: successful server startup


[01/Jul/1996:07:13:18] info:  Suspend Httpd Service


[01/Jul/1996:07:47:25] info: successful server startup


[02/Jul/1996:07:46:49] config: for host 205.163.44.8 trying to GET /misc/, send-error
reports: missing parameter (path)
```

```
[02/Jul/1996:07:47:21] warning: for host 205.163.44.8 trying to GET /misk/, send-file
reports: can't find e:/basis/misk (ERROR_FILE_NOT_FOUND)
```

```
[02/Jul/1996:10:46:10] info: successful server startup
```

Each error log entry consists of the date and time of the error, the type of error (such as `info` and `warning` in these examples), and the actual error message. Periodically examining the error log can help you understand what is going on behind the scenes with your server.

If you desire, you can also access the error log file outside of Netscape's programs entirely. This is possible because the file is stored in ASCII format, so you can easily manipulate it using a text editor. The error log is stored at the following location:

```
c:\netscape\server\servername\logs\errors
```

Make sure you replace the `servername` directory with the name of the server whose error log you want to access.

Access Log Formats

It seems there are almost as many log file formats on the market as there are servers. Unfortunately, different servers save their log information in different formats. FastTrack allows you to either save your access log files in a format called common logfile format, or to specify exactly what you want saved.

It would be impossible (and impractical) to examine every possible log format in this chapter. A couple of log file formats are worth examining, however. The next couple of sections look at two rather common formats, and then we'll take a look at how you can modify what is saved in the FastTrack access log.

EMWAC Log Format

EMWAC is the European Microsoft Windows NT Academic Centre. Many people, before switching to the FastTrack server, used the EMWAC server for the Web. (This server represented a good, low-cost starting point for many people making their first forays into the Web.)

Because many Windows NT sites are familiar with or have used EMWAC servers, you may already have programs that analyze EMWAC format log files. Unfortunately, Netscape does not provide any programs that convert from one log-file format to another. This means that if you do have such analysis programs, you will either need to change them to work with the format used by FastTrack, or abandon them altogether and use the analyzer built in to Netscape Server Manager.

Common Logfile Format

The NCSA has devised a standard way of saving access information to a log file. The purpose of this standard is to set the stage so that programs that use the log file data could work on any number of products. This standard, appropriately enough, is called the *common logfile format.*

The common logfile format is understood and used by many of the Web servers on the market, including the FastTrack server. Although it is possible to save more information that what is maintained in common logfile format, the information maintained is more than adequate for tracking what's happening at your site.

Log files are made up of individual records. Each record reflects an event to which your server responded. Fields in each record are separated by spaces, and a carriage return terminates a record. The following is a portion of an access log file saved in common logfile format:

```
Req->srvhdrs.clf-status% %Req->srvhdrs.content-length%
205.163.44.3 - - [30/Jun/1996:06:41:44 -0600] "GET /demo/wireframe/example3.html
HTTP/1.0" 200 187
205.163.44.3 - - [30/Jun/1996:06:41:45 -0600] "GET /demo/wireframe/models/hughes_500.obj
HTTP/1.0" 200 38020
205.163.44.3 - - [30/Jun/1996:06:43:18 -0600] "GET /demo/wireframe/example4.html
HTTP/1.0" 200 181
205.163.44.3 - - [30/Jun/1996:06:43:24 -0600] "GET /demo/wireframe/models/knoxS.obj
HTTP/1.0" 200 21872
205.163.44.8 - - [02/Jul/1996:08:28:03 -0600] "GET /misk/ HTTP/1.0" 404 1430
205.163.44.8 - - [02/Jul/1996:08:28:03 -0600] "GET /misk/e:\basis/DCI/Art/rainban.gif
HTTP/1.0" 404 1430
```

```
205.163.44.8 - - [02/Jul/1996:08:30:47 -0600] "GET /misk/ HTTP/1.0" 404 1426
205.163.44.8 - - [02/Jul/1996:08:30:47 -0600] "GET /misk/e:\errormsg\rainban.gif
HTTP/1.0" 404 1426
205.163.44.8 - - [02/Jul/1996:08:30:53 -0600] "GET /misk/ HTTP/1.0" 404 1426
205.163.44.8 - - [02/Jul/1996:08:31:57 -0600] "GET /misk/ HTTP/1.0" 404 1443
205.163.44.8 - - [02/Jul/1996:08:33:30 -0600] "GET /misk/ HTTP/1.0" 404 1445
```

This excerpt represents only 11 records from the file. Each record consists of six fields, separated by spaces. The divider between the first two fields, however, is space, dash, space.) If no data exists for a particular field, a hyphen appears as a placeholder. Table 19-1 details the meaning of the fields in each record.

Table 19-1   Common logfile format record fields.

Field	Meaning	Comments
1	Client's IP address	
2	User name	Valid only for non-anonymous login
3	Date and time	
4	HTTP request	Enclosed within quotes
5	Service status code	See below
6	Bytes transmitted	

Notice that the fifth field is a status code, which indicates the code returned by FastTrack. For instance, FastTrack generates a code 200 when an operation was completed successfully.

Logging Options

FastTrack allows you to configure exactly how your access log is created and what information is stored in each entry in the file. In order to change how FastTrack creates its access log, follow these steps:

1. Choose the Programs option from the Start menu. This displays the Programs menu.

2. Choose the Netscape option from the Programs menu. This displays the Netscape menu.

3. Click on the Administer Netscape Servers option. This starts Netscape Navigator, and shortly you will see a security dialog box asking for your user name and password.

4. Enter your user name and password as you specified it when installing FastTrack, then click on OK. This displays the Server Selector page.

5. Click on the name of the server whose log file you want to change. This displays the Netscape Server Manager.

6. In the toolbar in the upper frame, click on the Server Status button. This changes the information displayed in the lower frames.

7. In the lower-left frame, click on the Log Preferences option. Your screen should now look like what you see in Figure 19-2.

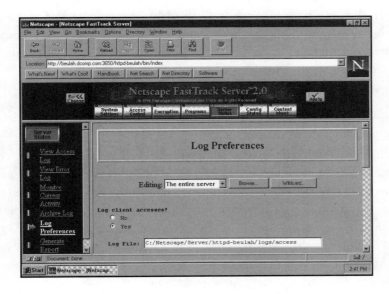

FIGURE 19-2

The Log Preferences page allows you to change how access logs are created.

The first option on the Log Preferences page allows you to indicate whether you want to even keep an access log. By default, an access log is maintained. (After all, it is a good idea for security purposes.) If you don't want to keep a log, you can click on the No radio button.

If you decide to keep an access log, you also need to specify where the log is to be created. By default, the access log is stored in the directory indicated in Figure 19-2. You can change to a different directory, if you want.

The balance of the options available from the Log Preferences page are discussed in the following sections. (You can view the options by scrolling through the Log Preferences page.)

What to Record

FastTrack gives you the opportunity to save either IP addresses in the access log, or domain names (DNS addresses). The example provided in the log file earlier showed that IP addresses were being logged. If you want domain names stored, then you must turn on the DNS feature of FastTrack. The DNS feature is controlled by the Performance Tuning option of the System Settings configuration category; it is discussed in Chapter 17, "The Netscape Server Manager."

If you specify that DNS names should be saved, and you have turned on the DNS feature, then FastTrack does a reverse lookup on all IP addresses it receives. While this is great information to have in your access log, it can slow down your server considerably. Most Web experts suggest that you don't use the DNS feature. Instead, store the IP addresses and then use a separate analyzer program to look up addresses.

Log File Format

Earlier in the chapter you learned that FastTrack typically saves information in the common logfile format. You are provided with quite a bit of flexibility in this area, however. FastTrack allows you to modify exactly what is stored in each log-file record. When you change the format of the file, however, remember that you are straying from the common logfile format. Since this format is used by many different servers, there are a wide variety of programs on the Internet that allow you to analyze and manipulate information stored in this format. When you change the format of your log file, you automatically make it non-compatible with those freeware or shareware programs.

There are 12 different pieces of information that FastTrack can save in the log file:

- Client hostname
- User name
- System date and time
- HTTP request
- Status

- Content length
- HTTP header, "referrer"
- HTTP header, "user-agent"
- Method
- URI
- Query string of the URI
- Protocol

The first six items in this field list are the same items recorded when using the common logfile format. The last six items are additional items which you can direct FastTrack to include.

Perhaps the most useful of these items is the field called HTTP header, "referrer." This allows you to record from where the user linked to your site. That way you can see where the most active sites are, and how people are getting to your site.

What to Exclude

The final option on the Log Preferences page allows you to indicate if anyone should be left out of the access log. This is a powerful feature that allows you to make your log files more meaningful. For instance, if you have a Web page that you want to develop statistics about, you can exclude your own accesses to the page. This helps you get a better picture of how popular the page really is. FastTrack allows you to either exclude host names (such as dcomp.com) or IP addresses.

Archiving Your Access Log

When you first install FastTrack, a single access log is established for your server. This means that all your access information is written to a single file, which keeps getting bigger and bigger. Periodically, it is a good idea to archive the access log so that you can work with the older files.

FastTrack allows you to either archive your logs manually, or to create archives automatically. Both methods are controlled from the Archive Log Files page, which is accessed in this manner:

1. Choose the <u>P</u>rograms option from the Start menu. This displays the Programs menu.

2. Choose the Netscape option from the Programs menu. This displays the Netscape menu.

3. Click on the Administer Netscape Servers option. This starts Netscape Navigator, and shortly you will see a security dialog box asking for your user name and password.

4. Enter your user name and password as you specified it when installing FastTrack, then click on OK. This displays the Server Selector page.

5. Click on the name of the server you want to configure. This displays the Netscape Server Manager.

6. In the toolbar in the upper frame, click on the Server Status button. This changes the information displayed in the lower frames.

7. In the lower-left frame, click on the Archive Log option. This displays the Archive Log Files page, as shown in Figure 19-3.

FIGURE 19-3

The Archive Log Files page is used to control how log files are archived.

At the top of the Archive Log Files page is a button, labeled Archive. If you click on this button, your current log files are immediately archived. What this means is that both the error and the access log are closed, renamed with the current date and hour appended to the file name, and a new log file opened. Thus, if you click the Archive button at 3:14 p.m. on August 14, the file access (which is the name of the access log) is renamed as access.14Aug-03PM, and a new access file is opened.

Archiving log files manually may not be feasible for most sites, either due to number of visits, availability of disk space, or how busy you are. In these instances, you can set FastTrack to automatically archive the log files without your intervention. You do this by clicking on the check box at the bottom of the Archive Log Files page, to the left of the word rotate. You can then specify how often you want the log files archived. The choices you have on the page allow you to archive anywhere from once to seven times a week (daily). You can also pick the time of day for the archival.

> **TIP:** Even though archival is not that difficult, nor does it consume a lot of time, you should pick a rotation time that is during your slower times. For many people, sometime in the middle of the night generally works best.

Using Log Files

As long as you have FastTrack maintaining log files for you, you need to worry about what to do with them. Exactly how you use log files may depend on your site needs. The following sections should give you some ideas on how you can use the log files created by FastTrack.

The Log File Analyzer

FastTrack includes a program called the Log File Analyzer. This program sifts through a log file and creates a summary overview of the information in the file. You can access any log file, including the one currently being used.

To use the Log File Analyzer, which is accessible through the Netscape Server Manager, follow these steps:

1. Choose the Programs option from the Start menu. This displays the Programs menu.

2. Choose the Netscape option from the Programs menu. This displays the Netscape menu.

3. Click on the Administer Netscape Servers option. This starts Netscape Navigator, and shortly you will see a security dialog box asking for your user name and password.

4. Enter your user name and password as you specified it when installing FastTrack, then click on OK. This displays the Server Selector page.

5. Click on the name of the server whose log file you want to analyze. This displays the Netscape Server Manager.

6. In the toolbar in the upper frame, click on the Server Status button. This changes the information displayed in the lower frames.

7. In the lower-left frame, click on the Generate Report option. Your screen should now look like what you see in Figure 19-4.

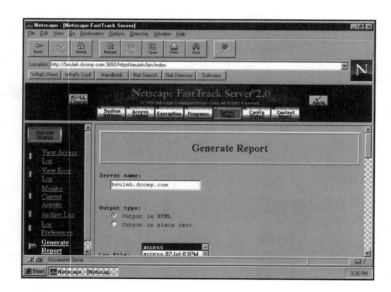

FIGURE 19-4

The Generate Report page is used to create a summary report from an access log.

In order to generate a report, there are three options you need to set, at a minimum:

♦ *Output Type.* There are two ways the Log File Analyzer can create output—either as an HTML file or as a text file. The former is great for simply viewing what is going on. The latter of helpful if you plan on including the report (or portions of it) in a different report being developed in your word processor.

♦ *Log File.* You can also pick the access log on which you want the summary report based. Remember that the access option, with no data and hour after it, is the current access log. All other files listed are archival in nature.

♦ *Output File.* If you supply a name for an output file, then the report is saved to disk. If you don't, then the file is displayed on the browser screen.

Outside of these three options, you don't need to specify anything else. The rest of the options on the Generate Report page allow you to control what is included in the summary report. The best way to use these options is to generate reports, figure out what you feel you don't need, make the changes, and generate again.

To generate a report, click on the OK button at the bottom of the Generate Reports page. Figure 19-5 shows what a full HTML report looks like.

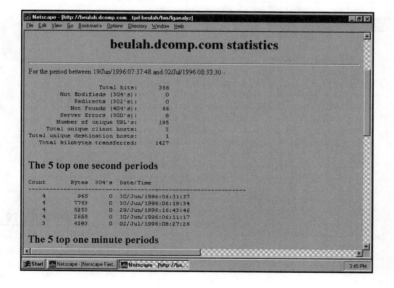

FIGURE 19-5

The Generate Report page is used to create a summary report from an access log.

Custom Programs

While the Log File Analyzer does provide some tremendous information, it is still limited. For instance, you can only use it to analyze a single log file. Thus, if you want a picture of how our site has done since the beginning of the year, it is difficult to get that information from the Log File Analyzer. This is where custom programs come in handy.

Because log files are written in plain ASCII text, writing a custom program to extract needed information shouldn't be that tough. You can use any programming language you want; if you use a program to transfer your log information to a database, you can use the programming features of the database to generate your reports.

As an example, we use a custom program (one we developed in-house) to transfer log information to an Access database. We then process our log files using Access. Once in Access, the information can be compiled into reports that provide the information we need to manage our site. Figure 19-6 shows an example of a log file that shows page-by-page activity on our Web site for the previous week. We use special filtering routines to weed out "bogus" activity events. For instance, we don't count visits from within our own network, and we have filtered out visits by robots from around the Web. The result is a nice, clean snapshot of how our site is doing.

Web Site Hits – Weekly/Monthly/Life to Date Summary

	7/30/96	7/31/96	8/1/96	8/2/96	8/3/96	8/4/96	8/5/96	Past 7 Days	Month to Date	Life to Date
Aladdin	8	10	3	7	11	5	9	53	35	1,219
Arrowhead Motel	6 4	6 2	11 2	5 1	4 1	6 1	3 1	41 12	29 6	1,123 292
Avalon Writing Center		2	1					3	1	35
Bear Lodge Motel	6 3	6 6	11 2	5 1	4 5	6 3	3 3	41 23	29 145	1,123 319
Bear Lodge Outfitters	4 6	6 9	8 17	3 7	13 11	10 12	9 12	53 75	43 59	1,100 1,336
Bell Fourche COC	3	11	6	4	7	9	5	45	31	411
Best Western	6	6 5	11 3	5	4 3	6 3	3 1	41 15	29 10	1,123 258
Business Climate	12 1	11 3	20 3	3 1	8 4	12 2	6 2	72 16	49 12	2,362 319
CanAm SD		2		1	2	6		2		22
Crook County	2		4		10		6	15	13	153
DCI - Authoring	14	25	16	29	10	13	26	133	94	800
DCI - Bear Lodge	5 17	3 14	15 6	1 10	1 5	9 3	5 5	39 60	31 29	674 317
DCI - Consulting		1	1	4			3	9	9	134
DCI - Fulfillment	11	7	5	9	8	8	12	60	42	578
DCI - Internet Advert.			2	2		1	5	5		60
DCI - Manufacturing	2	4	31	2	1		3	43	37	439
DCI - Publishing		1	7	2		6	16	15	187	
DCI - Search Engines		1	2		1			4	3	4
Devils Tower	16	39	24	15	11	14	15	134	79	3,785
Devils Tower Tr. Post	3	7	2			3	1	16	6	249
Discovery Computing	5 101	3 77	15 78	1 65	1 34	9 42	5 78	39 475	31 297	674 2,228
higbee's	6	6	11	5	4	6	3	41	29	1,123
Hulett										1
Hurd's Texaco	6	6	11	5	4	6	3	41	29	1,123
IMA Arizona	4	1	2		1			8	3	33
IMA California	14	4	12	5	2	5	9	51	33	126
IMA Colorado	5	2	2	3	2		2	16	9	38
IMA Facility Keys	5	9	4	9	2		3	32	18	112
IMA Idaho		1	1		2		2	4	4	15
IMA Illinois	4	1	3	2		2	1	14	9	40
IMA Kansas	1	1	1	2		1	1	7	5	20
8/6/96										1

FIGURE 19-6

A sample report created from log file entries in a database.

Managing the Log Files

Eventually you'll reach a point where you need to make some decisions about log files. Making those decisions early in the game can save you both time and hassle later on.

Perhaps the biggest decision is how long you're going to keep the log files generated by FastTrack. If you have an active site, the log files can mount up very quickly. Unless you have unlimited hard disk space, you probably need to set a time frame after which the log files are deleted or moved to an archive media.

Another option is to periodically toss out the information you no longer need from individual log file records. If you store information in the common logfile format, or in an expanded format, you can receive quite a bit of information, not all of it useful. At our site, we tend to throw out some fields (such as the server status code and the bytes transferred) just to make the information we maintain a bit more manageable.

You can also filter your records to pull out events you don't need. For instance, most people connected to the Internet are only interested in events generated by users outside their organization. You can use your IP address or subnet mask to filter out events generated by your own computers, as discussed earlier in this chapter. Depending on the number of people on your network, this could decrease your log file size quite a bit.

If you are running an intranet, you obviously can't filter out an entire subnet. Instead, you may want to filter specific client IP addresses—those used by your intranet content development staff, for example.

> **TIP:** If you are running an exclusive intranet, sort your log files by IP address to make sure that no unauthorized access from outside your organization is occurring. Looking through IP addresses for those that don't belong to your assigned IP address ranges makes this process easy.

Summary

Log files are the method by which you monitor and track what's happening at your Web site. They can be used for feedback and help in tailoring your site to meet the needs of your users. FastTrack lets you save your log files to a text file using any format you desire. This chapter has discussed the details of FastTrack log files, how you can use them, and how they can be most useful to you.

In the next chapter, you learn how to monitor and improve the performance of your site.

Chapter | 20

Monitoring and Improving Performance

If you've been using Windows NT for any length of time, you may already be familiar with the Performance Monitor. This tool enables you to graphically view the performance of your system, which is a great boon in optimizing. In this chapter, you learn how you can use the Performance Monitor with your Internet services.

It isn't the purpose of this chapter to provide an in-depth guide to how Performance Monitor is used. Instead, you learn the basics of the program, and then proceed with how you can use Performance Monitor for Internet service performance improvement.

The Task Manager

Historically, when someone mentions the Task Manager, most system administrators think of the task switcher in older versions of NT. In Windows NT 4.0, a new and improved Task Manager has been added. One of the features of the new Task Manager is that you can use it to monitor your system performance—at least to a degree.

To display the Task Manager, right-click on the Taskbar at the bottom of your screen. This displays a context menu, from which you should pick the <u>T</u>ask Manager option. When the Task Manager is displayed, notice that it has three tabs from which you can select. Click on the Performance tab, and your screen should appear as shown in Figure 20-1.

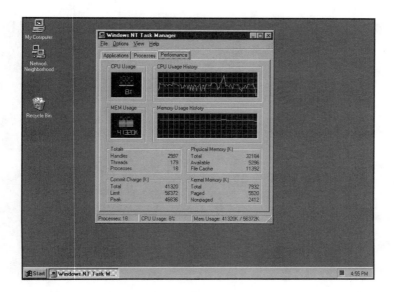

FIGURE 20-1

The Performance tab of the Task Manager can be used to display the general performance of your system.

Using the Task Manager, you can see how your system is doing in relation to your two primary resources: your CPU and your memory. If you double-click on the Task Manager (anywhere within the Performance Tab will do), you can see a larger representation of your CPU and memory usage graphs. This form of the Task Manager is shown in Figure 20-2. To return the Task Manager to normal, simply double-click on the graph again.

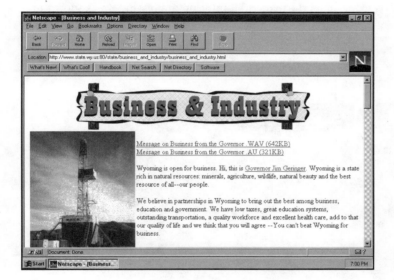

FIGURE 20-2

The Performance tab of the Task Manager can be used to display the general performance of your system.

Notice that at the right-side of the Taskbar is a small green square, right near the system time. This block, which appears when the Task Manager is active, displays a "gas gauge" that indicates how much of your CPU's capacity is being used. You can either minimize the Task Manager and keep an eye on the gas gauge, or you can choose <u>H</u>ide When Minimized from the <u>O</u>ptions menu and then minimize the Task Manager. (In this latter case, the Task Manager won't even show up on the Taskbar.) To again display the Task Manager, double-click on the gas gauge.

By keeping an eye on the Task Manager while you are in the middle of a normal day at your site, you can get a general idea of how your resources are holding up. If you need any more in-depth information, you will need to use the Performance Monitor, as discussed in the next section.

The Performance Monitor

The Performance Monitor is the one tool built into Windows NT that can help you make your system outstanding. Unfortunately, it's also one of the tools most commonly overlooked by system administrators. To start the Performance Monitor, choose Programs from the Start menu, then Administrative Tools (Common), and finally Performance Monitor. This displays the Performance Monitor program window, as shown in Figure 20-3.

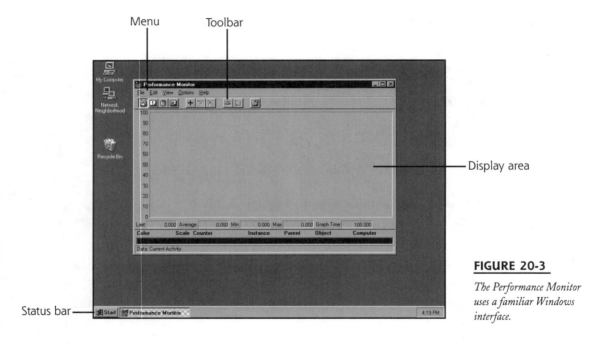

FIGURE 20-3

The Performance Monitor uses a familiar Windows interface.

The User Interface

The Performance monitor uses a typical Windows interface. The program window is divided into several areas. At the top of the program window is the menu bar, just above the toolbar. The majority of the program window is occupied by the display area. At the bottom of the program window is the status bar. Each portion of the user interface is discussed in the following sections.

The Menus

At the top of the program window is a menu with the choices File, Edit, View, Options, and Help. Most of the options available from the menus are also available from the toolbar, as described in the next section.

The choices available from the File menu vary, depending on which Performance Monitor window you're viewing. The purpose of each choice is the same; just the wording of the choices varies. The following list describes the major purpose of each File menu option:

- **New.** Eliminates all your current window settings and opens a new window, of the type you're currently using.
- **Open.** Enables you to load, from disk, any settings you have previously saved.
- **Save Settings.** Saves your current settings to disk, using a previously defined file name.
- **Save Settings As.** Saves your current settings to disk under a new file name.
- **Save Workspace.** Saves settings from all your Performance Monitor windows.
- **Export.** Lets you save your settings in a format other than the native Performance Monitor format.
- **Exit.** Exits the program.

Like the choices in the File menu, the wording of those in the Edit menu also changes depending on which Performance Monitor window you're viewing. The Edit menu includes the following options:

- **Add To.** Enables you to add an object to the current Performance Monitor window.
- **Edit.** Lets you change a chart line (in the Chart window) or an alert item (in the Alert window).
- **Time Window.** Allows you to modify the amount of detail displayed along the horizontal axis in the display area.
- **Clear Display.** Clears the information shown in the display area.
- **Delete From.** Removes an object from the current Performance Monitor window.

Use the <u>V</u>iew menu to choose which Performance Monitor window you want to show in the display area. The four choices are as follows:

- **<u>C</u>hart.** Shows a graphic representation of object performance over time.
- **<u>A</u>lert.** Shows alerts generated when the performance of an object passes a threshold which you define. You can also choose the action to be performed when the threshold is passed.
- **<u>L</u>og.** Allows you to specify the objects whose actions you want to monitor. The activity of those objects is then recorded in a log file for later analysis.
- **<u>R</u>eport.** Enables you to create reports based on the performance of objects in your system.

With the <u>O</u>ptions menu, you can control how information is derived, stored, or displayed by the Performance Monitor. Choices in the <u>O</u>ptions menu are fairly standard, but the first choice always varies based on the Performance Monitor window being viewed. (The first four items in the following list represent options displayed in the first menu position, based on which window is selected.)

- **<u>C</u>hart.** This option appears when working with the Chart window. It enables you to change display properties of the chart.
- **<u>A</u>lert.** This option appears when working with the Alert window. Select this option when you want to change how alerts are generated.
- **<u>L</u>og.** This option appears when working with the Log window. It allows you to change how the log file is created and where it's saved.
- **<u>R</u>eport.** This option appears when working with the Report window. Use it to change how often the report is updated.
- **<u>M</u>enu and Title.** When this option is selected, the menu and title bar are displayed.
- **<u>T</u>oolbar.** When this option is selected, the toolbar is displayed.
- **<u>S</u>tatus Bar.** When this option is selected, the status bar is displayed.
- **Always on Top.** When this option is selected, the Performance Monitor window appears on top of whatever other program windows are open on your screen.

◆ **Data From.** This option enables you to specify where Performance Monitor should obtain its information. Your choices are from current activity (real-time) or from a prerecorded log file.

◆ **Update Now.** This option forces the information in the display area to be updated.

◆ **Bookmark.** This option enables you to save text information with your log file. The bookmark is designed so that you can make notes about the log file.

The Toolbar

The Performance Monitor also includes a toolbar at the top of the program window. This toolbar, if not visible on your system, can be turned on by choosing Toolbar from the Options menu. The various tools on the toolbar perform many of the same functions you can select from the menus.

Notice that the tools are divided into four groups. The leftmost group, consisting of four tools, controls which window is currently shown in the display area. These four tools correspond to the four choices in the View menu. The first tool displays the Chart window, the second the Alert window, the third the Log window, and the fourth the Report window.

The second group of tools provide a way to quickly modify items added to the windows. The first option is for adding an object, the second for editing the object, and the third for deleting an object. These tools correspond to choices available on the Edit menu.

The third group of tools corresponds to the bottom two choices on the Options menu. The first tool in this group is used to update the information in the display window, and the second is used to set a bookmark in a log file.

The fourth group consists of a single tool. This tool provides the same purpose as the first choice on the Options menu—displaying the options for the current window you are viewing.

The Display Area

The display area of the Performance Monitor changes, based on which window you have selected from the View menu or from the toolbar. When you have selected the Chart window, the display area contains a chart. This chart displays the performance of selected objects over time. The vertical axis is a scale appropriate to the objects, and the horizontal axis represents time.

If you have the Alert window selected, the display area shows the alert log. At the bottom of the display area is the legend, which represents the objects on which you want to be alerted. The main part of the display area is the log of when those alerts have been triggered.

With the Log window selected, the display area shows a list of the objects you're logging, as well as the status of the log file itself. Finally, with the Report window selected, the display area shows the objects you have added to the report.

The Status Bar

At the bottom of the Performance Monitor program window is a status bar. This functions the same as the status bar on any other Windows program. Its primary purpose is informational, but it doesn't really provide a whole lot of information. If you select a menu item, a quick reminder of what the item is used for appears in the status bar. However, when you are working in the display area, the only thing shown is where the information in the window is derived from (current activity or log file).

To turn the status bar on or off, choose Status Bar from the Options menu. If a check mark appears next to the option, the status bar is on; if no check mark, the status bar is off.

Monitoring Objects

You can monitor objects in any window that makes the most sense for your purposes. To add an object, click the Add tool on the toolbar to display the Add To dialog box. The exact appearance of the dialog box differs, depending on the window currently displayed. For example, if you're working in the Chart window and you choose to add an object, the dialog box appears as shown in Figure 20-4.

Notice that the dialog box allows you to select a Computer, an Object, a Counter, and an Instance. These items are rather hierarchical in nature. When you select a computer, that determines the objects available. Likewise, selecting an object affects the counters available, and the counter affects the instances.

The objects available on a particular computer system are, to a degree, dependent on what's installed on that system. Different system components provide different Performance Monitor objects. Common objects include processors, memory, cache, threads, and processes. In addition, different application programs may add their own objects that the Performance Monitor can access.

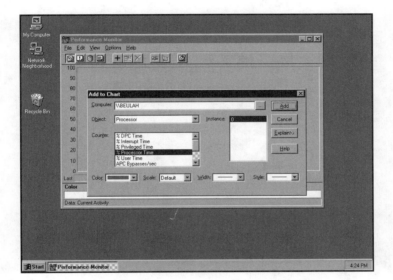

FIGURE 20-4

The Add To dialog box is used when adding an object to a window.

Within objects, you can monitor different counters or instances of counters. The counters vary depending on the object you have selected. For example, if you choose the processor object, you can monitor counters such as processor time or interrupt usage. If you pick an object such as threads, you can monitor counters such as thread state or thread wait reason.

TIP: If you want to know what a specific instance within an object represents, click the Explain button in the Add To dialog box. This action displays an explanation area at the bottom of the dialog box.

Refresh Rate

One of the items most often changed when using the Performance Monitor is the refresh time. This value determines how often the Performance Monitor samples the values necessary to update the display. By default, the Performance Monitor updates the information once every second. To change the refresh rate, click the Options tool on the toolbar, or choose the first option under the Options menu. Using either of these actions with the Chart window selected, for example, displays the Options dialog box shown in Figure 20-5.

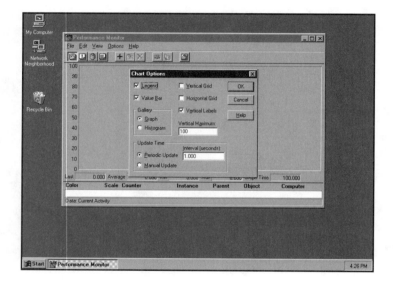

FIGURE 20-5

In the Options dialog box, you can change display and acquisition properties of the selected window.

To change the refresh rate, make sure that the Periodic Update radio button is selected, and then change the value in the Interval field. If you want, you can also choose the Manual Update radio button. If you choose this button, however, you can update the information in the Performance Monitor only if you click the Update tool on the toolbar, or choose Update Now from the Options menu.

> **TIP:** Use the other selections in the Options dialog box to change display properties of the current window as desired.

Printing Reports

Unfortunately, the Performance Monitor doesn't allow you to print results. In those instances where you need a hard copy of your performance results, you have one of two options. First, you can capture the contents of the screen, and then use a graphics editing program to print the screen. (This is particularly effective when displaying the Chart window.) For example, you can use the Paint accessory to do this by following these steps:

1. In the Performance Monitor, display the window you want to print.
2. Maximize the Performance Monitor program window.
3. Press the PrintScreen key. This action copies a "snapshot" of your desktop to the Windows Clipboard.
4. Minimize the Performance Monitor program window.
5. Open the Paint accessory.
6. Choose Paste from the Edit menu. The copy of the Performance Monitor program window should appear in Paintbrush.
7. Choose File, Print to open the Print dialog box.
8. Click OK. Your printout is sent to the printer.
9. Close the Paint accessory.

The other option for printing Performance Monitor information is to export the raw data generated by Performance Monitor to another program, and then use that program to print the information. Common programs you can use include spreadsheet and database programs. This method of printing Performance Monitor data allows you to add any additional information necessary to your report. You can also change the format or appearance of the information using the capabilities of your spreadsheet or database program. To export the information, follow these steps:

1. In the Performance Monitor, display the window containing the information you want to export.
2. Choose File, Export to open the Export As dialog box, shown in Figure 20-6.
3. In the Save as Type pull-down list (lower-left corner), select TSV or CSV. (TSV stands for tab-separated values; CSV is comma-separated values.)
4. In the File Name field, specify the name to be used for this file.

5. Select the drive and directory in which to store the file.

6. Click <u>S</u>ave to save the export file.

After the information is saved to a disk file, you can use your spreadsheet or database program to load the data and manipulate it. You can then print the information with that program.

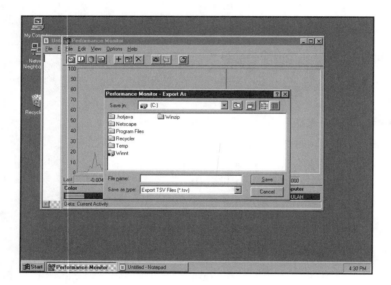

FIGURE 20-6

Using the Export As dialog box to create an export file from the Performance Monitor.

FastTrack Performance

The FastTrack server is a high-needs program that runs round the clock on your server. The more people you have visiting your site, the higher the resource needs of the system. By actively monitoring how your system performs with FastTrack running, you can come up with ways to make your system run even better. The advantage in doing this is faster access time for people visiting your site.

The value of measuring performance depends, to the largest extent, on how busy your site is. If you're only running a couple of hundred connections per day, it's questionable whether you really have enough to monitor. However, if you're running a couple of hundred connections per hour, you're getting into the range where you might be able to really benefit from a good analysis of how your site is being used.

Chances are good that the hardware on which you are running FastTrack is also running other servers, as well. For instance, you may be running an FTP server and DNS server on the same system as FastTrack. As you analyze the performance of your various servers, you may not see any real problems in any individual server, but instead detect problems in your entire site. These types of problems can typically be boiled down to the amount of memory in your server, or the type of CPU you're using. Before you run out and add more memory or another (or different) CPU, use Performance Monitor to check out the problem.

In the area of memory, remember that Windows NT uses a concept called *virtual memory*. This means your system uses as much RAM as it can; when it runs out, it swaps information to and from the hard disk in a page file. With this situation in mind, you can monitor the performance of two counters to see how they relate to each other.

First, examine the Pages/Sec counter of the Memory object. If this value is pretty high—say, above 5 on a consistent basis—consider adding more memory. You can clinch the decision by comparing the Pages/Sec counter to the Avg. Disk Sec/Transfer counter of the Logical Disk object. If these two counts are both high, your system is spending quite a bit of time swapping information to and from the disk. In this case, you could definitely benefit from adding memory to your system.

On the CPU side of the fence, there are a couple of counters you should check out. First, take a look at the % Processor Time counter of the Processor object. Add this to the Chart window, and then add the % Disk Time counter from the Physical Disk object. If the processor time is consistently high (over 75%) and your disk time is low (under 10%), you would probably benefit from an upgraded or additional CPU.

You may also want to look at the Processor Queue Length counter of the System object. If the queue length is greater than 2 for extended periods, the rest of your system is waiting inordinately long on your CPU. In a bottleneck situation like this, you need to add another CPU or upgrade the one you have.

Improving Performance

If you notice that your site is acting sluggish, and you think that you need to add some equipment to your site, investigate the following items, in this order:

- **Memory.** As you learned in Chapter 1, "Your Hardware," Netscape requires at least 32MB of memory to run properly. Check out how much time is being spent swapping information to disk. If it's a lot (as covered in the preceding section), consider more memory, going first to 48MB, and then even higher.

- **Hard drive.** The biggest problem here isn't necessarily hard drive space, but the speed of your hard drive. Internet services tend to be disk-intensive, as files are read from all over your disk and sent over the wire. If you're using an older hard drive that has an access time of 12 ms or greater, strongly consider a new one. You can get access times down near 8 ms now, and you'll notice a big improvement in response times.

- **CPU.** The more people you have simultaneously visiting your site, the more work your CPU needs to do. If you have quite a bit of activity, you could probably benefit from a speedy Pentium system. However, if you don't get that much activity (a couple of hundred hits per day), you should be able to get by with a fast 486 chip. (If your server also is working hard for people in your office, though, the Pentium chip becomes a big plus.)

- **Network connection.** When all else fails, you may need to get a faster Internet connection, but understand that this can be a very costly approach. (Internet connections are covered in Chapter 3, "Your Internet Connection.")

These items are listed in this order primarily for cost reasons, as well as their likelihood of being a problem. On a byte-per-byte basis, RAM costs more than hard drive space (even though it is coming down), but more often than not we try to get by with too little. But both of these items are cheaper than a new CPU, and much cheaper than a new network connection.

Don't rashly jump to any conclusions without using a tool such as the Performance Monitor to check out your suspicions. You can do this by applying the information covered in this chapter. Monitor the proper system counters, and then make sure that they support spending the money necessary for the additional hardware.

Summary

After your Internet site is up and running, part of your management routine should include checking the performance of your site. (This was mentioned in Chapter 18, "Day-to-Day Management.") The tool provided for this in Windows NT is the Performance Monitor. By effectively using the objects and counters in the Performance Monitor, you can determine how well your system is doing at all times.

INDEX

Symbols and Numbers
32-bit systems, 12
56Kb channel, 52
80486 family, 9-10

<A>....</A> **tag, 157-160, 214**
  HREF attribute, 157-160
access log files, 454-459
  archiving, 459
  changing how created,
    456-459
  common logfile format,
    455-456
  DNS addresses, 458
  EMWAC format, 454-455
  format, 458-459
  IP addresses, 458
  viewing, 420
  what to exclude, 459
  what to record, 458
access time, 15-16
accessing information
  basics, 212-223
  FTP (file transfer protocol)
    files, 213-221

Gopher files, 222-223
  URLs (Uniform Resource
    Locators), 212-213
Account Policy dialog box,
  359
  account lockout, 361
  password restrictions,
    360-361
accounts
  lockout, 361
  setting effective policies,
    359-361
  user, 361-371
Add To dialog box, 474-475
Add Users and Groups
  dialog box, 367
Add/Remove Programs
  dialog box, 119
Additional Document
  Directories frame, 84-85
<ADDRESS>....</ADDRESS> **tag,**
  161-163
Administer Netscape
  Servers shortcut, 121
administrator privileges, 69

admserv directory, 116-117
Albitz, Paul, 33
alert method, 301
anchor method, 313
anchors, 157-159
Applet Viewer, 335
<APPLET>...</APPLET> **tag,**
  338-339
  CODE attribute, 338-339
  HEIGHT attribute, 338,
    344
  WIDTH attribute, 338,
    344
applets, 326
  Control Panel, 37
  passing parameters to,
    345-348
  templates, 348-349
application log file, 42, 404
applications, 326
Archive Log Files page,
  459-461
archive log creation, 421
archiving access log files,
  459

archiving log files, 460-461
ARPA (Advanced Research Projects Agency), 47
ARPANET, 47
arrays, 315-316, 329
Assign a Style page, 447
attributes, 154
AU files, 131-132
audio file formats, 131, 132
auditing, 375-376
authoring tool, 25
automatic URL forwarding, 437

<B>....</B> tag, 151-152
back method, 306
beta, 32
big method, 313
BigFont object, 336-337
Blank command, 194
blink method, 313
body, 135-137
  displayed information, 137-139
<BODY>....</BODY> tag, 135-136, 191, 295
  attributes, 192
bold method, 313
bold text, 151
**
 tag, 139, 141-142, 179**
Browser Window
  differences between Netscape Navigator and Netscape Navigator Gold, 185-186
  text wrapping, 205

bulleted lists, 150, 203
ByRef keyword, 277

C language, 252
cc:Mail, 34
CD-ROM drives, 7
  speed, 17-18
<CENTER>....</CENTER> tag, 144-146, 155
centering
  paragraphs, 202
  text, 144-146
CERN image map file format, 99-100, 165-166
Certification Authority (CA), 380-381
CGI (Common Gateway Interface), 98, 230
  file types, 420
  programs and directories running from, 420
CGI scripts
  another way of configuring for, 420
  file name extensions, 445
CGI_Mail program, 281-284
CGI_Main routine, 274
changed link page script, 317-319
changing to Netscape FastTrack
  directory structure, 95
  file and directory names, 95-96
  HTML differences, 100

  image map files, 99-100
  log files, 96-97
  sample conversion, 101-105
  scripts, 97-98
  server differences, 94-101
  stepping through documents, 101
Character Format toolbar, 187
  Image tool, 204
  Make Link tool, 206
characters, formatting, 151-153
charAt method, 313
check boxes, 239-244
<CITE>....</CITE> tag, 153
Class A networks, 31
Class B networks, 31
Class C networks, 31
classes, 330
  collections of, 331-332
clear method, 305
clearTimeout method, 301
client side vs. server-side programs, 327
client software, 22
client/server basics, 22-23
client/server model, 22
clients, 22
close method, 301, 305
<CODE>....</CODE> tag, 153
color in HTML documents, 191-192
com domain, 29
comment fields, 246-248

comments <! - -> tag, 293-294

Common Log File Format, 97, 455-456

company logo and audio file applet, 339-344

HTML document, 342-344

methods, 341-342

compressed files, 128-129

computers

memory requirements, 13-14

requirements, 6

UNIX operating systems supported, 6

Windows NT hardware platforms supported, 6

concentrator, 8

configuration styles, 444-447

active assignments, 422

assigning, 447

assigning to URL, 422

defining, 444-447

deleting, 422

editing, 422, 447

encryption, 446

error messages, 446

new, 421

configuring Netscape FastTrack during installation, 72

configuring networks, 37-39

configuring Web server

additional document directories, 83-85

changing default port ettings, 81-83

controlling directory indexing, 80-81

default file, 76-79

hosting multiple sites, 85-91

confirm method, 301

connection types, 49-50

content directories, separating from executable files, 399

content pages

managing, 436-439

moving, 436-437

removing, 436-437

URL forwarding, 437-439

context menus, 188-189

CONTEXT.TXT file, 32

Control Panel

accessing, 37

applets, 37

icons, 37

Network applet, 37-39

Services applet, 39

conversion functions, 311-312

CONVERT command, 359

CoolPage function, 308

copyrighted information, 128

Web pages, 199

CPUs (central processing units)

80486 family, 9-10

Pentium family, 11

Pentium Pro, 11-12

speed, 9-12

Create Group page, 442-443

current date and time of where server located program, 279-281

Custom Error Responses page, 435

daemons, 39

data flow analysis, 12

data types, 309-310

date and time formatting, 278

day zero backups, 392-393

dedicated service, 50

DSU/CSU (data service unit/channel service unit), 51-52

phone lines, 52-53

required equipment, 50-53

routers, 50-51

default file, 76, 423

changing name of, 77-79

default HTML page, 108

default ports

changing settings, 81-83

HTTP commands, 81

Default Publish Location command, 186

Denny, Robert, 266
destroy( ) method, 342
`<DFN>....</DFN>` **tag, 153**
Dial-Up Networking, 36
dial-up service, 49
differences between servers, 94-101
  directory structure, 95
  file and directory names, 95-96
  HTML differences, 100
  image map files, 99-100
  log files, 96-97
  operating systems, 94-95
  sample conversion, 101-105
  scripts, 97-98
  security, 99
  virtual servers, 101
directories
  additional document, 83-85
  default home for content pages, 75
  differences in structure in servers, 95
  examining daily, 394
  installing Web servers in different, 114
  international character sets, 445
  organizing server, 62-65
  permissions, 263, 287, 371-374
  problems with changes in structure, 95
  Read permission, 399

  restricting access, 446
  running CGI programs from, 420
  structuring, 64-65
  tracking users, 375-376
  turning browsing on/off, 81
  URLs (Uniform Resource Locators), 62-63
  users can't access, 113-114
  watching structure, 393-394
Directory Auditing dialog box, 376
directory indexing, 65, 80-81, 423
directory names, differences between servers, 95-96
Directory Permissions dialog box, 263, 287, 372-373
directory structure, 126-127
Discovery Computing Inc.
  directory organization, 64-65
  directory structure, 126-127
displaying text message applet, 335-337
  adding to Web page, 338-339
  compiling, 337
DNS servers, 28-31
  BIND port, 32
  checking installation, 68
  commercial versions, 32
  difficulty in setting up, 33

  domain addresses, 28-30
  domain name, 56
  IP addresses, 30-31, 57
  Microsoft DNS, 32
  people can't locate Web server probem, 112
  when they are necessary, 31
  where to obtain, 32
document directories
  additional, 83-85, 423
  additional aren't visible, 114
  links pointing to files or documents in other, 114
document files, 399
document object
  methods, 304-305
  properties, 302-304
Document Preferences frame, 79
document.write function, 291
documents
  remote manipulation, 423
  remote user access, 446
domail.pl program, 250
domain addresses, 28
  domain name, 29-30
  domains, 28-30
  geographical domains, 30
  level of domain, 28-30
domain name, 29-30
  DNS server, 56
  fees, 56
  registering, 55-56
  selecting, 55

domains
complexity, 28-29
geographical, 30
levels of, 28-30
modifying access rights, 40
top-level, 29
DoPublishers subroutine, 282-284
dosimple function, 296
DoTitles subroutine, 282-283
drawString method, 337
DS3 bandwidth, 53
DSU/CSU (data service unit/channel service unit), 51-52
dynamic communications links, 46
Dynamic Execution, 11-12

e-mail
accounts, 224-225
servers, 33-34
sending, 224-225
User Agents, 33
Edit a Style page, 445-447
Edit Document command, 185
Edit tool, 186, 199
editing Web documents
adding graphics, 204-205
adding links, 206
text, 200-203
editor preferences, 189-193
Editor Preferences command, 186, 189

Editor Preferences dialog box, 189
Appearance tab, 191-192
General tab, 190-191
Publish tab, 192-193
Editor Window
activating links, 206
changing text attributes, 201-202
Character Format toolbar, 187
differences between Netscape Navigator and Netscape Navigator Gold, 186-189
editing Web documents, 199-206
empty, 194
File/Edit toolbar, 187
graphics, 205
HTML code creation, 208
loading Web documents from disk, 198
menus, 187
Paragraph Format toolbar, 187
pop-up menus, 188-189
setting preferences, 189-193
toolbars, 187
EDO RAM, 14
edu domain, 29
effective account policies, 359
account lockout, 361

password restrictions, 360-361
EIDE hard drives, 16
<EM>....</EM> **tag, 153**
embedded systems, 324
EMWAC, 33, 454-455
FTP server, 35
server, 102
equipment and Internet providers, 50-53
error log, 452-454
viewing, 420
error messages
meaningful, 430-431
testing, 436
error page creation, 432-434
errors
forbidden, 430
not found, 430
server, 431
unauthorized, 430
escape codes, 153, 256, 278
eval function, 311-312
event logs, 403-404
Event Viewer, 41-42
managing log files, 406
starting, 403
Event Viewer window, 41
events, 307-308
evt file extension, 406
example Java applets
company logo and audio file, 339-344
displaying text message, 335-339

**example JavaScript scripts,
317-321**
changed link page, 317-319
formatting input, 319-321
**example WinCGI program,
279-284**
CGI_Main program,
281-284
EXE files, 266
executable files
separating from content
directories, 399
site security, 400
Export As dialog box, 477
external URLs, 157
**extra header name value,
276**

f32d20.exe program, 69
Fast Page Mode RAM, 14
**FastTrack README
shortcut, 122**
**FieldPresent function,
275-277**
file formats, 130-132
audio, 131-132
compressed files, 129
graphics, 130-131
**file names, differences
between servers, 95-96**
File/Edit toolbar, 187
Save tool, 207
files
permissions, 371-374
tracking users, 375-376
users can't access, 113-114

**FindExtraHeader function,
275-276**
firewall, 390
fixed method, 313
fixed-width text, 151
fontcolor method, 313
fontsize method, 313
forbidden errors, 430
<FORM>...</FORM> tag, 231
ACTION attribute, 250,
267
METHOD attribute,
250-251, 267
FORMAT command, 358
formatting
characters, 151-153
input script, 319, 320, 321
paragraphs, 139-142, 202
forms
check boxes, 239-244
checking if value was
passed to your program
by server, 275-276
comment fields, 246-248
creation, 231-233
Enter button, 233
GET method, 267
limiting input, 237-238
linking to WinCGI, 267
POST method, 267
pull-down lists, 244-246
radio buttons, 239-244
renaming buttons, 236
Reset button, 235
retrieving value associated
with field, 276-277

scripts, 231-248
strings to scripts, 252-256
submission methods,
249-250
Submit button, 233,
235-236
Submit Query button, 241
submitting, 233-236
text boxes, 246-248
understanding, 231
user input, 231
forward method, 306
**From Template command,
194**
**From Wizard command,
196**
**FTP (File Transfer
Protocol), 34-35**
accessing from your Web
site, 213-221
directory links, 213-217
file links, 217-221
servers, 34-35
sites, 35, 215

garbage collection, 332
gateways, 395-396
**Generate Report page,
462-463**
geographical domains, 30
GET method, 249-250, 267
**GetAcceptTypes procedure,
274**
GetArgs procedure, 274
**GetExtraHeaders
procedure, 274**

GetFormTupples procedure, 274
getParameter method, 347
GetProfile procedure, 274
GetSmallField function, 275-277
GIF file format, 131, 156
global groups, 365
go method, 307
Gopher, 35-36
accessing files from your Web site, 222-223
servers, 35-36
site, 36
gov domain, 29
graphics
adding to Web documents, 204-205
changing properties, 205
clickable regions, 163
file formats, 130-131
file sizes, 156
GIF file format, 156
including in document, 154-156
tables, 178-181
graphics accelerators, 18
graphics adapter, 18
groups
global, 365
local, 364
managing, 442-443
putting to work, 443-444
user accounts, 364-365

\<H1\>....\</H1\> tag, 143-144, 179, 181
hard drives
access time, 15-16
backing up, 17
EIDE, 16
latency, 15
requirements, 6-7
RPM (revolutions per minute), 16
SCSI, 16
seek time, 15-16
sizes, 16
speed, 15-16
transfer rate, 15
hardware
networks, 8
requirements, 5-8
servers, 4-7
workstations, 7-8
hardware virtual servers, 87-89, 424
Hardware Virtual Servers frame, 88-89
head, 135-137
identification information, 136-137
specialized information to another program, 137
\<HEAD\>....\</HEAD\> tag, 135-136, 295
headings, 143-144
history object, 306-307
horizontal rule, 160-161
\<HR\> tag, 160, 161

HTML (HyperText Markup Language), 63, 134
differences between servers, 100
links to WinCGI, 267-269
source code editor, 190
versions, 135
HTML documents, 134-146, 182
authoring name, 190
body, 135-139
centering text, 144-146
color schemes, 191-192
company logo and audio file applet, 342-344
designing headings, 143-144
displayed information, 137-139
e-mail addresses, 160
footers, 424
formatting characters, 151-153
formatting paragraphs, 139-142
head, 135-137
horizontal rule, 160-161
identification information, 136-137
image editor, 190
image maps, 164-165
including graphics, 154-156
links, 157-160

lists, 146-150
MIME header, 256
on-the-fly creation, 256
organization/individual
    responsible for, 161-163
scroll bars, 156
special fonts, 161-163
structure, 135-139
tables, 166-181
tags, 134-135
templates, 190
title, 136
white space, 139
HTML tags, 134-135
attributes, 154
`<HTML>....</HTML>` **tag, 136**
**HTTP (Hypertext
Transport Protocol), 23**
command default port, 81
HTTP command, 63
**https-remove command,
104**
HTTPS.CPL file, 104
HTTPS.EXE file, 104
HTTPS.HLP file, 104
hub, 8

`<I>....</I>` **tag, 151-152**
**image map files, 99-100,
163-165**
creation of, 166
CERN format, 99-100
HTML tags, 164-165
NCSA format, 100
Netscape FastTrack, 100

shape definitions, 99
user creation, 208
`<IMG>` **tag, 154-155, 164**
ISMAP attribute, 165
SRC attribute, 154
img_url object, 347
import keyword, 336
**improving site
performance, 479-480**
**improving system
performance**
CPU capacity, 469
Performance Monitor,
    470-478
printing reports, 477-478
Task Manager, 468-469
improving throughput, 42
indexOf method, 314
**information, accessing
basics, 212-223**
**init( ) method, 341g- 342,
347**
InitializeCGI routine, 274
`<INPUT>` **tag, 231**
CHECKED attribute, 240,
    243
MAXLENGTH attribute,
    237-238
NAME attribute, 233, 241
SIZE attribute, 237
TYPE attribute, 233
types, 235
VALUE attribute, 236
**installing Netscape
Navigator Gold, 70-71**

**installing Netscape
FastTrack, 69-75**
configuration information,
    72
default home directory for
    content pages, 75
Internet address of Web
    server, 73
license agreements, 71
location of files, 71
server conversion example,
    104
Setup program, 69-75
user name and password for
    Netscape Server
    Manager, 73-74
Welcome screen, 69-70
instance variables, 330-331
int domain, 29
Internet
connection types, 49
definition of, 46
dynamic communications
    links, 46
history, 46-47
packet switching, 46-47
vs. intranet, 47
Internet providers, 48
billing, 49
communications, 49
connection types, 49-50
cost, 54
equipment, 48
obtaining IP addresses, 57
phone line links, 52

required equipment, 50-53
routers, 51
security, 54
selecting, 54
services, 49, 54
support, 54
Internet Shopper, 33-34
internetwork system, 47
InterNIC (Internet Network Information Center), 55-56
whois server, 56
Inter_Main subroutine, 273
intranet, 25
vs. Internet, 47
server-side programs, 327
IP (Internet Protocol) addresses, 28, 30-31
DNS server, 57
new server, 91
obtaining, 57
router, 57
servers, 63
IP ports, watching in real time, 421
ISDN (Integrated Services Digital Network) channel, 53
ISPs (Internet Providers). See Internet providers
italic text, 151
italics method, 314

Java
adding /java/bin directory to system path, 333-334
applets, 326
applications, 326
arrays and strings, 329
bytecode, 332
classes, 330
client-side vs. server-side programs, 327
compilers, 332-333
data types, 327-328
defining, 324
developing programs, 332-335
developing skills, 350-353
development cycle, 325
enabling for server-based programs, 420
example applets, 335-344
garbage collection, 332
instance variables, 330-331
interfaces, 331
JavaScript vs., 290
memory management, 332
methods, 330-331
multiple inheritance, 331
newsgroups, 352
objects, 329-332
operators, 328-329
packages, 331-332
passing parameters to applets, 345-348
resources in JDK (Java Developer's Kit), 350-352
speed, 326
subclasses, 330

template for applets, 348-349
virtual machine concept, 325-326
Web sites, 352-353
Java Developers Kit (JDK), 333-335
resources, 350-352
java.applet package, 331
java.awt package, 331
java.io package, 331
java.lang package, 331
java.net package, 331
java.util package, 332
JavaScript, 324
adding to Web pages, 291-296
arrays, 315-316
browsers and, 290
conversion functions, 311-312
creating windows, 299
data types and variables, 309-310
defining, 290
document object, 302-305
double quotes and command line, 308
events, 307-308
example scripts, 317-321
functions, 294-296
hiding code, 292-294
history object, 306-307
Java vs., 290
location object, 305-306
logical data type, 309

null data type, 309
number data type, 309
objects, 296-307
operators, 316-317
reserved words, 310
simulated events, 308
string data type, 309
strings, 310-315
switching between data types, 311
user events, 307-308
window object, 299-302
JPG file format, 131

<KBD>....</KBD> **tag, 153**
key pair file
changing password, 419
generating, 418

L2 cache, 12
LANs (local area networks), 8
lastIndexOf method, 314
latency, 15
<LI>....</LI> **tag, 146, 148, 150**
link method, 314
links, 24, 157-160
adding to Web documents, 206
Gopher servers, 222-223
pointing to files or documents in other document directories, 114

server differences, 95-96
testing, 159
lists
bulleted, 150, 203
nesting, 148-149
numbered, 146-147
ordered, 146-147
unordered, 150
Liu, Cricket, 33
LiveWire, interfacing with, 420
local groups, 364
local URLs, 157
location object, 305-306
Log File Analyzer, 461-463
log files, 41-42, 393
access, 454-459
analyzing, 461-463
archiving, 460-461
configuring settings, 405-406
custom programs, 463-464
deleting fields, 465
error log, 452-454
filtering records, 465
how information is written to, 446
keeping, 465
managing, 406, 464-465
parameters, 421
server differences, 96-97
sorting by IP address, 465
usage reports, 421
Log Preferences page, 457-459

Log Settings dialog box, 406

macros, 230
Main( ) procedure, 272
Main( ) subroutine and error handling, 274
MakeArray( ) function, 315
MakeEXE command, 279
management checklists, 448-449
managing
content pages, 436-439
server users, 440-444
managing Web site information
compressed files, 128-129
copyrighted information, 128
focusing on unique topics, 127-128
map files, 164-165
CERN format, 165-166
NCSA format, 165-166
shapes, 165
MapEdit, 100, 166
Mbps (millions of bits per second), 15
meaningful error messages, 430-431
configuring Netscape FastTrack to recognize, 434-435
error page creation, 432-434
testing error messages, 436

memory
nanoseconds, 14
Netscape FastTrack
requirements, 69
quantity requirements,
13-14
requirements, 13-14
server requirements, 7
service pack requirements,
67
services, 13
speed, 14
<META> **tag, 137**
attributes, 154
methods, 330-331
Mi'Mail, 34
Microsoft DNS server, 32
Microsoft Mail BackOffice
portion, 34
mil domain, 29
MILNET, 47
MIME header, 256
monitors, 7
MTA (Message Transfer
Agent), 33
multihoming, 101
multiple branch prediction,
12
multiple inheritance, 331
multiple Web sites
hardware virtual servers,
87-89
multiple Netscape
FastTrack instances,
89-91

software virtual servers,
85-87

named windows, 299-300
nanoseconds, 14
NCSA image map file
format, 100, 165-166
nesting lists, 148-149
net domain, 29
Netscape Browser
command, 205
Netscape FastTrack
beta versions, 68
changing to, 94-101
components, 23-25
configuring for running
WinCGI programs,
285-287
default HTML page, 108
image map files, 100
installing, 69-75
memory requirements, 69
multiple instances, 89-91
Netscape Navigator Gold,
25
Netscape Server Manager,
25
performance, 478-479
recognizing error messages
configuration, 434-435
removing from system,
117-122
requirements, 26-27
uninstall program, 120
UNIX operating systems
supported, 6

Web documents don't show
up after converting to,
115
Web server, 24-25
Welcome screen, 69
Windows NT 3.51, 26-27
Windows NT 3.51 Service
Pack, 27
Windows NT hardware
platforms supported, 6
Netscape FastTrack
server, 4
Netscape menu, 77, 80, 82
Netscape Navigator, 69
differences from Netscape
Navigator Gold,
184-189
Netscape Navigator Gold,
25, 69
Browser Window, 185, 186
differences from Netscape
Navigator, 184-189
Editor Window, 186-189
installing, 70-71
interface, 184
what it is, 184
Netscape Page Wizard,
196-197
Netscape Server Manager,
25, 78, 80, 82, 84, 261, 438,
462
Access Control category,
416-417, 440-443
applying configuration
changes, 413
category choices, 413

Config Styles category, 421-422, 445
configuration areas, 412-413
configuration categories, 414-424
configuration window, 413-414
Content Mgmt category, 422-424, 439
Encryption category, 418-419
networks, 424-426
Programs category, 419-420
script location, 97
Server Status category, 420-421
starting, 410-411
starting and stopping Web server tests, 110-111
System Settings category, 415-416
toolbar, 412-413
unable to get into, 116-117
user interface, 411-412
user name and password, 73-74, 116-117
viewing error log, 452-454
Netscape window, 121
Network applet, 37-39
networks
configuring, 37-39
environment, 4
hardware, 8
interface card, 8

LANs (local area networks), 8
Netscape Server Manager, 424-426
TCP/IP configuration, 38
New Document command, 185, 194, 196
New Local Group command, 365
New Local Group dialog box, 365
New User command, 363
New User dialog box, 363-364, 397
NewApplet class, 336
NewApplet.class file, 337
NewApplet.java file, 336-337
not found errors, 430
Notepad, 190
Now( ) function, 278
NTFS (Windows NT file system), 358-359
numbered lists, 146-147

objects, 296-332
instance variables, 330-331
methods, 330-331
monitoring, 474-475
octet, 30
`<OL>....</OL>` **tag, 146, 148**
OOP (object-oriented programming), 329-330
Open File command, 198
Open File in Browser command, 185

Open File in Editor command, 185
open method, 299-302, 305
operating systems, 94-95
operators, 316-317
option menus, 244-246
`<OPTION>` **tag, 244, 246**
Options dialog box, 476
ordered lists, 146-147
org domain, 29

`<P>....</P>` **tag, 139-141**
packages, 331-332
packet switching, 46-47
pages, 24
paint( ) method, 341-342
Paragraph Format toolbar, 187
Paragraph toolbar
Bulleted List tool, 203
Center tool, 202
paragraphs
bulleted lists, 203
centering, 202
formatting, 139-142, 202
`<PARAM>` **tag**
NAME attribute, 348
VALUE attribute, 348
ParseFileValue procedure, 274
parseFloat function, 311-312
parseInt function, 311-312
passwords
editing file, 116-117
enforcing, 395

restrictions, 360-361
users, 441
Pentium family, 11
Pentium Pro, 11-12
**people can't locate Web
server problem, 112**
**Performance Monitor, 42,
470-478**
display area, 473-474
Edit menu, 471
exporting information, 477
File menu, 471
menus, 471-473
monitoring objects,
474-475
Options menu, 472-473
printing results, 477
refresh rate, 475-476
status bar, 474
toolbar, 473
user interface, 470-474
View menu, 472
**Perl (practical extraction
and reporting language),
252, 260**
permissions, 371-374
phone lines, 52-53
**PlusToSpace subroutine,
275, 277-278**
**point-to-point connection,
52**
pop-up menus, 188-189
**ports, changing default
settings, 81-83**
**POST method, 249-250,
267**

post.office, 34
printing reports, 477-478
private profile file, 270-271
problems and solutions
addition document
directories aren't
visible, 114
installing Web server in
different directory, 114
people can't locate server,
112-113
unable to get into Netscape
Server Manager,
116-117
user getting error when
connecting to server, 113
users can't access some files
and directories, 113-114
users only see directory
when connecting to
server, 116
Web documents don't show
up after converting to
Netscape FastTrack, 115
**processing mailing list
request form script,
257-260**
programs
MapEdit, 100, 166
Netscape Navigator Gold,
25
WinCGI, 98
Programs menu, 77, 80, 82
Programs window, 121
prompt method, 301

**Properties dialog box,
204-205, 263, 287,
372, 375**
Publish tool, 193
pull-down lists, 244-246

**QUERY_STRING
environment variable, 254**

radio buttons, 239-244
**RAM (random access
memory), 14**
**RAS (Remote Access
Service), 36**
refresh rate, 475-476
**remote browsers, sending
HTTP response code 204
to, 278**
**removing Netscape
FastTrack from system,
117-120**
residual files and cleanup,
121-122
reports, printing, 477-478
**REQUEST_METHOD
environment variable, 250**
required equipment, 50-53
**Restrict Access page,
400-402, 443-444**
reviewing events
configuring log file settings,
405-406
managing log files, 406
viewing event logs,
403-404

robots, 137, 437
routers, 50-51
  IP address, 57
routine backups, 392
RPM (revolutions per minute), 16
running scripts, 261-263
running WinCGI program, 284
  configuring Netscape FastTrack, 285-287
  setting directory permissions, 287

`<SAMP>....</SAMP>` **tag, 153**
Save As command, 207
Save command, 207
Save Remote Document dialog box, 199
`<SCRIPT>...</SCRIPT>` **tag, 291, 294**
  LANGUAGE attribute, 292
scripts, 97-98
  basics, 230-231
  CGI (common gateway interface), 230
  choosing scripting language, 251-252
  creation, 249-260
  escape codes, 256
  forms, 231-248
  languages and conventions, 98
  located on server, 251

PRINT statements, 256
processing mailing list request form, 257-260
returning information to server, 256
running, 261-263
storing, 97-98
strings from form, 252-256
structure of information received, 255-256
understanding, 230
Visual Basic, 251-252
writing, 257-260
scroll bars, 156
SCSI hard drives, 16
SDRAM, 14
sec-key program, 377-378, 380
secure machines, 396
security
  differences between servers, 99
  Internet providers, 54
  reviewing events, 403-406
  server, 390-396
  site, 396-402
  SSL (Secure Sockets Layer), 376-387
  Windows NT, 358-376
security dialog box, 77
security log file, 42, 404
seek time, 15-16
`<SELECT>...</SELECT>` **tag, 244, 246**
Send subroutine, 275, 277

sending e-mail, 224-225
SendNoOp subroutine, 275, 278
server conversion example, 101-102
  bringing down old server, 103-104
  checking installation, 105
  converting information, 104-105
  installing Netscape FastTrack, 104
  planning move, 102
server errors, 431
server security
  backups, 392-393
  developing security plan, 390-396
  enforcing passwords, 395
  gateway machines, 395-396
  guest account, 395
  log files, 393
  secure machines, 396
  watching directory structure, 393-394
  watching programs used, 394-395
  written plan, 391-392
Server Selector page, 77, 80, 82, 111, 261, 410-411, 435, 445
server software, 4, 22
servers, 4, 22
  adding, 89-91, 424
  bringing down old, 103-104

CD-ROM drives, 7
certificate management, 419
computers, 6
CPU speed, 9-12
databases of users, 417
differences between, 94-101
differences in file and directory names, 95-96
directory indexing, 65
DNS-related information, 415-416
domain address, 63
editing existing user, 416
editing groups, 417
encryption system on/off, 418
error responses, 415
groups, 417
hard drives, 6-7
hardware requirements, 5-7
importing collection of users, 417
IP address, 63
key pair file, 418
limiting access to, 400-402, 417
listing groups, 417
listing users defined, 416
managing, 410-411
managing users, 440-444
memory quantity requirements, 13-14
memory requirements, 7

modifying information sent to browser, 424
on/off, 415
operating systems, 94-95
organizing directories, 62-65
parsing Web pages, 446
password for key pair file, 419
performance tuning, 415-416
restoring configuration, 415
scripts returning information to, 256
security standards, 418
sending output to file to send back to, 277
services, 13
setting up, 65-69
user definitions, 416
user name and password in relation to operating system, 415
video system, 7
viewing settings, 415
Service dialog box, 398
service pack, 66-68
obtaining, 27
services, 28-36, 39
memory, 13
modifying, 39
Services applet, 39
starting and stopping Web server tests, 109

Services dialog box, 39, 103, 109, 398
SetFont method, 336
setTimeout method, 301
setting up site
domain name, 55-56
lead time, 57-58
obtaining IP address, 57
Setup program, 69-75
SGML (standard generalized markup language), 134
shape definitions, 99
shortcuts, deleting, 121-122
simulated events, 308
site security
document files, 399
executable files, 400
FastTrack only user account, 396-399
limiting access to server, 400-402
separating content directories and executable files, 399
sites
network environment, 4
setting up, 55-58
small method, 314
software virtual servers, 85-87, 424
defining, 86
Software Virtual Servers frame, 87
sound_url object, 347

sp4_351i.exe file, 66
special characters, 153
Special File Access dialog box, 373-374
speculative execution, 12
SSL (Secure Sockets Layer)
  authentication, 376
  enabling, 386
  encryption, 376
  enrolling site, 380-381
  generating key file, 377-380
  implementing, 377
  installing certificate, 384-386
  integrity, 377
  registered Certification Authority (CA), 377, 380-381
  registered encryption key, 377
  requesting certificate, 381-384
  usage differences, 387
Start Menu window, 121
start( ) method, 341-342
stop( ) method, 341-342
strike method, 314
strings, 312, 329
  converting plus signs into spaces, 277
  methods, 313-315
<STRONG>...</STRONG> tag, 134, 153
sub method, 314
substring method, 314

subsystems, 42
sup method, 315
superVGA cards, 18
system log file, 42, 403
system objects, 42
system performance, improving, 468-478
System Properties dialog box, 333-334

T1 channel, 52-53
T3 channel, 53
<TABLE>....</TABLE> tag, 166
  BORDER attribute, 168-169, 179
  CELLPADDING attribute, 169
  CELLSPACING attribute, 169
tables
  aligning cell contents, 175-177
  attributes, 168-169
  borders, 168-169
  cells, 166
  filler in cells, 171
  graphics in, 178-181
  headings, 166-167
  rows, 166
  skipping cells, 170-171
  space between cell contents and border, 169
  spanning columns, 171-174
  spanning rows, 174-175
  user creation, 208
  width of cell dividers, 169

Task Manager, 468-469
TCP/IP network configuration, 38
<TD>....</TD> tag, 166, 171
  ALIGN attribute, 176
  COLSPAN attribute, 172-173
  ROWSPAN attribute, 175
templates, 194-195
  applets, 348-349
  URL (Uniform Resource Locator), 194
  user-created, 196
testing Web server installation, 108-111
text
  bold, 151, 202
  centering, 144-146
  centering paragraphs, 202
  changing attributes, 201-202
  entering, 200-201
  fixed-width, 151
  formatting paragraphs, 202-203
  italic, 151
  logical styles, 152-153
  physical styles, 151-152
  underlined, 151
text boxes, 246-248
<TEXTAREA>...</TEXTAREA> tag, 246
  COLS attribute, 248
  GET method, 250
  NAME attribute, 248
  ROWS attribute, 248

`<TH>....</TH>` **tag, 166-167**
ALIGN attribute, 176
throughput, improving, 42
`<TITLE>....</TITLE>` **tag, 136-137**
toLowerCase method, 315
toolbar
Bold tool, 202
changing text attributes, 201-202
Content Mgmt button, 79-80, 84, 86
Edit tool, 199
Heading 1 tool, 201
Programs tool, 262
Publish tool, 193
System Settings tool, 82
top-level domains, 29
toUpperCase method, 315
`<TR>` **tag, 166**
ALIGN attribute, 176-177
transfer rate, 15
`<TT>....</TT>` **tag, 151**

`<U>....</U>` **tag, 151**
`<UL>....</UL>` **tag, 150**
unauthorized errors, 430
underlined text, 151
Unescape function, 275, 278
uninstall program, 120
unique topics for Web sites, 127-128
UNIX
daemons, 39
FTP daemon, 35

hard drive requirements, 6-7
operating systems supported, 6
Pentium Pro, 12
workstation requirements, 8
unordered lists, 150
update command, 67
URL forwarding, 438-439
URLs (Uniform Resource Locators)
assigning configuration styles, 422
associating international character set with, 424
directories, 62-63
directory path, 63
executable script file, 250
external, 157
forwarding requests for, 423
HREF attribute, 157
linking to WinCGI, 268-269
local, 157
mailto: resource type, 224
main URL mapped on hard drive, 423
resource types, 63, 212-213
server address, 63
single slash (/) after resource type, 63
templates, 194
user accounts
FastTrack only, 396-399
groups, 364-365

new, 363-364
user rights, 366-371
User Agents, 33
user events, 307-308
User Manager, 40-41
User Manager program, 359
Administrator privileges, 362
groups, 363-365
new user account, 363-364
starting, 362
user rights, 366-371
users, 363
User Manager window, 40-41
user rights
advanced rights, 369-371
regular rights, 367-369
User Rights Policy dialog box, 366-367
users
can't access some files and directories, 113-114
can't locate Web server, 112
getting error when connecting to Web server, 113
group, 441
managing, 440-444
only see directory when connecting to server, 116
password, 441
putting to work, 443-444
real name, 441
user name, 441

<VAR>....</VAR> **tag, 153**
variables, 309, 310
VB40032.DLL file, 279
VBRUN300.DLL file, 279
VGA cards, 18
video cards, 7, 18-19
video systems, 7
  VGA cards, 18
  video cards, 18-19
View Error Log page, 453-454
virtual machine concept, 325-326
virtual memory, 479
  Windows NT, 13
virtual servers
  differences between servers, 101
  hardware, 87-88
  software, 85-87
Visual Basic
  scripts and, 251-252
  WinCGI, 266
  WinCGI framework file, 271-274

WAV files, 131-132
Web browsers, 23
  active window, 299
  JavaScript and, 290
  locating information with URLs, 62
  logical styles, 152-153
  Netscape Navigator Gold, 25

single slash (/) after resource type, 63
testing links, 159
Web document creation, 193
  blank pages, 194
  existing pages, 198-199
  Netscape Page Wizard, 196-197
  templates, 194-196
Web documents, 24
  adding graphics, 204-205
  adding JavaScript, 291-296
  adding links, 206
  copyrights, 199
  displaying text message applet, 338, 339
  don't show up after converting to Netscape FastTrack, 115
  e-mail accounts, 224-225
  editing, 199-206
  footers, 446
  links, 24
  loading from disk, 198
  loading from Web, 198-199
  objects, 297-307
  referencing information and handling images, 193
  saving, 207
  transferring information to remote system, 193
Web Page Starter command, 186

Web robots, 137
Web servers, 23-25
  administrator privileges, 69
  checking your system, 68-69
  common problems and solutions, 111-117
  configuring, 76-91
  disabling others, 69
  hosting multiple sites, 85-91
  installing in different directory, 114
  installing service pack, 66-68
  Internet address, 73
  people can't locate, 112-113
  setting up, 65-69
  testing installation, 108-111
  testing starting and stopping, 109-111
  user getting error when connecting, 113
  users only see directory when connecting to, 116
Web sites
  accessing FTP (file transfer protocol) files, 213-221
  accessing Gopher files, 222-223
  directory indexing, 65
  directory structure, 126-127
  hosting multiple, 85-91
  improving performance, 479-480

Java, 352-353
managing every aspect of, 25
managing information, 127-129
restricting access to, 443-444
services, 28-36
time availability, 50
turning directory browsing on/off, 81
WebDate function, 275, 278
white space, 139
whois server, 56
WinCGI, 98
adding code, 275-278
checking if value was passed to your program by server, 275-276
compiling program, 279
converting string plus signs into spaces, 277
defining, 266
example program, 279-284
extra header name value, 276
formatting date and time, 278
forms linking to, 267
how information is passed, 270-271
HTML links to, 267-269
private profile file, 270-271
program creation, 271-278

program has no response for information passed to it, 278
programs as EXE files, 266
programs on different drive than server, 285
removing escape codes from raw HTTP text, 278
retrieving value associated with field, 276-277
running programs, 284-287
sending output to file to send back to server, 277
speed of programs, 281
storing programs, 267, 420
URLs (Uniform Resource Locators) linking to, 268-269
versions, 266
Visual Basic, 266
WinCGI framework file, 271, 273
InitializeCGI routine, 274
Inter_Main subroutine, 273
Main( ) procedure, 272
obtaining, 272
window object, 299-300
methods, 301-302
properties, 300
windows, 299-300
Windows 95 Dial-Up Networking, 36
Windows CGI, 266
Windows NT
32-bit programs, 251

Administrators group, 365
Control Panel, 37-39
Event Viewer, 41-42
FTP server in Windows NT Resource Kit, 35
hard drive requirements, 6-7
hardware platforms supported, 6
log files, 41-42
Pentium Pro, 12
Performance Monitor, 42
removing Netscape FastTrack from system, 118-119
tools, 36-42
User Manager, 40-41
video system requirements, 7
virtual memory, 13, 479
workstation requirements, 8
Windows NT 3.51, 26-27
installing latest service pack, 66-68
Windows NT 3.51 Service Pack, 27
Windows NT 4.0
deleting shortcuts, 121-122
removing Netscape FastTrack residual files and cleanup, 121-122
service pack, 27
Windows NT security, 358-359
auditing, 375-376
FAT system, 358-359

NTFS (Windows NT file system), 358-359
permissions, 371-374
setting effective account policies, 359-361
user accounts, 361-371
Windows NT Server
RAS (Remote Access Service), 36
Windows NT Server 3.51, 26

Windows NT Server 4.0, 27
installing Netscape FastTrack, 69
Windows NT Workstation 3.51, 26
Windows NT Workstation 4.0, 27
workstation requirements, 7-8
write method, 305

writeln method, 305
WWW (World Wide Web), 24
growth, 24-25
loading Web documents from, 198-199
pages, 24
robots, 137

x2c function, 278

FILL IN AND MAIL TODAY

Prima Publishing
P.O. Box 1260BK
Rocklin, CA 95677-1260

USE YOUR VISA/MC AND ORDER BY PHONE:
1-800-632-8676 extension 4444

OR, TO ORDER BOOKS ONLINE:
sales@primapub.com

YOU CAN ALSO VISIT OUR WEB SITE:
www.primapublishing.com

Please send me the following titles:

Quantity	Title	Amount

Subtotal	$
Postage & Handling ($4.00 for the first books plus $1.00 each additional books)	$
Sales Tax	
7.25% Sales Tax (California only)	
8.25% Sales Tax (Tennessee only)	
5.00% Sales Tax (Maryland only)	
7.00% General Service Tax (Canada)	$
TOTAL (U.S. funds only)	$

❏ Check enclosed for $_____ (payable to Prima Publishing)

Charge my ❏ Master Card ❏ Visa

Account No. _____

Exp. Date _____

Signature _____

Your Name _____

Address _____

City/State/Zip _____

Daytime Telephone _____

Satisfaction is guaranteed—or your money back!
Please allow three to four weeks for delivery.
THANK YOU FOR YOUR ORDER

Other books from Prima Publishing, Computer Products Division

ISBN	TITLE	RELEASE DATE
0-7615-0064-2	Build a Web Site	Available Now
1-55958-744-X	The Windows 95 Book	Available Now
0-7615-0383-8	Web Advertising and Marketing	Available Now
1-55958-747-4	Introduction to Internet Security	Available Now
0-7615-0063-4	Researching on the Internet	Available Now
0-7615-0693-4	Internet Information Server	Summer 1996
0-7615-0678-0	Java Applet Powerpack, Vol. 1	Summer 1996
0-7615-0685-3	JavaScript	Summer 1996
0-7615-0684-5	VBScript	Summer 1996
0-7615-0726-4	The Webmaster's Handbook	Summer 1996
0-7615-0691-8	Netscape Fast Track Server	Summer 1996
0-7615-0733-7	Essential Netscape Navigator Gold	Summer 1996
0-7615-0759-0	Web Page Design Guide	Summer 1996